Disenfranchising Democracy

The first wave of democratization in the United States – the removal of property and taxpaying qualifications for the right to vote – was accompanied by the disenfranchisement of African American men, with the political actors most supportive of the former also the most insistent upon the latter. The United States is not unique in this respect: other canonical cases of democratization also saw simultaneous expansions and restrictions of political rights, yet this pattern has never been fully detailed or explained. Through case studies of the USA, the UK, and France, *Disenfranchising Democracy* offers the first cross-national account of the relationship between democratization and exclusion. It develops a political institutional perspective to explain their co-occurrence, focusing on the politics of coalition building and the visions that political community coalitions advance in support of their goals. Bateman sheds new light on democratization, connecting it to the construction of citizenship and cultural identities.

David A. Bateman is Assistant Professor of Government at Cornell University. He is co-author of *Southern Nation: Congress and White Supremacy After Reconstruction* (2018).

Disenfranchising Democracy

Constructing the Electorate in the United States, the United Kingdom, and France

DAVID A. BATEMAN

Cornell University, New York

CAMBRIDGE
UNIVERSITY PRESS

CAMBRIDGE
UNIVERSITY PRESS

University Printing House, Cambridge CB2 8BS, United Kingdom

One Liberty Plaza, 20th Floor, New York, NY 10006, USA

477 Williamstown Road, Port Melbourne, VIC 3207, Australia

314–321, 3rd Floor, Plot 3, Splendor Forum, Jasola District Centre,
New Delhi – 110025, India

79 Anson Road, #06–04/06, Singapore 079906

Cambridge University Press is part of the University of Cambridge.

It furthers the University's mission by disseminating knowledge in the pursuit of
education, learning, and research at the highest international levels of excellence.

www.cambridge.org
Information on this title: www.cambridge.org/9781108470193
DOI: 10.1017/9781108556323

First published 2018

Printed in the United States of America by Sheridan Books, Inc.

A catalogue record for this publication is available from the British Library.

Library of Congress Cataloging-in-Publication Data
NAMES: Bateman, David A., author.
TITLE: Disenfranchising democracy : constructing the electorate in the United States,
the United Kingdom, and France / David A. Bateman.
DESCRIPTION: New York : Cambridge University Press, 2018.
IDENTIFIERS: LCCN 2018018157| ISBN 9781108470193 (hardback) | ISBN
9781108455459 (paperback)
SUBJECTS: LCSH: Democratization – United States. | Democratization – Great Britain. |
Democratization – France. | Suffrage – United States. | Suffrage – Great Britain. |
Suffrage – France.
CLASSIFICATION: LCC JK1764 .B385 2018 | DDC 320.973–dc23
LC record available at https://lccn.loc.gov/2018018157

ISBN 978-1-108-47019-3 Hardback
ISBN 978-1-108-45545-9 Paperback

To Mary, Robert, Kate, Chris, Justin,
Mary-Alma, and Martina

Contents

Figures

Tables

Preface

This is a book about democratization, the transformation of institutions to make them more responsive to a larger share of persons subject to their authority or determining influence. More narrowly, it is about distinct moments in the construction of a mass electorate in three countries, a historical process through which the right to register a binding choice over the leadership of a state was expanded beyond small cliques and narrow social classes to include a much larger body identified with "the people." And because "the people" never has a predetermined identity, it is ultimately a book about the ways in which particular political communities were delineated and given form, about how democratization reshaped the social foundations of the state.

Given these subjects, however, the book starts in an unusual place and with an unusual question: asking why democratization in the early nineteenth-century United States was accompanied by the *disenfranchisement* of black Americans.

Nationalist conceits to the contrary, it is not obvious that the United States has much to teach the world about democracy. In fact, the very conditions that seemed to facilitate its early but stunted emergence in America would eventually make the country a poor guide for developments elsewhere. The democratic transformations in Europe during the late nineteenth and early twentieth centuries, for example, seemed to require a focus on conflict between economically defined classes – the peasantry, proletariat, bourgeoisie, and landed aristocracy that still populate our stories about this period. The initial wave of democratization in America, by contrast, was more often explained in terms of a supposed muting of class conflict and especially by the absence of feudalism and its profoundly antagonistic class relations. The United States even seemed to lack a precise moment of transition, a definite date at which it could be said that it had ceased to be an autocratic regime and become a democratic one. As Alexis de Tocqueville remarked, "The great advantage of the Americans is to have come to democracy without having to endure democratic revolution and to have been born equal rather than become so."[1]

The seeming exception to America's ostensibly exceptional history was the enfranchisement of African American men after the Civil War, which in many ways fit the comparative patterns that would emerge in the rest of the world. Paradoxically, however, this case seemed to only further mark America as an outlier. Unlike in Europe, the fight over African American voting rights was organized along not only a vertical axis of class conflict but also a horizontal one of racial differentiation. It was not simply the "masses against the classes," but black Americans arrayed against whites across social classes. And it was ultimately defeated, a clear case of democratic reversal but one often neglected in the comparative literature on democratization. For decades afterward, conflict over black political and civil rights would often be interpreted not through the lens of democratization but through that of "race relations," a formulation that framed conflict over political rights in terms of managing frictions inherent to a diverse society, and in which the aspirations of black Americans to equal citizenship was a problem to be regulated, generally unconnected to America's regime type. And so the case of democratization in America that aligned most closely with the comparative pattern has itself often been seen as a different matter altogether.[2]

If the book's starting place in America is unconventional, so too is its focus on disenfranchisement, the act of stripping a social group of political rights and, more broadly, the state of being denied political and civic standing. If mass enfranchisement is a defining feature of democratization, then disenfranchisement would seem to be its negation, the active undoing of its achievements or a frontier beyond which it has not yet occurred.

---

[1] Alexis de Tocqueville, *Democracy in America*, trans. Arthur Goldhammer (New York: Literary Classics of the United States, 2004), 588–89.

[2] Some of the most important exceptions are Barrington Moore, Jr., *Social Origins of Dictatorship and Democracy: Lord and Peasant in the Making of the Modern World* (Boston: Beacon Press, 1966); W. E. B. Du Bois, *Black Reconstruction in America, 1860–1880* (New York: The Free Press, 1998 [1935]); and most recently, Robert Mickey, *Paths Out of Dixie: The Democratization of Authoritarian Enclaves in America's Deep South, 1944–1972* (Princeton, NJ: Princeton University Press, 2015).

If you want to understand a phenomenon, starting from its negation in a seemingly deviant case is not usually the best strategy. And yet my guiding premise has been that democracy and democratization might be productively studied by examining their exclusions, and that this might provide new insights into their occurrence.[3] This requires us to cast a new look on familiar cases, reexamining the primary record and historical sources from a new perspective, telling these stories in different ways, and asking whether our existing theories are compatible with the new stylized histories we produce. The objective in doing so, however, was not so much to invalidate or contradict earlier accounts, but to see what sorts of stories we tell in light of different questions. The downside is that by changing the focus of the analysis and dealing with specific cases rather than aggregate patterns, we are not directly testing alternative theories of democratization. The upside is that by attending to the *possibility* that democratization might have been accompanied by disenfranchisement – whether this actually occurred in any given case – we might gain new insights that would have been overlooked if not studied with this in mind.

One such insight is that democratization is not only a process by which political rights are extended but also a deliberate effort to change the composition and character of a particular community, reallocating influence, the benefits and costs of public policy, and social and civic prestige across different groups. Democracy, in this light, is never simply a neutral set of procedures for deciding upon political leadership: it is also a form of government that rests its legitimacy on a claim to constitute and represent a particular "people." And so democratization is, perhaps inevitably, a conflict over *people making*, occurring not only in institutional and material realms but on the level of discourse and imagination.

If understanding the connection of democratization to disenfranchisement requires us to attend to discursive and institutional processes of people making, then it also suggests that the historical study of democratization needs to expand the cast of actors beyond the narrowly defined economic classes to which we usually assign the leading roles. We must grapple with the variegated ways in which class and other forms of social differentiation and group identity were given form and meaning through locally specific institutions that assigned worth, rights, and standing. In examining the historical record, students of democratization are

---

[3] This had many sources, but among the most important was Teri L. Caraway, "Inclusion and Democratization: Class, Gender, Race, and the Extension of Suffrage," *Comparative Politics* 36, no. 4 (2004): 443–60.

confronted by this fact all the time. The work we produce carries the traces of this encounter, often resulting in an acknowledgment that interests and identities are socially constructed and so will result in nationally specific differences; but if our goal remains nonetheless limited to identifying a "locus classicus" of historical democratizations in the enfranchisement of an urban, male (white) proletariat, we will likely miss much of the story.[4] Our stories of democratizations can instead be enriched by considering a wider variety of intersecting classes, social groups, and not-straightforwardly-economic hierarchical relations, paying attention to the political processes by which these groups – and the actors who claimed to represent them – defined their separate and collective interests, negotiated with others around these interests, and ultimately created new understandings of common purpose and collective identity.[5]

Reading democratization through the lens of disenfranchisement might also help make our stories about its historical occurrence more relevant to contemporary readers. Democracies around the world are being buffeted by the rise of a form of politics that simultaneously appeals to portions of the electorate in democratic terms, as representing the will of a coherent "people," even as it threatens civic and political disenfranchisement for some. This development is often connected to what a number of scholars have identified as "*the* defining political question of our times," namely the seemingly "growing proliferation of antagonism around cultural difference."[6] Relative to these trends, the historical study of democratization can often seem far removed, concerning ostensibly less diverse societies and focusing on conflicts organized around definite material interests rather than seemingly more subjective understandings of identity, status, or culture.

When viewed through the perspective of disenfranchisement, however, the nineteenth century looks a lot more diverse, with myriad identities and a proliferation of ideologies and ideas about interests that are not straightforward implications of the structural position of a given class. Much like contemporary conflicts, struggles over historical democratizations weave together questions of status, culture, identity, power, and material and

---

[4] Ruth Berins Collier, *Paths Toward Democracy: The Working Class and Elites in Western Europe and South America* (Cambridge: Cambridge University Press, 1999), 27.
[5] For a project that embodies these imperatives and that has helped me appreciate their importance, see Dawn Langan Teele, *The Political Origins of the Female Franchise* (Princeton, NJ: Princeton University Press, 2018).
[6] Kobena Mercer, ed., "Introduction," in Stuart Hall, *The Fateful Triangle: Race, Ethnicity, Nation* (Cambridge, MA: Harvard University Press, 2017), 11.

economic position in ways that can never be wholly disentangled. The past is a foreign country, and the nineteenth century was different, very different, from today. But perhaps in some ways it was less different than is generally appreciated.

If such a perspective helps make historical democratizations more legible to us today, it might also shed light on contemporary democratic struggles. Many instances of democratic backsliding in recent years have combined the undermining of democratic institutions with the affirmation of democratic identities. In some cases, these have been political projects aiming not only at reconfiguring state or economic institutions, but also at constructing a broadly shared sense of peoplehood that will help sustain it at a popular level. The "peoples" they construct will be varyingly exclusive in their symbols, institutions, and assignation of civic worth, but for many they will provide a reason to believe that one is part of something valuable, even if its value is defined in part by what is denied to others. This might help explain why democratic backsliding can be experienced not as a fall into authoritarianism but as a democratization, as the reconfiguration of the state to better represent, even if only in public discourse, a particular definition of "the people."

We should not concede the words *democratization* or *democracy* to such projects. But we should take seriously the possibility that their contested popularity rests on their creation of an image of community and a hierarchy of worth that provides potential constituents with a sense that they are valued and that their state *represents* them in some meaningful sense (even if its officers are fleecing them in a more material sense).

Those of us who believe that a further and genuine democratization of social, economic, and political life is urgently needed, and that democratizing projects to level inequalities and expand liberties can be pursued without resting these on disenfranchisements, should take note of what these faux democratizers have understood. Democratization has always required its advocates to work out new senses of collective belonging, new peoples that can meaningfully connect a multiplicity of identities into a shared emancipatory and democratic purpose. Its occurrence and consolidation in turn rest in part on connecting individuals and communities with a commitment to a broader political project, one that is both imagined – in the sense that all such communities require us to imagine who "we" are – and yet anchored in either the antagonisms and differentiations of social life or in real improvements and opportunities clearly connected to the democratizing project itself. Imagining and constructing such egalitarian and emancipatory visions of popular community must count among the vital tasks of a democratizing movement today.

America has only briefly lived under a democracy, and its geographic and social scope has only gradually (and somewhat feebly) been expanded. There is no particular reason to think it should endure. But I do not expect American democracy will be killed by a public opinion that turns against the *idea* of democracy or its presumptive values in the abstract, or that rediscovers animosities of race, origin, gender, language, or religion. Authoritarian values have always been with us. White racism, sexism, and other chauvinisms never went away: they are embedded in and daily reconstituted by our form of economic organization, our governing institutions, our social relations, and our senses of self, and they have buttressed forms of undemocratic rule that were successfully defended by large segments of America's political elites, with the backing of broad publics, until quite recently. The current danger, as is generally the case, is to be found in certain political elites who see in the degradation of democratic institutions – through voter suppression, the harassment and physical terrorizing of activists, the deportation of community leaders, continued attacks on the collective organizations of working people, especially those of importance to people of color, and the legal dismantling of the institutional gains of previous democratic revolutions – an opportunity to hold on to or expand their own power through denying the status and membership of certain classes of Americans. To cite just one example, the last several decades have seen many of America's elites, of both political parties, delight in the destruction of a limited form of democratic organization in the workplace, one of the few organizations that seek to provide the majority of America's inhabitants with a concrete ability to shape the conditions under which they live. And this is done in the name of unleashing capital and entrepreneurship, shifting the balance of America's public priorities from one vision of the people to another.

If America continues to undermine and roll back its democratic institutions, the danger is not likely to come from "below," in the form of illiberalism among a mass and variegated public. We should instead expect the denigration and corruption of democratic institutions to be undertaken by political elites pursuing their own interests, whether for love of self, power, or a form of principle. But history suggests that in doing so, they will seek to rest their project on a popular warrant, harnessing widely held identities and America's quasi-official civic statuses for their own ends, offering a seemingly democratic identity that affirms care and worth for some, telling them that their lives matter, even if no one else's does.

In this case, I expect that a good many Americans will not only not notice democracy's passing – after all, many did not notice its centuries-long denial – but will experience it instead as a moment when a particular vision of the "people" was again represented in the symbols and discourse of the government. It will be a democratization for some, resting on the substantive disenfranchisement of others.

***

There would be no book in front of you had it not been for the collective and individual efforts of scores of people, whose assistance and guidance can never be repaid. I arrived at the University of Pennsylvania knowing only a little about political science, less about politics, and next to nothing about anything else. What little I did know I owe to Axel Huelsemeyer and Leander Schneider, who had encouraged me to apply to graduate school. And I was lucky to arrive with a wonderful cohort whose friendship enriched my life and profoundly shaped my scholarship. Graduate workers are the bones and sinew of intellectual inquiry, and their friendships and solidarities define the discipline: it is well past time for your labor to be recognized as such and for your inalienable right to organize collectively to be affirmed.

The persons most responsible for shaping this project, and my own intellectual development, are Brendan O'Leary and Rogers M. Smith. Brendan provided me with much-needed mentorship and support, introduced me to and guided me through the study of comparative politics, encouraged me as I developed an interest in American politics, helped find funding for me when I was broke, counseled me when my immigration status seemed imperiled, and at every stage of a lengthy process was a generous friend and inspiring role model. Rogers introduced me to the study of American politics, the study of ideas, and the value of politically engaged political science. Through the Penn Program on Democracy, Citizenship, and Constitutionalism, he anchored a rich and stimulating intellectual community from which I greatly benefited, and his counsel over the years has fundamentally shaped my approach to research, pedagogy, and the practice of citizenship. I am profoundly privileged to be one of the many whom Brendan and Rogers have mentored and supported.

Many of the ideas and insights for this project had their genesis in courses taught by Adolph Reed, Jr., Tulia Falleti, Rudy Sil, Ian Lustick, and John Lapinski, who taught me to think critically and introduced me to the historical study of institutions, democratization, ideologies of race and class, and political representation. This book bears the imprint of their insights and courses.

I have been fortunate in receiving support for this research from the Penn Program in Ethnic Conflict and the Penn Program on Democracy, Citizenship, and Constitutionalism, as well as a Penn Dissertation Completion Fellowship. Funding from these sources would have only gone so far had it not been for the generous assistance provided by the archivists at the National Archives in Kew, the Archives nationales and the Bibliothèque nationale de France in Paris, the Ohio History Center, the State Archives of Rhode Island, the Wisconsin Historical Society, and the Bodleian Library. A postdoctoral research position at the Center for the Study of Democratic Politics provided additional time and resources and a stimulating environment in which to work and learn. I owe much to Jean-François Godbout, Miguel R. Rueda, and Kyle Dropp, as well as Paul Frymer, Nolan McCarty, Charles Cameron, and Michele Epstein for enriching my time there.

Special thanks are owed to Sara Doskow, Danielle Menz, Robert Judkins, Lisa Yambrick, Sunantha Ramamoorthy, Robert Swanson, and the team at Cambridge University Press, Integra, and Arc Indexing. Chapter and paper drafts have benefited from the feedback of workshop participants at the Center for the Study of Democratic Politics, the Ohio State University, the University of California, Berkeley, Northwestern University, Fordham University, and the Université de Montreal. Megan Ming Francis, Pamela Brandwein, Carol Nackenoff, Ira Katznelson, Adam Sheingate, and Jason Frank provided extremely helpful critical responses to a version of Chapter 4, while Didi Kuo provided exceptionally valuable comments to a draft of Chapter 5. Sid Tarrow, Jamila Michener, Josh Chafetz, Zachary D. Clopton, Michael Dorf, Matt Evangelista, Mary Katzenstein, Joe Margulies, and Aziz Rana provided helpful feedback to draft chapters, as well as a supportive and intellectually rewarding forum in which to present and engage with new work. Van Gosse generously shared portions of his research on black disenfranchisement with me and offered encouragement in pursuing this project. Matthew Holden and the participants of the Wepner Symposium on the Lincoln Legacy helped me better understand black disenfranchisement and the processes of counteremancipation. Professor Holden's support and engagement with younger scholars stand as an inspiring model of what political science ought to be, and I am forever grateful for his encouragement.

I am especially thankful to Dawn Langan Teele for providing feedback on several chapters and for inviting me to participate on truly wonderful panels examining democratization through rich new lenses: the discussions that were generated on these occasions, in addition to what I have learned from her work, have deeply informed my thinking and shaped the book in front of you.

Richard Valelly, Paul Frymer, Stephen Skowronek, and Robert Mickey gave generously of their time and advice, sharpening the book's argument and clarifying its comparative structure; I am deeply grateful for their feedback and encouragement. Richard Valelly merits special praise and appreciation. I have learned enormously from his work but possibly even more from his example: he has been a wonderfully supportive and encouraging reader, a valuable resource, and critical and stimulating interlocutor.

The project was enriched through conversations with Alex Livingston, Peter Enns, Sergio Garcia-Rios, Adam Seth Levine, Bryce Corrigan, Steven Ward, Elizabeth Sanders, Sabrina Karim, Jill Frank, and Nic van de Walle, whose feedback helped me considerably in revisions, and all of my colleagues at Cornell University. Suzanne Mettler has been a generous and wonderful mentor and friend. And above all, Richard Bensel, whose guidance, criticism, encouragement, and enthusiasm have made this a much better book and me a better scholar.

I am deeply thankful to Stephan Stohler, Tim Weaver, Meredith Wooten, Chelsea Schafer, Emily Thorson, Rhoneil Eurchuk, Joanna Richman Weaver, Pitou Devgon, Anand Vaidya, Jyothi Natarajan, Mik Kinkead, Vani Natarajan, Vanessa Hamer, Ali Garvey, Laura Louise Tobin, Kevin James Holland, and Sam Allingham, who have each provided generously of their time as intellectual interlocutors and as wonderful friends. I could not imagine a more wonderful family than Robert, Kate, Chris, Justin, Mary-Alma, and Martina Bateman, and Çetin, Melike, Müge, and Cormac. Most of all, I am grateful to Begüm Adalet, my lung and fellow traveler, whose support, critical engagement, and example, in scholarship, teaching, and life, are an ongoing inspiration, and whose comradeship is my greatest joy.

As this book nears completion, I have become ever more aware of its limitations, of advice that I should have heeded, of work from which it would have benefited, of voices I should have attended to more, and of critiques that I have insufficiently addressed. I have no excuses, for of the many ways in which I have been privileged, none is greater than the opportunity to have learned from such a supportive community. The failure to listen more attentively was mine alone.

The Puzzle of Democratic Disenfranchisement

We affirm the promise of our democracy. We recall that what binds this nation together is not the colors of our skin or the tenets of our faith or the origins of our names. What makes us exceptional – what makes us American – is our allegiance to an idea, articulated in a declaration made more than two centuries ago: "We hold these truths to be self-evident, that all men are created equal."

> – Barack Hussein Obama[1]

Government requires make believe. Make believe that the king is divine, make believe that he can do no wrong or make believe that the voice of the people is the voice of God. Make believe that the people *have* a voice or make believe that the representatives of the people *are* the people. Make believe that governors are the servants of the people. Make believe that all men are equal or make believe that they are not. The political world of make-believe mingles with the real world in strange ways, for the make-believe world may often mold the real one.

> – Edmund Morgan[2]

Like all peoples, Americans tell stories about who they are, about what unites them and sets them apart from others. In the canon of American self-narratives, few themes loom as large as that of progressive democracy, a story about how the "general triumph of democratic principles" is the defining feature of American history.[3] This story has been told most

---

[1] "Inaugural Address by President Barack Obama," January 21, 2013, https://obamawhite house.archives.gov/the-press-office/2013/01/21/inaugural-address-president-barack-obama.

[2] Edmund Morgan, *Inventing the People: The Rise of Popular Sovereignty in England and America* (New York: W. W. Norton, 1988), 13–14.

[3] Frederic Ogg and P. Orman Ray, *Introduction to American Government* (New York: Century Co., 1922), 199.

insistently in recent years by former President Barack Obama, who sought to rally Americans around his political program by narrating a story of "what makes us exceptional – what makes us American." In his telling, American identity is rooted in the country's shared allegiance to the principles of equality and liberty, and above all by its commitment to democracy, "the constant struggle to extend rights to more of our people, to give more people a voice." The faithful pursuit of this struggle was the cornerstone of American identity. "We, the people," he announced in his second inaugural address, "declare today that the most evident of truths – that all of us are created equal – is the star that guides us still."[4]

The story of progressive democracy is a powerful political myth, one that offers its listeners an interpretation of common purpose and shared identity. By staging American history as a sequence of democratizing struggles – from "the patriots of 1776" through to "Seneca Falls, and Selma, and Stonewall" – President Obama invited a diverse audience to identify with the past triumphs or future promises of a meaningful political community, one supposedly defined by its dedicated pursuit of egalitarian reform.[5] At its best, the story is a call to imagine bonds of solidarity that extend beyond the limits of citizenship and status, the prejudices and exclusions of a given place and time.

But by distilling a progressive direction to American history, the story implicitly treats as inessential those patterns that seem to contradict it. This is often reflected in a peculiar sort of amnesia. Examples abound of American history being characterized as "a gradual movement toward democracy with no reverses," of comforting declarations that "the arc of American history has always moved toward expanding the electorate" or that "including as many Americans as possible in our electoral process is the spirit of our country. It is why we have expanded rights to women and minorities but never legislated them away."[6]

Even a partial listing of American disenfranchisements, however, suggests that these were anything but exceptions. Freed Southern black men

---

[4] https://obamawhitehouse.archives.gov/the-press-office/2013/01/21/inaugural-address
-president-barack-obama;.https://obamawhitehouse.archives.gov/the-press-office/2015/0
9/28/remarks-president-obama-united-nations-general-assembly.

[5] Ibid.

[6] Daron Acemoglu and James Robinson, *The Economic Origins of Democracy and Dictatorship* (Cambridge: Cambridge University Press, 2009), xi; "Attorney General Eric Holder Speaks at the NAACP Annual Convention," July 10, 2012, https://www.justice.gov/opa/speech/attor ney-general-eric-holder-speaks-naacp-annual-convention; Charlie Crist, "The Voter ID Mess," *Washington Post*, July 20, 2012.

and their male children were ejected from the franchise in the decades following Reconstruction, after thirty years of exercising the right to vote.[7] Free black men in both Northern and Southern states had also been purged from the electorate during the Jacksonian "age of democracy."[8] Many noncitizen immigrants lost the right to vote in the early twentieth century.[9] Women lost the suffrage on only two occasions – in New Jersey in 1807 and Utah in 1887 – but their exclusion was successfully defended against an extensive social movement for almost seventy years.[10] Many of the country's indigenous peoples were effectively denied the vote for decades after the extension of citizenship in 1924, while formal and informal language tests denied access to the polls for many non-English speakers into the mid-1970s.[11]

Nor is disenfranchisement safely confined to the past. Restrictions on the franchise excluded working-class persons of all races and genders in the early twentieth century, but they threaten to do so again in the twenty-first, as restrictive voter identification laws impose onerous burdens on poor citizens' right to vote.[12] Even more severe are the laws that exclude convicted felons. More than fifty years after the Voting Rights Act, the intersection of intensive policing, aggressive prosecutorial practices, and felon disenfranchisement laws has

---

[7] J. Morgan Kousser, *The Shaping of Southern Politics: Suffrage Restrictions and the Establishment of the One-Party South, 1880–1910* (New Haven, CT: Yale University Press, 1974); Richard Valelly, *The Two Reconstructions: The Struggle for Black Enfranchisement* (Chicago: University of Chicago Press, 2004).

[8] Christopher Malone, *Between Freedom and Bondage: Race, Party, and Voting Rights in the Antebellum North* (New York: Routledge, 2008); Alexander Keyssar, *The Right to Vote: The Contested History of Democracy in the United States*, rev. edn. (New York: Basic Books, 2009).

[9] Ron Hayduk, *Democracy for All: Restoring Immigrant Voting in the United States* (New York: Routledge, 2006).

[10] Corrine M. McConnaughy, *The Woman Suffrage Movement in America: A Reassessment* (Cambridge: Cambridge University Press, 2015); Dawn Langan Teele, *The Political Origins of the Female Franchise* (Princeton, NJ: Princeton University Press, 2018).

[11] Daniel McCool, Susan M. Olson, and Jennifer L. Robinson, *Native Vote: American Indians, the Voting Rights Act, and the Right to Vote* (Cambridge: Cambridge University Press, 2007); Laughlin McDonald, *American Indians and the Fight for Equal Voting Rights* (Norman: University of Oklahoma Press, 2011); David H. Hunter, "The 1975 Voting Rights Act and Language Minorities," *Catholic University Law Review* 25, no. 2 (1976): 250–70; Juan Cartagena, "Latinos and Section 5 of the Voting Rights Act: Beyond Black and White," *National Black Law Journal* 18, no. 2 (2004–05): 201–23; John A. Garcia, "The Voting Rights Act and Hispanic Political Representation in the Southwest," *Publius: The Journal of Federalism* 16, no. 4 (1986): 49–66.

[12] Lorraine Minnite, *The Myth of Voter Fraud* (Ithaca, NY: Cornell University Press, 2010).

resulted in nearly 8 percent of adult black Americans being denied the right to vote, a number that stands at nearly 12 percent for the South and more than 20 percent in the states of Florida, Kentucky, and Virginia.[13]

In the story of progressive democracy, these are obstacles to be overcome and not constitutive of the country's character. As President Obama remarked in regard to contemporary voting restrictions, "That's not who we are. That shouldn't be who we are."[14]

For many, however, the recurring patterns of disenfranchisement reveal precisely what the country is and has always been about. As the many writers who have detailed America's disenfranchisements remind us, one of the more prominent features of the country's history has been the active and explicit rejection of democratic ideals. W. E. B. Du Bois's *Black Reconstruction*, for example, tells the story of how America offered a "vision of democratic self-government" only to turn violently against it.[15] Richard Valelly notes that the disenfranchisement of black Americans at the turn of the twentieth century was the largest such extrusion by an otherwise stable democracy in world history, and he shows that voting rights today rest not on any progressive tilt to history but on political organizations and institutions whose persistence is by no means guaranteed.[16] And in a powerful intervention into public discourse, Michelle Alexander has argued that American history is not a process of progressive democratization but of successively reconstituted racial control regimes: slavery, Jim Crow, and now mass incarceration.[17]

The contrast between the storylines of progressive democracy and persistent exclusion is stark; at times it is difficult to imagine how they could be referring to the same country. But they do, and the premise of this

---

[13] Jeff Manza and Christopher Uggen, *Locked Out: Felon Disenfranchisement and American Democracy* (New York: Oxford University Press, 2008); Elizabeth Hull, *The Disenfranchisement of Ex-Felons* (Philadelphia: Temple University Press, 2008); Katherine Irene Pettus, *Felony Disenfranchisement in America: Historical Origins, Institutional Racism, and Modern Consequences* (Albany: State University of New York Press, 2013); Christopher Uggen, Sarah Shannon, and Jeff Manza, "State-Level Estimates of Felon Disenfranchisement in the United States, 2010," *The Sentencing Project*, 2012, 17–18.

[14] "The President's News Conference, Jan. 18, 2017," http://www.presidency.ucsb.edu/ws/index.php?pid=50589.

[15] Du Bois, *Black Reconstruction in America*, 30.

[16] Valelly, *The Two Reconstructions*, 1.

[17] Michelle Alexander, *The New Jim Crow: Mass Incarceration in the Age of Colorblindness* (New York: The New Press, 2010).

book is that we cannot understand either democratization or disenfranchisement in America without understanding the relationship between them.

The story I tell in *Disenfranchising Democracy* connects these supposed opposites, first in America and then as a more general pattern. The defining feature of democratization in nineteenth-century America, I argue, was the construction of an extensive and vibrant democracy that was being simultaneously circumscribed along racial lines, both through the country's heavy reliance on slavery and in the constriction of the status of enfranchised citizen to white men. I will show that debates over black citizenship and voting rights, and contestation over their relationship with democratization for white men, were of vital importance to American politics from the very beginning of the Republic, well before Reconstruction made their extension and protection the defining question of American political development.

Of particular importance is the pattern by which democracy and exclusion were joined. The constitutional conventions and state legislatures that extended the right to vote by abolishing property and taxpaying qualifications tended to simultaneously curtail the voting rights of black American citizens, with those who were most supportive of the first simultaneously the most supportive of the second. This pattern raises several important questions. Why was white democratization in America associated with black disenfranchisement? Was this co-occurrence mere coincidence, or does it reflect a deeper connection? If so, is this connection unique to America – a sui generis phenomenon explained by the many peculiar characteristics of the country's historical development – or might it reflect a more general pattern, with implications for how we study democratization elsewhere?[18]

Some of the most compelling work to grapple with these questions argues that democratization in America was premised upon disenfranchisement or that racial disenfranchisement was an inevitable consequence of democratization. The reasons include the claim that democracy requires a high level of racial and ethnic homogeneity;[19] that racial exclusion provided the conceptual foundation upon which white Americans

---

[18] Valelly highlights the most important of these, America's "unprecedented marriage of slavery and political democracy." Richard Valelly, "How Suffrage Politics Made – and Makes – America," *The Oxford Handbook of American Political Development*, ed. Richard Valelly, Suzanne Mettler, and Robert Lieberman (Oxford: Oxford University Press, 2016), 445–72.

[19] Rebecca Kook, *The Logic of Democratic Exclusion: African Americans in the United States and Palestinian Citizens in Israel* (Lanham, MD: Lexington Books, 2002).

could imagine equal citizenship among themselves;[20] or that working-class white Americans were so intensely committed to white supremacy that any expansion of their influence was sure to lead to intensified racial oppression.[21]

I offer a new account, rooted in politics, institutions, and the ideological narratives that political actors construct in the pursuit of power. I argue that the conjunction of democratization and disenfranchisement was neither inevitable nor unique to America. It was the result of deliberate choices made by elite political coalitions looking to gain and hold on to power but operating within institutional and ideological contexts that shaped their strategies and behavior. Different contexts and different choices could have produced different patterns in the United States, just as they did produce different patterns elsewhere.

However, this does not mean that their association was merely coincidental. There is a deeper connection between democratization and disenfranchisement, one that requires us to look at both from a new perspective. What links these seeming opposites is that they are two paths to the same goal: each is a manifestation of a particular type of political project, one that aims to reconstitute the set of groups and communities who are the principal beneficiaries of a regime's public policies and whose support is crucial for its survival. Such projects are pursued by political coalitions that are looking to gain power and secure their priorities over the long term, and that have decided that this would be best achieved by changing the composition and identity of "the people" whose votes will help arbitrate, however indirectly, who governs and in whose interests. Democratization, then, is never simply a process by which members of a preexisting political community are enfranchised: it is a political project through which the boundaries and character of the "people" are redefined, with inclusions and exclusions not only compatible but also potentially reinforcing means to achieve this.

The story of democratization in nineteenth-century America is that of the political construction and partial dismantling of the *white man's*

---

[20] Edmund Morgan, *American Freedom, American Slavery: The Ordeal of Colonial Virginia* (New York: W. W. Norton, 1975); Edmund Morgan, "Slavery and Freedom: The American Paradox," *The Journal of American History* 59, no. 1 (1972): 5–29; Aziz Rana, *The Two Faces of American Freedom* (Cambridge, MA: Harvard University Press, 2010).

[21] David Roediger, *The Wages of Whiteness: Race and the Making of the American Working Class*, rev. edn. (London: Verso, 1999 [1991]); Joel Olson, *The Abolition of White Democracy* (Minneapolis: University of Minnesota Press, 2004).

republic, a discursive and institutional formulation that helped certain political actors define and maintain a political community of value to themselves, its architects, but also to many of their constituents, to whom it offered a space of democratic egalitarianism unprecedented in the modern world. The terms of the white man's republic were always contested, and during the revolutionary years of the Civil War and Reconstruction, it would be rejected by many as a coherent vision of national purpose. Under pressure from organized constituencies of black and white antislavery activists, supported by allied legislators, it was dislodged from many of the country's governing institutions, at the national level and, more unevenly and momentarily, in the states. It was deeply woven into the fabric of America's political institutions and national mythology and would not be easily displaced. But it was also the product of political coalition making and institution building and could be challenged and defeated.

The ideology of the white man's republic was intended to provide a compelling vision of political community that would appeal broadly, and as a story of the American "people" it endured well beyond the end of the Civil War, not always as the ethos of the governing national regime but as a resonant theme available for reinterpretation and synthesis. It has persisted in some localities and discursive communities as a defining feature of a regional culture, as an imagined ideal for the future, or as the endangered inheritance of the past.[22] And at times, ambitious office seekers, seeing in its tropes a potentially resonant frame for mobilizing true believers and for reframing the concerns of a broader public, have brazen-throated revived its tropes on the national stage, warning of threats to "*our* history and *our* heritage."[23]

The remainder of the chapter will provide more detail on this argument, on how it relates to the broader literatures on democratization and on disenfranchisement, and on the possible pathways by which these might be brought together or kept apart. For the moment, however, I want to highlight three points.

The first is that while projects that aim to reconstitute a political community – such as the white man's republic – can enjoy broad support and

[22] Ulrich B. Phillips, "The Central Theme of Southern History," *The American Historical Review* 34, no. 1 (1928): 30–43.
[23] Jaqueline Thomsen, "Trump: Media Is Trying to Take Away Our History and Our Heritage," *The Hill*, August 22, 2017, http://thehill.com/homenews/administration/347587-trump-media-is-trying-to-take-away-our-history-and-our-heritage.

elicit popular mobilizations, their terms will ultimately be defined through the collective efforts of a relatively small number of actors whose motivations cannot be assumed to be identical with the preferences or aspirations of the social classes or groups they might claim to represent. Their particular goals might include political liberation, the reconstruction of society, or the protection of capital; they might amount to nothing more than winning office or pecuniary gain. But whether and how democratization and disenfranchisement are brought together will depend largely on their collective choices. The regime they establish will bear the imprint of their goals and the commitments they have made to their allies or negotiated with their opponents; and it will reflect their efforts to appeal through policy and discourse to the constituencies upon which they hope to found a new regime.

The second point is that while an electoral calculus – enfranchising supporters and disenfranchising opponents in order to maximize the likelihood of winning – can be an important part of the story, it is not all of it. These projects aim to recompose not just the legal electorate but also the more nebulous concept of political community, a discursive construct that details how a particular group of persons is united by something more meaningful than an arbitrary association.[24] This is both because coalitions pursuing changes to the regime are pushed to articulate a rationale in terms of broader principles about how the state should relate to society, and who should and should not be included; and because framing their projects in terms of political community can help connect their particular goals with the aspirations and identities of a broader public. Changes to political rights, for instance, are generally defended not as a set of arbitrary qualifications, let alone as an instrument to power, but as attempts to better represent a particular vision of community in the institutions of the state. And aspiring leaders cultivate popular support not just by offering a litany of policies but by appealing to potential constituents as members of a distinct people, with obligations to each other and a collective purpose to realize. Like President Obama's story of progressive democracy, these appeals invite some listeners to connect their own interests and aspirations, their own experiences and identities, with those of a broad and meaningful community. And like the story of progressive democracy, these stories bear the imprint of a particular political project: whether

---

[24] Benedict Anderson, *Imagined Communities: Reflections on the Origin and Spread of Nationalism* (London: Verso, 1991 [1984]), 6.

subtly or tendentiously, they contain prescriptions for a "common program to realize."[25]

Our accounts of democratization often abstract away from these narratives, in part because they seem to be merely rhetorical cover for material interests. A core contention of this book is that they matter. When considered from the perspective of "people-making," enfranchisement and disenfranchisement appear as two ways of marking out the boundaries of this "people," offering potential constituents a civic identity whose value might derive as much from its exclusions as from its inclusions. And by framing their projects in terms of a meaningful political community, political coalitions look to gain not just a momentary numerical superiority in an electorate, but a more durable source of public authority: at the extreme, they hope that their particular goals might become inscribed on the identities and civic statuses of constituents, whose support will hinge not on any particular policy but on the ability of aspiring leaders to connect their claim to govern with the ideals and boundaries of this community.

The final point relates to the book's comparative methodology: while the argument I present here will be developed most extensively with regard to the United States, its logic should apply wherever there is an effort to change a political regime. If democratization always involves a political project that aims to reallocate power and influence across social groups, then the possibility of disenfranchisement is always implicit in its occurrence. This does not mean it will always happen or that the form it takes will look the same everywhere. But it suggests that the histories of other democratizing moments should be reexamined with this possibility in mind.

In order to attend to this possibility, the book is divided into two parts. The focus of the first is on disenfranchising democratization in the United States, while the second extends the analysis to two other cases of nineteenth-century democratization, the United Kingdom and France. While the analysis is comparative, I encourage the reader to think about not just the similarities or differences between the cases but also the transnational connections between them. Nineteenth-century Americans regularly toasted the progress of revolutions abroad and denounced the monarchical machinations they blamed for their defeat. And tens of thousands of European democrats and reformers, including Thomas Paine, the

---

[25] Ernest Renan, *Qu'est ce qu'une nation? Conférence faite en Sorbonne, le 11 mars 1882* (Paris: Calman Lévy, 1882), 27.

Marquis de Lafayette, Mathew Carey, William Cobbett, John Binns, William Duane, Georges Clemenceau, Carl Schurz, Thomas Francis Meagher, John Mitchel, and others, arrived on America's shores as refugees or supporters of its cause, leaving an indelible mark on its politics.[26] Their visions of democracy were forged by connecting their local struggles with similar contests and aspirations elsewhere. They were never tidily solidaristic or chauvinistic, but the stories they told of their local communities bore the traces of these broader visions and engagements. To understand these stories, we must attempt to study them in the broader context in which they had meaning.

* * *

The remainder of this chapter considers possible explanations for disenfranchising democratization and outlines my own account. The empirical case studies are divided between two parts. Part I details the gradual emergence of a pattern of disenfranchising democratization in the United States. Chapter 2 looks at the upsurge of democratic politics during the American Revolution and argues that at this juncture, these were *not* generally connected to disenfranchising reforms. Chapter 3 focuses on the forging of the Jeffersonian coalition in the early American Republic, the recurring divisions within this coalition over the question of black citizenship, and the ultimate solution in the discursive and institutional formulation of the white man's republic. Chapter 4 examines how this formulation structured democratization and disenfranchisement in the antebellum United States.

Part II extends the analysis to the United Kingdom and France, highlighting similar impulses toward exclusion amid democratization but tracing how different institutions and political coalitions resulted in distinctive patterns. Chapter 5 looks at the overthrow of a particular formulation of political community in the United Kingdom – the Protestant Constitution – and the conjoined enfranchisement of the middle classes and disenfranchisements of Irish farmers and portions of the working class. Chapter 6 examines the French critical juncture of the 1870s, a decade in which the disenfranchisement of the industrial working classes

---

[26] Seth Cotlar, *Tom Paine's America: The Rise and Fall of Transatlantic Radicalism in the Early Republic* (Charlottesville: University of Virginia Press, 2011); W. Caleb McDaniel, *The Problem of Democracy in the Age of Slavery: Garrisonian Abolitionists and Transatlantic Reform* (Baton Rouge: Louisiana State University Press, 2013).

was heatedly debated and only narrowly defeated, even as other exclusions were reinforced and given a new durability.

In the book's conclusion, I consider the contemporary importance of these nineteenth-century patterns and reflect on the possibility that the dynamic of disenfranchising democracy might be an inherent, but variable, feature of democratic life.

DEMOCRATIZATION AND AMERICAN EXCEPTIONALISM

Our story begins with a puzzling fact about democratization in America. The United States is generally recognized as the first country to establish a stable regime in which political power at most levels of government was allocated by a binding choice of a mass electorate. And yet even as this democracy was being constructed, through the extension of voting rights and the use of elections for more public offices, it was being constricted along racial lines, with free African-American men denied a right to vote that many had exercised since the founding.

Disenfranchisement and democratization came together in America in distinct ways. As institutional reforms, they occurred in conjunction with each other, so that expansions in voting rights along class lines were accompanied by their restriction along racial lines. But they were also associated at the level of behavior and political ideology, with the persons most supportive of removing property and taxpaying qualifications also the most insistent on denying free persons of color the right to vote. This conjunction was evident in voting patterns, in the rationales that legislators and others provided for their positions, and in the ideological construction of these positions as part of a more coherent and principled philosophy.

Understanding the puzzle of American democratization requires a theory that can encompass the institutional, behavioral, and ideological dimensions of this conjunction.

Democratization in America

Democratization is often studied by looking at the decisions made by incumbent elite. Why would an elite concede to a peaceful transfer of power, place constitutional limits on their authority, or extend the right to vote? To answer these questions, social scientists often look for mechanisms by which an incumbent elite can be encouraged to do the democratic right thing.[27] For example, elites might concede power when they have negotiated pacts that will guarantee the protection of their essential interests, or they might accept constraints on their power as a way to commit to policies needed to secure the cooperation of some important actor.[28]

So why would an elite decide to extend the right to vote? Accounts of suffrage extension generally provide two types of answers: first, that an elite will make concessions in order to preserve some of its own prerogatives against the threat of more far-reaching changes; and second, that the elite or a segment of it will reach out to the excluded classes for support in a political or military project, offering rights as an inducement or reward.[29]

Consider the first case. When faced with the threat of revolution, an incumbent elite can either repress opposition or extend rights and democratize. If they choose the latter, they will likely lose some of their privileges and wealth, as the newly enfranchised seize opportunities once closed to them and as the political system becomes more responsive to their preferences. If the elite choose to repress, they might retain their wealth and political power, but they risk losing everything if they fail. The key factors determining whether an elite will undertake democratizing reforms, then, will be the anticipated costs it would impose weighed against the perceived ability of the excluded classes to organize opposition and the capacity of the elite to repress this if needed.[30]

Variations on this argument have a rich lineage. Barrington Moore, for example, emphasized the uniquely antidemocratic role played by the landed aristocracy, an economic and social class so totally dependent upon the expropriation of labor that it was nearly everywhere committed

---

[27] Adam Przeworski, *Democracy and the Market: Political and Economic Reforms in Eastern Europe and Latin America* (New York: Cambridge University Press, 1991), chapter 2.

[28] Tom Ginsburg, *Judicial Review in New Democracies: Constitutional Courts in Asian Cases* (New York: Cambridge University Press, 2003); Barry Weingast and Sonia Mittal, "Self-Enforcing Constitutions: With an Application to Democratic Stability in America's First Century," *Journal of Law, Economics, and Organization* 29, no. 2 (2013): 278–302; Barry Weingast, "The Political Foundations of Democracy and the Rule of Law," *American Political Science Review* 91, no. 2 (1997): 245–63.

[29] Adam Przeworski, "Conquered of Granted? A History of Suffrage Extensions," *British Journal of Political Science* 39, no. 2 (2009): 291–321; Ruth Berins Collier, *Paths Toward Democracy: The Working Class and Elites in Western Europe and South America* (New York: Cambridge University Press, 1999), 11–12.

[30] Daron Acemoglu and James Robinson, "Democratization or Repression?" *European Economic Review* 44 (2000): 683–93.

to maintaining despotic power over the rural population. Democratization, he argued, could only occur once this intractably hostile aristocracy had been displaced by another not so directly threatened by the extension of political rights, namely the industrial or commercial bourgeoisie: "no bourgeoisie, no democracy," he famously concluded.[31] Others have placed greater stress on the ability of the subordinated classes to organize collective action and make the costs of repression unsustainable, emphasizing, among other things, the changed opportunities for mass action that accompanied industrial capitalism.[32]

The second type of account sees the extension of political rights less as an extracted concession than as an appeal by the elite to the excluded classes for assistance. Social scientists have long noted that military conflict is often accompanied by expansions of civil, political, and social rights for those who fight, a pattern that reflects elites' need to secure the loyalty and willing participation of the population in the war effort. As ruling classes have sometimes discovered too late, war is not an opportune moment to find your soldiery unwilling to fight, your landowners and tenants unwilling to pay higher taxes, or your workers ready to strike.[33] Appeals to the excluded classes might also result from divisions within the elite itself. This was the stylized history traced by Marx and Engels in the *Communist Manifesto*: the rising bourgeoisie, locked in a fight with the aristocracy, reached out for assistance from the urban working classes and peasantry by offering political rights and limited land reform in exchange for support in the streets and on the battlefields.[34]

---

[31] Moore, *Social Origins of Dictatorship and Democracy*, 418.

[32] Elisabeth Jean Wood, *Forging Democracy from Below: Insurgent Transitions in South Africa and El Salvador* (New York: Cambridge University Press, 2000); Göran Therborn, "The Rule of Capital and the Rise of Democracy," *New Left Review* 1, no. 103 (1977): 3–41, 29; Dietrich Rueschemeyer, Evelyne Huber Stephens, and John D. Stephens, *Capitalist Development and Democracy* (Chicago: University of Chicago Press, 1992).

[33] Charles Tilly, "Where Do Rights Come From?" in *Contributions to the Comparative Study of Development*, ed. Lars Mjoset (Oslo: Institute for Social Research, 1992), 10; Philip A. Klinkner and Rogers M. Smith, *The Unsteady March: The Rise and Decline of Racial Equality in America* (Chicago: University of Chicago Press, 1999).

[34] The role of a divided elite is a central theme in the democratization literature, whether this division is generated by nonpolitical processes such as the structure of the economy or by the efforts of insurgents or social movements themselves. Karl Marx and Friedrich Engels, *Marx/Engels Selected Works*, vol. 1 (Moscow: Progress Publishers, 1969), 98–137; Wood, *Forging Democracy from Below*, 14; Przeworski, *Democracy and the Market*, 55–57; Guillermo O'Donnell and Philippe C. Schmitter, *Transitions from Authoritarian Rule: Tentative Conclusions About Uncertain Democracies* (Baltimore: The Johns Hopkins University Press, 1986), 19–20.

In a similar vein, scholars have argued that political rights can be extended by a political party looking for a competitive advantage over its rivals, enfranchising some constituencies in the hopes of securing their electoral support. Here the focus is less on conflict between broad social classes than on a more quotidian jockeying for partisan advantage, but the logic is the same: the pursuit of a particular political project leads a faction of the elite to extend political rights in order to recruit allies against their rivals.[35]

What insight do these stories provide on democratization in America? And what, if anything, can they tell us about its co-occurrence with disenfranchisement? Perhaps most important, they implicitly or explicitly condition the likelihood of democratization on the level and form of social and economic equality within society: when a small ruling clique owns the vast majority of wealth (especially if that wealth is immovable), then democratizations threaten a drastic redistribution of property, making repression a more appealing option and outreaches to new constituencies a dangerous gambit. If the enfranchised and disenfranchised are not very different in social and economic standing, however, then the costs of democratization will be much lower, easing its acceptance.[36]

This insight is critical to understanding democratization in America. A long line of historians and social scientists have argued that frontier conditions in the New World produced an abundance of land and scarcity of labor, a configuration that facilitated the acquisition of property by the laboring classes and that checked the emergence of any overweening aristocracy.[37] Repeated efforts to recreate the social and economic structure of Europe were foiled when the needed workers and tenants moved and claimed land for their own use. As many American agricultural laborers became landowners themselves, the property-based voting

---

[35] E. E. Schattschneider, *The Semi-Sovereign People: A Realist's View of Democracy in America* (New York: Holt, Rinehart, and Winston, 1964), 98–99; Valelly, "How Suffrage Politics Made – and Makes – America," 445–72, 463; Humberto Llavador and Robert J. Oxoby, "Partisan Competition, Growth, and the Franchise," *The Quarterly Journal of Economics* 120, no. 3 (2005): 1155–92.

[36] Carles Boix, *Democracy and Redistribution* (New York: Cambridge University Press, 2003), 3; Carles Boix and Susan Stokes, "Endogenous Democratization," *World Politics* 55, no. 4 (2003): 517–49, 540.

[37] Tocqueville, *Democracy in America*, 50; Du Bois, *Black Reconstruction*, 6; Louis Hartz, *The Liberal Tradition in America* (New York: Harcourt, Brace, and World, Inc., 1955); Evsey Domar, "The Causes of Slavery or Serfdom: A Hypothesis," *Economic History Review* 30, no. 1 (1970): 18–32; Stanley Engerman and Kenneth Sokoloff, "The Evolution of Suffrage Institutions in the New World," *Journal of Economic History* 65, no. 4 (2005): 891–921.

qualifications that might have restricted political power proved insufficient at preventing most free adult men from claiming a right to vote. And because the potential costs of further democratization were already low, competition among political parties, mobilization for war, efforts to attract immigrants, and occasional pressure from below led to expansions of the suffrage that quickly resulted in the country being an "(almost) full democracy."[38]

This story is lacking much necessary detail, taking for granted the political and military investments and institutions that undergirded the abundance of land and the deliberate efforts of America's settlers to devise institutions restricting the mobility of the laboring classes. We will complicate it further in Chapters 2 through 4. But as an abstract story, it contains an important insight: the early occurrence of democratization in America was fundamentally shaped by the distinctive features of settlement in the New World, which had the effect not of eradicating class conflict but of potentially reorganizing some of the antagonisms within America's settler society and, from the perspective of the wealthy elite, muting some of democracy's dangers.

What does this imply for understanding the co-occurrence of democratization with disenfranchisement? Perhaps not surprisingly, accounts in the democratization literature that do try to explain the persistent exclusion of black Americans often begin by treating race as constitutive of a particular class relationship or class position. While "there have also been racial restrictions on voting," note Acemoglu and Robinson, "the racial groups disenfranchised have always been poor."[39] The significance of "race" in these accounts is that it serves as a marker for a distinctive class position, that of being a slave or available for enslavement or part of the "American peasantry" or just simply poor. Slavery is in turn treated as a system of labor control more extreme than, but comparable in kind, to that exercised by aristocratic landlords over serfs and peasants. American slaveholders then can be cast in the role played elsewhere by Anglo-Irish landlords, French nobles, or German junkers: a social class with an existential material stake in opposing democratization.[40]

---

[38] Rueschemeyer, Stephens, and Stephens, *Capitalist Development and Democracy*, 125; Donald Ratcliffe, "The Right to Vote and the Rise of Democracy, 1787–1828," *Journal of the Early Republic* 33, no. 2 (2013): 219–54.

[39] Acemoglu and Robinson, *Economic Origins of Dictatorship and Democracy*, 119.

[40] This is clearest in Moore's analysis of the Civil War as a bourgeois revolution in *Social Origins of Dictatorship and Democracy*, chapter 1. For a discussion of the particularities of labor-repressive agriculture, see Wood, *Forging Democracy from Below*, 6-8; Robert

The treatment of American slavery as a particular type of coercive labor regime is important, as it helps place American democratization into a broader comparative framework and reminds us that it was a material investment around which particular classes and political commitments were formed. One possible answer to our question, then, might be to tell a slightly modified story of American democratization, reaffirming its fortunate status but circumscribing this along lines of geography and race. In the North, the relatively low cost of obtaining land defeated efforts to erect a rent-collecting aristocracy, and so democratization could proceed without much serious opposition. In the South, a particular type of aristocracy was established and empowered, one that rested on the ability to own and control black slave labor. This group – which included large planters, mid-sized farmers, and the region's aspiring middle classes – would be willing to risk violent secession and terroristic campaigns to oppose democratization, eventually carving out "authoritarian enclaves" that persisted into the latter half of the twentieth century.[41] In this story, it is the elites – and in particular, the slave-owning class – that was most invested in disenfranchisement.[42]

The limit of such an account, however, is that disenfranchisement was not restricted to enslaved African Americans nor to the South: before the Civil War, racial disenfranchisement had gradually come to encompass nearly all persons categorized as nonwhite, regardless of whether they were held in slavery or lived in those states dominated by the slave-owning class. It is not clear from this story, for instance, why Pennsylvania, a state that began abolishing slavery in 1780, would disenfranchise black men in 1838. Nor is it apparent why the vast majority of nonslave states, including newly settled territories eager to attract labor and capital, would disenfranchise all free black men, including the wealthy. Nor can sole

---

W. Mickey, "The Beginning of the End for Authoritarian Rule in America: Smith v. Allwright and the Abolition of the White Primary in the Deep South, 1944–1948," *Studies in American Political Development* 22, no.2 (2008): 143–82.

[41] This version of the story is perhaps most explicitly laid out by Rueschemeyer, Stephens, and Stephens, *Capitalist Development and Democracy*; on the characterization of the South post-Reconstruction as "authoritarian enclaves," rather than a form of "democracy for whites only," see Robert Mickey, *Paths Out of Dixie: The Democratization of Authoritarian Enclaves in America's Deep South, 1944–1972* (Princeton, NJ: Princeton University Press, 2015).

[42] I refer to this class interchangeably as slave-owners and slaveholders, with the first used to highlight the fact that the United States recognized a property claim in persons and on this basis ensured that the full weight of local, state, and federal government would be brought to bear on the side of the "owner."

responsibility be straightforwardly attributed to the slave-owning classes when black disenfranchisement had so much support among all classes of white Americans.

The few answers one can find in the democratization literature rely heavily on the claim that "race" served as a conceptual category that could somehow restrict the process of democratization in ways that rendered it safe for the southern elite. In their study of American democratization, for example, Dietrich Rueschemeyer, Evelyne Huber Stephens, and John D. Stephens argue that the ostensible racial distinction between whites and blacks made it "plausible [for the southern elite] to think that inclusion of poor whites would not be a precedent for blacks."[43]

But why shouldn't the inclusion of poor whites have been a precedent? As we will see, free and enslaved blacks certainly claimed that it was, and they were joined in this belief by anxious slave-owners, who complained regularly that the precedent of democracy and equal rights encouraged insurrection. "Race," as a category of law and social practice, does not so much resolve the question as raise another: through what mechanisms did it work to cordon off democracy?

Disenfranchising American Democracy

Fortunately, we have other stories that focus directly on this question – stories that interrogate what Aziz Rana has eloquently described as the "two faces of American freedom."[44]

Exclusion as a Functional Requisite of Democracy

One category of answer argues that disenfranchisement reflects a general tendency of democratic regimes toward exclusion. For democracies to persist, it is argued, they require the cultivation of a strong sense of collective identity achieved through exclusionary policies that reinforce in-group solidarity. This claim grows out of a research tradition that looked for the foundations of stable democratic government in the economic and demographic characteristics of society, and that concluded that ethnic, racial, or religious heterogeneity undermined democracy by reducing societal consensus. One possible implication of this research is that cultivating a strong sense of in- and out-group identities might be an essential condition for the survival of democratic regimes. Charles

---

[43] Rueschemeyer, Stephens, and Stephens, *Capitalist Development and Democracy*, 125.
[44] Rana, *The Two Faces of American Freedom*.

Taylor, for instance, has argued that democratic exclusion is "a by-product of the need, in self-governing societies, of a high degree of cohesion" that can only be achieved through the creation of a "people with a strong collective identity."[45] Expanding on this logic, Rebecca Kook has maintained that "democratic regimes always exclude groups or individuals" and do so precisely in order "to maintain the exclusivity necessary for the identity to function as an efficient mechanism of cooperation."[46] The implication for our question is that the simultaneous expansion of democracy and the exclusion of nonwhites in American history might have been neither coincidental nor politically contingent but functionally related and necessary companions.

While there is an elegance to this answer, neatly accounting for the limits of democracy by drawing attention to its ostensible functional needs, it shares the drawbacks of most functionalist arguments: it requires us to presume either that democracies naturally "produce" the exclusions they ostensibly need, or that state-builders aim to maintain a high degree of social cohesion rather than pursue their own ambitions; and it has difficulty accounting for dramatic changes over time in the scope and porousness of democracy's boundaries and the rigidity of its internal hierarchies.

Racial Hierarchy as Constitutive of American Democracy

Another set of arguments suggests this conjunction is not a necessary feature of all democracies but just of American democracy, the historical development of which was conditional upon racialized slavery. Edmund Morgan's account of colonial Virginia, for instance, details how laws that fragmented the colony's laboring class into rigid racial categories helped local elites mitigate the threat of insurrection. In response to persistent threats from below, the Virginia elite acquired and opened up new lands for settlement, enabling the broad diffusion of property that Tocqueville and others took as a natural condition of American life. At the same time, however, they codified a system of labor regulation and racial hierarchy that subjected those of African descent – slaves as well as free persons – to an extraordinary system of social control. Since access to property by former white agricultural workers often included acquiring slaves, ties of sympathy and convergent interests were created between this new middle class and the large planters, making a broadly participatory public life

---

[45] Charles Taylor, "The Dynamics of Democratic Exclusion," *Journal of Democracy* 9, no. 4 (1998): 143–56, 143–44.

[46] Kook, *The Logic of Democratic Exclusion*, 6, 34.

much less threatening to the latter. "Racism," Morgan argues, "made it possible for white Virginians to develop a devotion to the equality that English republicans had declared to be the soul of liberty," and it absorbed "the fear and contempt that men in England, whether Whig or Tory, monarchist or republican, felt for the inarticulate lower classes."[47] This racism was not a free-floating belief in human difference or simply an individual prejudice toward people of different backgrounds: it was a rigidly enforced legal and social code, one that was constructed with a distinct political and economic purpose in mind.

Aziz Rana tells a similar, but distinctive, story about how the democratic ideals trumpeted as essential characteristics of American peoplehood "gained strength and meaning through frameworks of exclusion."[48] Rana notes that colonial Americans believed property ownership was an essential condition for republican citizenship, but rightly emphasizes the degree to which control over property in *settler colonial societies* is especially dependent on the successful projection of coercive power. American conceptions of freedom, he argues, have always rested on a foundation of coercion, which was necessary for the settler community to vanquish in the conflicts their freedom engendered, whether it was to displace and eliminate the indigenous populations, to suppress slave insurrections, or to aggressively police disproportionately immigrant working classes.

Perhaps the most important variant of this type of argument is to be found in the literature on "whiteness," a diverse body of scholarship that rests on three broad claims: that "white" is a meaningful and socially constructed racial identity; that this identity does political work, reconciling a large segment of the American working class with the country's elite; and that the white working classes' psychic investment in this identity ensures that they take primary responsibility for articulating and enforcing white supremacy. Drawing on the work of W. E. B. Du Bois, whiteness scholars have argued that the category of "white" is the product of a cross-class coalition of a segment of the working class and their masters, employers, and landlords in which the latter gained a "public and psychological wage" as compensation for their loss of status or economic independence in an increasingly market-based society.[49] "The cross-class

---

[47] Morgan, *American Freedom, American Slavery*, 386.
[48] Rana, *Two Faces of American Freedom*, 7, 12.
[49] Du Bois, *Black Reconstruction*, 700; W. E. B. Du Bois, "Marxism and the Negro Problem," *Crisis* 40, no. 5 (1933): 103–4, 104; Roediger, *Wages of Whiteness*, 12.

alliance," writes Joel Olson, "is the class foundation of the white democracy," ensuring "the social stability of American democracy by reconciling political equality with economic exploitation through a system of racial privilege and subordination."[50]

But if white supremacy is based on a cross-class alliance, particular emphasis is placed on the role of the white working class in enforcing its strictures. "White labor," writes David Roediger, "does not just receive and resist racist ideas but embraces, adopts and, at times, murderously acts upon those ideas."[51] In terms of our question, whiteness scholarship regularly suggests that it was the white working classes that pressed for the disenfranchisement of African Americans during the antebellum era.[52]

These are a very diverse set of texts, with perhaps more differences than similarities. But they share a core theme: it was not the absence of inequality or class conflict that was the defining feature of American history but rather its reorganization along lines of race. Racial hierarchy was from the outset a constitutive feature of American democracy, providing the conceptual basis or material conditions for equal citizenship among white Americans.

Disenfranchisement as the Product of Partisan Competition

A final set of accounts takes a very different tack, emphasizing the contingent character of disenfranchisement and treating it as a product of short-term political calculations. The starting point for these accounts is E. E. Schattschneider's observation that political parties in danger of losing their majority might expand the right to vote in the hopes that incoming electors will support them. Party-based accounts of disenfranchisement argue that the logic also applies in reverse – that under certain conditions, parties will seek electoral advantage by disenfranchising constituencies that support their opponents, increasing the size of their majority without having to reach beyond their base.[53]

J. Morgan Kousser inaugurated the comparative study of disenfranchisements with his analysis of the exclusion of African Americans in the late

[50] Olson, *Abolition of White Democracy*, xxiv, 16, 29, 39; Evelyn Nakano Glenn, *Unequal Freedom: How Race and Gender Shaped American Citizenship and Labor* (Cambridge, MA: Harvard University Press, 2004), 30; Alexander, *New Jim Crow*, 34.

[51] Roediger, *Wages of Whiteness*, 12; Noel Ignatiev, *How the Irish Became White* (New York: Routledge, 1995); Du Bois, *Black Reconstruction*, 30.

[52] Roediger, *Wages of Whiteness*, 56–59; Glenn, *Unequal Freedom*, 29–30.

[53] Schattschneider, *The Semi-Sovereign People*; Valelly, *The Two Reconstructions*; Valelly, "How Suffrage Politics Made – and Makes – America," 445–72.

nineteenth century, concluding that "evidence of a partisan intent" underlying the disenfranchisements was "overwhelming."[54] Similar arguments
have been made about the disenfranchisement of free blacks during the
antebellum era.[55] Frances Fox Piven, Lorraine Minnite, and Margaret
Groake have extended this argument to include strategies of voter suppression, such as restrictive voter identification laws or effort to limit
access to polling stations, which become more likely when appeals to
new voters would strain a party's existing policy commitments and
when they can be targeted at voters "whose discordant cultural identities
and contentious political demands make them easier to isolate."[56]

In general, party-based accounts stress a built-in incentive under competitive electoral institutions for incumbents to manipulate electoral qualifications. Richard Valelly, however, adds the important insight that its
occurrence is conditional on whether the group targeted for disenfranchisement has access to institutions that will enable them to effectively resist
their exclusion.[57] The implication for our question is that the association
of white democratization in America with the disenfranchisement of
nonwhites was a historically contingent one, produced by partisan competition and the contours of American institutions.

Toward a Common Story

These stories provide different perspectives on the relevant actors and
motivations underlying democratization and disenfranchisement and on
the mechanisms by which they might have been connected. The literature
on democratization outlines a set of strategic interactions framed largely
around the divergent preferences over economic redistribution held by
varyingly unified blocs of elites, industrial workers, and rural peasants.
From this we could distill a possible story of black disenfranchisement in
the United States in which the group most invested in excluding African
Americans from the electorate would be economic elites, particularly
slave-owners.

---

[54] Kousser, *Shaping of Southern Politics*, 259.
[55] Malone, *Between Freedom and Bondage*; Paul J. Polgar, "'Whenever They Judge
It Expedient': The Politics of Partisanship and Free Black Voting Rights in Early
National New York," *American Nineteenth Century History* 12, no. 1 (2011): 1–23.
[56] Frances Fox Piven, Lorraine C. Minnite, and Margaret Groarke, *Keeping Down the
Black Vote: Race and the Demobilization of American Voters* (New York: The New
Press, 2009), 16, 17, 21.
[57] Valelly, *The Two Reconstructions*.

By contrast, a prominent theme of accounts focusing on racial exclusion in America is that the impetus for disenfranchisement came from below, from working-class whites who were psychically invested in a racial identity premised upon their civic, social, and biological superiority over black Americans; or from a more broadly distributed preference for white supremacy in a society where freedom was conceptually based on black subordination.[58] Social cohesion and party-based accounts often implicitly downplay the importance of varying preferences across social classes and place the motivation for disenfranchisement and democratization in the contingent choices of state builders looking to foster a strong communal identity and party leaders looking for electoral advantage.

The first question that we need to resolve, then, is that of agency and motivation. It is common shorthand to attribute agency to broad social categories, such as the "working class" or "elite," who are presumed to share material interests around which stable and coherent preferences over public policy can be formed. This provides a convenient rubric for researchers to compare agents and motivations across countries and historical periods; indeed, if the ambition is to explain the "origins of dictatorship and democracy," then reliance on such categories is an almost essential analytical strategy, precisely because they abstract away from the multiplicity of potential identities and social cleavages that are found in any complex society.[59]

But this leaves unaddressed the critical questions of how collective action was organized and how interests and policy objectives were determined. For the "working class" or "the elite" to be constituted politically, it must be given organized form through which their particular class interests can be defined and expressed, whether this is done through labor unions, formal political organizations, diffuse social movements, or the amorphous but identifiable combination of old families, corporate directors, political and state officials, and military men that C. Wright Mills characterized as the "power elite."[60] This step from putative class

---

[58] Morgan places important stress on the deliberate construction of racism but also argues that it was this that eventually allowed Virginians – and America, he writes, was "colonial Virginia writ large" – to conceptualize republican equality and a more democratic organization of public life. Morgan, *American Slavery, American Freedom*, 387.

[59] The presence of cross-cutting cleavages, however, does have a long lineage in social science research on democratization.

[60] C. Wright Mills, *The Power Elite* (Oxford, UK: Oxford University Press, 1956); C. Wright Mills, "The Structure of Power in American Society," *The British Journal of*

interests to organized groups inevitably means that not all of a class's potential interests will be represented, that some additional interests will sneak in, and most importantly that a relatively small set of agents operating within particular organizations will have to interpret and define these interests and select which should be prioritized.[61]

This is an important strength of accounts that place the emphasis on political parties. The empirical advantage is that the choices made by parties over how to define their interests, which to prioritize, and the appropriate strategy for their achievement can be more or less definitely identified by looking at their internal deliberations or their activities in campaigns and legislative bodies. The theoretical advantage is that party-centered accounts assign motivation to a set of agents capable of realizing their goals in policy, rather than a more amorphous class whose ability to act collectively is far from clear.

Party-centered accounts, however, can at times go too far in the other direction, treating parties as almost exclusively motivated by the electoral interests of office seekers and neglecting the ways in which social groups or aligned constituencies might have shaped the decisions of partisan actors. Political scientists often think of parties as organizational frames for advancing the interests of ambitious individual office seekers.[62] But political parties also rely heavily on alliances with organized groups that seek specific policy goals.[63] These groups – labor unions, public interest groups, professional associations, networks of issue activists – can sometimes be represented directly in the institutions of the party, or an alliance might be formed around regular participation in shared endeavors, coordinating support for election campaigns or legislative proposals. Insofar

Sociology 9, no. 1 (1958): 29–41; Adam Przeworski and John Sprague, *Paper Stones: A History of Electoral Socialism* (Chicago: University of Chicago Press, 1986).

[61] As Daniel Ziblatt notes, "'Upper-class' and 'lower-class' groups are not the only relevant actors, and it is certainly incorrect to treat economic groups as if they themselves were *directly* fighting over democracy.... What is missing is a theoretical account that comes to terms with the fact that it was often *political parties* that only partially represented societal and political elites who were the key players in fights over democratization." Daniel Ziblatt, *Conservative Parties and the Birth of Democracy* (Cambridge: Cambridge University Press, 2017), 20; C. Wright Mills, "Letter to the New Left," *New Left Review* 5 (September–October 1960).

[62] John Aldrich, *Why Parties? A Second Look* (Chicago: University of Chicago Press, 2011).

[63] Kathleen Bawn, Martin Cohen, David Karol, and Seth Masket, "A Theory of Political Parties: Groups, Policy Demands, and Nominations in American Politics," *Perspectives on Politics* 10, no. 3 (2012): 571–97; Daniel Schlozman, *When Movements Anchor Parties: Electoral Alignments in American History* (Princeton, NJ: Princeton University Press, 2015).

as these groups actually represent broader constituencies, their alliances with parties suggest the possibility of a reciprocal relationship connecting parties, groups, and different types of social constituencies. Groups such as labor unions, for example, might attempt to represent and give shape to the protean interests and identities of their social base, advocating for these within a larger coalition. And through engagement with this coalition, a particular construction of common purpose and identity might be disseminated back to their constituents. Parties or other organized coalitions can consequently serve as a vehicle joining macro-historical perspectives that stress the interests of discrete social classes, the analytical need to root agency in organizations able to act collectively, and the frequently observed fact that groups' subjective understandings of interest and identities are politically and socially constructed.

Specifying the actors involved and the particular ways in which they understood their goals and interests is an essential first step. But political change is always shaped by an institutional context that conditions behavior, allocates influence, and molds the identities and goals of political actors. This is a key point developed by Richard Valelly, whose account of black voting rights during the "two Reconstructions" emphasizes strategic calculations over partisan advantage but also the institutional context in which these calculations took place. Valelly argues that while the post–Civil War Republican party had a partisan incentive to defend the voting rights of southern blacks, and the southern Democratic party had a partisan motive to support disenfranchisement, it was the course of institution building in the region that ultimately determined which of these two goals would be realized. The dismantling of institutions for protecting voting rights, and the failure to build new ones, left southern (black) Republican constituencies at the mercy of local disenfranchising coalitions.[64] To understand policy change, then, means that we need to examine how governing institutions shaped the opportunities for different actors to achieve their objectives, by empowering them directly, by enabling them to persuade a broader range of actors to support their position, or by imposing steep hurdles for exercising influence.

DISENFRANCHISING DEMOCRACY

The account I offer is a political-institutional one, focusing on the motivations of organized coalitions, rather than broad social classes; on the

---

[64] Valelly, *The Two Reconstructions*, chapter 6.

institutional context that structured their efforts and conditioned their prospects for success; and on the visions of political community they advanced in support of their goals. I first discuss the argument as it pertains to the United States; I then distill from it a more generalizable account of the relationship between democratization and disenfranchisement that can be applied elsewhere.

The United States of America

The American pattern of simultaneous democratization and disenfranchisement, I argue, was the product of a national political coalition that saw an electoral advantage and ideological purpose in facilitating the mobilization of lower class whites into politics and yet was responsive to the organized demands of slaveholders, who came to see free black citizenship as posing an integral threat to their own well-being. This coalition, which first appeared in the form of Thomas Jefferson's Republican Party, was organized to take advantage of the US Constitution's implicit requirement that aspiring political leaders appeal to constituencies in both the South and the North. But the early years of the Republic repeatedly revealed that state and national legislators fundamentally differed over their understandings of national citizenship, particularly about whether the republican commitments most of them extolled should be applied to the growing class of free African Americans.

In an ongoing effort to keep the coalition together, Republican legislators gradually worked out a narrative of political community that they hoped would resolve this tension. The narrative around which they eventually coalesced was the *white man's republic*, which held that America's political community had always been intended as a racially circumscribed republic, its founding principles of civic and political equality applicable to white men only. This story was invoked in concrete political fights, election campaigns, and judicial contests, and seemed to reconcile the democratic and egalitarian commitments of some of the party's most active members with the anxieties of its most important aligned constituency. Throughout the antebellum period, the political parties that inherited the Republican mantel – and especially the Democratic Party – sought to disseminate this view among their activists, aligned interest groups, and a more diffuse public opinion. In doing so, they helped foster a political culture premised on and organized around the defense of *white* democracy, one that was strongest among Democratic-leaning constituencies and Democratic partisans but that permeated much of American society.

How does this story relate to the accounts of democratization and disenfranchisement presented above? Following the literature on democratization, I argue that the most important social class opposed to black political rights were slaveholders who worried that voting by free blacks would blur the rigid equation of black and slave upon which their material existence rested. But it was not "race" as a conceptual category that reassured slaveholders that democratization for whites would not be a precedent for blacks. There were specific institutional mechanisms that served this purpose. For the slaveholding elite to secure the reassurance they needed, they had to work through a political organization that united them with constituencies in the North, and so they gradually negotiated and encouraged the exclusion of black Americans across the nation through the elite networks that constituted the party coalition.

This is not an argument that widespread white racism was unimportant, or that it was the product of southern influence, or that the political parties were the only organizations responsible for its dissemination in public opinion. American racism has diverse origins, including a longstanding denigration of persons of African descent in Anglo-American culture and a colonial-era codification of "race" as a civic status defined through its connection to slavery, which fostered a culture in which the meaning of liberty and equality was always inflected by an awareness of and participation in the subjugation of others.[65] These legacies, along with the emergence of an international discourse about inherent racial difference, provided a conceptual frame and language into which calculations over economic competition or anxieties over status could be slated.[66] Political leaders, participants in an extensive

---

[65] The timing and origins of modern forms of racial prejudice, as a distinct belief in inherent difference, has long been a point of disagreement among historians. Oscar Handlin and Mary F. Handlin, "The Origins of the Southern Labor System," *The William and Mary Quarterly* 7, no. 2 (1950): 199–222; Carl Degler, "Slavery and the Genesis of American Race Prejudice," *Comparative Studies in Society and History*, 2, no. 1 (1959): 49–66; Oscar Handlin, Mary F. Handlin, and Carl N. Degler, "Letters to the Editor," *Comparative Studies in Society and History* 2, no. 4 (1960): 488–95; Winthrop D. Jordan, *White Over Black: American Attitudes Toward the Negro, 1550–1812* (Chapel Hill: University of North Carolina Press, 1968); Ibram X. Kendi, *Stamped from the Beginning: The Definitive History of Racist Ideas in America* (New York: Nation Books, 2016), 15–76; David Brion Davis, "The Culmination of Racial Polarities and Prejudice," *Journal of the Early Republic* 19, no. 4 (1999): 757–75; see the contributions to the *William and Mary Quarterly* special issue on "Constructing Race."

[66] Bruce Dain, *A Hideous Monster of the Mind: American Race Theory in the Early Republic* (Cambridge, MA: Harvard University Press, 2002); Nicholas Hudson, "From 'Nation' to 'Race': The Origin of Racial Classification in Eighteenth Century Thought,"

transatlantic literary culture, military officials, and regular whites of all backgrounds and regions contributed to the construction of an image of black Americans, as well as the indigenous nations, as separate from, dangerous to, and, paradoxically, inferior to the white community.[67] Within this political and cultural matrix, white Americans learned early and with strong reinforcement to differentiate themselves from black Americans, producing no unity or solidarity among whites themselves but spawning attitudes ranging from vituperative animosity to condescending sympathy toward persons of color.

Northern racism was in no way a Southern import. But it *was* organized politically, given ideological coherence, and intensified and mobilized in political campaigns by parties whose most important leaders were Southerners and that relied heavily on Southern money and Southern votes for their national viability. The strength of Northern racism undoubtedly made black disenfranchisement more politically palatable, and its intensification over the antebellum era certainly made opposing it politically as well as socially difficult. But it was only with the organization of the Jeffersonian coalition that democratization for white men and disenfranchisement for black men came to be *conjoined* politically, a pattern that rested on the fact that those Northern politicians who in the antebellum era were most responsible for democratization were also affiliated with a national party that rewarded the organization of white supremacy. It was the governing institutions at the national level, especially the political parties, that helped stitch the inclusive and exclusionary dimensions of the American experience into a coherent vision of national community.

The association between democratization and disenfranchisement was not inevitable, and alternative configurations were possible. An important theme of Chapters 2 and 3 is that before the appearance of the Jeffersonian coalition, democratization and disenfranchisement each tended to have distinct bases of support, were pushed

---

Eighteenth-Century Studies 29, no. 3 (1996): 247–59; James Brewer Stewart, "The Emergence of Racial Modernity and the Rise of the White North, 1790–1840," *Journal of the Early Republic* 18, no. 2 (1998): 181–217.

[67] Alexander Saxton, *The Rise and Fall of the White Republic: Class Politics and Mass Culture in Nineteenth Century America* (London: Verso, 1990); Reginald Horsman, *Race and Manifest Destiny: The Origins of American Racial Anglo-Saxonism* (Cambridge, MA: Harvard University Press, 1981); Robert G. Parkinson, *The Common Cause: Creating Race and Nation in the American Revolution* (Chapel Hill: University of North Carolina Press, 2016).

onto the policy agenda by different groups, and tended not to occur in conjunction or with explicit rhetorical reference to the other. It was only as this coalition was institutionalized that they became linked, the Jeffersonian and later Democratic Party the principal vehicles for both. In turn, activists who hoped to make alternative configurations a reality – such as a race-neutral but class-limited suffrage, or manhood suffrage, or even the more genuinely universal suffrage that was put on the agenda after Seneca Falls – recognized the need to confront the Democratic Party and the vision of political community it helped popularize.

A Generalized Story

This story of America's disenfranchising democracy has been pieced together by my reading of secondary sources, historical debates, and the analyses I will present in Part I. But we can also reframe the question as a more general one: under what conditions do democratization and exclusion occur in conjunction with each other?

The theoretical accounts of democratization outlined above focused on the decisions made by an incumbent elite and suggested that the key determinant of democratization is what elites choose to do when confronted by popular demands or internal divisions. Before this critical moment arrives, however, there has to be the organization of an alternative. "What is threatening to authoritarian regimes," writes Adam Przeworski, "is not the breakdown of legitimacy but the organization of counterhegemony: collective projects for an alternative future."[68] Such alternative projects of rule articulate a new vision of how the relationship between state and different social groups should be organized, and they propose institutional reforms to realize this vision in practice. These might aim at the eradication of the existing elite, or its replacement by a counter-elite, or even just integration into the established regime on equal terms.[69] They might even be intended to secure the interests of

---

[68] Przeworski, *Democracy and the Market*, 54–55; see also Valerie J. Bunce and Sharon L. Wolchik, "Defeating Dictators: Electoral Change and Stability in Competitive Authoritarian Regimes," *World Politics* 62, no. 1 (2010): 43–86, 67.

[69] The "primary objective" of many within the African National Congress in opposing apartheid, according to Moeletsi Mbeki, "was inclusion into the existing system." Peter S. Goodman, "End of Apartheid in South Africa?" *New York Times*, October 24, 2017.

incumbent elites themselves, changing the form of the regime in order to retain the privileges of its social base.[70]

Insofar as these projects are aimed at regime transformation, however, their proponents will need to take control of state institutions or force incumbents to negotiate. This will usually require bringing together a diverse set of groups and actors into a coalition, whether in the form of a social movement, an elite political party, a cabal of military officers, or something else.[71] How broad this coalition needs to be, which specific elements are most important to include, and what types of activities it will engage in will be conditioned by the institutional context. Some of these actors will be motivated by the perceived interests of a social group, while others will be focused more on personal enrichment. Many of the "allies in the struggle" will rank among the already enfranchised; some will be found among the incumbent elite; and sometimes the unenfranchised might be missing from the struggle altogether, the recipients rather than conquerors of rights. But many will be regular people, moved to action by persistent injustice and looking to secure political and economic liberation or a valued civic status for themselves or others. Whatever their particular motivations or backgrounds, they are united by a negotiated belief that their goals cannot be realized within the constraints of existing institutions.

Once we recognize, as much theorizing in comparative politics has done, that democratization does not pit a "mass" against an "elite" but a varyingly diverse coalition seeking a change to the regime against another varyingly diverse coalition seeking its preservation,[72] then we can begin to see it not as a sliding scale of inclusion but as a political contest over which assemblage of individuals and groups will be given greater weight in deciding questions of collective allocation.

Democratization as a political project, then, can be understood as a calculated effort, never fully controlled or predictable, to reconstitute the social basis of the state by changing the set of groups and communities

---

[70] "Unless we ourselves take a hand now, they'll foist a republic on us. If we want things to stay as they are, things will have to change." Giuseppe di Lampedusa, *The Leopard*, trans. Archibald Colquhoun (New York: Pantheon Books, 2007 [1960]), 28.

[71] Marc Morjé Howard and Philip G. Roessler, "Liberalizing Electoral Outcomes in Competitive Authoritarian Regimes," *American Journal of Political Science* 50, no. 2 (2006): 365–81.

[72] Institutionalizing the coalition of incumbent elites in the form of a political party might be especially useful. Jason Brownlee, *Authoritarianism in an Age of Democratization* (New York: Cambridge University Press, 2007).

that are the principal beneficiaries of its policies and whose support is crucial for its survival.[73] That democratization involves a reconstitution of the social basis of the state is implicit in the theoretical literature on the subject, much of which rests on the assumption that the policies of a postdemocratization regime will differ from those of its predecessor precisely because of the changed social preferences to which policymakers will be responsive.[74] What is distinct about the perspective I offer is that it underscores the importance of coalition building in shaping how this project is conceived, negotiated, and defined;[75] it makes clear that democratization can involve a mix of inclusionary and restrictive reforms; and it highlights the need for a democratizing coalition to collectively envision the terms of their reconstitutive project and to devise an electoral basis that could sustain it.

This coalition-focused account helps answer the question of disenfranchising democratization. Enfranchisement and disenfranchisement will occur in conjunction when: (1) the institutional or political context encourages those conspiring to change the regime to build a broad

[73] There is a long literature that examines the mutual constitution of states and societies, as well as related questions of the degree to which the state can operate autonomously from the preferences of those classes that constitute its base. Joel Migdal, *State in Society: Studying How States and Societies Transform and Constitute One Another* (New York: Cambridge University Press, 2001); Timothy Mitchell, "The Limits of the State: Beyond Statist Approaches and Their Critics," *American Political Science Review* 85, no. 1 (1991): 77–96; Ralph Miliband, *The State in Capitalist Society* (London: Weidenfeld & Nicholson, 1969); Nicos Poulantzas, "The Problem of the Capitalist State," *New Left Review* 58 (1969): 67; Fred Block, "The Ruling Class Does Not Rule: Notes on the Marxist Theory of the State," *Socialist Revolution* 33, no. 7 (1977): 6–28.

[74] Allan Meltzer and Scott Richard, "Why Government Grows (and Grows) in a Democracy," *Public Interest* 52 (1978): 111–18; T. S. Aidt, Jayasri Dutta, and Elena Loukoianova, "Democracy Comes to Europe: Franchise Extension and Fiscal Outcomes, 1830–1938," *European Economic Review* 50, no. 2 (2006): 249–83; Daron Acemoglu and James Robinson, "Why Did the West Extend the Franchise? Democracy, Inequality, and Growth in Historical Perspective," *The Quarterly Journal of Economics* 115, no. 4 (2000): 1167–1200; Llavdor and Oxoby, "Partisan Competition, Growth, and the Franchise," 1155–92; Alessandro Lizzeri and Nicola Persico, "Why Did the Elites Extend the Suffrage? Democracy and the Scope of Government, with an Application to Britain's 'Age of Reform,'" *The Quarterly Journal of Economics* 119, no. 2 (2004): 707–65.

[75] The importance of coalition building is a theme developed by a number of scholars of democratization. Adrienne LeBas, *From Protest to Parties: Party-Building and Democratization in Africa* (New York: Oxford University Press, 2011); Bunce and Wolchik, "Defeating Dictators"; Howard and Roessler, "Liberalizing Electoral Outcomes in Competitive Authoritarian Regimes"; Leonardo R. Arriola, *Multiethnic Coalitions in Africa: Business Financing of Opposition Election Campaigns* (New York: Cambridge University Press, 2012).

coalition uniting actors with separate interests in empowering some classes and excluding others; (2) these groups are able to articulate a shared vision of the changes they want to pursue, one that can reconcile their different goals and forestall fractures; (3) and through their coalitional efforts, rhetorical appeals, and policy promises, they can cultivate sufficiently broad support among their putative base to neutralize opposition from the to-be-disenfranchised, depriving them of allies and anchoring a willingness to use the coercive institutions of the state against them if needed. *in summary: people cut deals*

Forging a Coalition and Constructing a "People"

This argument draws our attention to two problems faced by an emerging counterelite: the need to reconcile potential divisions within its coalition, and the need to secure the support of not just organized groups or influential individuals but of broader publics.[76] The diversity of interests represented in any coalition will inevitably create disagreement about priorities and strategies and raise the possibility of fracture. A particularly important source of tension within democratizing coalitions will be in deciding how their envisioned alternative will allocate institutional influence across different social groups, determining which should be included and the relative weight to be accorded to their voices.

So long as there exist multiple lines of potential antagonism within society, there is the possibility that some actors will perceive an interest in disenfranchisement. It is perhaps likely that labor-repressive agriculturalists will be especially invested in disenfranchisement, since their material existence is predicated upon denying the aspirations of their tenants or the enslaved. But it can be true of any group that "perceive[s] the danger to their property, privileges, and persons" as likely to be "endemic and unmanageable" if particular social groups are accorded political influence or civic standing.[77] These antagonisms need not fall strictly along lines of economic class: civic privileges are often allocated on the basis of religion, descent, gender, language, or other factors, and while these can form the basis for economic relationships or property accumulation, the perceived danger need not lie strictly in the economic realm. As the literature on party-motivated disenfranchisement reminds us, the threat might even

[76] For a similar claim, see Charles Tilly, *Stories, Identities, and Political Change* (Lanham, MD: Rowman and Littlefield, 2002), 89.

[77] Dan Slater, *Ordering Power: Contentious Politics and Authoritarian Leviathans in Southeast Asia* (New York: Cambridge University Press, 2010), 5.

exist only for a narrow class of officeholders. But whatever the basis of the antagonism, it is a line around which group and individual preferences over who should be enfranchised can form.

When brought into a coalition, whether in the form of a political party or something else, the diversity of these preferences is likely to occasion disagreement as participants try and forge a joint project of regime transformation out of their distinct visions for how the relationship between the state and different social groups should be structured. Coalitions try to reconcile these divisions by negotiating compromises and working out a set of shared principles that seem to render their diverse interests coherent and even mutually reinforcing. In other words, they articulate an ideology,[78] a principled rationale intended to persuade potential supporters that there is some long-run alignment between their diverse interests and aspirations, justifying their different goals as manifestations of a common principle or political project.[79] For many, this might amount to nothing more than agreed-upon opposition to the incumbent, "simply coalesc[ing] around a shared goal of ousting the ruling party."[80] But even when coalitions do not seek to build a common party, most will be impelled to negotiate a set of common objectives around which they can work together, and will communicate this to their constituents. Democratizing coalitions, in short, will often attempt to distill a set of common principles that justify their efforts at regime transformation while reassuring themselves and each other that the changes they bring about will take a form that they can live with.[81]

---

[78] Hans Noel, *Political Ideologies and Political Parties in America* (New York: Cambridge University Press, 2013), 42; Philip E. Converse, "The Nature of Belief Systems in Mass Publics," in *Ideology and Its Discontents*, ed. David E. Apter (New York: The Free Press of Glencoe, 1964), 211.

[79] This is one of the central functions of party platforms: they articulate a set of policy priorities around which different groups in a party can unify during a campaign, embedding these within a grander narrative that can appeal to a variety of audiences. John Gerring, *Party Ideologies in America, 1828–1996* (New York: Cambridge University Press, 1998).

[80] Danielle Resnick, "Do Electoral Coalitions Facilitate Democratic Consolidation in Africa?" *Party Politics* 19, no. 5 (2013): 735–57, 736.

[81] An ideological narrative is especially important if a coalition aims to endure beyond a regime transition. But it will also be a factor for coalitions with shorter horizons. John Wilson, *Introduction to Social Movements* (New York: Basic Books, 1973), 91–134, 126; Doug McAdam, John D. McCarthy, and Mayer N. Zald, *Comparative Perspectives on Social Movements: Political Opportunities, Mobilizing Structures, and Cultural Framings* (New York: Cambridge University Press, 1996), 6.

Defining the composition of the electorate, or the balance of rights and influence allocated across groups, will involve drawing equivalences and differences between various groups, articulating a common and compelling reason why some should be included or prioritized and others not.

This will likely occur in at least two registers, one concerned with who is instrumentally desirable to have within the electorate, and the other with how a particular "people" is defined and ought to be represented.[82] This second register will serve as an important means by which coalitions cultivate mass support, a task for which comprehensive ideologies and detailed platforms, let alone nakedly instrumental arguments, might be less useful.[83] For this reason, political coalitions often frame their appeals in terms that connect their ideological program with the diversity of identities, cultural attachments, and political ideals existing within society. Political parties, for example, often try to cultivate a sense among different constituencies that together they form a relatively coherent and meaningful public, one whose interests and values are well served by supporting this party politically.[84] Parties select certain identities as socially relevant and valued and try to associate themselves with these in the public mind. They can also cast others as worthy of denigration and try to associate these with their opponents. In short, they piggyback on the resonance of existing social identities and narratives of political

---

[82] This is similar to the distinction between coordinative and communicative discourse. Vivien Schmidt, "Discursive Institutionalism: The Explanatory Power of Ideas and Discourse," *Annual Review of Political Science* 11 (2008): 303–26.

[83] Voters tend not to respond to party manifestos – although they are sensitive to perceptions of party extremism – and are much less ideological than political elites. James Adams, Lawrence Ezrow, and Zeynep Somer-Tocu, "Do Voters Respond to Party Manifestos or to a Wider Information Environment? An Analysis of Mass-Elite Linkages on European Integration," *American Journal of Political Science* 58, no. 4 (2014): 967–78; Donald R. Kinder and Nathan P. Kalmoe, *Neither Liberal nor Conservative: Ideological Innocence in the American Public* (Chicago: University of Chicago Press, 2017).

[84] Decades of research into political socialization and preference formation have found that support for particular parties tends to be based less on calculations of material gain or consistent ideological positions than on socially constructed beliefs about what a given party stands for in terms of its broad values or the different social groups it is perceived to represent. Donald Green, Bradley Palmquist, and Eric Schickler, *Partisan Hearts and Minds: Political Parties and the Social Identities of Voters* (New Haven, CT: Yale University Press, 2002).

community, even as they try to rearticulate these into new and more favorable combinations.[85]

Democratizing coalitions do the same. In negotiating the terms of their common project, they narrate stories about the purpose and boundaries of political community and the proper relationship between the state and different social groups. These stories detail how a community is tied together by something – descent, choice, providential fate, a purposeful history – in such a way that their association entails something more meaningful than being simply "the same people living in the same place."[86] Democratizing coalitions rely on these stories to justify their projects, including the recomposition of the electorate, to themselves and to possible constituents. They promise to reform the institutions and iconography of the state – its definition of political rights, the civic statuses it supports, and the terms of its public discourse – so that these will better approximate this narrative and the values and interests it embodies. And they invite listeners to recognize their own experiences, interests, and aspirations in a particular construct of political community and to lend a coalition their support in this project.[87]

This process of discursively constructing a "people" is central to understanding how democratizing coalitions define the terms of their common projects and connect these with a mass public. While never under the total control of its proponents, it is through this process that the particular terms of a reconstitutive project are defined, imagined, and articulated to potential constituents, potentially anchoring the support needed to sustain its particular inclusions and exclusions over the long term.[88] This can be especially important if the coalition gains power, reconstitutes the regime, and disseminates its vision of political community from a position of political and cultural strength. In this case, the new political order will shape expectations about what types of discourse and political activities will help one advance politically or socially. Representatives of the new regime, for instance, will be likely to continue to recount this narrative, tying the opportunities and material benefits the regime provides back to this broader vision of community. The particular exclusions

---

[85] Cedric de Leon, Manali Desai, and Cihan Tugal, *Building Blocs: How Parties Organize Society* (Stanford, CA: Stanford University Press, 2015).

[86] James Joyce, *Ulysses* (London: Egoist Press, 1922), ep. 12, 1419–31; 523–54.

[87] Rogers M. Smith, *Stories of Peoplehood: The Politics and Morals of Political Membership* (Cambridge: Cambridge University Press, 2003), 32.

[88] Seymour Martin Lipset and Stein Rokkan, *Party Systems and Voter Alignments: Cross-National Perspectives* (Toronto: Free Press, 1967).

and inclusions that have been enacted can then become objects of popular civic loyalty, markers of the reconstituted relationship between state and society and the real and symbolic benefits that have flowed from this.

THE LOGIC OF COMPARISON

Disenfranchisement is a possibility wherever lines of antagonism exist within society or political life, such that a group involved in reshaping governing institutions could believe it will benefit from excluding portions of the population. This does not mean that it will be common, or that it will always be associated with democratization, or that it will always take the same form. It will be most likely in circumstances where social and political rivalries are fiercest, where countervailing institutions have been neutralized, or where those targeted for exclusion lack influential allies and the ability to organize resistance. It will be associated with democratization when a coalition brings together those who see an interest in expanding political rights with those who see an interest in excluding a distinct social group, and these actors are able to work out a narrative of political community that makes these contrary movements seem compatible and even complementary.

Part I of this book will show how this argument explains America's pattern of disenfranchising democracy. But given that the theory was constructed through engagement with the American case, it is important to see whether it can explain patterns elsewhere. Part II extends the analysis to the democratizing junctures of 1828 to 1832 in the United Kingdom and 1870 to 1877 in France.

These examples were chosen for a variety of reasons, the most important of which is that from the standpoint of theory and historical practice, these are three extremely influential cases. The United States, the United Kingdom, and France are seminal cases of democratization's "first wave," as well as paradigmatic examples of distinct paths to democracy around which many of our social scientific theories of franchise expansion were framed. Moreover, through their example and imperial ligaments, they have each wielded an enormous influence in shaping how democratization has unfolded across the globe.

Their selection also follows from a logic of iterative theory-building and -testing. The three cases are similar in key respects, while showing important variations in outcomes. Democratizing reforms were accompanied by disenfranchisement in the United States and United Kingdom, with somewhat different patterns of political support; and while France only narrowly averted the disenfranchisement of urban workers, the processes I describe above undergirded exclusions that would define the Republic for decades. This combination of similarity and variation allows me to examine whether the additional cases accord with the theory, even if it does not establish a general rule.

I begin with the United States because it is the country where disenfranchisement has been most extensively studied and is thus an appropriate case for considering the strengths and weaknesses of existing theories and for building a new one. It is the paradigmatic case, however mistaken, of an easy democratization resting on abundant land and scarce labor. I then turn to the United Kingdom, a paradigmatic case of gradual democratization.[89] It is similar to the American case along key dimensions: like the United States, the United Kingdom had relatively competitive elections before mass enfranchisement,[90] was broadly but not fully liberal in its rights protections, and was relatively diverse along lines of religion (Anglican, established Church Presbyterian, various shades of dissenting Protestantism, Catholicism, Judaism, and "free-thinkers"), nationality (English, Welsh, Scottish, Irish, with urban communities from European nations, a growing Jewish population centered in London's East End, free and enslaved persons of color, whether in seaports or in the country's burgeoning industrial cities, and, of course, the diversity of peoples circulating through the connecting threads of the empire), and economic class (from haute financiers, bourgeois industrialists, aristocratic grandees, middle-class professionals, an urban proletariat, and agricultural tenants living under conditions ranging from middle-class independence to near-servitude). Both countries were undergoing a pronounced shift in the relative importance of different economic sectors, and both combined a national state with regionally distinctive allocations of rights, whether through federalism or the different national legal systems. I conclude with the French case, the paradigmatic case of all-or-nothing democratization. France is perhaps the most

---

[89] This analysis focuses on the United Kingdom, rather than England or Britain, as the Union was the political unit in which questions of democratic rights were decided. While the administrative relationship of Ireland to England was one of colonialism, representatives from all the constitutive nations sat in Parliament; and while democratization could proceed at a different pace across the constituent units, as it did in the United States, every contest over democratization in any one nation immediately implicated the others.

[90] They had liberalized along a public contestation dimension more than they had democratized along an inclusive dimension. Robert Dahl, *Polyarchy: Participation and Opposition* (New Haven, CT: Yale University Press, 1972), 6.

distinct of the three. While there were competitive elections before 1870, they were less consequential than in either the United Kingdom or the United States. The country was also much more centralized than the other two, although considerable variation existed in the colonies, which were treated during the republican periods as departments with voting rights. And while in some sense there was less religious diversity, one of the country's main fault lines was between Catholics and various shades of anticlericalism, a cleavage with deep roots in the country's revolutionary history.

The book's narrative arc, then, moves from the site of theory building to progressively less similar cases. The comparisons are intentionally kept at the level of broad histories, rather than a finely structured juxtaposition of a few key elements. Still, each story is organized around the basic sequence of conditions listed above: the context in which a broad coalition uniting diverse interests is formed, the discursive and ideological work undertaken in order to reconcile this coalition and forestall fractures, and their efforts to dislodge an incumbent regime and institutionalize their own vision of the proper relationship between the state and society, offering constituents a compelling narrative of political community that could anchor the particular exclusions that they might also pursue.

There are other cases that could have been selected. Perhaps the most obvious, given their relative size, would be the 1948 disenfranchisement of Tamil plantation workers in Sri Lanka, the 1895 revisions to the Italian electoral list that purged nearly a third of the electorate – targeting the socialist base of support among the working classes – or the disenfranchisement of "black" (1959) and "coloured" (1968) voters in the Cape Province of South Africa. Proportionally smaller cases could also have been selected, such as the disenfranchisements of certain categories of indigenous voters by the Liberal government of Canada in 1898, the disenfranchisement of non–property owning and indigenous men in Liberia in 1847, the higher property qualifications introduced into the upper chamber of Denmark in 1866, or the multiple restrictions on voting rights imposed by Latin American countries in the years following independence.[91]

---

[91] Stefano Bartolini, *The Political Mobilization of the European Left, 1860–1980: The Class Cleavage* (New York: Cambridge University Press, 2007), 220–21; Adam Przeworski, *Democracy and the Limits of Self-Government* (New York: Cambridge University Press, 2010), 50; Richard H. Bartlett, "Citizens Minus: Indians and the Right to Vote," *Saskatchewan Law Review* 44, no. 2 (1980): 163–94; Malcolm Montgomery, "The Six Nations Indians and the Macdonald Franchise," *Ontario History* 57, no. 1 (1965):

Perhaps the most glaring omission from this study, however, is the process by which African Americans were enfranchised and then disenfranchised after the Civil War. The reason for this is twofold. While the enfranchisement of African Americans from 1867 to 1870 was associated with corresponding disenfranchisements in the North – through restrictive voter registrations and supervision procedures – and, more briefly, in the South – through anti-Confederate oaths – the disenfranchising juncture of 1890–1910 was associated with no corresponding expansion of political rights. It was disenfranchisement straight, without anything added. I decided that this would take us away from the focus on the conjunction with which I began. But another reason is that my account of disenfranchisement has already been deeply influenced by my reading of the extensive literature on this specific period. In part because the literature on this period was so generative of my own perspective, it seemed useful to begin with a period that has been less extensively studied.

One final point is worth noting. While the comparative analysis is important in demonstrating the possible generalizability of the argument to other countries, it is empirically tested not primarily by their macro-outcomes but by examining micro-level evidence of political processes within each country. The benefit of framing the study around a few in-depth case studies is that it allows me to increase the number of theoretically relevant observations within each case, tracing the unfolding political drama back to the hypothesized processes I outlined above.[92]

The data for this project came from extensive engagement with the secondary literature as well as analyses of primary sources. For the United States, I read what I believe to have been every recorded debate in legislatures and constitutional conventions on the right to vote, whether to expand or restrict it along class lines, gender lines, race lines, citizenship lines, or something else altogether, between the Revolution and the Civil War. Contemporary newspapers were extensively searched for words relating to black suffrage and black citizenship, as were the variety of online databases of nineteenth-century publications.[93] I additionally

---

13–25; Kenneth D. Bush, *The Intra-Group Dimensions of Ethnic Conflict in Sri Lanka* (London: Palgrave Macmillan, 2003), chapter 4; Valli Kanapathipillai, *Citizenship and Statelessness in Sri Lanka: The Case of the Tamil Estate Workers* (London: Anthem Press, 2009), chapter 3; Hermann Giliomee, "The Non-Racial Franchise and Afrikaner and Coloured Identities, 1910–1994," *African Affairs* 94, no. 375 (1995): 199–225.

[92] Ziblatt, *Conservative Parties and the Birth of Democracy*, 53.

[93] Especially useful were Google Books, www.archive.org, the Hathi Trust Digital Library, Readex's *Archive of Americana* – including the American Broadsides and Ephemera, the

compiled all recorded votes on black suffrage and political and constituency demographic data for American state legislators, which form the basis for Tables 2-2, 3-2, and 3-3 and Figures 4-1 and 4-2. Similar sweeps of parliamentary debates were conducted for France and the United Kingdom, from 1870 to 1940 and 1800 to 1885, respectively. While only a portion of this period is studied here, the analysis is informed by this broader perspective. For each country, every distinct speech act regarding the right to vote was compiled in a database of stated positions and rationales, allowing for rough evaluations of the comparative importance of different positions and their development over time.

The argument of the book emphasizes coalition building, the institutional and ideological constraints that shaped this process, and the efforts to articulate a narrative of political community and reconfigure governing institutions in this image. Through content analysis of legislative debate, political pamphlets, public writings, private correspondence, and government memoranda, as well as through process tracing of the adoption of policy positions and institutional reforms, I connect the content of the different institutional and discursive formulations to the strategic decisions and political projects pursued by political actors.

While I tack between these different sources, using different methods where appropriate, I try to give the reader a flavor of how participants understood the meaning of enfranchisement and disenfranchisement through extensive reliance on their own words. Only through contact and engagement with the words chosen by these speakers and writers can we begin to imagine the meaning they attributed to their decisions, and thus begin to discern the reasons for their choices. Democratizers and disenfranchisers spend a lot of time talking about the character, boundaries, and purpose of "the people." To understand their collective choices, I suggest we should listen and take seriously what they were saying.

Early American Imprints Series, and the Historical Newspapers Series – and www .newspapers.com. For the UK cases, the wonderful work undertaken by Andrew Eggers and Arthur Spirling, the Libraries of the House of Commons and House of Lords, and the History of Parliament Trust (https://hansard.parliament.uk/; https://parlipapers.proquest .com/parlipapers), in digitizing Hansard debates, compiling election results and division lists was extremely useful and was supplemented by extensive analyses of archival records and primary publications. See Andrew C. Eggers and Arthur Spirling, "Electoral Security as a Determinant of Legislator Activity, 1832–1918: New Data and Methods for Analyzing British Political Development," *Legislative Studies Quarterly* 39, no. 4 (2014). The French case relied heavily on the resources made available at www.gallica .bnf.fr and on hard copies of the legislative debates available at the Archives nationale.

PART I

THE UNITED STATES

2

Revolutionary Democracy

A black, tawny or reddish skin is not so unfavorable an hue to the genuine son of liberty, as a tory complection.

– William Gordon[1]

SETTLER COLONIALISM IN AMERICA

How did democracy come to America? Was it inevitably premised upon racial oppression and exclusion? Perhaps the most useful way to begin answering these questions is by considering the United States' origins in an historical process of settler colonialism, one that began soon after Europeans arrived in the Western Hemisphere and that has continued to shape America's political development for centuries since.

Settler colonialism matters for our story in a few ways. The first is how the particular configuration of land and labor in the North American colonies shaped patterns of social inequality. A common story holds that natural resources and agricultural land along the Eastern Seaboard were abundant, attracting settlers and speculative corporations looking for productive investments, while the costs of importing European workers meant that there was a persistent scarcity of labor. This structural configuration allowed early settlers to escape the bonds of feudal dependence, to establish individual ownership of productive property, and ultimately to gain a measure of economic security that was out of reach for most persons in Europe. As one colonial-era lieutenant governor

[1] *The Independent Chronicle and the Universal Advertiser*, January 8, 1778, 1.

43

noted, "The hopes of having land of their own & becoming independent of Landlords is what chiefly induces people into America & they think they have never answer'd the design of their coming till they have purchased land."[2]

With relatively low levels of economic inequality, a measure of democracy could be established without threatening elite privileges or property. It is for this reason that the United States often appears as an exceptionally propitious site for democratization.[3] An extensive historical literature was founded on the argument that America was "born free," that it was essentially a "middle-class democracy" during the colonial period, with the Revolution changing relatively little in terms of political rights.[4]

Settler colonialism, however, required ongoing engagements with the indigenous nations, armed encroachments into their homelands, and a succession of wars to acquire and sustain territory. If access to land was a condition for American democratization, from the outset it was premised upon the ability of the colonizing power and the colonial settlers to project force and defend their plunder. As Paul Frymer has demonstrated, this ability rested on the armed and concentrated settlement of small white communities, whose strategic placement defended the settler project while fostering intense antagonisms between them and the

---

[2] Michael G. Kammen, *Colonial New York: A History* (New York: Oxford University Press, 1975), 299.

[3] Louis Hartz, *The Founding of New Societies: Studies in the History of the United States* (Orlando, FL: Harper, Brace, Jovanovich, 1964); Tocqueville, *Democracy in America*; Engerman and Sokoloff, "The Evolution of Suffrage Institutions in the New World."

[4] Robert E. Brown, "Democracy in Colonial Massachusetts," *The New England Quarterly* 25, no. 3 (1952): 291–313; Robert E. Brown, *Middle-Class Democracy and the Revolution in Massachusetts, 1691–1780* (Ithaca, NY: Cornell University Press, 1955); Robert E. Brown and B. Katherine Brown, *Virginia, 1705–1786: Democracy or Aristocracy?* (East Lansing: Michigan State University Press, 1964); B. Katherine Brown, "The Controversy over the Franchise in Puritan Massachusetts, 1954–1974," *The William and Mary Quarterly* 33, no. 2 (1976): 212–41; Richard McCormick, *The History of Voting in New Jersey: A Study of the Development of the Election Machinery, 1664–1911* (New Brunswick, NJ: Rutgers University Press, 1953); Charles Sydnor, *Gentlemen Freeholders: Political Practices in Washington's Virginia* (Chapel Hill: University of North Carolina Press, 1952); Milton Klein, *Democracy and Politics in Colonial New York* (New York: New York State Historical Association, 1959); J. R. Pole, "Historians and the Problem of Early American Democracy," *The American Historical Review* 67, no. 3 (1962): 626–46; Robert Dinkin, *Voting in Provincial America: A Study of Elections in the Thirteen Colonies, 1689–1776* (Westport, CT: Greenwood Press, 1977), 28–49; John G. Kolp, *Gentlemen and Freeholders: Electoral Politics in Colonial Virginia* (Baltimore: The Johns Hopkins University Press, 1998), 38–49; Ratcliffe, "The Right to Vote and the Rise of Democracy," 221–22.

indigenous nations.[5] And as Aziz Rana has shown, settler colonialism helped generate a particular understanding of liberty as resting on coercion.[6] Settler colonialism, then, may have provided European settlers with a form of economic and political liberation that rested on the dispossession of the indigenous nations and the maintenance of armed outpost communities engaged in sporadic warfare and violence.

Settler colonialism is implicated in our story in another way: not only would-be independent small farmers but also speculative corporations and aspiring gentry looking to gain control over the products of other people's labor were attracted to America. In fact, the ability of the settlers to open up large areas of land created a range of possibilities for how property and labor relations could be organized in the New World. If there were no restrictions on mobility or on acquiring land, frontier conditions had the potential to support widely diffused property ownership and a relatively egalitarian social structure among settlers. But if a settler community or colonial corporation wanted to create a nonworking landowning class, it could close off land for settlement or develop a coercive apparatus for limiting laborers' mobility. In this case, the conditions of American settlement could result in property ownership and labor relations more closely approximating slavery or serfdom than independent small proprietor farming.[7] Many of the colonies would do just that: more than the other mainland colonies, authorities and settlers in Virginia and the Carolinas decided – through corporations, legislatures, and dispersed market decisions – to invest in a form of coerced labor that would come to rest on the ascription of a particular civic status to those of African descent, legally binding these laborers and their descendants to individual owners.[8]

---

[5] Paul Frymer, *Building an American Empire: The Era of Territorial and Political Expansion* (Princeton, NJ: Princeton University Press, 2017).

[6] Rana, *Two Faces of American Freedom.*

[7] Domar, "The Causes of Slavery or Serfdom," 20.

[8] Edward Countryman, "Indians, the Colonial Order, and the Social Significance of the American Revolution," *The William and Mary Quarterly* 53, no. 2 (1996): 342–62; Kenneth Lockridge, "Land, Population and the Evolution of New England Society, 1630–1790," *Past & Present* 39 (April 1968): 62–80; Jack M. Sosin, *Whitehall and the Wilderness: The Middle West in British Colonial Policy, 1760–1775* (Lincoln: University of Nebraska Press, 1961); Ashton Wesley Welch, "Law and the Making of Slavery in Colonial Virginia," *Ethnic Studies Review* 27, no. 1 (2004): 1–13; Darold Wax, "'New Negroes Are Always in Demand': The Slave Trade in Eighteenth-Century Georgia," *The Georgia Historical Quarterly* 68, no. 2 (1984): 193–220; Edgar McManus, *Black Bondage in the North* (Syracuse, NY: Syracuse University Press, 1973), 57; Winthrop D. Jordan, "The Influence of the West Indies on the Origins of New England Slavery,"

Settler colonialism in America, then, provided for a range of possible outcomes and fostered a cultural matrix in which liberty and coercion could be conceptually joined. But it was ideas and choices about how to best organize settler society and exploit its commercial and economic opportunities – and political institutions that empowered some interests and choices over others – that ultimately determined the extent of democracy and oppression in colonial America. Without attention to these choices, settler colonialism as an answer to our question risks exaggerating the importance of structural conditions in shaping America's democratic and disenfranchising development, underestimating the Revolution's role in broadening the suffrage and reconstructing the terms of political engagement, and neglecting the role that political institutions and organizations played in ultimately wedding these seemingly contradictory concepts together.

The Franchise in Colonial America

The extent of popular representation in colonial America was determined by the institutional arrangements of elections and the franchise, which in turn reflected local and imperial decisions and English intellectual traditions about the proper basis and boundaries of political community. In colonial America, these institutions and ideas buttressed a political order that fell far short of a democracy.

The specific qualifications for the right to vote varied considerably across the colonies, but generally required electors to own a defined amount or type of property, have an independent legal status,[9] be in allegiance to the Crown,[10] and be a free adult male. These restrictions

The William and Mary Quarterly 18, no. 2 (1961): 243–50; Lorenzo J. Greene, *The Negro in Colonial New England, 1629–1776* (New York: Columbia University Press, 1942); Morgan, *American Slavery, American Freedom.*

[9] Anglo-American political thought considered freedom as a civic status arising out of one's location in a hierarchy of material relations: the dependent, including propertyless men, tenant farmers, wage laborers, women, slaves, and indentured servants were subject to the will or influence of their masters or employers. Chilton Williamson, "American Suffrage and Sir William Blackstone," *Political Science Quarterly* 68, no. 4 (1953): 552–57.

[10] All of the colonies except Georgia either explicitly or through restrictions on land ownership limited the franchise to natural born or naturalized subjects of the Crown. Edward Hoyt, "Naturalization under the American Colonies: Signs of a New Community," *Political Science Quarterly* 67, no. 2 (1952): 250n9, 257n27; Charles Sullivan, "Alien Land Laws: A Re-Evaluation," *Temple Law Quarterly* 36 (1962): 15; McKinley, *The Suffrage Franchise in the Thirteen English Colonies in America,* 475; A. H. Carpenter, "Naturalization in England and the American Colonies," *The American Historical Review* 9, no. 2 (1904): 297.

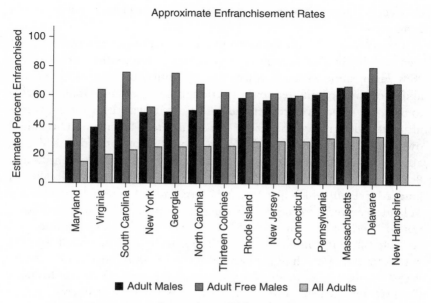

FIGURE 2.1   Approximate Enfranchisement Rates

marked the boundaries of both the American and English political communities. But principles that produced a small electorate in Great Britain here had the opposite effect. Figure 2.1 compares the rates of enfranchisement in the colonies, produced by averaging across various estimates provided by secondary historical sources.[11] A total enfranchisement rate for all nonindigenous persons in the colonies was approximately 9 percent, similar to the rate in the larger English borough constituencies at this time. Authority was vested in a varying combination of Crown-appointed officials and a small number of active citizens, drawn largely from wealthy families and resting on either the deference or indifference of the enfranchised population. Even among those who could vote, very few did; and widespread nonparticipation ensured that the "overwhelming majority"

[11] The sources include Chilton Williamson, *American Suffrage: From Property to Democracy, 1760–1860* (Princeton, NJ: Princeton University Press, 1960); Dinkin, *Voting in Provincial America*; John Cary, "Statistical Method and the Brown Thesis on Colonial Democracy," *The William and Mary Quarterly* 20, no. 2 (1963): 251–64; Brown, "Democracy in Colonial Massachusetts"; Brown, *Middle-Class Democracy and the Revolution in Massachusetts*; Brown and Brown, *Virginia, 1705–1786*; Kolp, *Gentlemen and Freeholders*.

of elected representatives were from the wealthiest portion of the community.[12]

The colonies with the highest enfranchisement rates among free adult men were likely South Carolina and Georgia on the southern frontier and New Hampshire on the northern frontier. But while the varying availability of land contributed to the portion of the free male population able to meet the respective property qualifications, it was the institutions that ultimately determined the size of the electorate. Massachusetts required ownership of land that produced an annual income of forty shillings, approximately three months' wages, and enfranchised between 70 and 80 percent of its adult free population despite declining availability of land. Maryland, which like Massachusetts had a diminishing availability of land, required a freehold of fifty acres or a personal estate worth forty pounds sterling and enfranchised far fewer. New York's electorate was restricted by the combination of a steep freehold requirement and the concentration of much of the population in a few counties dominated by very large landholders, itself a product of the strength of the Iroquois Confederacy (which impeded westward expansion), deliberate policy choices undertaken by the colonial state to sustain the manorial estates, and the withholding of millions of acres from the market by the manorial elite.[13]

Nor did New World settlement produce a dynamic of democratization. Not only was the rate of property ownership falling in many colonies, but the legislative trend also was toward restricting the electorate. Of twenty-three significant changes to voting qualifications in the colonies between 1700 and 1776, fourteen were aimed at narrowing the franchise, while only nine were aimed at its expansion. These trends were exacerbated by English policy, which limited western settlements and required governors to disallow legislation that would enlarge the electorate.[14]

---

[12] Richard Beeman, "The Varieties of Deference in Eighteenth-Century America," *Early American Studies: An Interdisciplinary Journal* 3, no. 2 (2005): 311–40; Jackson T. Main, "Government by the People: The American Revolution and the Democratization of the Legislatures," *The William and Mary Quarterly* 23, no. 3 (1966): 391–407.

[13] Kammen, *Colonial New York: A History*, 299.

[14] Dinkin, *Voting in Provincial America*, 44, 46; Allan Kulikoff, *From British Peasants to Colonial American Farmers* (Chapel Hill: University of North Carolina Press, 2000), 132–33; Lockridge, "Land, Population and the Evolution of New England Society, 1630–1790," 62–80; McKinley, *The Suffrage Franchise in the Thirteen English Colonies*, 27–28, 31, 77, 161–62, 379.

Racial Hierarchy in the Colonies

Democracy did not exist in colonial America. This is especially apparent once we turn our attention to persons of African descent. The most important means by which African Americans were disenfranchised was through the civic status of "slave," which denied the enslaved an ability to claim standing before or rights under the law. The position of free blacks, however, was more ambiguous. At the time of the Revolution, only Virginia, Georgia, and South Carolina *explicitly* restricted the right to vote to white men, although across all the colonies, free blacks were commonly prohibited from testifying against whites in court and barred by law or custom from serving on juries or in the militias.

The variety of restrictions on free blacks seems to have been part of a broader strategy to regulate labor relations and maintain planter rule, to safeguard investments in human property and agricultural capital against the very real dangers of insurrection and invasion. By the early eighteenth century, this had led to a detailed code of regulations governing interactions between the different classes of population in the colonies. "It has been allways the policy of this govert to creat an aversion in [Indians] to Negroes," wrote the outgoing governor of South Carolina to his successor in 1758, explaining why these groups must not be allowed to combine.[15] It was at least as important to establish rigid boundaries separating European and African laborers and to cultivate a clear sense of social difference between them. Virginia and other slaveholding colonies "deliberately did what [they] could to foster the contempt of whites for blacks and Indians" in order to "separate dangerous free whites from dangerous slave blacks."[16]

These strategies fragmented the colony's laboring classes through an elaborate code of regulations that strictly enforced a racial hierarchy defined along lines of descent and that prohibited forms of fraternization that did not uphold this hierarchy. When necessary to gain their support in intra-elite conflicts or to put down insurrections, some of the colonial elite

[15] William S. Willis, "Divide and Rule: Red, White, and Black in the Southeast," *The Journal of Negro History* 48, no. 3 (1963): 157–76.

[16] Morgan, *American Slavery, American Freedom*, 328, 331; Kenneth Stampp, *The Peculiar Institution: Slavery in the Antebellum South* (New York: Penguin, 1989 [1956]), 16; A. Leon Higginbotham, Jr. and Greer Bosworth, "Rather than the Free: Free Blacks in Colonial and Antebellum Virginia," *Harvard Civil Rights–Civil Liberties Law Review* 26 (1991): 17–66; Jordan, *White Over Black*, 176–77; Theodore W. Allen, *The Invention of the White Race: Volume II: The Origin of Racial Oppression in Anglo-America* (London: Verso, 1997), chapter 13.

were willing to extend rights or benefits to European settlers, providing a further social foundation to the legally inscribed distinctions. In Virginia, for example, the demarcation between black and white was accompanied by the opening of new territory for white settlement, creating an opportunity for many whites to acquire property and to participate in slaveholding themselves. Ties of sympathy, convergent interests, and a shared civic status of "white freemen" could then constitute the basis for uniting the colony's European population, as persons of African descent were marked out as subordinate and subject to intense social control.

Racial disfranchisement seems to have first appeared in colonial America as part of this strategy. A formal racial qualification for voting or office holding was first imposed in the Carolinas and Virginia, where it was framed as a response to threatened or actual insurrections.[17] When Virginia disenfranchised free blacks in 1723, the law was denounced by the English attorney of the Board of Trade, who could not see how it could be just "to strip all free persons of a black Complexion (Some of whom may perhaps be of Considerable substance) from those Rights which are so justly valuable to any Freeman." When later called upon to justify the legislation, the colonial governor explained that:

there had been a Conspiracy discovered amongst the Negros to Cutt off the English, wherein the Free-Negros & Mulattos were much Suspected to have been Concerned, (which will for-ever be the Case) and tho' there could be no legal Proof, so as to Convict them, yet such was the Insolence of the Free-Negros at that time, that the next Assembly thought it necessary, not only to make the Meetings of the Slaves very Penal, but to *fix a perpetual Brand upon Free Negros and Mulattos by excluding them from that great Priviledge of a Freeman*, well knowing they always did, and ever will, adhere to and favour the Slaves. And 'tis likewise said to have been done with design, which I must think a good one, to make the free Negros sensible that a distinction ought to be made between their offspring and the Descendants of an Englishman, with whom they never were to be Accounted Equal.... As most of them are the Bastards of some of the worst of our imported Servants and Convicts, it seems no ways Impolitick, as well for discouraging that kind of Copulation, as to preserve a decent Distinction between them and their Betters, to leave this mark on them, until time and Education has changed the Indication of their spurious Extraction, and made some Alteration in their Morals.

[17] McKinley, *The Suffrage Franchise in the Thirteen English Colonies in America*, 36, 92, 151, 474; William M. Wiecek, "The Statutory Law of Slavery and Race in the Thirteen Mainland Colonies of British America," *The William and Mary Quarterly* 34, no. 2 (1977): 258–80; Jordan, *White Over Black*, 169.

As Winthrop Jordan has noted, "Freemen in America – *Negro* freemen – lost their franchise because Negro slaves alarmed their white masters."[18]

Free blacks, however, were not explicitly excluded from the franchise in the other principal slaveholding colonies of Maryland, Delaware, or, after 1734, North Carolina. And despite fears of slave insurrections in the North, race was never used as an explicit basis for electoral disfranchisement in any of these colonies, although other civil disabilities were imposed on free persons of African descent, and few if any free men of color ever sought to cast a vote.[19]

REVOLUTIONARY DEMOCRATIZATION

This political and social order would be radically disrupted by the American Revolution. The unprecedented democratization of American political institutions that followed was produced through a combination of elite outreach and popular mobilization, with divided elites looking to shore up their authority and newly mobilized communities taking advantage of the conflict to press their own claims to political inclusion.

Even before Bunker Hill, divisions within the colonial elite over whether to resist British authority had led different factions to compete for the support of communities that had generally been excluded or stayed out of politics. Conservatives in the Georgia Assembly, for example, voted to extend the right to vote to owners of town lots equal in value to a fifty-acre freehold. The South Carolina provincial congress, an extralegal body, went one better and provided representation to the previously unrepresented back country in an explicit attempt to secure the inhabitants' loyalty to the resistors' cause.[20]

With the intensification of the crisis and outbreak of hostilities, new political institutions were organized to mobilize small farmers or propertyless laborers behind the independence cause. Participation or

---

[18] Jordan, *White Over Black*, 126–27; Evans, "A Question of Complexion," 413–15; Allen, *The Invention of the White Race*, vol. 2, 249; McKinley, *The Suffrage Franchise in the Thirteen English Colonies*, 37.

[19] Jordan, *White Over Black*, 123; Ira Berlin, *Slaves Without Masters: The Free Negro in the Antebellum South* (New York: New Press, 1974), 7–9.

[20] Main, "Government by the People," 397; Williamson, *American Suffrage*, 89; Elisha Douglass, *Rebels and Democrats: The Struggle for Equal Political Rights and Majority Rule During the American Revolution* (Chapel Hill: University of North Carolina Press, 1955), 36–37.

representation within these in turn created opportunities for the excluded to press their own interests and for "new men, more radical and more organized than their predecessors," to advocate for an expansion of political rights.[21] In Philadelphia, the German associations "called for all taxables to have the right to vote," which would have marked a substantial expansion of the franchise, while allying themselves with Scots-Irish Presbyterians and Philadelphia artisans in enforcing the non-importation agreements.[22]

The militias were especially important in mobilizing support for suffrage reform.[23] The privates of the Military Association of the City and Liberties of Philadelphia petitioned for the inclusion of all persons who bore arms in defense of the country, regardless of whether they were indentured apprentices, of legal age, or natural-born or naturalized subjects of the Crown, especially important given the colony's large German population. When the Maryland provincial congress decided to support independence, it called for elections to a constitutional convention on the basis of the existing property qualifications. Members of the militias protested and insisted that "that every taxable bearing arms, being an inhabitant of the country, had an undoubted right to vote for representatives at this time of public calamity." When judges ruled that they could not vote under the existing qualifications, at least a few persons suggested that they should "lay down their Arms and go Home" if "they were Denied the privilege of Voting for it was their Right and they ought not to be deprived of it." In five counties, the returning judges were replaced with men who allowed any man who bore arms to vote. The revolt was uncoordinated, and the Annapolis convention promptly voided

[21] Charles Olton, *Artisans for Independence: Philadelphia Mechanics and the American Revolution* (Syracuse, NY: Syracuse University Press, 1975), 74; Douglass, *Rebels and Democrats*, 38.

[22] R. A. Ryerson, "Political Mobilization and the American Revolution: The Resistance Movement in Philadelphia, 1765 to 1776," *The William and Mary Quarterly* 31, no. 4 (1974): 565–88; T. H. Breen, *American Insurgents, American Patriots: The Revolution of the People* (New York: Macmillan, 2010), 189; Douglas Bradburn, *The Citizenship Revolution: Politics and the Creation of the American Union, 1774–1804* (Charlottesville: University of Virginia Press, 2009), 32.

[23] Steven Rosswurm, "Arms, Culture, and Class: The Philadelphia Militia and 'Lower Orders' in the American Revolution, 1765 to 1783" (PhD diss., Northern Illinois University, 1979), 110; Steven Rosswurm, *Arms, Country, and Class: The Philadelphia Militia and the Lower Sort During the American Revolution, 1775–1783* (New Brunswick, NJ: Rutgers University Press, 1989), 11.

the elections, reappointed the original judges, and held new elections under the old rules.[24]

As the committees and militias became dominated by men of modest economic standing, they also came to be viewed with disfavor by many elites, with one conservative describing the new members as "needy desperate Men, who could not lose anything but might gain something by the Contest."[25] The increasingly radical tenor of their rhetoric had already caused consternation among some of the richest Americans. Staughton Lynd's study of Dutchess County, New York – a county with a particularly large tenant population and a very low enfranchisement rate – revealed the wealthy manorial landlord Robert R. Livingston hesitating "long on the brink of independence," and William Smith, the loyalist chief justice of the colony, warning that the "landed interest" of the country had "no Foresight of the natural Consequences of a republican Spirit in a poor Country, where Gentlemen of Fortune are but few." Once war had broken out, the militias pressed demands for the confiscation of Loyalist property, demands that some believed would soon be extended to the "Tenanted estates." Livingston's mother prayed for "Peace and Independence and deliverance from the persecutions of the Lower Class who I forsee will be as dispotic as any Prince (if not more so) in Europe." "The people," remarked Thomas Tillotson, "want nothing but to be a little more impoverished to prepare them for it."[26]

But Dutchess County was not America writ large, and the fears of its manorial elite would generally prove unwarranted. The redistribution of

[24] *Proceedings of the Conventions of the Province of Maryland, Held at the City of Annapolis in 1774, 1775, & 1776* (Baltimore: James Lucas, 1836), 211; Gary B. Nash, *The Unknown American Revolution: The Unruly Birth of Democracy and the Struggle to Create America* (New York: Viking, 2005), 284; Ronald Hoffman, *A Spirit of Dissension: Economics, Politics, and the Revolution in Maryland* (Baltimore: The Johns Hopkins University Press, 1973), 169–71; Mark W. Kruman, *Between Authority and Liberty: State Constitution Making in Revolutionary America* (Chapel Hill: University of North Carolina Press, 1997), 99–100; Williamson, *American Suffrage*, 108; Douglass, *Rebels and Democrats*, 49–50.

[25] Olton, *Artisans for Independence*, 73; Ryerson, "Political Mobilization and the American Revolution," 576; Williamson, *American Suffrage*, 88; Rosswurm, "Arms, Culture, and Class," 112, 149, 162–63.

[26] Staughton Lynd, "Who Should Rule at Home? Dutchess County, New York, in the American Revolution," *The William and Mary Quarterly* 18, no. 3 (1961): 330–59; Staughton Lynd, *Class Conflict, Slavery, and the United States Constitution* (Indianapolis, IN: Bobbs-Merrill, 1967); William H. W. Sabine, ed., *The Historical Memoirs from 12 July 1776 to 25 July 1778 of William Smith* (New York: Colburn and Tegg, 1958), 280.

property was an important feature of the revolutionary ferment, with Virginia debating a proposal to redistribute slaves from wealthy planters to poor white militiamen, Pennsylvania debating whether to allow the state to limit large landholding, New York tenants threatening to side with the Loyalists and then pressing for the confiscation and redistribution of their property, and post-Revolution governments providing land grants to veterans on territory conquered from the indigenous nations.[27] But the Revolution did not see expropriations for the benefit of landless tenants, whether in the manorial districts of New York or in southern counties where tenancy was a widespread feature of commercially oriented crop production. The Livingston Manor – with over 100,000 acres and hundreds of tenant families – would remain largely intact until the 1840s, while the confiscated Loyalist property mostly "passed into the hands of men of wealth."[28]

Democratization during the Revolution was not produced by the threat of an internal revolution, staved off by adroit policy concessions from imperiled elites. Indeed, the most radical voices in favor of the war, and often of confiscating Loyalist property, were to be found among the "businessmen, lawyers, and landowning gentry."[29] But in denying the existing organization of political authority, the revolutionaries were compelled to found new states that could muster enough constituency support to sustain their cause. Even if the patriot elite stood to materially gain from greater independence from Britain, the people beyond their ranks could not be simply conscripted into revolution but had to be persuaded through promises of symbolic and material gains, the reminder of real and symbolic outrages, and, where necessary, the application of a disciplinary compulsion. And so, while the Revolution was not motivated by a simmering internal struggle over "who should rule at home," the mobilization of thousands of previously excluded or quiescent communities brought with it a profound reconfiguration of

---

[27] Michael McDonnell, "Class War? Class Struggles During the American Revolution in Virginia," *The William and Mary Quarterly* 63, no. 2 (2006): 305–44; Nash, *The Unknown American Revolution*, 275–76.

[28] Lewis C. Gray, *History of Agriculture in the Southern United States to 1860*, vol. 1 (Washington, DC: Carnegie Institution, 1933), 386–91; James Livingston and Sherry H. Penney, "The Breakup of Livingston Manor," *The Hudson Valley Regional Review* 4, no. 1 (1987): 56–73; Allan Kulikoff, "Revolutionary Violence and the Origins of American Democracy," *The Journal of the Historical Society* 2, no. 2 (2003): 229–60, 243.

[29] Richard B. Morris, "Class Struggle and the American Revolution," *The William and Mary Quarterly* 19, no. 1 (1962): 3–29.

governing authority, radically changing the terms of political representation and voting rights.[30]

The Expansion of Political Representation

New Jersey, Maryland, and South Carolina reduced their property qualifications. New Hampshire replaced a fifty-pound real estate qualification
with a poll tax, while North Carolina enfranchised all freemen who had
paid taxes and been resident for one year (it maintained a fifty-acre freehold franchise for the Senate). New York lowered the value of freehold
property that entitled one to vote and created an alternative for men who
rented farms or tenements valued at forty shillings a year. The enfranchisement rate of Dutchess County went from around one-quarter of adult
white men to around 55 percent, with similar gains in other counties with
large tenant populations. Only Virginia, Rhode Island, Connecticut, and
Delaware retained their pre-Revolution franchise unaltered.[31]

The most dramatic change came in Pennsylvania. For years, the colony's politics had been divided between the Quaker "mercantile oligarchy," hesitant about the American cause, and Philadelphia mechanics,
German and Scotch-Irish farmers, and other lower and middle-class
groups who keenly felt their exclusion from the colony's politics and
representative institutions.[32] Their organization into militias, correspondence committees, and nonimportation associations, as well as the deep
divisions among the commercial and political elite, enabled members of
these communities to assert themselves into the colony's political life.
In 1776, the militias gained control over the commonwealth's conference
of committees and quickly organized elections to a constitutional conven-

---

[30] Carl Becker, "History of Political Parties in the Province of New York, 1760–1776" (PhD diss., University of Wisconsin, 1907), 22; Michael McDonnell, *The Politics of War: Race, Class, and Conflict in Revolutionary Virginia* (Chapel Hill: University of North Carolina Press, 2007); Eliga Gould, "The Question of Home Rule," *The William and Mary Quarterly* 64, no. 2 (2007): 255–58.

[31] Ratcliffe, "The Right to Vote and the Rise of Democracy," 228–29; McCormick, *The History of Voting in New Jersey*, 77, 85; Jonathan Clark, "Taxation and Suffrage in Revolutionary New York," *Hudson Valley Regional Review* 1, no. 1 (1984): 23–33; Keyssar, *The Right to Vote*, 16, 19.

[32] Gordon Wood, *The Creation of the American Republic, 1776–1787* (Chapel Hill: University of North Carolina Press, 1998), 85; Robert Gough, "Charles H. Lincoln, Carl Becker, and the Origins of the Dual-Revolution Thesis," *The William and Mary Quarterly* 38, no. 1 (1981): 97–109; Williamson, *American Suffrage*, 86.

tion in which all militia associators would be entitled to vote so long as they were above the age of twenty-one, were resident in the colony for one year, and had paid *any* tax levied from *any* public source. This expansion was accompanied by one new exclusion, disenfranchising any man who refused to support the revolutionary cause. With the colonial elite pushed out of power, "radicals like [Tom] Paine, David Rittenhouse, James Cannon, Christopher Marshall, Timothy Matlack, and James Wilson, many of them recent immigrants or ethnic outsiders ... rushed in to fill the political vacuum."[33] The convention, presided over by Benjamin Franklin, had a large militia representation but also included schoolteachers, mechanics, farmers, and immigrants, and it produced a constitution with a unicameral legislature elected by "every Freeman" resident one year and having paid state, county, or municipal taxes, with voting conducted by ballot, equal districts to be reapportioned every ten years, and a clause vesting in the citizenry the right to reject legislation before it went into effect.[34]

The Pennsylvania constitution influenced radicals elsewhere.[35] Vermont was effectively founded by a militia that wrote a constitution that enfranchised "all freemen, having a sufficient evident common Interest with, and Attachment to the Community," resident one year and of "a quiet and peaceable Behaviour." The revolutionary committees in Georgia – composed of "a Parcel of the Lowest people, chiefly carpenters, shoemakers, blacksmiths, etc., with a Jew at their head" – organized a provincial congress in 1775, where they secured a consensus in favor of revolution and an agreement that the committees would be broadened to include all those who had paid the general tax.[36] Competing factions of conservatives and radicals each "sought popular approval," and in 1777, a provincial congress dominated by radicals – and led by a delegate returned from Philadelphia and inspired by that state's model – wrote a constitution that lowered the franchise qualifications for white men from ownership of fifty acres of land to possession of ten pounds and

[33] Dee E. Andrews, *The Methodists and Revolutionary America, 1760–1800: The Shaping of an Evangelical Culture* (Princeton, NJ: Princeton University Press, 2000), 51.

[34] Nash, *The Unknown American Revolution*, 269; J. Paul Selsam, *Pennsylvania Constitution of 1776: A Study in Revolutionary Democracy* (New York: Octagon Books, 1936), 148–49.

[35] Douglass, *Rebels and Democrats*, 340, 344; Robert F. Williams, "The State Constitutions of the Founding Decade: Pennsylvania's Radical 1776 Constitution and its Influences on American Constitutionalism," *Temple Law Review* 62 (1989): 541–85.

[36] Norman Risjord, *Jefferson's America: 1760–1815* (Lanham, MD: Rowman and Littlefield, 2010), 119.

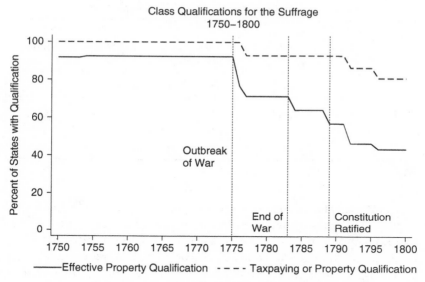

FIGURE 2.2   Changes in Suffrage Qualifications

liable to pay tax in the state, or – desperate for skilled immigrants – any white man resident six months who engaged in a mechanic's trade.[37]

Figure 2.2 shows the proportion of colonies or states with an effective property or taxpaying qualification for voting rights from 1720 until the turn of the century. Immediately upon the outbreak of war, eight states made liberalizing adjustments to their franchise qualifications. Twenty-five years later, fewer than 50 percent of the states required ownership of property in order to vote, and nearly 20 percent of states did not even require payment of taxes.

These institutional reforms undergirded a more democratic politics than had existed in colonial America. Historians have documented a clear increase in the proportion of adult white men who could vote, and Jackson Turner Main has detailed how these reconfigured electorates returned a different class of representatives.[38] Table 2-1 shows the class

---

[37] Harvey H. Jackson, "Consensus and Conflict: Factional Politics in Revolutionary Georgia, 1774–1777," *The Georgia Historical Quarterly* 59, no. 4 (1975): 388–401; Kenneth Coleman, *Georgia History in Outline* (Athens: University of Georgia Press, 1978), 17–22.

[38] Ratcliffe, "The Right to Vote and the Rise of Democracy"; Main, "Government by the People," 404–5; Kruman, *Between Authority and Liberty*, 85.

TABLE 2.1 *Class Distribution of Elected Representatives*

	New Hampshire, New York, and New Jersey		Massachusetts		Maryland, Virginia, and South Carolina	
	Pre-1776	Post-1783	Pre-1776	Post-1783	Pre-1776	Post-1783
Wealthy	36%	12%	17%	7%	52%	28%
Affluent	47%	26%	33%	15%	36%	42%
Moderate	17%	62%	40%	52%	12%	30%

Adapted from Main, "Government by the People."

distribution of elected representatives across seven states before and after 1776. A large majority of representatives before 1776 had been from what Main classified as the wealthy (top 2 percent of society) and affluent (top 10 percent). After the Revolution, the portion of representatives from these classes had declined considerably, while the "moderate" classes – those in the top 30 percent of the colonies' wealth distribution – had come to new prominence.

The Revolution was also accompanied by "a broad rejection of the fundamental philosophies which maintained the status quo," as the mobilization of "ordinary people in small farm communities" gave voice to segments of the population that had largely been shut out from political participation.[39] Through committee discussions, musterings of the militias, town councils, newspaper correspondence, and the conversations that occurred in an extensive transatlantic network linking seaports, they articulated new bases for political inclusion premised on one's having a stake in society, having made a material contribution to the common good, or on a natural right to consent to the laws.[40] By the mid-1770s, the language of natural rights and equality, including a republican opposition to artificial distinctions of rank, had become nearly ubiquitous in American public discourse.[41]

---

[39] Bradburn, *The Citizenship Revolution*, 14; Breen, *American Insurgents, American Patriots*, 12, 52.

[40] Michael Durey, *Transatlantic Radicals and the Early American Republic* (Lawrence: University Press of Kansas, 1997); David S. Wilson, *United Irishmen, United States: Immigrant Radicals in the Early Republic* (Ithaca, NY: Cornell University Press, 1998); Richard J. Twomey, *Jacobins and Jeffersonians: Anglo-American Radicalism in the United States, 1790–1820* (New York: Garland Publishing, 1989).

[41] Keyssar, *The Right to Vote*, 10–13.

A Philadelphia newspaper debate in 1776, for instance, arrayed "advocates of prevailing political theory" against a "radical middling cadre whose base of support was in the militia." In demanding an expansion of the suffrage, the Pennsylvania militias were seeking to break the link between property and participation in political governance.[42] "Great and over-grown rich Men will be improper to be trusted," the committee warned, as they would "be too apt to be framing Distinctions in Society, because they will reap the Benefits of all such Distinctions.... We are contending for the Liberty which God has made our Birthright: All Men are entitled to it, and no Set of Men have a Right to any Thing higher. Let no man represent you, who would be disposed to form any Rank above that of Freeman."[43] Only the common people could be trusted to defend republican government, because only they lacked the lust for emoluments, offices, or distinctions of rank.[44]

The Pennsylvania militias were the most effectively organized for political action. But throughout the colonies, the Revolution saw a push for suffrage expansion in terms that went well beyond the argument that property was necessary for political independence. Allegiance to the cause of America and material contributions to the war effort and society were instead becoming more common as the basis for claiming a positive right to vote. "Shall these poor adult persons," asked the citizens of Northampton, Massachusetts, "who are always to be taxed as high as our men of property shall prevail to have them set ... who have gone for us into the greatest perils and undergone infinite fatigues in the present war ... shall they now be treated by us like villains and African slaves?"[45]

THE REVOLUTION AND SLAVERY

The potential for an internal revolution did exist, but it appeared in a different form than often assumed; while the militias were pushing for political inclusion, enslaved persons of African birth and descent were

---

[42] Rosswurm, "Arms, Culture, and Class," 211; Rosswurm, *Arms, Country, and Class*, 12.

[43] Thomas Nevil et al., *To the Several Battalions of Military Associators in the Province of Pennsylvania* (Philadelphia: n. p., 1776).

[44] Nash, *The Unknown American Revolution*, 269; Williams, "The State Constitutions of the Founding Decade," 553.

[45] Samuel E. Morison, "The Struggle Over the Adoption of the Constitution of Massachusetts," *Proceedings of the Massachusetts Historical Society* 50 (June 1917): 353–412; Keyssar, *The Right to Vote*, 12; McKinley, *The Suffrage Franchise in the Thirteen English Colonies*, 149; Kulikoff, "Revolutionary Violence and the Origins of American Democracy," 233.

seizing the opportunity to demand and strike out directly for a freedom that had been much more thoroughly and oppressively denied them than any white American colonist.[46]

In 1775, the royal governor of Virginia organized an insurgent campaign in the Chesapeake, calling on slaves to join his forces in exchange for their freedom. George Washington worried that if he were "not crushed before Spring, he will become the most dangerous man in America. His strength will increase like a snowball rolling down a hill. Success will depend on which side can arm the Negroes the faster." This would be a dynamic of elite competition that could lead to an unacceptable result: the immediate liberty and arming of the oppressed population on whose backs much of the wealth of elites throughout the mid-Atlantic and Southern colonies rested. Within a few years, Congress recommended the enlistment of enslaved men; by war's end, between five thousand and eight thousand black soldiers had served in the revolutionary army, often in exchange for freedom (many more had served in the British forces and were subsequently evacuated).[47]

The impact of the Revolution on American slavery was complex. On the one hand, the threat that the colonists would be defeated by the efforts of enslaved persons, as well as indigenous peoples, led the founding generation's military and civil leadership to actively encourage the belief that these were peoples irrevocably antagonistic to the American cause.[48] The belief that persons of African descent were a potential fifth column would persist into the early Republic.[49] This was in addition to existing commitments to racial hierarchy: when Thomas Kench applied to raise

---

[46] Gary Nash, *Race and Revolution* (New York: Rowman and Littlefield, 1990), 57–60; Gary Nash, "Forging Freedom: The Emancipation Experience in the Northern Seaport Cities, 1775–1820," in *Slavery and Freedom in the Age of the American Revolution*, ed. Ira Berlin and Ronald Hoffman (Charlottesville: University of Virginia Press, 1986); Allan Kulikoff, "Uprooted People: Black Migrants in the Age of the American Revolution, 1790–1820," in Berlin and Hoffman, *Slavery and Freedom in the Age of the American Revolution*, 144; Merton L. Dillon, *Slavery Attacked: Southern Slaves and Their Allies, 1619–1865* (Baton Rouge: Louisiana State University Press, 1990).

[47] Klinkner and Smith, *The Unsteady March*, 18–21; Benjamin Quarles, *The Negro in the American Revolution* (Chapel Hill: University of North Carolina Press, 1996 [1961]).

[48] The Committee of Safety in Orange County, New York, issued a wartime decree regulating the movements of "negro slaves" after "many menacing speeches" and "an unusual going and coming, and getting themselves into companies and procuring to themselves arms." *The New York Journal, or, the General Advertiser* (New York), April 11, 1776, 3; Parkinson, *The Common Cause*.

[49] Nash, *Race and Revolution*, 60.

a detachment of African Americans for military service, riots broke out in Boston among those "offended at the thoughts of their servants being free."[50]

The growing numbers of free people of color, however, led to the formation of the earliest free black communities, which began to appear in small and large towns across the mid-Atlantic, stretching into New England and down the seaboard to Charleston, South Carolina. These communities would renew and keep vibrant a language of republicanism, pushing its boundaries beyond the narrow confines many of the patriot founders had envisioned.[51] In the years after the Revolution, Benjamin Banneker – the most prominent figure in Maryland's free black community – would invoke the Declaration of Independence in a letter to Thomas Jefferson:

> recall to your mind that time, in which the arms and tyranny of the British crown were exerted, with every powerful effort, in order to reduce you to a state of servitude.... [Y]our abhorrence thereof was so excited, that you publicly held forth this true and invaluable doctrine, which is worthy to be recorded and remembered in all succeeding ages: "We hold these truths to be self-evident, that all men are created equal."[52]

Others published an attack on slavery in the *Maryland Gazette*, adopting the language of the Revolution and treating the claim that a "disparity in colour" should lead to a "disparity in rights" as an "absurdity." "Attend to your own declarations," wrote *Vox Africanorum*, "these truths are self-evident – all men are created equal."[53]

Black Americans were transforming the signifiers of the Revolution's language, and a considerable number of whites were following them. Methodists – who were proselytizing extensively – became among the most ardent promoters of abolition and manumission, regretting that "prejudice of education and want of not weighing the matter thoroughly" had impeded them from seeing this before the Revolution. The itinerant preacher William Colbert attacked slavery and expressed his hopes to meet all persons in heaven, "for the Lord has many precious in this part of

---

[50] George Henry Moore, *Notes on the History of Slavery in Massachusetts* (New York: D. Appleton and Co., 1866), 195.

[51] Arthur Zilversmit, *First Emancipation: The Abolition of Slavery in the North* (Chicago: University of Chicago Press, 1967), 616–17.

[52] Ira Berlin, *Many Thousands Gone: The First Two Centuries of Slavery in North America* (Cambridge, MA: Belknap Press, 1998), 232.

[53] *Maryland Gazette*, May 15, 1783, 3; see also Celeste Condit and John Lucaites, *Crafting Equality: America's Anglo-African Word* (Chicago: University of Chicago Press, 1993), 85.

the world that are clothed with black bodies," and Ezekial Cooper published a series of attacks on slavery, deploring the sight of "enlightened citizens" influenced by *"groundless, absurd* prejudices."[54]

Religious organizations had some success in pushing for more liberal manumission laws and slave codes in the South, in securing restrictions on the slave trade, and in encouraging individual manumissions, although many of these policies aligned with the economic interests of merchant slaveholders.[55]

The North saw more dramatic changes. In 1780, Pennsylvania's radical government passed the first general abolition law, and while this and others that followed were extremely slow moving – giving slave-owners time to divest themselves of their "investment" – they stopped the progress of what had been a growing institution. One writer, describing a gradual abolition proposal in Rhode Island, placed the bill in the context of a progressive overcoming of feudal oppressions. "The Humane and Benevolent" of the world, he wrote, often despaired of achieving human liberation, only for some event to show them that the "same Principle of Compassion is planted in the Breast of all Mankind, but is buried in Rubbish." The "rapid Progress of the Sentiment against domestic Slavery for Ten Years past," as expressed in Pennsylvania and Rhode Island's abolition bills as well as in a liberal manumission law in Virginia, was one such event. "To attempt to prove to *an American*" that Africans were "by Nature Free, and that they have at this Time, an undoubted Right to have their Liberty, appears to me like repeating the letters of the Alphabet. – It is a first principle, and is felt by all Freemen who reflect upon the Feelings of their own Minds." All that was left was to work "to stir up and kindle the Sparks of Compassion in the human Breast," and "gradually call [it] forth into Action."[56]

Republicanism Against Disenfranchisement

Edmund Morgan famously argued that slavery provided the conceptual basis for American republicanism, as it allowed slaveholders – and

---

[54] Andrews, *The Methodists and Revolutionary America*, 129–31.
[55] Eva Sheppard Wolf, *Race and Liberty in the New Nation: Emancipation in Virginia from the Revolution to Nat Turner's Rebellion* (Baton Rouge: Louisiana State University Press, 2006).
[56] *The United States Chronicle* (Providence, RI), January 29, 1784, 1; *The Independent Gazetteer* (Philadelphia), March 12, 1785, 2.

Virginia slaveholders in particular – to envision a society in which the threat posed to republican government by the poor had been solved; the votes of the poor could not be purchased by would-be aristocrats, because the poor themselves had been shackled by chains and legal disabilities. "The most ardent American republicans were Virginians," he wrote, "and their ardor was not unrelated to their power over the men and women they held in bondage."[57]

It is certainly true that America would not have been able to forge a successful union during the Revolution without the support of Virginia, which meant that slavery could not be too aggressively challenged outside of the Northern states; and concerns with not alienating the South were an important rationale for denying black political and civil rights.

But while Virginians were important, America was no more "colonial Virginia writ large" than it was Dutchess County.[58] Outside Virginia, we do not find any evidence during the revolutionary period of what would eventually become a defining feature of American democratization: the strong correlation between favoring the removal of property and taxpaying qualifications with support for racial disenfranchisement.[59] While almost all of the states democratized their colonial suffrage qualifications, not a single constitution or franchise law enacted from the outbreak of hostilities in 1774 to their cessation in 1781 included a racial disfranchising clause where one had not existed already. One near-exception was the proposed 1778 constitution for Massachusetts, which would have explicitly excluded free blacks, Indians, and mulattoes from the right to vote. Not only was this never ratified, but it also was met with a broadside of opposition to the racial exclusion.

The draft constitution, which had a property qualification for the upper house and governor, is considered to have been "the most conservative in the North." But while the state's conservative elite may have played an outsized role in the first attempt outside the South to "disenfranchise free blacks and Indians," as suggested by Gary Nash, they could not have been

---

[57] Morgan, *American Slavery, American Freedom*, 381, 386.   [58] Ibid., 387.

[59] Virginia itself was not a democracy for white men, either: the state was one of the few to retain steep property qualifications during the Revolution and for decades afterward. A law allowing manumissions divided farmers from areas more reliant on slavery and lawyers, merchants, and farmers from areas with fewer slaves; of those coded as being of "humble origin," 71 percent voted in favor of the manumission bill against only 42 percent of "prominent old families." Jackson Turner Main, *Political Parties Before the Constitution* (Chapel Hill: University of North Carolina Press, 1972), 259–63.

alone: only 18 of 101 delegates voted to remove the racial restriction in the one vote on the question.[60]

Most details of the drafting process and convention debates have been lost. But a future Jeffersonian Republican, John Bacon, asked a Massachusetts newspaper to publish a speech he had given in the convention opposing the racial distinction. Bacon insisted that racial disfranchisement would undermine the cause of republicanism and "sap the foundation of liberty." Excluding free blacks from the franchise would "contradict the fundamental principle on which we engaged in our present opposition to [Britain] . . . that representation and taxation are reciprocal."[61]

Bacon's speech is useful for highlighting some of the arguments given by supporters of black disenfranchisement. "It is," he noted, "urged by gentlemen on the other side, 'that these persons are *foreigners*, and therefore not intitled to a voice in our legislation.' But how does this appear, Mr. President? What, unless it be their colour constitutes them foreigners? Are they not Americans? Were they not (most of them at least) born in this country?" Bacon then turned to what was perhaps the most important objection raised to black voting.

"That by erasing this clause out of the constitution, we shall greatly offend and alarm the southern States.". . . Can this be supposed, Mr. President, that any of the sister States will be offended with us, because we don't see fit to do that which they themselves have not done? Nay, more, will they be offended or alarmed that we do not violate those essential rights of human nature which they have taken the most effectual care to establish and secure?

Bacon hoped the people would show virtue "enough to trample under foot a form of government which thus saps the foundation of civil liberty, and tramples on the rights of man."[62] The claim that racial exclusion was necessary to reassure Southerners was also emphasized by the chaplain of the Massachusetts legislature, who had come from Britain to support the American cause; he likewise dismissed this as unfounded and warned that disenfranchisement would signal to the world that "they mean their own rights only, and not those of mankind, in their cry for liberty."[63] In an

---

[60] Oscar Handlin and Mary Flug Handlin, *Popular Sources of Political Authority: Documents on the Massachusetts Constitution of 1780* (Cambridge, MA: Belknap Press of Harvard University Press, 1966), 186; Nash, *The Unknown American Revolution*, 296; *The Independent Chronicle and the Universal Advertiser*, September 23, 1779, 1.

[61] *The Independent Chronicle and the Universal Advertiser*, September 23, 1779, 1.

[62] Ibid.   [63] *The Continental Journal and Weekly Advertiser* (Boston), July 9, 1778, 1.

open letter proposing a variety of democratic reforms, he asked whether it would not be "ridiculous, inconsistent and unjust, to exclude *freemen* from voting for representatives and senators, though otherwise qualified, because their skins are black, tawny or reddish?" Black skin, he argued, was not "so unfavorable an hue to the genuine son of liberty, as a tory complection." He urged the convention to include a declaration of rights that would show that Massachusetts residents "do *verily* believe that *God hath made of one blood all nations of man*, whether black, white, or otherwise coloured."[64]

The town meetings of the state voted overwhelmingly against the constitution, and although it is unlikely that black disenfranchisement was the decisive factor, approximately 35 percent of towns that gave reasons for their decision listed their opposition to the policy "of depriving the Africans" of the right to vote.[65] The town of Dartmouth, for example, complained that the racial exclusion "deprives them of the natural right all men have to make their own laws," while the citizens of Sutton denounced the draft as wearing the "very gross complexion of slavery" and repugnant to the "grand and Fundamental maxim of Human Rights, viz. *'That Law to bind all must be assented to by all.'*"[66]

Patterns of support for black voting rights in Massachusetts did not have a clear relation to support for an expanded suffrage along class lines. The town of Charlemont opposed both black disenfranchisement and the retention of a property qualification for voting for the senate, governor, and lieutenant governor, as did the town of Boothbay. Many towns expressed their opposition to the suffrage qualification in general terms as being contrary to the principle that "all men were born equally free and independent" or as violating the privileges and immunities clause of the Articles of Confederation, but did not expressly note whether they were opposed to black disfranchisement, the property qualification, or both. One town opposed disenfranchising of free blacks unless "exempted from

---

[64] Emil Olbrich, *The Development of Sentiment on Negro Suffrage to 1860* (Master's thesis, University of Wisconsin, 1912), 12; *The Independent Chronicle and the Universal Advertiser*, January 8, 1778, 1; *The Boston Gazette and Country Journal*, December 7, 1778, 1; Moore, *Notes on the History of Slavery in Massachusetts*, 186.

[65] Moore, *Notes on the History of Slavery in Massachusetts*, 191–200; Bradburn, *The Citizenship Revolution*, 245; Handlin and Handlin, *Popular Sources of Political Authority*.

[66] *The Continental Journal and Weekly Advertiser* (Boston), June 18, 1778, 4; Nash, *The Unknown American Revolution*, 297; Harry A. Cushing, "History of the Transition from Provincial to Commonwealth Government in Massachusetts," *Studies in History, Economics and Public Law* 7, no. 1 (1896): 218.

publick Taxes" and demanded the emancipation of all slaves; another wanted the franchise to be as near to universal as possible, although it saw this as encompassing "every freeman of suitable property." There was only one town – Sutton, which wrote that black exclusion carried "a very gross complextion of slavery" – that opposed black disenfranchisement while expressly supporting a high property qualification, and while several towns were silent on the proposed restriction to "whites," none expressly endorsed it. The evidence is thin, but it does not suggest that those supportive of democratization along class lines were more likely to favor racial disfranchisement. The lack of a racial disenfranchisement in the 1780 constitution prompted no discussion.[67]

It is possible that a few black men had cast a vote in Massachusetts: in 1795, Jeremy Belknap recalled that he knew of only one man of color who had been elected, "a town-clerk in one of our country towns."[68] But the defeat of the disenfranchisement clause did not lead to a recognition of the voting rights of men of color. An article published by the *Liverpool Mercury* in 1811 described the efforts of Paul and John Cuffe to secure their voting rights in Dartmouth, despite the town itself having forcefully rejected a racial qualification at the state level. It noted that the "people of colour had never been considered as entitled to the privilege of voting at elections, nor of being elected to places of trust and honour."[69] A petition prepared by the Cuffe brothers to the general assembly, signed by Adventurer Child, Samuel Gray, Pero Howland, Pero Russell, and Pero Coggeshall, asked to be relieved from taxation, citing both the unique conditions of their economic circumstances and the deprivation of their political rights. "By reason of long bondage and hard slavery," they began, "we have been deprived of enjoying the profits of our labor or the advantage of inheriting estates from our parents, as our neighbours the white people do." They were now for the first time being taxed, and noted that "while we are not allowed the privilege of freemen of the State, having no vote or influence in the election of those that tax us, yet many of our colour (as is well known) have cheerfully entered the field of battle in the

[67] See the sources in Handlin and Handlin, *Popular Sources of Political Authority*.
[68] Jeremy Belknap, "Judge Tucker's Queries Respecting Slavery," *Collections of the Massachusetts Historical Society* 4, no. 1 (1835): 191–211.
[69] *Connecticut Journal* (New Haven), January 24, 1814; "Memoir of Captain Paul Cuffee," *Christian Observer* 10 (Appendix): 825–32.

defence of the common cause, and that (as we conceive) against a similar exertion of power (in regard to taxation), too well known to need a recital in this place." The assembly gave little heed to their request, and so they refused to pay their poll tax and petitioned the town of Dartmouth to decide whether "all free negroes and mulattoes shall have the same privileges ... as the white people have." Shortly after, the taxes of both men were accepted and receipts given, and since at least the second decade of the nineteenth century, this has been cited as confirming the rights of free men of color to vote in Massachusetts.[70]

In Pennsylvania, the radical "Constitutionalists" – those who supported the democratic constitution against the conservatives who wanted it overturned – guided through the gradual abolition bill of 1780. Opponents of abolition argued that it would threaten relations with the Southern states, who would see in it an encouragement for insurrection. But they also warned that "we could not agree to their being made free citizens in so extensive a manner as this law proposes," insisting that free blacks should not have been given the "right of voting for, and being voted into offices, intermarrying with white persons," at least not "during the limited time of their servitude."[71]

The leader of the Constitutionalists, the Scots-Irish George Bryan, took a central role in passing the bill, which he later claimed was the public act in which he took the "greatest pride."[72] The state's democratic constitution was praised for creating the context in which the measure could pass. "This act of humanity, wisdom and justice," according to one, flowed out of the "constitution of Pennsylvania, which declares, 'that all men are born equally free and independent, and have certain natural and unalienable rights.'"[73] Another writer, signing himself a "Liberal," praised

---

[70] Nell, *The Colored Patriots of the American Revolution*, 87–90; Nash, *The Unknown American Revolution*, 298; Henry Noble Sherwood, "Paul Cuffe," *The Journal of Negro History* 8, no. 2 (1923): 153–229; *Connecticut Journal* (New Haven), January 24, 1814.

[71] The abolition law changed the status of all born of an enslaved mother after 1780 to that of an indentured servant, to be legally independent at the age of twenty-eight. The complaint suggested that during this interim period it would be inappropriate for the indentured to be able to exercise equal political rights. *Journals of the House of Representatives of the Commonwealth of Pennsylvania, Beginning the Twenty-Eighth Day of November, 1776, and ending the second day of October 1781* (Philadelphia: John Dunlap, 1782), 435, 436.

[72] John W. Jordan, *Genealogical and Personal History of the Allegheny Valley, Pennsylvania*, vol. 2 (New York: Lewis Historical Publishing Company, 1913), 434–35.

[73] *New Jersey Gazette* (Trenton), February 23, 1780, 3.

abolition and credited the constitution for securing "to every one equal liberty, to strangers as well as natives."[74] In contrast, a "Whig" wrote that abolition threatened the southern alliance. Political rights might be well and good for those black men who had been raised free since childhood, but those raised in slavery were "unfit for good commonwealth's men from their having all the habits of servitude deep rooted in their minds."[75] A Presbyterian minister, disheartened that some of his co-religionists signed a petition opposing the bill, wrote a fellow minister urging him to embrace abolitionism and disseminate its principles. "It is very suitable, that in a democratical state, as ours is," he wrote, "that there should neither be nobility on the one hand nor inferior inhabitants on the other: All should be citizens, invested with equal privileges." He noted that a central objection to abolition was that it would cause difficulties for the Southern states, but he was optimistic that abolition was gaining favor there as well.[76]

In 1790, Pennsylvania conservatives won control of the state and called for a convention to revise the democratic constitution. The unicameral legislature was replaced with a bicameral assembly, the governor was given extensive authority to nominate state officers, the right of the people to disallow legislation was removed, and the suffrage was restricted by lengthening the residency period from one year to two and by limiting the types of taxes that qualified a freeman to vote. No racial proscription was included, however, despite the steadily growing free black population. As Albert Gallatin, the future Jeffersonian Republican secretary of the treasury, would later recall, "I have a lively recollection that, in some stages of the discussion, the proposition pending before the convention, limited the right of suffrage to 'free white citizens,' and the word 'white' was struck on my motion." Gallatin generally voted with the more democratic members of the convention, a majority of which wanted to keep the new constitution free of an explicit racial disenfranchisement.[77]

While Pennsylvania seems to have deliberately chosen not to exclude free blacks, the New York assembly attempted to do the opposite. When a gradual emancipation bill was being debated in 1785, a majority in the assembly insisted that emancipation be accompanied by disenfranchisement.

[74] *The Pennsylvania Packet or General Advertiser*, March 25, 1780, 2–3.
[75] *New Jersey Gazette* (Trenton), October 10, 1780, 1.
[76] *The Pennsylvania Packet or General Advertiser*, January 1, 1780, 1–2.
[77] John Agg, *Proceedings and Debates of the Convention of the Commonwealth of Pennsylvania*, 10 vols. (Harrisburg, PA: Packer, Barrett, and Parke, 1837–39), 10:45.

The senate twice refused to pass a bill with a disenfranchising clause, arguing that it would create an aristocracy of race, while the assembly twice refused to pass a bill without it. When the senate eventually conceded, Robert Livingston, the wealthy manorial landlord and future Jeffersonian, drafted an opinion of the Council of Revision that vetoed the bill on the grounds that it would deprive free blacks of the "privileges of citizens" and was an outrage against "those principles of equal liberty which every page in that Constitution labors to enforce." The council listed other reasons:

[the bill] holds up a doctrine which is repugnant to the principles on which the United States justify their separation from Great Britain, and either enacts what is wrong or supposes that those may rightfully be charged with the burdens of government who have no representative share in imposing them. . . .. This class of disfranchised and discontented citizens, who at some future period may be both numerous and wealthy, may under the direction of ambitious and factious leaders, become dangerous to the State and effect the ruin of a Constitution whose benefits they are not permitted to enjoy. . . .. The creation of an order of citizens who are to have no legislative or representative share in the government, necessarily lays the foundation of an aristocracy of the most dangerous and malignant kind, rendering power permanent and hereditary in the hands of those persons who deduce their origin through white ancestors only.

Republican ideology – that those who contribute to the government should have a say in the laws that bind them, that legal distinctions between citizens were odious and tended toward aristocracy, and that government had to be founded on the affections and sovereignty of the people – was used to insist upon a measure of racial equality in law.[78]

And in New York as well, there does not seem to have been any association between positions on racial disenfranchisement and class democratization. While there were not well-developed party organizations in 1785, we can examine differences on black suffrage across the factional divisions in the assembly, which generally mapped on to differences in social class and different positions on economic policies. One faction, organized around Governor George Clinton and led in the assembly by the "levelling" radicals Matthew Adgate and Jacob Ford, supported protection for debtors, paper money, the establishment of a loan office, the seizure and redistribution of Loyalist lands, a state import tariff, and the incorporation of

---

[78] David N. Gellman, *Emancipating New York: The Politics of Slavery and Freedom, 1777–1827* (Baton Rouge: Louisiana State University Press, 2006), 49; Alfred B. Street, *The Council of Revision of the State of New York* (Albany, NY: William Gould, 1859), 268.

TABLE 2.2 *Support for Abolition and Black Voting Rights in New York State, 1785*

Faction	Abolition		Black Voting Rights	
	Support	Oppose	Support	Oppose
Future Anti-Federalist or Republican	68%	32%	56%	44%
Future Federalist	57%	43%	43%	57%
Radical Faction	95%	5%	65%	35%
Conservative Faction	64%	46%	40%	60%
Supported Mechanics' Charter	81%	19%	53%	47%
Opposed Mechanics' Charter	62%	38%	50%	50%
Total	67%	33%	48%	52%

a Society of Mechanics. Another, organized around Philip Schuyler and Alexander Hamilton, was much more conservative on economic issues and generally attacked Clintonians as a threat to property. Most wealthy legislators were anti-Clintonians, while legislators of more moderate economic standing tended to support Clinton.[79]

Table 2-2 shows the proportion of legislators from the different factions who voted for or against gradual abolition and for or against dropping the black disfranchisement provision. The first two rows show the relative proportions for legislators whose future political affiliation could be identified as either Anti-Federalist or Republican or as Federalist. The next pair of rows show the relative proportions for legislators who could be identified as belonging to the radical Clintonian or conservative anti-Clintonian bloc in 1785, either by reliance on primary or secondary sources or by the degree to which they voted with other members of this

[79] Main, *Political Parties Before the Constitution*, 148–50.

bloc.[80] Because some legislators could not be reliably affiliated with any of these factions, we can also look at the relative proportions for legislators who voted for or against chartering the Society of Mechanics that year, the most significant political demand made by an organized white working-class constituency. Each row shows the same basic pattern: whether looking at future party affiliation, voting behavior, or the support for the Society of Mechanics, the more economically radical group was consistently more supportive of abolition and of dropping the provision disenfranchising black voters, although only weakly so.

Conservatives such as John Jay, Alexander Hamilton, and Gouverneur Morris often appear in an outsized role in promoting abolition within the state, and not without reason: Jay seems to have lost support in his bid to defeat Governor Clinton because of fears that he was "for making the negroes free, and let them stay amongst us, that they mix their blood with white people's blood, and so make the whole country bastards and outlaws." But conservatives were far from alone in supporting either abolition or black political rights: while some Clintonians attacked Jay for his abolitionism, Clinton was attacked by some Federalists for his insistence that black New Yorkers be "entitled to *all the* Priviledges of *Freemen*," and for his characterization of racial disfranchisement as an "odious Distinction."[81]

What was more important in determining legislator voting patterns was the proportion of the population held in slavery, which ranged from 33 percent in Kings County to less than 1 percent in Washington County. Representatives of counties with more persons held in slavery, as well as those who personally owned slaves, were much more likely to oppose both abolition and disenfranchisement. The average enslaved population in districts whose legislators voted against abolition was 12 percent, compared with 5 percent for those who voted for abolition; 10 percent for those who voted to disfranchise free black voters, versus 5 percent for those who voted to allow black suffrage. "Educated men," noted Jackson Turner Main, "opposed Negro rights more than those without learning"; the legislators from the frontier were strongly in favor of black political rights, those from Albany and New York divided equally, and those from

[80] Voting blocs were identified by estimating an ideal point for each member of the legislature and separating those on one side of the median member from the other. The blocs map on to those in Main, *Political Parties Before the Constitution*.

[81] Gellman, *Emancipating New York*, 134; John R. Kaminski, *George Clinton: Yeoman Politician of the New Republic* (New York: Rowman and Littlefield, 1993), 206.

the large commercially oriented farm districts where slavery was especially prominent were strongly opposed.[82] When the bill was defeated, some New Yorkers blamed it on "Whig Slave Holders," while Republicans in Pennsylvania remarked scathingly that its defeat would be to "the lasting honour of those *disinterested* professors of republican principles," suggesting that those with a personal stake in slave ownership had conspired to defeat the bill.[83]

Arguments both in support of and opposition to black suffrage were advanced in the *New-York Packet*, a newspaper with broad readership among the city's mechanics. One writer simply mocked the idea of black equality, pretending to be an African American disappointed that "de Legislatermen no make de poo nega free las Sataday."[84] Another provided an actual argument, drawing on worries that the sizeable Loyalist population in the state might appeal to free blacks' votes in their efforts to regain control. While "An American" acknowledged that it was "without doubt" a violation of the principles of independence, he argued that disenfranchisement was justified if needed to protect the community: free blacks, "in combination with their friends the Quakers, would give every assistance to our enemies, as we have already experienced their fidelity in the late contest, when they fought against us by whole regiments. . . . The moment the period of emancipation of negroes arrives, it will cause [the Quakers], with others who wish to join them, to have a greater influence in the government." The result of black equality would be the return to British subjection. "If they were free and on an equal footing with us," he concluded, "God knows what use they would make of their power."[85]

There were also persistent defenses of both abolition and political equality. One writer, calling himself Tiberius Gracchus after the Roman tribune whose agrarian laws transferred land from the rich to the urban poor, quoted the Declaration of Independence and called to mind the pleasure that "every good man, every well wisher of the human race" must have felt when they read it. "At last," he wrote, "a nation is found to wipe out the oppressions of Kings and Princes – a nation that establishes liberty, as nature has established it, upon *universal principles*; without exception of rank, of country, of complexion." But America has been

---

[82] Main, *Political Parties Before the Constitution*, 142.

[83] *The Pennsylvania Evening Herald and the American Monitor* (Philadelphia), March 12, 1785, 3; *New-York Packet*, March 31, 1785, 3.

[84] *New-York Packet*, March 31, 1785, 3.   [85] *New-York Packet*, April 4, 1785, 2.

misconceived, he regretted. "Persons who have not paid rent and taxes *are not men*" and so could not vote or hold office. "Persons of a black colour are evidently *no men*," for they were held in slavery and were to be denied political equality.[86]

Opposition to civil, political, and social rights for free blacks undermined the prospects for gradual emancipation in New York State. But there was a sizeable minority – nearly half the assembly – that was willing to accept black suffrage in order to secure abolition, and this group was disproportionately composed of men associated with the state's democratic and radical factions, such as the mechanic-endorsed shoemaker William Goforth, the "levelers" Matthew Adgate and Jacob Ford, and future Republicans John Smith, Edward Savage, and Ebenezer Purdy.[87] When gradual emancipation eventually passed in 1799, "no attempt was made by any of the lawmakers to hedge emancipation with political or social restrictions," and Federalists and Democratic-Republicans provided nearly equal proportions of the favorable votes.[88]

CONCLUSION

In the immediate postrevolutionary years, there were likely few white Americans who had given much thought to the possibility of black political equality. Most evidence suggests that a majority would have been opposed, although perhaps not all to the extreme taken by one writer's acquaintance, who declared that he "should rather chuse to go to hell than to heaven" if blacks were to be his equals in paradise.[89] Colonial understandings of political community had generally assumed that full political membership was limited to whites of property and social standing, with blackness frequently standing in as a synonym or metaphor for slavery. Americans of all ranks and classes were acutely aware of their relative positions within a civic hierarchy that arrayed inhabitants by intersecting categories of wealth, race, gender, indigeneity, allegiance, and religion, whose anti-black ordering was perhaps strongest but certainly not limited to the Southern colonies, and whose social and civic differentiation of

[86] *New-York Packet*, March 28, 1785, 2.
[87] Only Goforth and Dirck Brinckerhoff were from working-class backgrounds, and while Goforth took the racially egalitarian position on every vote, Brinckerhoff voted against abolition and insisted on restricting black rights. *New-York Packet*, March 14, 1785, 2.
[88] Edgar J. McManus, *A History of Negro Slavery in New York* (Syracuse, NY: Syracuse University Press, 1966), 175.
[89] *Dunlap's American Daily Advertiser* (Philadelphia), January 13, 1792, 3.

whites along lines of religion, property, and allegiance was perhaps most bitterly felt in the upper South, the mid-Atlantic, and lower New England.

This order was unsettled by the Revolution, and the new states that were founded had to accommodate new demands for enhanced social and civic statuses, for political rights and representation, and for public policy to be organized in pursuit of the aspirations and material interests of broader constituencies. The new civic and political order that would ultimately be established after the Revolution would sustain some of these demands, roll back others, and consolidate a form of democratic politics for male citizens on a national scale, one that would gradually be constrained to white men.

While limited, the democratizations of the revolutionary era were real: they were much more than simply the institutional ratification of a democracy produced by favorable structural circumstances. For its time, and for more than a century after, democratization in America was rightly seen as a radical event. And at least part of its radicalism was its destabilization of slavery and racial oppression.

Even in national forums, there was opposition to explicitly restricting the terms of American citizenship on the basis of race. New Jersey's congressional delegation, for instance, quoted the Declaration of Independence in a motion to expunge the word "white" from the proposed Articles of Confederation. And when South Carolina moved to add the word "white" before "free inhabitants" in the privileges and immunities clause, the amendment was defeated with only two states in support, one divided, and eight against.[90]

Yet while some white Americans were willing to both push forward and follow through on the egalitarian implications of republican ideology, perhaps listening to the claims of black Americans themselves, a great many were also willing to go on buying and selling and appropriating the labor of human captives. As one Jamaica newspaper remarked with sarcasm, "It certainly appears strange that American papers should teem with essays and paragraphs against slavery, and yet the inhabitants should shew such an avidity to purchase slaves when cargoes arrive."[91] This strange conjunction would have profound implications for the course of American democratization.

---

[90] Immediately after, South Carolina proposed to limit its application to "the law of such states respectively for the government of their own free white population"; this too was defeated. Jonathan Elliot, *The Debates in the Several State Conventions on the Adoption of the Federal Constitution*, vol. 1 (Philadelphia: J. B. Lippincott Company, 1901), 89–90; Bradburn, *The Citizenship Revolution*, 246.

[91] *The Maryland Journal* (Baltimore), March 19, 1785, 2.

3

The "Monstrous Spectacle" of Jeffersonian Democracy

What an insult to common sense!
                   – Thomas Branagan[1]

What changed in American politics to realign positions on class and race suffrage, so that by the mid-nineteenth century, support for one would be strongly associated with opposition to the other?

The most important factor was the US Constitution, which encouraged the organization of political coalitions across the country's main geographic divisions. It was the pressures of coalition building and maintenance that would ultimately yoke democracy and disenfranchisement together in the United States. In their efforts to build a coalition capable of winning national offices, the Republican Party, centered on Thomas Jefferson, presented itself as the defender of an embattled republican and democratic cause. Upon coming to power, Jeffersonian politicians promoted institutional changes that expanded the scope of democracy for many Americans, including more liberal terms for naturalization, land laws that encouraged a more dispersed ownership of property, and an extension of voting rights to citizens who paid taxes, worked on the highways, served in the militia, or were even just resident in the state or county for a fixed amount of time.

But Jeffersonians from across the country were also increasingly responsive to heightened worries about the place of free blacks within the Republic. It was a mainstay of Southern discourse during this period that free persons of color posed a unique danger to social stability in

---

[1] Thomas Branagan, *Preliminary Essay, on the Oppression of the Exiled Sons of Africa* (Philadelphia: John W. Scott, 1804), 214.

a slave society. After the successful insurrection in St. Domingue/Haiti – along with suppressed ones in Virginia and Louisiana – Southern representatives would increasingly demand that the civic statuses of free black Americans be further diminished. In the North, a growing free black population was viewed with unease and antipathy by many whites, who both listened to Southern warnings and resented persons of color for their increasing assertion of political and civil equality. Republicans would repeatedly find themselves divided over the question of free black citizenship, but they gradually converged on an institutional and discursive formulation that helped reconcile these tensions, working out in successive debates a vision of the proper boundaries of American political community.

THE U.S. CONSTITUTION AND NATIONAL COALITIONS

State governments looking to establish their authority and popular legitimacy during and after the Revolution rewarded constituencies who had chosen the American side, providing policies that were more responsive to their needs and aspirations. Loyalists' property was seized and sold at depreciated prices – largely to patriot wealth-holders such as Robert R. Livingston, Jr. – while those who remained were often subject to civil and political disabilities, further strengthening the hand of the new state leadership. Laws and constitutional provisions granting debtors some security from their creditors proliferated, and the issuance of state money produced inflation that eased debt obligations.[2] In order to cut off the legs from any incipient aristocracy in the country, laws revising inheritance rights and prohibiting primogeniture and entail – which in Europe were crucial mechanisms for building up large estates – were passed in Virginia, Georgia, North Carolina, Pennsylvania, Delaware, and elsewhere.[3] Some states began liberally incorporating private enterprises such as banks and turnpike, bridge, and canal companies, or

---

[2] Herbert Aptheker, *The American Revolution, 1763–1783* (New York: International Publishers, 1960), 255–57; Bruce Mann, *Republic of Debtors: Bankruptcy in the Age of American Independence* (Cambridge, MA: Harvard University Press, 2002); David Ramsay, *The History of the American Revolution*, vol. 2 (Trenton, NJ: James J. Wilson, 1811), 177.

[3] Claire Priest, "The End of Entail: Information, Institutions, and Slavery in the American Revolutionary Period," *Law and History Review* 33, no. 2 (2015): 277–319; Stanley N. Katz, "Republicanism and the Law of Inheritance in the American Revolutionary Era," *Michigan Law Review* 76, no. 1 (1977): 1–29; C. Ray Keim, "Primogeniture and Entail in Colonial Virginia," *The William and Mary Quarterly* 25, no. 4 (1968): 545–86.

passing general incorporation laws allowing corporations and societies to form without the cumbersome process of gaining legislative support. Others, concerned that incorporation would result in state-supported monopolies against the public interest, pushed in the other direction, prohibiting their establishment in the text of their constitutions.[4]

Both the tendency and diversity of state policies provoked a reaction. For instance, when the British restricted American trade to Europe and the Caribbean, some states refused to authorize a national response, leaving those that imposed retaliatory duties at a disadvantage.[5] The authority of the new nation was also called into question by the continued British presence along the frontier, its strategic weakness relative to the indigenous nations, and its inability to maintain order within its borders. By the mid-1780s, a growing number of political elites had come to believe that the country needed new powers to raise revenue, regulate international relations, and assert its authority on a continentwide scale. The exercise of popular sovereignty needed to be rechanneled into institutional arrangements that could better protect the "sacred rights of property," which Alexander Hamilton and James Madison agreed was a "principal cause of the Union which took place among good men to establish the National Government."[6]

The new Constitution did much to insulate policymaking from the democratic politics that was developing in the states: it shifted authority over trade and monetary policy to the national level, away from annually elected state legislatures whose deliberations could be closely monitored by local crowds; it required legislation to be passed by two chambers, chosen by different constituencies at different times, and signed by a president selected by an electoral college whose members were appointed by the states; the president was named commander-in-chief, oath-bound

---

[4] Brian P. Murphy, *Building the Empire State: Political Economy in the Early Republic* (Philadelphia: University of Pennsylvania Press, 2015); Pauline Maier, "The Revolutionary Origins of the American Corporation," *The William and Mary Quarterly* 50, no. 1 (1993): 51–84.

[5] Lawrence Peskin, "From Protection to Encouragement: Manufacturing and Mercantilism in New York City's Public Sphere, 1783–1795," *Journal of the Early Republic* 18, no. 4 (1998): 589–615.

[6] Stuart Bruchey, "The Impact of Concern for the Security of Property Rights on the Legal System of the Early American Republic," *Wisconsin Law Review* 6 (1980): 1135–58, 1142; James Madison, *The Debates in the Federal Convention of 1787 Which Framed the Constitution of the United States of America*, ed. Gaillard Hunt and James Brown Scott (New York: Oxford University Press, 1920 [1787]), 620; Robert Olwell, *Masters, Slaves, and Subjects: The Culture of Power in the South Carolina Low Country, 1740–1790* (Ithaca, NY: Cornell University Press, 1998).

to defend the Constitution and given the authority to use the militia to suppress insurrections or invasions; prohibitions on the impairment of contracts and the restriction of state-issued money reassured property holders across the country, and a new Supreme Court was empowered to enforce these rules.

For all its insulation of policymaking from popular politics, however, the Constitution also fostered new forms of national political engagement. By empowering the federal government in certain policy areas, it invited aspiring politicians and interests to direct their ambitions and attentions toward its institutions. This required the organization of coalitions that could cultivate support across a more extensive and diverse array of interests and publics than had heretofore been necessary. The coalitions that would form in support of a given presidential candidate, the state legislative coalitions that would select senators, and the representatives chosen from relatively large congressional districts were each expected to coordinate around men known for their talents and discretion: "It is only in remote corners that demagogies arise," wrote James Wilson. "Nothing but real weight of character can give a man real influence over a large district."[7]

But the particular constraints imposed by the Constitution ensured that the building of a national majority would require sectional accommodations. As Madison had recognized, divisions centered on "the institution of slavery & its consequences" posed the greatest obstacle to a closer union. This was not just because Southerners feared that a national legislature might follow the example of Pennsylvania and Rhode Island in abolishing slavery, but also because distinct forms of commercial activity – and cultural and social priorities – were organized around slavery.[8] The Constitution accordingly provided Southern slaveholders with an additional set of textual commitments – the prohibition on taxing exports, the requirement that federal and state governments participate in the return of fugitive slaves, the prohibition on regulating the slave trade for twenty years – and, more importantly, a structural advantage in the allocation of governing authority. The three-fifths clause increased Southern representation in the House from 38 percent under the Articles of Confederation to 45 percent in the first Congress, while inflating Southern numbers in the new electoral college. The Senate provided

[7] Bernard Manin, *The Principles of Representative Government* (Cambridge: Cambridge University Press, 1997), 121–22.
[8] Madison, *Debates in the Federal Convention of 1787*, 195, 257.

more representation to the eight states of the North over the five states of the South, but the quick admission of Kentucky and Tennessee, in addition to Vermont, helped bring this into closer balance. The national government was empowered, and accession to its highest office required the formation of a coalition that bridged the country's sectional divide. Responsibility for holding the Union together rested not only on the constitutional text but on the calculations of aspiring leaders.[9]

Early Republican Peoplehood

By the middle of the 1790s, two competing coalitions had adherents in almost every state. While there was considerable overlap in their constituencies, they nonetheless tended to draw on the support of distinct social groups defined by intersecting axes of religion, region, and economic circumstances.[10] Federalists drew support from the commercial elite, including merchants from Massachusetts to South Carolina, and from farmers in New England and the mid-Atlantic.[11] The Republicans found their strongest supporters among what Jefferson referred to as the "southern interest," the defense of whose priorities he claimed were his "sole object" for engaging in national politics.[12] Many Southern communities had been alienated by Hamilton's economic program, which threatened to prioritize commercial and financial interests over agriculture and aroused Republican fears of centralized authority. Their worries grew deeper after the administration's support for Britain led to an embargo by France, an increasingly important purchaser of Southern tobacco, a former ally, and

[9] Paul Finkelman, *Slavery and the Founders: Race and Liberty in the Age of Jefferson*, 3rd edn. (Armonk, NY: M. E. Sharpe, 2014), 21.

[10] Philip A. Crowl, "Anti-Federalism in Maryland, 1787–1788," *The William and Mary Quarterly* 4, no. 4 (1947): 446–49; Noble Cunningham, Jr., *The Jeffersonian Republicans: The Formation of Party Organization, 1789–1801* (Chapel Hill: University of North Carolina Press, 1957); Harry M. Tinkcom, *The Republicans and Federalists in Pennsylvania, 1790–1801* (Harrisburg: Pennsylvania Historical and Museum Commission, 1950); Kenneth W. Keller, "Rural Politics and the Collapse of Pennsylvania Federalism," *Transactions at the American Philosophical Society* 72, no. 6 (1982): 1–73.

[11] James H. Broussard, *The Southern Federalists: 1800–1816* (Baton Rouge: Louisiana State University Press, 1978).

[12] Subsequent to writing his letter in which he described the protection of the "southern interest" as his "sole object," either Jefferson or one of his contemporaries cross out the word "southern" and replaced it with "republican." James Roger Sharp, "Unraveling the Mystery of Jefferson's Letter of April 27, 1795," *Journal of the Early Republic* 6, no. 4 (1986): 411–18.

a country experiencing its own republican revolution. Moreover, the tariff and excise taxes that Federalists had established as the principal sources of revenue required the employment of large numbers of revenue and custom officials, potential agents of local influence and patronage from which the Federalist party could build an electoral base.[13]

Winning office in the new institutional environment, however, required an expansion beyond this Southern base. Jeffersonian Republicans consequently sought to stitch together a broad coalition of former anti-Federalists, urban mechanics and artisans, backcountry farmers, and immigrant constituencies such as the Scots-Irish and political refugees from Europe.[14] Republicans drew heavily on the organizational legacy and rhetorical appeals of the Democratic-Republican Societies – political clubs formed in the early 1790s with the aim of defending republicanism – as well as the numerous fraternal, occupational, and immigrant societies that had emerged since the Revolution. Many of these had articulated radically democratic and egalitarian understandings of American community, embracing the Fourth of July as an opportunity to celebrate equality and the rights of man (a sharp contrast to Federalist toasts to "the constituted authorities – may they be reverenced in place of equality").[15] They praised the French Revolution, toasted the ambassador from revolutionary France – who was organizing privateering expeditions out of Charleston without federal permission – and toasted the "courageous and virtuous mountain," i.e., the Montagnards of France, the most radical of the Jacobins.[16] The "ultra-democratic" Society of Master Sailmakers in New York toasted the "Fourth of July, a free press, freedom for African slaves, and ... 'the societies of America as nurseries of

---

[13] Herbert E. Sloan, *Principle and Interest: Thomas Jefferson and the Problem of Debt* (New York: Oxford University Press, 1995), 119.

[14] Norman K. Risjord, "The Virginia Federalists," *The Journal of Southern History* 33, no. 4 (1967): 486–517; Richard E. Ellis, "The Market Revolution and the Transformation of American Politics, 1801–1837," in *The Market Revolution in America: Social, Political, and Religious Expressions, 1800–1880,* ed. Melvyn Stokes and Stephen Conway (Charlottesville: University of Virginia, 1996), 146–76; Carl E. Prince, *New Jersey's Jeffersonian Republicans: The Genesis of an Early Party Machine, 1789–1817* (Chapel Hill: University of North Carolina Press, 1964); Alfred E. Young, *The Democratic Republicans of New York: The Origins, 1763–1797* (Chapel Hill: University of North Carolina Press, 1967).

[15] David Waldstreicher, "Federalism, the Style of Politics, and the Politics of Style," in *Federalists Reconsidered,* ed. Doron S. Ben-Atar and Barbara B. Oberg (Charlottesville: University of Virginia Press, 1998): 99–117, 110, 115.

[16] William Cobbett, *A Bone to Gnaw, for the Democrats; or, Observations on a Pamphlet, entitled, "The Political Progress of Britain"* (Philadelphia: Thomas Bradford, 1795), 44.

Republicanism.'"[17] The newly founded Tammany Society of New York City – later infamous as a bastion of corruption, white working-class incorporation, and antiblack racism – toasted the cause of abolition.[18] Others insisted that preserving the democratic character of the Republic depended on the vigilance and political activism of the working classes. New York mechanics' committees wrote that they had "equal rights with the merchants and that they are as important a set of men as any in the community," and insisted that it would be "the mechanics and farmers, or the poorer class of people (as they are generally called) that must support the freedom of America."[19] The Democratic-Republican Societies faded after being denounced by Washington and associated with the Whisky Rebellion in western Pennsylvania, but their networks in many cases merged with the "election machinery" of the Republican Party.[20]

Jeffersonian politicians also sought to cultivate the support of the growing population of immigrants. In 1798, Federalists had amended the naturalization law to require a residence period of fourteen years and passed the Alien and Sedition Acts, enabling the president to deport politically active aliens and criminalizing the publication of "malicious" writings against governmental officials.[21] Jeffersonians offered support to émigré printers and pledged to repeal the new laws. They organized the Society for the Assistance of Persons Emigrating from Foreign Countries, encouraged the formation of immigrant organizations such as the United Irishmen of New York, the Hibernian Provident Society, the Hibernian Militia Volunteers, and the Caledonian Society, and regularly carried news in the Republican press of the Irish, French, and Polish struggles

[17] Eugene P. Link, *Democratic-Republican Societies, 1790–1800* (New York: Columbia University Press, 1942), 94–96, 181–82.

[18] *The Herald* (New York), January 28, 1795, 4; Alfred Young, "The Mechanics and the Jeffersonians: New York, 1789–1801," *Labor History* 5, no. 3 (1964): 247–76, 272.

[19] *New York Journal*, March 30, 1791, February 22, 1792; *The Herald* (New York), January 28, 1795.

[20] Matthew Schoenbachler, "Republicanism in the Age of Democratic Revolution: The Democratic-Republican Societies of the 1790s," *Journal of the Early Republic* 18, no. 2 (1998): 237–67, 250–51; Young, "The Mechanics and the Jeffersonians," 252, 271–72; Roland M. Baumann, "Philadelphia's Manufacturers and the Excise Taxes of 1794: The Forging of the Jeffersonian Coalition," *The Pennsylvania Magazine of History and Biography* 106, no. 1 (1982): 3–39; Sean Wilentz, *The Rise of American Democracy: Jefferson to Lincoln* (New York: W. W. Norton and Co., 2006), 74–75; Howard B. Rock, *Artisans of the New Republic: The Tradesmen of New York City in the Age of Jefferson* (New York: New York University Press, 1979).

[21] *Annals of Congress*, H. R., 3rd Cong., 2nd sess., 1021–22, 1030–40; H. R., 5th Cong., 2nd sess., 1567.

for liberty. Many of these organizations became hotbeds of radicalism, voicing strong support for the Volunteer Movement in Ireland, the French Revolution, and the rights of man.[22] These different societies would become the backbone of Republican political strength, providing a grassroots organization to complement the efforts of the political elite in forging a national coalition.[23]

Jeffersonians offered policy gains for these different constituencies but also laid out a vision of the purpose and character of the United States. Needing a resonant appeal to justify their aspirations for office, Republicans framed Federalist policies as part of a broad conspiracy to overturn republican government and establish a monarchy. This message was rapidly spread through the party's growing network of newspapers, the "principal spokesman, supplier of ideology, and enforcer of party discipline."[24] It was an explicitly populist appeal, intended both to rouse the people to political action and to define them in opposition to the Federalist "monocrats."[25] The cause of America, they insisted, was the cause of democratic government, of a political equality that ennobled the laboring classes; Jefferson and his associates were presented as "friends to the people," committed to social equality and opposed to aristocratic efforts to establish distinctions of rank.[26]

For almost a decade, Federalists had been crafting citizenship laws, land settlement policies, financial institutions, and a revenue system that advantaged their core constituencies and reflected their vision of

[22] Young, "The Mechanics and the Jeffersonians," 269; Bradburn, *The Citizenship Revolution*, 163.

[23] Bradburn, *The Citizenship Revolution*, 209, 226; Sean Wilentz, *Chants Democratic: New York City and the Rise of the American Working Class, 1788–1850* (New York: Oxford University Press, 1984), 39; Wilentz, *The Rise of American Democracy*, 87; Edward C. Carter II, "'A Wild Irishman' Under Every Federalist's Bed: Naturalization in Philadelphia, 1789–1806," *The Pennsylvania Magazine of History and Biography* 94, no. 3 (1970): 331–46, 333–34.

[24] Jeffrey L. Pasley, "1800 as a Revolution in Political Culture: Newspapers, Celebrations, Voting, and Democratization in the Early Republic," in *The Revolution of 1800: Democracy, Race, and the New Republic*, ed. James J. Horn, Jan Ellen Lewis, and Peter S. Onuf (Charlottesville: University of Virginia Press, 2002), 121–52, 135–38.

[25] Peter S. Onuf, *Jefferson's Empire: The Language of American Nationhood* (Charlottesville: University of Virginia Press, 2000), 88–89.

[26] Alan Taylor, "From Fathers to Friends of the People: Political Personae in the Early Republic," in Ben-Atar and Oberg, *Federalists Reconsidered*, 225–45, 227; Merrill D. Peterson, *The Jefferson Image in the American Mind* (Charlottesville: University of Virginia, 1998 [1960]), 67; Joyce Appleby, "Thomas Jefferson and the Psychology of Democracy," in Horn, Ellen Lewis, and Onuf, *The Revolution of 1800: Democracy, Race, and the New Republic*, 155–71, 157–58.

nationally led commercial development. The election of Jefferson and a Republican House and Senate in 1800 provided Republicans with an opportunity to roll back some of these changes, to shore up their own authority and advance their own priorities and aspirations. "My great anxiety," wrote Jefferson to John Dickinson after his election, "is to avail ourselves of our ascendancy to establish good principles and good practices: to fortify republicanism behind as many barriers as possible, that the outworks may give time to rally and save the citadel, should that again be in danger."[27]

They repealed or revised the Naturalization and Alien laws, and Jefferson pardoned the Republican editors still in jail under the Sedition Act, which they allowed to expire in 1800. They attempted a modest restructuring of the laws governing settlement and democracy in the territories, supporting the division of public lands into smaller tracts and allowing down payments to be made with four years to pay off the balance for the express purpose of making land available to the "poor class" of citizens so that they could "exercise their own [political] will," which they could not do if "they were obliged to become tenants to others." They also put the representative institutions of the territories on a more democratic foundation, gradually establishing "the principle of universal suffrage."[28] They accelerated land acquisitions and, most dramatically, arranged for the purchase of the extensive Louisiana Territory; but they did not break with the Federalists' policy of gradual expansion organized around concentrated settler communities.[29]

[27] Thomas J. Randolph, ed., *Memoirs, Correspondence, and Private Papers of Thomas Jefferson*, vol. 3 (London: Henry Colburn and Richard Bentley, 1829), 495.

[28] *Annals of Congress*, H. R., 4th Cong., 1st sess., c. 858; H. R., 10th Cong., 1th sess., January 1808, c. 1359; Wilentz, *Rise of American Democracy*, 111; Stanley Elkins and Eric McKitrick, "A Meaning for Turner's Frontier: Democracy in the Old Northwest," *Political Science Quarterly* 69, no. 3 (1954): 321–53, 337; Alan Taylor, "Land and Liberty on the Post-Revolutionary Frontier," in *Devising Liberty: Preserving and Creating Freedom in the New American Republic*, ed. David Thomas Konig (Stanford, CA: Stanford University Press, 1995), 84; "Enabling Act for Ohio, 1802," *Ohio Archaeological and Historical Quarterly* 5 (August 1897): 75.

[29] Frymer, *Building an American Empire*; Reginald Horsman, "American Indian Policy in the Old Northwest, 1783–1812," in *The American Indian: Past and Present*, 3rd edn. (New York: Alfred A. Knopf, 1986), 137–49; Robert M. Owens, "Jeffersonian Benevolence on the Ground: The Indian Land Cession Treaties of William Henry Harrison," *Journal of the Early Republic* 22, no. 2 (2002): 405–35; Robert W. McCluggage, "The Senate and Indian Land Treaties, 1800–1825," *Western Historical Quarterly* 1, no. 4 (1970): 415–25.

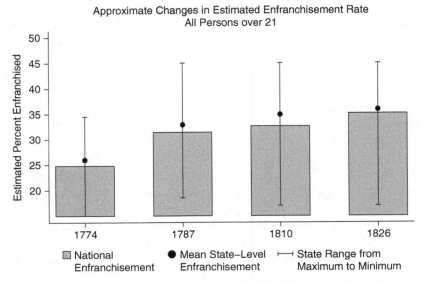

FIGURE 3.1 Changes in Estimated Enfranchisement Rates

Republicans in the states and Congress generally came out in favor of further democratizations of the right to vote, seeing in suffrage reform a potential issue that could back up their pretensions to being the supporters of democracy against aristocracy. Between 1789 and 1826 ten states – most of them with Republican majorities – revised their voting qualifications, while a succession of new states was admitted whose voting laws had been liberalized first by congressional Republicans and then by the local party in constitutional conventions. By the third decade of the nineteenth century, only three states continued to require ownership of property to vote – Virginia, Rhode Island, and North Carolina for the state senate – with the accession of Republicans to office a major factor in the expansion of voting right.[30]

The result was a steady but modest expansion of the right to vote. Figure 3.1 shows an estimate of the proportion of the free adult male national population that could vote and the range of state-level enfranchisement rates, based on secondary sources and statistical estimates of the level of disenfranchisement produced by different types of qualifications. The post-1787 changes did not produce as sharp an expansion of the

[30] Ratcliffe, "The Right to Vote."

electorate as the Revolutionary period, but within forty years, approximately 85 percent of the free adult male population was likely enfranchised.

COALITIONAL TENSIONS AND THE PLACE OF FREE BLACKS

For the first time, however, many of these democratizing reforms were accompanied by the simultaneous disenfranchisement of black voters. Table 3-1 lists the major changes to the suffrage qualifications from 1789 to 1826. The last column notes whether the reforms saw the pairing of democratization and black disenfranchisement, with a star noting those that were passed by Congress. Fourteen of twenty expansions of the franchise for white men also saw black disenfranchisement imposed simultaneously; thirteen of fifteen did so if we look only at the period after 1800. By 1822, the proportion of states or territories with a property qualification had fallen to under 10 percent, while the proportion with a racial disenfranchising clause had risen to 65 percent.

The emergence of this pattern at this juncture was not the result of a coherent and explicit commitment to white republicanism, where "white egalitarians" were motivated simultaneously by a desire to extend the right to vote and the hopes of depriving free black Americans of any claim to equal civic status. There was, in fact, no straight line connecting the ongoing democratization of American institutions and their simultaneous constriction on racial lines, and only gradually would the Republican party actively try to coordinate its members around a white male standard and offer an ideological narrative that could help justify this association.

There were, however, some common factors across the country that impelled black disenfranchisement. Most important was the broadly shared belief among white Americans that free blacks were degraded and that association with them would itself be degrading unless in the position of paternalistic or employer control, although this was not yet an elaborate scientific ideology of inherent racial difference and hierarchy. As black Americans began in small numbers asserting their right to vote, white Americans revealed that their egalitarian commitments were not as catholic as they had seemed to suggest during the heady days of revolution and the founding of new republics. As the population of former slaves grew, subjected to intense discrimination in labor markets and without any source of inherited wealth or savings, white Northerners were confronted with a level of intense poverty that was relatively new in the

TABLE 3.1 *Democratizing and Disenfranchising Changes, 1789–1826*

State or Territory	Class Qualification	Racial Qualification	Paired
Georgia (1789)	Removes property qualification	*Only whites were state citizens*	No
South Carolina (1790)	Effectively ends property qualification	*Black disenfranchisement already established*	—
Vermont (1791)	Residence requirement	—	No
Delaware (1792)	Replaces property with taxpaying qualification	White male citizen standard imposed	Yes
Kentucky (1792)	No property or tax qualification; two-year residence	—	No
Tennessee (1796)	Allows freemen resident six months in county to vote	—	No
Kentucky (1799)	—	Race qualification imposed	No
Maryland (1801)	Replaces property with residence qualification	White male citizen standard imposed	Yes
Ohio (1802)	Congressional enabling act replaces property with taxpayer qualification; liberalized in constitution	White male inhabitant standard imposed in constitution	Yes
New Jersey (1807)	Replaces property with taxpaying qualification	White male citizen standard imposed	Yes
Indiana (1808)	Liberalizes property qualification	White male citizen standard imposed by Congress	Yes*
Mississippi (1808)	Liberalizes property qualification	White male citizen standard imposed by Congress	Yes*

(continued)

South Carolina (1810)	Replaces taxpaying with residence qualification	*Black disenfranchisement already established*	—
Maryland (1810)	Reduces residency qualifications	*Black disenfranchisement already established*	—
Louisiana (1811–12)	A taxpaying qualification established by Congress; a restrictive taxpaying qualification established by constitution	White male citizen standard imposed by Congress and maintained in new constitution	Yes*
Indiana (1811)	Taxpaying qualification established by Congress	*Black disenfranchisement already established*	—
Missouri (1812)	Taxpaying qualification established by Congress	White male citizen standard imposed by Congress	Yes*
Illinois (1812)	Taxpaying qualification established by Congress	White male citizen standard imposed by Congress	Yes*
Mississippi (1814)	Residence qualification established by Congress	*Black disenfranchisement already established*	—
Connecticut (1813)	Property qualification is increased by statute	—	No
Connecticut (1814)	—	Nonwhites barred from freemanship	No
Indiana (1816)	Residence qualification established in constitution	A racial qualification was not included in the congressional enabling act, but was included in the constitution	Yes
Mississippi (1817)	Replaces residence with a tax or militia qualification	Continued racial qualification established by Congress	—
Connecticut (1817–18)	Replaced property with taxpayer qualification for elections to constitutional convention; constitution establishes taxpaying qualification	Nonwhites barred from voting for constitutional convention, and constitution imposes racial qualification unless already had the freemanship	Yes

(continued)

TABLE 3.1 *(continued)*

State or Territory	Class Qualification	Racial Qualification	Paired
Illinois (1818)	Enabling act establishes residence qualification, maintained in the constitution	*Black disenfranchisement already established.* White male citizen standard included in enabling act and in constitution	—
Alabama (1819)	Continued residence qualification established by Congress	*Black disenfranchisement already established*	—
Maine (1819)	Replaces requirement with a residence qualification	*Black disenfranchisement proposed but defeated*	No
Michigan (1819)	Taxpaying qualification established by Congress	White male citizen standard imposed by Congress	Yes*
Missouri (1820)	Enabling act establishes residence qualification, maintained in the constitution	*Black disenfranchisement already established.* White male citizen standard included in enabling act and in constitution	—
Massachusetts (1820)	Replaces property with a taxpaying qualification	—	No
New York (1821)	Replaces property with a taxpaying qualification	All but extremely wealthy free blacks are disenfranchised	Yes
Rhode Island (1822)	Removal of property qualification defeated by legislature	Nonwhites barred from admission to freemanship	No
Florida (1823–26)	Territorial council establishes residential qualifications for delegate and (1826) council	White male citizen standard imposed	Yes
New York (1826)	Replaces property with a taxpaying qualification	*Black disenfranchisement already established*	—

* indicates territories in which Congress altered the suffrage qualifications.

88

American experience: much overwrought fretting that persons of color would be forced to cast (or induced to sell) their vote to please the employers upon whom they were dependent ensued, establishing what would become one of the more important and enduring racist tropes against equal voting rights.

But even as states began to explicitly disenfranchise black voters, support was not immediately associated in members' voting patterns or stated preferences with support for class democratization. It was not yet rooted in a political ideology of white democracy.

Stirrings of Sectional Conflict

Soon after the Haitian revolution, a Republican from Connecticut – Abraham Bishop – wrote "The Rights of Black Men," in which he implored his fellow Americans to show that "we have not been hypocrites in the cause of freedom." "The American Declaration of Independence," the "spirit of freedom" that had animated the American army, "Paine's *Common Sense*," and "the articles of our liberating societies" all demanded that the country recognize the rights of the enslaved persons of St. Domingue to freedom.[31]

Bishop's father was later appointed collector of customs by Jefferson as a reward for his son's services to the party, and he would soon be appointed to that position himself. Even as he rose to prominence in the party and began calling for a democratization of state politics, Bishop remained committed to this egalitarian position. As with many Northern Republicans during this period, Bishop's entry into a national alliance with slaveholders did not lead him to instantly abandon his egalitarian views. Similarly, John Bacon – who had spoken eloquently in favor of black suffrage in 1778 Massachusetts – insisted as a Republican member of Congress in 1803 that black Americans were citizens and had been such "previous to the time of forming the Constitution, and actually had a voice in the adoption of that solemn compact." As citizens, they had rights that could not be abridged, as any racial "distinction between the citizens of the United States is not only unknown, but repugnant to the radical principles and general tenor of the Constitution." To his surprise,

---

[31] Tim Matthewson, "Abraham Bishop, 'The Rights of Black Men,' and the American Reaction to the Haitian Revolution," *The Journal of Negro History* 67, no. 2 (1982): 148–54, 153.

he was met with "affected sneers" and "inhuman threats" from at least one Southern Republican.[32]

William Pinkney, later attorney general under President James Madison, encouraged the Maryland assembly in 1789 to retain a law allowing for voluntary emancipation, asking whether slavery was "correspondent with *the principle of a democracy*? Call that principle what you will, the love of *equality*, as defined by some; of *liberty*, as understood by others; such conduct is manifestly in violation of it." The claim of slaveholders to be "the zealous partizans of freedom, cannot but astonish a person who is not casuist enough to reconcile antipathies." Pinkney concluded that incorporating freed slaves as citizens would strengthen the Republic. Rather than being the "convenient tools of usurpation," as claimed by opponents of abolition, "freed-men" had always "reanimated the drooping spirit of democracy" when incorporated into the body politic, "bound by gratitude" to the government that emancipated them. "Is their colour, Mr. Speaker, the mark of a divine vengeance, or is it only the flimsy pretext upon which we attempt to justify our treatment of them?"[33]

The organization of the Jeffersonian coalition, however, would bring new pressures for its aligned members to render some of their divergent commitments consistent. The party's self-presentation as the defender of the Republic was juxtaposed against a Federalist narrative that stressed the preservation of political order and property. Southern Federalists warned that "democracy and insurrection were blood brothers" and that slaves were learning that "equality is the natural condition of man."[34] A Northern Federalist paper asked sardonically whether the attention given to slavery "might embolden the black citizens of our southern states to attempt erecting a democratical republic, after the moddle [sic] of Mr. Jefferson, and other friends to the rights of Negro Men."[35] In 1800, South Carolinian Federalist Henry William de Saussure warned against electing Jefferson because he "entertains opinions unfriendly to the property, which forms the efficient labor of a great

---

[32] *Annals of Congress*, 7th Cong., 2nd sess., February 1803, 467.

[33] *The Freeman's Journal; or, The North-American Intelligencer* (Philadelphia), April 27, 1790, p. 2; William Pinkney, *Speech of William Pinkney, Esq.: 1789, in the legislature of Maryland* (Philadelphia: J. Van Court, 1842), 3

[34] Link, *Democratic-Republican Societies, 1790–1800*, 184–86; Joseph C. Carroll, *Slave Insurrections in the United States, 1800–1865* (Mineola, NY: Dover Publications, 2004 [1938]), 41–45.

[35] *Russell's Gazette* (Boston) 5, no. 28 (December 12, 1798): 2.

part of the southern states." Jefferson's writings, he argued, indicated that he "wishes the 500,000 blacks in America should be emancipated – he wishes their condition, both of body and mind *raised*."[36]

When a conspiracy organized by the enslaved Virginian Gabriel Prosser was discovered, a widely reprinted letter warned that the plot had originated "with some vile French Jacobins, aided and abetted by some of our own profligate and abandoned democrats. Liberty and equality have brot the evil upon us. A doctrine, however intelligible, and admissible, in a land of freemen, but dangerous and extremely wicked in this country [eastern Virginia], where every white man is a master, and every black man a slave." The doctrine of political equality was also blamed for the revolution in St. Domingue/Haiti, and it was noted that this doctrine had been "imprudently propagated, at many of our tables, while our servants have been standing behind our chairs, for several years past." "Democracy . . . in Virginia," the correspondent concluded, "is like virtue in hell. The Ethiopian can never be washed white. The slave holder can never be a democrat."[37] While Northern Federalists praised Governor James Monroe for suppressing the plot, they sarcastically remarked on the inconsistency of the "democratic Governor" not recognizing "the holy right of insurrection in citizen Gabriel."[38]

Federalists in Congress were also willing to connect the dots between the democratic radicalism advanced by many Jeffersonian activists and the threat of slave insurrections. When a body of free persons of color organized by Absalom Jones presented petitions to Congress, Federalists responded with outrage that they dared claim the rights of citizens to petition their government. "Already," warned South Carolinian John Rutledge, "had too much of this new-fangled French philosophy of liberty and equality found its way and was too apparent among these *gentlemen*." Robert Harper told the House that "a temper of revolt" was "more perceptible" among Southern slaves as a result. It was not just Southerners who opposed the petition. Harrison Gray Otis of Massachusetts believed the measure to be "dangerous," as it would "teach them the art of assembling together, debating, and the like, and would soon, if encouraged, extend from one end of the Union to the other." Samuel Dana of Connecticut announced

---

[36] William Henry de Saussure, *Address to the Citizens of South-Carolina on the Approaching Election of President and Vice-President of the United States* (Charleston, SC: W. F. Young, 1800), 15–16.
[37] *The Independent Gazetteer* (Worcester, MA), October 14, 1800, p. 4.
[38] *New-Hampshire Sentinel*, October 4, 1800, p. 2.

that he would have opposed the petition had it contained the usual "farago of the French metaphysics of liberty and equality," which would "produce some of the dreadful scenes of St. Domingo." Other Northern Federalists expressed their opposition to any expression of liberal sentiment by Northerners that might encourage "slaves to come from the Southern States to reside as vagabonds and thieves among them."[39]

Northern Federalists attacked Republicans from both sides, accusing them of threatening property and instigating violence but also for their alliance with slavery, a charge that became more prominent as their own bisectional coalition fell apart. One New Englander attacked "Citizen James Monroe," who was "born and educated in that *favorite* spot of Freedom and Jacobinism, in which the shades of Liberty and Slavery are as nicely interwoven as the colours of its inhabitants."[40] The English reformer William Cobbett, writing as a Federalist pamphleteer, remarked that in the North, "order walks hand in hand with the most perfect liberty," while in the South, "anarchy revels, surrounded with its den of slaves."[41] Other Federalists reminded Southerners that they would need the support of Northern Federalists to suppress any slave rebellions. "If you carry your principles much farther," wrote one author, "your slaves will take you at your word – they will say, they are born free and equal, as well as other men, and they will form a Democratic Society among themselves.... Your safety is in a union with your northern brethren who are determined to maintain our government."[42]

Some Federalists also took aim at Jefferson's infamous suggestion – presumptuously offered as a suspicion only – that blacks and whites were not of the same species. William Linn, president of Rutgers University, denounced Jefferson's speculation as "directly opposite to divine revelation," and noted that for all his abstract support for black emancipation, he had "raised one of the greatest obstacles, by denying them to be the same species as whites."[43] Another attacked New Jersey Republican James Sloan, asking how he could support a president who believed

[39] *Annals of Congress*, H. R., 6th Cong., 1st sess., January 2, 1800, cc. 229–32.
[40] "A Citizen of New England," *The Antigallican; or, The Lover of His Own Country* (Philadelphia: William Cobbett, 1797), 59.
[41] Cobbett, *A Bone to Gnaw*, 44.
[42] *The Daily Advertiser* (New York), April 14, 1794, p. 2; *The Mirrour* (Concord, NH), June 9, 1794, p. 4.
[43] William Linn, *Serious Considerations on the Election of a President* (New York: John Furman, 1800), 11–14; see also *Federal Gazette and Baltimore Daily Advertiser*, August 12, 1800, p. 2.

Africans were "a race of beings inferior to the whites." The Republican party presented a "MONSTROUS SPECTACLE" of slaves being held by "*republican task-masters*," giving the lie to their self-professed "superior regard to liberty, equality ... the rights of man ... [and] the *genuine principles of our independence*."[44] An open letter to Jefferson asked him how he could still "profess yourself the friend to the rights of man" given his shocking speculation. "The citizens of the northern states who are friends to liberty and government, and equally enemies to tyranny and anarchy, would be very happy to have an explanation of your conduct."[45]

A considerable body of historical research has detailed the formation and extent of white racist attitudes in the late colonial and early republican periods, and there is little doubt that white Americans in the early nineteenth century generally treated both free and enslaved African Americans as "a rank of beings far below others."[46] But racist beliefs did not neatly translate into political positions or party support, nor were they always a paramount priority. Federalist attacks on Jefferson's racist "suspicions" and on Southern slaveholding, as well as their warnings that democratic rhetoric would encourage insurrection, were intended to undermine Republicans' position in public opinion, and Northern and Southern Republicans certainly worried that it would have this effect. Pressured by the inconsistency of loudly supporting egalitarian principles while relying on slaveholders for their political strength, Northern Republicans in particular were forced to respond. And yet instead of asserting Jefferson's racist statements as truths, they engaged in convoluted efforts to reinterpret his position and reframe the question.

Northern Republicans, for instance, emphasized Jefferson's statements in favor of emancipation and asked whether the acknowledged evil of slavery should be compounded by the evil of Federalist aristocratic rule.[47] William Duane, the editor of the Republican newspaper *Aurora*, tried to

---

[44] Christianus, *An Address to the Professors and Friends of the Christian Religion Residing in the State of New Jersey* (Trenton, NJ: Sherman, Mershon, and Thomas, 1801), 16; William Boyd, *To the Electors of the State of New-York* (Albany, 1809), 1, 6.

[45] *The Connecticut Courant*, February 11, 1793, p. 1.

[46] Richard Newman, ed. *Black Preacher to White America: The Collected Writings of Lemuel Haynes, 1774–1833* (New York: Carlson Publishing, 1990), 82; Joanne Pope Melish, "The 'Condition' Debate and Racial Discourse in the Antebellum North," *Journal of the Early Republic* 19, no. 4 (1999): 651–72, 663; Lois E. Horton, "From Class to Race in Early America: Northern Post-Emancipation Racial Reconstruction," *Journal of the Early Republic* 19, no. 4 (1999): 629–49.

[47] Americanus, *Address to the People of the United States, with an Epitome and Vindication of the Public Life and Character of Thomas Jefferson* (Philadelphia: James Carey, 1800).

dissuade "friends of the blacks in the city of Philadelphia" from turning against Jefferson in the election of 1800, insisting that the presidential candidate had dedicated his entire life to emancipation and accusing Federalists of trying to break up the Union.[48] Levi Lincoln, who had opposed slavery as a Massachusetts lawyer, denounced Federalist efforts to place "prejudices" between the "the northern and the southern states, *Republicans* and *Republicans*."[49] The *Albany Register* argued that Federalists' broadsides against Southern slavery were the rhetorical legacy of earlier efforts by Great Britain to keep the colonies divided, while the *National Aegis* claimed that it was an attempt "to divide the northern from the southern States, and on the ruins of such division, to erect a Monarchical Government."[50] Hezekiah Niles attempted to rouse public indignation by highlighting Federalist placards that called for the separation of the Northern states – "the Potomac the boundary – the Negro States by themselves."[51]

Some suggested that the continued disenfranchisement of whites was equivalent to slavery. Many of the inhabitants of Virginia, noted one writer – likely Abraham Bishop – "have no voice in elections, being denied the freeman's oath because they are BLACK. Many inhabitants of Connecticut ... have no voice in elections, being denied the freeman's oath because they are POOR. Virginia disfranchises the poor black man. Connecticut disfranchises the poor white man." Virginia, of course, did more than merely *disenfranchise* persons of color, and its denial of equal rights for black Americans was premised not on property or wealth but on descent. But in this case, at least, the author was not making an explicit appeal to Northern racism nor arguing that it was especially degrading to be on the same rank as a black slave. "A disfranchised black man, is like a disfranchised white man," the writer continued, "except that one is black and the other white. Our federal papers have repeatedly called on us to resent this insult. Insult! Good heavens!" Between the disenfranchised voter of the North and the Southern slave, "there is no political difference."[52]

[48] Padraig Riley, *Slavery and the Democratic Conscience: Political Life in Jeffersonian American* (Philadelphia: University of Pennsylvania Press, 2015), 80.

[49] Levi Lincoln, *A Farmer's Letters to the People* (Robert Johnson, 1802); Riley, *Slavery and the Democratic Conscience*, 36.

[50] *The Times and District of Columbia* (Alexandria, VA), October 14, 1800, p. 2.

[51] Hezekiah Niles, *Things as They Are, or, Federalism Turned Inside Out* (Baltimore: Evening Post, 1809), 50.

[52] *American Mercury*, September 16, 1802, p. 2; David Waldstreicher and Stephen R. Grossbart, "Abraham Bishop's Vocation; or, the Mediation of Jeffersonian Politics," *Journal of the Early Republic* 18, no. 4 (1998): 617–57, 648; *American Mercury*, August 1, 1805, p. 2.

This was not solidarity with the enslaved, and like many variants of "all lives matter," its effect was to refocus public sympathies on disenfranchised white men, and thus by implication away from those subjected to what was a much harsher oppression. But in this author's hands it was less a tactic of minimization than an insistence that readers should be profoundly outraged at both disenfranchisement and enslavement and should see in their own political exclusion a manifestation of the broader denial of republican equality that was slavery.

Southerners regularly complained that whenever slavery was brought up, sectional friction was the result. Worryingly, these debates would be "published in Newspapers" and read elsewhere, potentially endangering "the peace and security of these States holding slaves." One Southerner, ostrich-like, announced that he was "unwilling to think much less to speak on this subject."[53] And many Northern Republicans reciprocated, avoiding discussions of slavery or showing considerable reticence when it was brought up. John Smilie, a former leader of the radically democratic Pennsylvania Constitutionalists, was quite taken aback when Southerners attacked the right of free black citizens to petition the government. Still, he felt "a contrary impulse" against speaking on the matter, preferring to not discuss slavery "from motives of prudence," a line that he and other Republicans would return to repeatedly.[54]

In a particularly influential intervention, Mathew Carey – a refugee printer from Ireland who had fled prosecution for his support of Catholic emancipation – published a *Calm Address to the Eastern States on the Subject of the Representation of Slave* and the bestselling *The Olive Branch*, in which he argued that sectional tensions needed to be set aside for the sake of the Union and representative democracy: "The result of our governmental experiment will operate on millions yet unborn. Should it fail by our folly or guilt, it will afford encouragement to future despots in their attempts upon human liberty and human happiness." The message to Republican politicians and constituencies across the country was that

---

[53] Everett S. Brown, "The Senate Debate on the Breckinridge Bill for the Government of Louisiana, 1804," 353.

[54] Another remarked that "I abhor slavery. I am opposed to it in every shape.... I am very sorry the question is *now* called up. I have done every thing I could to prevent it – but since gentlemen, (and many of them from Slave States) will stir the questions, I am prepared and will on all occasions vote against slavery." *Annals of Congress*, H. R., 6th Cong., 1st sess., January 2, 1800, cc. 229–232; H. R., 11th Cong., 3rd sess., c. 937; Brown, "The Senate Debate on the Breckinridge Bill for the Government of Louisiana, 1804," 352.

while slavery might be an evil, a worse injustice would be the dismemberment of the national project, and with it the cause of democracy and republican government.[55] The full scope of republican commitments that supposedly defined America needed to be set aside in order to preserve America, marking out the country's purpose, solicitude, and public care as extending to white people alone.

Whatever their personal beliefs about slavery and political equality, the activists who aligned with the Jeffersonian party were partners in a coalition "commanded by Virginia gentry slaveholders." And while they provided a narrative of political community that connected "the fate of American equality to the political well-being of the middling classes," they were repeatedly pulled toward a defense of Jefferson and their Southern allies, which they framed as a defense of the Union itself.[56] Their efforts to reconcile these commitments would come under increasing strain as Southern representatives began demanding additional protections for slavery, including its extension into the new states.

"An evil far greater than slavery itself"

According to Southern political writers, free black Americans constituted a unique threat to the existence of Southern society and the well-being of its white residents. It was Thomas Jefferson who had most influentially articulated the belief that even were slavery entirely abolished, freed persons of color could not be granted an equal political status within American society, proposing in his *Notes on the State of Virginia* that they be colonized west of the Mississippi. "Why not retain and incorporate the blacks into the state," he asked? The answer would be among the most consequential passages in American political thought:

> Deep rooted prejudices entertained by the whites; ten thousand recollections, by the blacks, of the injuries they have sustained; new provocations; the real distinctions which nature has made; and many other circumstances, will divide us into parties, and produce convulsions which will probably never end but in the extermination of the one or the other race.

cool
excerpt
bro

---

[55] Riley, *Slavery and the Democratic Conscience*, 37; Mathew Carey, *A Calm Address to the People of the Eastern States* (Philadelphia: M. Carey, 1814), 5; Mathew Carey, *The Olive Branch: Or, Faults on Both Sides* (Philadelphia: M. Carey, 1814).

[56] Wilentz, *Chants Democratic*, 74; Wilentz, *Rise of American Democracy*, 97–98.

Free blacks would remember their oppression, while the attitudes of whites had been formed in the context of rigid racial distinctions essential to the functioning of American slavery, leaving them unable to recognize the social equality necessary for equal political rights.[57] "If they be emancipated," wrote Fernando Fairfax, "it would never do to allow them *all* the privileges of citizens," as they would then form a separate and hostile interest "from the rest of the community." Only intermarriage could "form one common interest," and the "prejudices, sentiments, or whatever they may be called," against this would be "insurmountable." Only by deporting black Americans could emancipation be rendered compatible with the security of white communities.[58] St. George Tucker's proposed abolition plan would remove black Americans through a form of "self-deportation," denying them citizenship rights and subjecting them to legal harassment – unlike most writers at this juncture, Tucker was insistent that while republican principles might support the abolition of slavery, they carried no implication of civil or political equality. His plan to make life miserable for free African Americans so that they might remove themselves would in effect become a strategy employed across the South, in New England towns from which persons of color from other states were "warned out" – a longstanding practice of evicting people from towns in which they supposedly lacked a right to inhabitancy or had in some way contravened its standards or propriety[59] – and in many frontier territories and states that passed "black laws" limiting the civil rights of free persons of color for the express purpose of dissuading them from migrating. Like Jefferson and Fairfax, however, Tucker blamed the prejudices of white society for why black Americans could never be accorded equal rights and thus should be encouraged to leave. "The habitual arrogance and assumption of superiority, among the whites" meant they would never accept blacks as their social equals.[60]

cool!

---

[57] Thomas Jefferson, *Notes on the State of Virginia* (London: John Stockdale, 1787), 265–71.

[58] Fernando Fairfax, "Plan for Liberating the Negroes," *The American Museum or Universal Magazine* 8 (December 1790): 285–87.

[59] In Rhode Island, 22 percent of the households warned out between 1750 and 1800 were headed by persons identified as indigenous or of African or partial African descent, and 13 percent were headed by women of color, despite constituting less than 5 percent of the total population; half of the households warned out were headed by women. Ruth Wallis Herndon, "'Who Died an Expence to this Town': Poor Relief in Eighteenth-Century Rhode Island," in *Down and Out in Early America*, ed. Billy G. Smith (University Park: Pennsylvania State University Press, 2004), 135–62.

[60] St. George Tucker, *A Dissertation on Slavery* (Philadelphia: Mathew Carey, 1796), 77.

The cross-class belief among whites that they shared a racial status elevating them over black Americans had long been cultivated by the planter elite; it was now being deployed by these same elites to frustrate the implications of their professed republican commitments.

If whites would not accept black Americans as their equals in social intercourse, then liberty could only result in a racial contest for political power. Given the extreme disparities of American society, the argument went, a victory by a party solicitous to black Americans would result in the expropriation of the whites, while a victory by the party of the whites would leave African Americans embittered and willing to throw their support to foreign powers. John Taylor denounced the efforts of an "amiable and peaceful religious sect" – likely the Quakers or Methodists – "to plunge three fourths of the union, into a civil war." "The history of parties in its utmost malignancy," he wrote, "is but a feint mirror for reflecting the consequences of a white and a black party. If badges and names have been able to madden men in all ages, up to robbery and murder in their most atrocious forms, no doubt can exist of the consequences of placing two nations of distinct colours and features on the same theatre, to contend, not about signs and sounds, but for wealth and power." The danger, as a range of Southern writers expressed it, was that any postabolition parties would be organized around racial categories that mapped on to real distinctions in property. Could it be supposed "that the negroes could be made free, and yet kept from property and equal civil rights; or that both or either of these avenues to power could be opened to them, and yet that some precept or incantation could prevent their entrance? As rivals for rule with the whites, the collision would be immediate, and the catastrophe speedy." And if they were free but "divested of equal civil rights and wealth to prevent this rivalship . . . they would constitute the most complete instrument for invasion or ambition."[61]

Taylor and others pointed to the insurrection in St. Domingue/Haiti for proof of his argument, and in the years after 1791 it became "a conventional belief among white North Americans that the colony's free population of color had been a leading cause of the catastrophe."[62] The Southern recitation of the case held that by enfranchising the free persons of color,

---

[61] John Taylor, *Arator, Being a Series of Agricultural Essays* (Georgetown [Washington, DC]: J. M. and J. B. Carter, 1813), no. 28.

[62] Eberhard Faber, *Building the Land of Dreams: New Orleans and the Transformation of Early America* (Princeton, NJ: Princeton University Press, 2015), 71.

the French National Assembly had encouraged the organization of distinct racial factions, whose intensifying conflicts provided the opportunity for the slaves to rebel.

After the Haitian revolution and Gabriel's rebellion, southern Republicans began insisting on policies that would explicitly deny rights for free black citizens, part of a larger process of reversing the liberalizations of the slave laws that had followed the Revolution.[63] When they proposed a bill that would have prohibited all persons of color, free or enslaved, from landing in any Southern port, Republicans found themselves divided on sectional lines over the question of black citizenship. Supporters of the bill, which responded to a public panic that vessels were disembarking insurgents from St. Domingue, argued that it was "only such as the imminent danger of the Southern States called for." But it was opposed by a number of Republicans, including John Bacon, John Smilie, John Nicholson of Maryland, Ebenezer Elmer of New Jersey, and others, on the grounds that it would "destro[y] and abridg[e] the rights of free negroes and persons of color."[64]

A proposal to prohibit the slave trade likewise caused sectional tensions, with Southerners arguing that enslaved persons captured under bill's enforcement provisions should be sold and Northerners opposing the federal government auctioning off slaves. When James Sloan proposed an amendment that would have required captured slaves to be freed, it was met with a violent backlash. Peter Early of Georgia explained:

> Those who, from experience, know the extent of the evil [slavery], believe that the most formidable aspect in which it can present itself, is by making these people free among them. Yes, sir, though slavery is an evil, regretted by every man in the country, to have among us in any considerable quantity persons of this description [free persons of color], is *an evil far greater than slavery itself*. Does any gentleman want proof of this. I answer that all proof is useless; *no fact can be more notorious.*

ha! ha! fun!

He demanded that the bill be amended not just to prohibit the "importation" of slaves, but an "evil ... still greater," the "introduction of persons of color from the West India islands, who under the existing laws were not considered slaves." To require Southerners to consent to the emancipation of forfeited slaves or the admission of free persons of color was "opposed to the principle of self-preservation, and to the love of family," for it would "turn loose, in the bosom of the country, firebrands that would consume them."[65] Nathaniel Macon insisted that "the owners of slaves do

---

[63] Bradburn, *The Citizenship Revolution*, 260–71.

[64] *Annals of Congress*, H. R., 7th Cong., 2nd sess., February 1803, c. 459, 469, 472.

[65] *Annals of Congress*, H. R., 9th Cong., 2nd sess., December 1806, cc. 173–75, 177.

not wish such free blacks mingling with the slaves, teaching them liberty or insurrection."[66] Were any considerable number of free blacks introduced into Southern communities, noted one representative, Southern whites would, "in self-defence – gentlemen will understand me – get rid of them in some way," so that "not one of them would be left alive in a year." Sloan and Smilie were shocked at the extremism of their co-partisans.[67]

When a committee again proposed a bill to prohibit the slave trade in 1807, Sloan included a proviso that any person freed under the act would be sent to live in a state that had already abolished slavery. "The Southern gentlemen," he explained, "have said if we would take away the negroes from them, they would be satisfied. We have exerted every stretch of our genius to do this, we have agreed to take them ourselves."[68] This was a risky gambit given the force of Northern racism, but it too was unacceptable. The problem was not just free blacks in the South, but free blacks anywhere in the nation.

Southern representatives repeatedly made the case that free blacks were a fundamental threat to social order. "Free men of colour," complained Wilson Nicholas of Virginia in a debate on prohibiting the importation of slaves into Louisiana, "have a very ill effect upon slaves – they do much more mischief than strangers conceive of."[69] In Virginia, fears about the danger posed by free blacks led to a proposal to prohibit the emancipation or manumission of any enslaved person. Republican Thomas Robertson warned that "if the blacks see all of their color slaves, it will seem to them a disposition of Providence, and they will be content. But if they see others like themselves free, and enjoying rights, they are deprived of, they will repine." It was the "free blacks who instill into the slaves ideas hostile to our peace," and it was they who in freely "passing from place to place in society" were best situated to "organize insurrection." Republican James Semple warned that "there are now 20,000 free blacks among us [in Virginia]. When they shall become more numerous, they will furnish the officers and soldiers around whom the slaves will rally."[70] The "proof"

---

[66] *Poughkeepsie Journal and Constitutional Republican*, December 30, 1806, p. 2.

[67] Only nineteen members voted for Sloan's proposal, but an amendment to exclude from the country all persons of color was also defeated. *Annals of Congress*, H. R., 9th Cong., 2nd sess., December 1806, cc. 173–77, 181–83.

[68] *Annals of Congress*, H. R., 9th Cong., 2nd sess., February 1807, 477.

[69] Brown, "The Senate Debate on the Breckinridge Bill for the Government of Louisiana, 1804," 352.

[70] *The Argus* (Richmond, VA), January 17, 1806.

for these often-lurid fantasies of race war, noted Winthrop Jordan, "lay in St. Domingo."[71]

The Virginia bill was defeated by a vote of seventy-five to seventy-three, but "there was apparent agreement that drastic police measures were necessary, and very little objection to placing free negroes under any surveillance and restriction that seemed to be necessary for the safety of society." If the right of owners to manumit was not impaired, legislators hoped to impose "such conditions upon freedmen as would make liberty undesirable," including a law expelling all newly free persons of color from the state. They would find that they were not often welcome elsewhere: within a year, Maryland, Kentucky, and Delaware had passed legislation forbidding free persons of color from other states from taking up residence.[72]

MAKING THE WHITE REPUBLIC

Disenfranchisement in the Mid-Atlantic and Ohio Valley

This was the context in which black disenfranchisement came on to the political agenda. From the Revolution until the end of the century, only two states had revised their laws to disenfranchise black voters: Delaware, which introduced a racial restriction in 1792 during the height of public concern with the insurrection in St. Domingue, and Maryland, which in 1783 denied the suffrage to newly freed men of color – but not those born free – as part of a compromise bill to end the slave trade.[73]

These two states would be joined in 1799 by Kentucky. Newly arrived in the state, Henry Clay threw his support behind the movement for a new constitutional convention, one that was hoped might provide an opportunity to gradually abolish slavery. In print he referred to black Americans as "part of the people" and urged voters to reject conservative plans to limit the franchise to freeholders. While he conceded that enslaved persons were not yet fit for "enjoying the rights of a freeman," he insisted that this would not apply to their children, who should be entitled to all "the rights

---

[71] Jordan, *White Over Black*, 581.

[72] John H. Russell, *The Free Negro in Virginia, 1619–1865* (Baltimore: The Johns Hopkins University Press, 1913), 69–72; Jordan, *White Over Black*, 224; Beverly Tomek, "'From Motives of Generosity, as Well as Self-Preservation': Thomas Branagan, Colonization, and the Gradual Emancipation Movement," *American Nineteenth Century History 6*, no. 2 (2005): 121–47; Wolf, *Race and Liberty in the New Nation*, 122–26.

[73] Delaware in 1787 had also restricted the rights of newly freed blacks.

of a citizen."[74] Proslavery forces argued that property rights were under threat given popular anger at the speculators and large planters who had acquired much of the land set aside for revolutionary veterans, and emphasized the dangers to society posed by free blacks as instigators of insurrection and sources of racial "contamination."[75] The right to vote for white men was not curtailed, but it was denied to free men of color and the indigenous inhabitants.

Maryland would be the next state to explicitly bar black voters. A few years after the partial disenfranchisement of 1783, a total ban on black voting had been proposed "in the wake of the conflict over France's extension of voting rights to the free mulattoes of Santo Domingo." No vote was held on the proposal. A few years later, in 1797, Michael Taney introduced a constitutional amendment that would have lowered the property qualification for voting; this was amended so that "all *free born men* above the age of twenty-one years" who had been resident one year would be able to vote. The effect would have been to gradually increase the number of free black voters in the state.[76]

Joseph Nicholson, a key Jeffersonian in the state, led the opposition that defeated the amendment. Free blacks, he explained later, should be entitled to complete "protection in their persons and property," but "stern necessity, nay, self-preservation itself, compels us to observe a rigorous policy, and to stop here. The French Revolution has taught us a lesson on this subject, which ought never to be forgotten – the history of the island of St. Domingo." The French decision to enfranchise free black men had "roused into action the people of colour; increasing conflicts took place between them and the whites; the slaves flew to arms and a rebellion ensued."[77]

---

[74] *Kentucky Gazette*, February 28, 1799; James F. Hopkins, ed., *The Papers of Henry Clay: Volume 1: The Rising Statesman, 1797–1814* (Lexington: University of Kentucky Press, 1959), 13–14; see also Gustavas Vasa, "To the People of Kentucky," *Stewart's Kentucky Herald*, February 12, 1799, p. 1.

[75] Federalists wanted a high property qualification for voting, but the suffrage was left unchanged except for a racial disenfranchisement clause attached. Jeffrey Brooke Allen, "The Origins of Proslavery Thought in Kentucky, 1792–1799," *The Register of the Kentucky Historical Society* 77, no. 2 (1979): 75–90, 88.

[76] Davis S. Bogen, "The Maryland Context of Dred Scott: The Decline in the Legal Status of Maryland Free Blacks, 1776–1810," *American Journal of Legal History* 34, no. 4 (1990): 381–411, 396n59.

[77] *The Republican Star, or Eastern Shore General Advertiser* (Easton, MD), September 20, 1803.

For the next few years, Maryland legislators repeatedly debated amendments to the constitution that would abolish the property qualification for voting but would also impose an absolute prohibition on black suffrage. When one reform was under debate in 1800, a delegate moved to strike the word "white," which would not only continue existing black voting rights but also enfranchise the black population freed since 1783. This was supported by only a quarter of the legislature, the size of the majority strong evidence that full and immediate political equality had little appeal. John Johnson – a Republican who had won the votes of twelve of the fifteen free men of color who had cast a vote in Annapolis – voted in favor of black suffrage; Allen Quynn – a Federalist who had won the votes of six men of color – voted against.[78]

The assembly then voted to strike out a property qualification that had been inserted by the senate. Thirty-two percent of Republicans had voted to strike the word "white," and all of these also voted to reject the property qualification. Only 16 percent of Federalists voted to strike "white," and all but one of these voted to retain a property qualification and opposed the bill after this was defeated. The bill was then killed in the Senate, but it became a central partisan issue during the next election and was passed after a resounding Republican victory.[79]

Shortly after the amendment's ratification in 1803, Greenbury Morton, a nephew of Banneker, learned upon approaching the polls that he was no longer entitled to vote. Shaken by the degradation, Morton is reported to have addressed the crowd in "a strain of true and passionate eloquence," which kept them in "breathless attention."[80]

The next state to pair an extension of voting rights to white men with the disenfranchisement of black voters was Ohio. In the campaign for the Ohio statehood convention, Republican corresponding societies launched an attack against proposals to introduce slavery into the state. The New Market Township Republican Society argued that slavery was inconsistent with republican government, where "every citizen has rights with another, standing on the same footing, on the ground of equality." They rejected any constitution that would make "any of the sons of liberty" slaves or allow others "to live on the fruit of their fellow labor," and called

---

[78] David S. Bogen, "The Annapolis Poll Books of 1800 and 1804: African American Voting in the Early Republic," *Maryland Historical Magazine* 86, no. 1 (1991): 57–65, 63.

[79] *Votes and Proceedings of the House of Delegates of the State of Maryland, November Session 1800* (Annapolis, MD: F. Green, 1800), 51.

[80] Bogen, "The Annapolis Poll Books of 1800 and 1804," 63; J. H. B. Latrobe, *Memoir of Benjamin Banneker* (Baltimore: John D. Toy, 1845), 6.

for the right to vote to be extended to all men, regardless of race, without any property or taxpaying qualification to vote or hold office. For these activists, odious distinctions of race or property were both "unacceptable to any 'true' republican."[81]

The campaign saw the issues of slavery and black civil and political rights interwoven in candidates' rhetoric, with Republicans staking out an egalitarian position on both.[82] While there were a few examples of Republican candidates openly endorsing a restriction of free blacks' political or civil rights – such as William Craig, who opposed slavery but was also against allowing any "negro giving testimony against any white person, in any controversy whatever, or to have a vote in any election for office or officer"[83] – it was more common for candidates to emphatically denounce slavery as inconsistent with republicanism and to call for a constitution that would "set the natural rights of the meanest African and the most abject beggar, upon an equal footing with those citizens of the greatest wealth and equipage."[84]

Antislavery Republicans were prominent in the frontier town of Cincinnati and surrounding Hamilton County. Much of the organizational strength of the party, however, lay in Ross County, the heart of the Virginia Military District (V.M.D.), territory set aside for land grants to Virginia's revolutionary war veterans.[85] Republican candidates from the V.M.D. opposed slavery but tended to frame their opposition in terms that would resonate with their Southern-born constituents. Since many of the settlers here were farmers who had been pushed out of Virginia or Kentucky, Republicans warned that "our present equal distribution of property would be destroyed by the accumulation of large estates," impoverishing the white working man while creating a class of idle rich who would look down on labor as degrading. For them, one of the great accomplishments of the Revolution had been the expansion of

[81] John Craig Hammond, *Slavery, Freedom, and Expansion in the Early American West* (Charlottesville: University of Virginia Press, 2007), 85–87, 140, 205n24; *Scioto Gazette*, September 11, 1802; Helen M. Thurston, "The 1802 Constitutional Convention and Status of the Negro," Ohio History 81 (1972): 15–37.

[82] Thurston, "The 1802 Constitutional Convention and Status of the Negro," 29; Barbara A. Terzian, "Ohio's Constitutional Conventions and Constitutions," in *The History of Ohio Law*, vol. 1, ed. Michael Les Benedict and John F. Winkler (Athens: Ohio University Press, 2004), 80n49.

[83] *Scioto Gazette*, October 2, 1802.

[84] *Scioto Gazette*, July 17, 1802; Stephen Middleton, *The Black Laws: Race and the Legal Process in Early Ohio* (Athens: Ohio University Press, 2005), 28–29.

[85] The V.M.D. in 1801 included Clermont, Adams, Fairfield, and Ross Counties.

landholding opportunities in the Ohio Valley: the egalitarian potential of this conquest for whites, however, was already being foreclosed in Kentucky and would be further threatened were wealthy slave-owners able to establish their estates north of the Ohio River. Another danger was also invoked, that slavery would bring with it the constant danger of "insurrections, murders, house burnings" that were "daily" reported in the South. Republicans argued that slavery was such an odious oppression that it justified a violent response by the enslaved; as a result, all classes of whites would be forced to live in constant terror of righteous retribution. "Whenever the slaves should become numerous," noted Michael Baldwin, "we should be in continual danger of having our throats cut."[86]

Even when campaigning among Southern-born voters, however, only two of twenty Republican candidates gave their explicit support for restricting black civil and political rights, and both of them lost quite badly. A number of candidates instead called for delegates to "cheerfully grant [African Americans] the privileges of freemen."[87]

Republican egalitarianism persisted in the convention, but here the party's Southern leadership worked to coordinate their members around a white male standard for political and civil rights. The committee charged with drafting the suffrage qualifications, appointed by the "Chillicothe Junta" – the dominant Republican faction led by Edward Tiffin, Thomas Worthington, and Nathaniel Massie, also nicknamed the "Virginia party" for the origins of its members, constituents, and strong ties to the national party – proposed a clause that limited the vote to "white male inhabitants."[88]

This caused an immediate and prolonged fight: a motion was introduced to strike the word "white," and a number of Republicans, including John Browne, an ardent antislavery editor, and William Goforth, Jr., the son of the radical shoemaker who had opposed disenfranchisement in New York in 1785, came out in favor of black rights.[89] A majority of Republicans from Hamilton County voted for a racially equal franchise,

[86] *Scioto Gazette*, October 2, 1802, September 4, 1802, August 21, 1802, August 28, 1802; Middleton, *The Black Laws*, 28–29.

[87] Hammond, *Slavery, Freedom, and Expansion in the Early American West*, 84, 93.

[88] Thurston, "The 1802 Constitutional Convention and Status of the Negro," 29; Terzian, "Ohio's Constitutional Conventions and Constitutions," 41, 43; William T. Utter, "Saint Tammany in Ohio: A Study in Frontier Politics," *Mississippi Valley Historical Review* 15, no. 3 (1928): 231–40.

[89] The elder Goforth, now living in Ohio, was widely recognized as a stalwart opponent of slavery and defender of republican equality. Fred J. Milligan, *Ohio's Founding Fathers* (Lincoln, NE: iUniverse, 2003), 64.

but only two of the ten Republicans from the V.M.D. stood with them. Federalists from Washington County, where the population was disproportionately from New England or were Quakers who had left North Carolina over slavery, voted five to two in favor of black voting rights, with only the Virginia-born John McIntire and the New Englander Samuel Huntington voting against it, the latter having been expressly promised a judgeship in exchange for voting with the junta.[90] The motion was defeated nineteen to fourteen.

Supporters of black suffrage then offered a compromise to relieve the main objection raised against black suffrage: that recognizing voting rights would lead free blacks pushed out of the South to look for refuge in Ohio. An amendment was proposed that would continue the right to vote of free men of color currently resident in Ohio, which passed nineteen to fifteen with five Republicans changing their votes. The next proposal was to enfranchise the male descendants of currently resident black Ohioans, but this was defeated seventeen to sixteen, with two Republicans returning to the Chillicothe fold. Even the limited voting rights that had been defended would be lost: on a subsequent roll call, three Republicans – James Grubb, Joseph Darlinton, and John Smith, all from the V.M.D – changed their votes to support a total disenfranchisement. The vote was seventeen to seventeen, and Edward Tiffin, the Republican president of the convention and soon to be the first governor of Ohio, cast the deciding vote in favor. He would later explain "that the immediate neighborhood of two slave-holding States made it impolitic to offer such an inducement for the influx of an undesirable class to the new State."[91]

The voting patterns in Ohio present the first occurrence of a clear relationship between support for racial disenfranchisement and positions on class democratization.[92] Republicans were more likely than Federalists to support liberalizing voting rights on class lines but also to support the disenfranchisement of black voters. Table 3-2 shows the proportion of

---

[90] Jeffrey P. Brown, "The Ohio Federalists, 1803–1815," *Journal of the Early Republic* 2, no. 3 (1982): 261–82, 262; Milligan, *Ohio's Founding Fathers*, 252; Randolph Downes, "The Statehood Contest in Ohio," *The Mississippi Valley Historical Review* 18, no. 2 (1931): 170.

[91] William E. Gilmore, *Life of Edward Tiffin: First Governor of Ohio* (Chillicothe, OH: Horney and Son, 1897), 76; Terzian, "Ohio's Constitutional Conventions and Constitutions," 49.

[92] *Journal of the Convention of the Territory of the United States North West of the Ohio* (Columbus, OH: George Nashee, 1827).

TABLE 3.2 *Voting on Disenfranchisement in Ohio, 1802*

	Keep "White"	Strike "White"	Average Percent of Votes Cast for Black Rights
Republican	65%	35%	41%
Federalist	29%	71%	76%
V.M.D. or Southern Republican	70%	25%	28%
Non-V.M.D. or Northern Republican	43%	57%	73%
Keep Tax Qualification	56%	44%	55%
Strike Tax Qualification	63%	38%	31%
Strike Exemption for Highway Labor	50%	50%	60%
Keep Exemption for Highway Labor	62%	38%	43%

delegates who voted to keep or strike the word "white," as well as the average percentage of votes they cast for black rights during the convention. Hamilton County Republicans – whose electoral committees had "recommended that voters elect delegates who were willing to grant suffrage to every male inhabitant of Ohio, including blacks"[93] – were largely in favor of black civil and political rights, splitting six to four in favor of striking "white," nine to one in favor of black resident suffrage, eight to two in favor of black legacy voting, and seven to three against another proposal to restrict black civil rights. By contrast, all but three of the ten delegates from the military district voted at every turn to reject black political or civil rights. Those who supported black disenfranchisement were slightly more likely to support striking the taxpaying requirement and to keep the highway labor alternative, but the difference amounts to one delegate.[94]

---

[93] Middleton, *The Black Laws*, 28.

[94] A chi-squared test of the difference between the observed and expected frequencies is not significant for either the highway labor exemption or the vote on the tax qualification. It is significant at the 0.1 level for party.

Most historians of the convention conclude that the decisive switch of the three Republicans was the result of pressure from the junta.[95] In 1803, two of these members were defeated in their election campaigns, which one member of the junta blamed on their having "lost much credit" with their constituents due to their "negro votes." The leadership had hoped that Darlinton in particular – who was defeated by only seven votes – would have been elected and regretted that "ninety nine good turns are forgoten [sic], if the hundredth is omitted." But elsewhere in the state, more forceful Republican defenders of black rights were elected to state legislative office, often with large majorities.[96] Voters' commitments to white supremacy could be important, as Darlinton learned; but they were not uniform across the state, nor did they explain the dynamics within the convention. As one historian remarked, it was ultimately "the former Virginia planters" who decided the issue, "even though voters seemed at best undecided about the status of free blacks in Ohio." [97]

Disenfranchisement in the Territories

The silence from Washington over the disenfranchisement of free blacks encouraged a further "testing" of the waters.[98] The territory of Indiana soon denied free blacks the right to testify in court in cases involving a white person and passed three bills providing for the exclusion of blacks from the territory. At any point, Congress could have signaled its opposition; instead, it did the opposite, foisting a racial prohibition on territorial governments and creating a template for a racially exclusive right to vote that would soon be extended into the territories of the Louisiana Purchase.

[95] David M. Massie, *Nathaniel Massie, A Pioneer of Ohio: A Sketch of his Life and Selections from His Correspondence* (Cincinnati, OH: Robert Clarke Co., 1896), 86, 88; Donald J. Ratcliffe, "The Changing Political World of Thomas Worthington," in *The Center of a Great Empire: The Ohio Country in the Early Republic*, ed. Andrew R. L. Clayton and Stuart D. Hobbs (Athens: Ohio University Press, 2005), 36–61, 37; Downes, "Statehood Contest in Ohio," 155–71, 167, 169.

[96] Thurston, "The 1802 Constitutional Convention and Status of the Negro," 24n21; Duncan M'Arthur to Thomas Worthington, January 17, 1803, Thomas Worthington Papers, 1796–1827 (microfilm), Ohio History Center.

[97] Hammond, *Slavery, Freedom, and Expansion in the Early American West*, 93–94.

[98] The new state of Ohio soon passed a series of "black laws" intended to discourage free blacks from settling in the state. Eugene H. Berwanger, *The Frontier Against Slavery: Western Anti-Negro Prejudice and the Slavery Extension Controversy* (Urbana: University of Illinois Press, 1967), 22.

In 1803, a petition from Indiana requested an extension of voting rights, the extinction of Indian land titles, and the introduction of slavery into the territory. The second was already being pursued, but the other two requests were rejected by a committee chaired by Virginian John Randolph along with two Federalists and two Republicans.[99] The same requests were more favorably considered in the subsequent three Congresses, each time by committees composed exclusively of Republicans, mostly from slave states. In 1804, a committee composed exclusively of Southerners recommended allowing slavery for a period of ten years and joined to this a recommendation to extend the right to vote – stressing the "the vital principle of a free Government" that taxpayers be represented – and endorsing a quickened extinction of Indian title, so that the lands could be "an asylum to the oppressed of all countries." Without any trace of irony, it also recommended limiting the suffrage to "every white free man."[100]

These proposals went nowhere, and soon a new petition arrived denouncing property qualifications as an "invidious" distinction (but again said nothing about black voting). A new committee of Republicans recommended an extension of the suffrage to "every white freeman" resident twelve months and the introduction of slavery in order to encourage settlement and avert the danger of "too large a black population existing in any one section of the country."[101] Congress still refused to act.

The next year, a Massachusetts Republican was named speaker, and he sent the petitioners' requests to a committee composed of Northerners and chaired by an ardent antislavery Republican from Philadelphia. This committee firmly rejected the request to allow slavery.[102] But the speaker also separated the question of the territorial franchise from that of slavery, which allowed suffrage reforms for both Indiana and Mississippi to advance through Congress: the owners of town lots were to be enfranchised, but a new racial disenfranchisement would be imposed. This would be the first federal law to impose a racial qualification for voting rights, and it received little attention and no debate.[103]

[99] Jacob P. Dunn, *Slavery Petitions and Papers* (Indianapolis, IN: Bowen-Merrill Co., 1894), 21, 24; Report No. 76, 7th Cong., 2nd sess., March 2, 1803.

[100] Report No. 173, 8th Cong., 1st sess., February 17, 1804.

[101] Dunn, *Slavery Petitions and Papers*, 34–35, 53; Report No. 203, 9th Cong., 1st sess., February 14, 1806.

[102] *Annals of Congress*, 10th Cong., 1st sess., November 1807, c. 816; Dunn, *Slavery Petitions and Papers*, 77.

[103] *Annals of Congress*, 8th Cong., 2nd sess., c. 1012; H. R. 10th Cong., 1st sess., January 1808, c. 1359; 10th Cong., 1st sess., February 1808, c. 1616.

This would not be the case a few years later, when a proposal to exclude free men of color from voting in Louisiana met with substantial opposition. The proposal to admit Louisiana produced considerable controversy, with Northeastern Federalists opposed because it would further diminish the importance of their region and some Republicans opposed because the bill would enfranchise the French population, whom they saw as holding allegiances to a foreign power. Pleasant Miller of Tennessee disliked the French but also worried that the territory's large class of free black citizens would have influence enough that they "might elect a person of color to the National Legislature; with whom Mr. M[iller] said he should feel no inclination to act." After the territorial delegate noted that many of these persons were "very wealthy and respectable," Miller's proposal to disenfranchise free black citizens was defeated, with only seventeen votes in favor.[104]

After the bill authorizing a statehood convention passed the House, it was sent to a bipartisan committee in the Senate, which reported an amendment that only "white male citizens" should have the right to form a new state. Twenty-four senators supported adding the word "white," including all Federalists; eight Republican senators voted against disenfranchisement.[105] The bill was then returned to the House. The aging Pennsylvanian radical John Smilie argued that Congress "could not, upon republican principles, and the principles of the American act of independence and of the constitution, exclude any portion of the free male inhabitants of that territory, from the common privileges of free citizens." He and others insisted that "the American act of independence and constitution, guaranteed equal privileges, and a republican form of government – That the latter would be in vain without the former – That if we were about establishing a free government for these people, let it be free, and not provide (which would be the same in principle) that a freeman to be entitled to vote, shall be 40 years old, 6 feet high, or of a particular shade of color." The issue, he noted, had been "so delicate" that the drafters of the US Constitution had "on this point ... used only the word 'persons,'" and he concluded that "the amendment could answer no good purpose, and an agreement to it would not be very honorable to the House."[106]

---

[104] *Annals of Congress*, 11th Cong., 3rd sess., January 1811, 498, 513.
[105] *Annals of Congress*, 11th Cong., 3rd sess., c. 98, 107.
[106] *Commercial Advertiser* (New York), February 16, 1811; *Annals of Congress*, H. R. 11th Cong., 3rd sess., 937.

And the House agreed with him; it *rejected* the amendment, by a vote of forty-nine to sixty, despite knowing that their insistence on black suffrage would threaten passage of the bill. Sixty-six percent of Republicans voted in support of continued black voting, while 70 percent of Federalists voted against; only two of the thirty-five Northern Republican representatives voted to disenfranchise free men of color, while half of Northern Federalists joined all of their Southern co-partisans in support. There was even a substantial minority of Southern Republicans – 41 percent, largely from districts with comparatively few persons held in slavery – who supported the continuation of black voting rights in the territory.

The Republicans were under considerable pressure to pass the statehood enabling act, and so when the bill went back to the Senate, Charles Tait of Georgia proposed that the chamber back down. Although there was now more support for an equal franchise, his proposal to drop the word "white" was defeated by a vote of eleven to nineteen.[107]

The most vocal supporters of black suffrage in the House continued to stand firm, but they were met with a phalanx of Southerners who insisted on accepting the Senate's amendment. Thomas Gholson, Daniel Sheffey, and John Eppes of Virginia, Nathanial Macon of North Carolina, Richard Johnson of Kentucky, and the territorial delegate from Mississippi ridiculed the claim of Smilie and others that any question of republican equality was at stake. "It was absurd to talk of equality," they argued. "We are not all equal – the God of Nature had made a difference." They asked their colleagues how they would feel "in going to the polls, or sitting in this Legislature with a Negro." Eppes mocked Smilie's invocation of the Declaration of Independence, insisting that "when it spoke of men being equal, it meant, *white* men – when we speak of the equality of men, we always mean the equality of *white* men." In the coming decades, this rhetorical effort to reconcile the terms of the Declaration with an insistence on black disenfranchisement would become quite common: at this moment, however, it contradicted how many Republicans had interpreted the Declaration. "Northern men," Eppes concluded, "who knew nothing of the difficulty of managing this species of population, were not competent to judge upon this subject." The constriction of the civic status of free black Americans was again being justified as needed to control slave labor.[108]

---

[107] *Annals of Congress*, 11th Cong., 3rd sess., February 1811, c. 151.
[108] *Commercial Advertiser* (New York), February 16, 1811.

Pressure to pass the statehood bill led most Republicans to drop their opposition. Smilie, however, stood firm, joined by Robert Whitehill – another former Pennsylvania Constitutionalist – by John Bacon's son Ezekiel, Samuel L. Mitchill of New York, and by Erastus Root, an important leader of the Tammany Hall wing of the New York Republican party. Fourteen of their Northern co-partisans, and all but two of the seventeen Southern Republicans who had supported black suffrage, now voted to accept disenfranchisement. Eight Northern Federalists also switched their vote, now opposing a racial qualification they had earlier endorsed. With time quickly running out, Northern and Southern Republicans in Congress aligned behind a white male citizen standard for political rights.[109]

This would later be ratified by the Louisiana convention, which produced a conservative document that distributed power between the Francophone aristocracy of New Orleans and incoming Anglo-American slaveholding settlers. The new constitution restricted voting rights for white men as well, limiting it to those who had paid a state *property* tax or to those who had purchased land directly from the United States. There seems to have been little question of continuing the voting rights of free blacks, especially after an insurrection in 1812 was interpreted as providing further proof of the oft-repeated warning that "one free negro is more dangerous where there are slaves than 100 slaves," and that any increase in the size of the free black community – especially those from the Caribbean, "known for their revolutionary principles" – was inviting catastrophe.[110]

Electoral Competition and Disenfranchisement in the Northeast

Republican support for a white male citizen standard remained more a matter of coalitional expediency than a manifestation of a coherent ideology of white democracy. But the alliance of Northern Republicans with slaveholders was creating a new and more local incentive for black disenfranchisement, as Republican politicians found that a growing number of free black men were supporting their partisan rivals.

---

[109] *Annals of Congress*, H. R. 11th Cong., 3rd sess., February 13, 1811, c. 964.
[110] Faber, *Building the Land of Dreams*, 71, 165; Dunbar Rowlands, *Official Letter Books of W. C. C. Claiborne, 1801–1816*, vol. 4 (Jackson, MS: State Department of Archives and History, 1917), 387; Brown, "The Senate Debate on the Breckinridge Bill for the Government of Louisiana, 1804," 352.

While it is often suggested that free blacks had a "natural" inclination to vote for Federalists, Republicans actively competed for free black support throughout the mid-Atlantic and Northeast.[111] Certainly many Republicans threw themselves into what one person of color called the "vile business of defamation," accusing free blacks of having encouraged the British to "give freedom to us and enslave their own colour" during the War of 1812, always "cry[ing] tory, tory, while they are themselves the greatest tories to true republican patriotism."[112] But the Federalists were not much better. Even as they attacked Republicans for their alliance with slaveholders, they were perfectly willing to engage in race-baiting of their own, complaining of Republicans celebrating "Negro Voters" at their "St. Jefferson's festival."[113] White racism was widespread, but it was not firmly ideological in the sense of being tethered to other issue positions or partisan affiliation.[114]

[margin annotation: like white feminism]

But the national Republican administration was engaging in repeated actions that could only repulse the growing population of black voters. Jefferson had imposed an explicitly racist embargo against Haiti, a country that many African Americans looked to with hope and pride, and had prohibited American shipping to Europe, crippling one of the few industrial sectors in which free blacks had been able to gain a foothold.[115] During the War of 1812, Madison refused to enlist free blacks – "the slippery slope to slave revolts" according to one historian – even as the Republican secretary of war insisted that "we must get over this nonsense." Free black Americans argued that they could expect very little

---

[111] The Republican party press of New York, for instance, carried the meetings of Republican men of color who insisted that "Republican principles are favorable to the equal rights of mankind, and to the preservation of Life, Liberty, and Property." Dixon Ryan Fox, "The Negro Vote in Old New York," *Political Science Quarterly* 3, no. 2 (1917): 252–75, 255–56; Polgar, "Whenever They Judge It Expedient," 3, 7.

[112] *The Evening Post* (New York), July 7, 1814, p. 3; Paul Finkelman, "The Problem of Slavery in the Age of Federalism," in Ben-Atar and Oberg, *Federalists Reconsidered*; Charles H. Wesley, "Negro Suffrage in the Period of Constitution-Making, 1787–1865," *Journal of Negro History* 32, no. 2 (1947): 143–68, 155; Fox, "The Negro Vote in Old New York," 187; McManus, *A History of Negro Slavery in New York*, 187.

[113] *Balance and Columbian Repository* 3, no. 29 (July 17, 1804): 229; *Balance and Columbian Repository* 4, no. 14 (April 2, 1805): 107; *Columbian Centinel and Massachusetts Federalist* 41, no. 37 (July 4, 1804): 2; *Connecticut Journal*, October 22, 1812, p. 1; Gellman, *Emancipating New York*, 218, 148.

[114] Polgar, "Whenever They Judge It Expedient," 7.

[115] Finkelman, "The Problem of Slavery in the Age of Federalism," 150.

"from a quarter that supports the doctrine of slave representation, and consequently the paradox of a republican holding slaves."[116]

As free black communities became more prominent and pronounced in opposition to the Jeffersonians, local Republicans were given a new partisan and electoral reason to pursue black disenfranchisement.[117] In 1808, Republican poll watchers in New York began challenging the qualifications of black voters at the polls.[118] In 1811, the party regained control of the state legislature from the Federalists – whom they believed had won the year before because of the support from black voters – and introduced a bill that would have required black men to obtain and present certificates proving that they were free. Federalists denounced the bill as unconstitutional, and a "humiliating" disenfranchisement on the unrepublican basis of race.[119] It passed on a straight party line vote but was rejected by the council of revision for imposing a requirement solely on the basis of color and for establishing a distinction between freemen in violation of the republican constitution. Republicans tried again in 1813 and 1814, when the bill was passed over the council's veto.[120]

Free black New Yorkers met the news with "astonishment."[121] Perhaps more astonishing was that Republicans continued to campaign for their votes, even having "the audacity to tell the people of color" in their local meetings "that it was the federalists who made it necessary for them to produce certificates of their freedom at the polls."[122] A large flag

---

[116] The Secretary was astounded by the "depths and shoals of southern prejudice." Alan Taylor, *The Civil War of 1812: American Citizens, British Subjects, Irish Rebels, and Indian Allies* (New York: Alfred A. Knopf, 2010), 326–28; "Selections from the Duane Papers," *The Historical Magazine* 4, no. 1 (1868): 60–75, 63; *The Evening Post* (New York), July 7, 1814, p. 3.

[117] In 1804, Republicans in the New York State legislature expanded the municipal suffrage of New York City in order to reenfranchise the city's white working-class freemen, but the new qualifications allowed *any* male resident who paid twenty-five dollars in rent to vote. In 1801, black voters were said to have supported the Republican mayoral candidate "to a man." As a result, he reportedly began to issue cartmen licenses to black New Yorkers, although this was quickly stopped "on discovering it would raise too much of a hubbub among the white cartmen." *The Evening Post* (New York), May 15, 1806, p. 3.

[118] Fox, "The Negro Vote in Old New York," 256; Graham Russell Hodges, *Slavery, Freedom, and Culture among Early American Workers* (Armonk, NY: M. E. Sharpe, 1998), 16–17.

[119] *The Balance, and State Journal* (Albany, NY), April 16, 1811, p. 122.

[120] Street, *The Council of Revision*, 362–64; Polgar, "Whenever They Judge It Expedient," 11.

[121] *The Evening Post* (New York), July 7, 1814, p. 3.

[122] *The Evening Post* (New York), April 22, 1813, p. 2.

was prepared showing Republican Governor Daniel Tompkins shaking hands with John Teasman, a prominent black Republican and vice president of the African Society (whose politics would eventually cause him to be fired by the Federalist-dominated New York Manumission Society). But even Teasman's vote was reportedly "twice rejected for want of a proper certificate of his freedom."[123]

In New Jersey, a similar concern with the impact of black voting led to a bipartisan disenfranchisement of women, noncitizens, and free persons of color. Free African Americans in the state had voted in the early Republic, and while the election law was controversial, this was largely because it enfranchised some classes of women and noncitizens. In 1799, Federalist William Griffith outlined a list of problems with the suffrage qualifications, including its admission of females and aliens and the loose interpretation of its property qualification, but he did not explicitly complain of the inclusion of free persons of color.[124] When a bill based on his recommendations was considered by the Senate that year, it limited voting to "all free male" citizens, but said nothing about race.[125] A few years later, a proposal to restrict the suffrage to "free white males" saw 68 percent of Republicans voting against it, joined by 43 percent of Federalists. While the measure would have disenfranchised single and widowed women as well, support was concentrated in the counties with the largest number of enslaved persons and among the bloc of legislators who had also tried to delay the abolition of slavery.[126]

Republicans in the state had argued that every freeman, "whether he is of exotic or domestic birth, whether he is black or white, or red or

[123] Manisha Sinha, *The Slave's Cause: A History of Abolition* (New Haven, CT: Yale University Press, 2016), 116–17; Leslie M. Alexander, *African or American? Black Identity and Political Activism in New York City, 1784–1861* (Urbana: University of Illinois Press, 2008), 44–46; *The Evening Post* (New York), April 28, 1813, p. 2.

[124] William Griffith, *Eumenes: Being a Collection of Papers, Written for the Purpose of Exhibiting some of the More Prominent Errors and Omissions of the Constitution of New-Jersey* (Trenton, NJ: G. Craft, 1799), 34–36; Jan Ellen Lewis, "Rethinking Women's Suffrage in New Jersey, 1776–1807," *Rutgers Law Review* 63 (2010): 1017, 1034; Judith Apter Klinghoffer and Lois Elkis, "'The Petticoat Electors': Women's Suffrage in New Jersey, 1776–1807," *Journal of the Early Republic* 12, no. 2 (1992): 159–93, 189.

[125] New Jersey, *Journal of the Proceedings of the Legislative-Council of the State of New-Jersey, Being the First Sitting of the Twenty-Fourth Session* (Trenton, NJ: Sherman, Mershon, and Thomas, 1799), 30.

[126] New Jersey, *Votes and Proceedings of the Twenty-Seventh General Assembly of the State of New-Jersey* (Trenton, NJ: Sherman and Mershon, 1802), 110, 117.

yellow," should have the right to vote.[127] By 1807, however, free blacks were beginning to support Federalist candidates, and after an egregiously fraudulent election was interpreted as revealing the problems with the state's electoral qualifications, an exclusively Republican committee – claiming that the "vote of a [female] negro slave, the property of another negro slave, [had] elected one of the members" of the assembly a few years before – proposed to restrict the right to vote to white male citizens, disenfranchising blacks along with aliens and women.[128] To justify the new exclusions, Lewis Condict, a rising Republican legislator, gave a widely applauded speech in which he argued that "no one could suppose that the framers of the constitution intended under the term 'all inhabitants' to include married women, Negro slaves, and aliens of every description as entitled to suffrage." The framers of the state constitution must have meant "white male citizens," a statutory reinterpretation that helped disenfranchise voters without formally amending the constitution.[129] The restrictions received bipartisan support, and seem to have been motivated by a broadly shared belief that the state's elections should be made more "respectable" and orderly.

In Connecticut, disenfranchisement took another route. The state's politics were a tightly closed oligarchy, with a Federalist government that had responded to electoral competition by passing successive laws to restrict voting rights in order to keep out "Irish patriots," the "refuse of the gaol, and the gibbet, and by the candidates for Newgate, and the gallows."[130] Unlike New York and New Jersey, there is relatively little evidence that free men of color voted in the state, and when they did, it seems to have caused a scandal: when two black Republicans were admitted as freemen in Wallingford in 1803, outraged Federalists called for a legislative investigation of the state's suffrage qualifications.[131]

---

[127] *The Centinel of Freedom* (Newark, NJ), September 30, 1806, p. 2, October 14, 1806, p. 1.
[128] *Trenton Federalist* (Trenton, NJ), November 30, 1807, p. 3; *New Jersey Journal* (Elizabethtown, NJ), April 14, 1807, p. 2.
[129] *Trenton True American*, November 23, 1807; Marion Thompson Wright, "Negro Suffrage in New Jersey," *Journal of Negro History* 33, no. 2 (1948): 168–224; Edward R. Turner, "Women's Suffrage in New Jersey, 1790–1807," *Smith College Studies in History* 1, no. 4 (1916): 163–87, 184.
[130] *The Connecticut Courant*, September 12, 1804, p. 3.
[131] Federalists complained when Republicans brought forward "a Negro fellow by the name of Toby," who was subsequently learned to have been convicted of attempted rape. I am indebted to Professor Van Gosse for informing me of this event and for generously sharing notes on disenfranchisement in Connecticut and Rhode Island. *Connecticut Centinel* (Norwich, CT), May 10, 1803, p. 3; *The Connecticut Courant*,

Eleven years later, a heavily Federalist legislature decided that going forward, only white men would be able to acquire voting rights, a year after they revised the property qualification to require real estate to be free of any mortgage. Soon after, it rejected a petition from two free black men – Bias Stanley and William Lanson – asking to be exempted from taxation if denied the vote. The petitioners wrote that while "God hath made of one blood all the nations of men, they are well aware that the feelings and prejudices of this community are so strong respecting the descendants of Africans that your Petitioners will not complain of their disfranchisement." Their disclaimer to the contrary, it is likely that their main motive in petitioning the assembly was to be enfranchised. The *Connecticut Courant* had recently published an account of Paul Cuffe's petitioning Massachusetts for an exemption from taxation unless his right to vote was recognized, which was credited with having secured black suffrage in that state.[132] And the petitioners concluded by suggesting that "there is no class of men in this community who if such an exemption were offered them as compensation for disfranchisement would consent to be disfranchised."[133]

During the first decade of the nineteenth century, Abraham Bishop and other Connecticut Republicans had made suffrage reform a key plank of their campaign platforms, arguing that without the suffrage, poor men had few rights that a rich man must respect and denouncing the Federalists as an aristocracy with "a radical contempt for stone cutters and saddlers."[134] But Bishop and others gradually decided that to win power, they needed to forge an alliance with disaffected Episcopalian Federalists and credit-starved manufacturers, placing the disestablishment of the Congregationalist Church and the chartering of new banks at the top of their platform.[135] They continued to call for suffrage reform, but also reported that otherwise sympathetic Federalists were worried that it would "bring in all the blacks and the town's poor to vote and the rich will

May 11, 1803, p. 1, May 18, 1803, p. 3, September 7, 1803, p. 3; *American Mercury* (Hartford, CT), May 26, 1803, p. 3.

[132] *Connecticut Journal* (New Haven, CT), January 24, 1814.

[133] Douglas M. Arnold, *The Public Records of the State of Connecticut*, vol. 37 (Hartford, CT: The Office of the State Historian, 2000), 544–46.

[134] *American Mercury* (Hartford, CT), January 16, 1806, p. 3, January 9, 1806, p. 3.

[135] Richard J. Purcell, *Connecticut in Transition, 1775–1818* (Washington, DC: American Historical Association, 1918), 221–22; Jeffrey L. Pasley, *The Tyranny of Printers: Newspaper Politics in the Early American Republic* (Richmond: University Press of Virginia, 2001), 379.

lose all their property."[136] In response, Republicans denied wanting to admit "every man to vote, whatever be his color, condition, or character." Instead, they argued that only men with a "fair character," who had paid taxes and performed militia duty should be enfranchised.[137] When Republicans finally came to power, they called a constitutional convention to be elected by white men who had paid taxes or served in the militia, expanding the suffrage along class lines while retaining and extending the racial standard passed earlier by the Federalists.

In the convention, a few Federalists now argued against a racial disqualification, but for the most part they focused their opposition on the impropriety of enfranchising laborers and working men. Republicans defended the class enfranchisement but said little – if anything – about the racial exclusion. The drafter of the convention bill, however, explained that he "followed the very expressions adopted in many of the constitutions." As the "white male citizen" standard gradually became more common across the country, it also became a template for reformers in different states, a model of what American citizenship should look like.[138] The few black men who could already vote in the state would retain the right while they lived, but no new black voters were to be recognized.

"WE, THE WHITE PEOPLE"

The pattern of disenfranchisement for black Americans being associated with democratization for whites was first evident in institutional reforms, and only gradually appeared in the policy positions and votes of legislators and delegates to constitutional conventions. What remained was an explicit ideological rationale that could link these different positions.

When Federalists attacked them for their alliance with slaveholders, Northern Republicans had initially parried with the argument that while slavery might be distasteful, the true injustice would be the abandonment of the national project. Some, however, also began to advance arguments that had been most commonly made by slaveholding Southerners: that

---

[136] *American Mercury* (Hartford, CT), January 2, 1806, p. 3.

[137] Character requirements were common in New England, but the restriction to those who served in the militia would have amounted to an implicit racial disenfranchisement given the federal Militia Law's restriction to white men and to prevailing racist exclusions by the states and localities. *American Mercury* (Hartford, CT), August 25, 1808, p. 3, June 7, 1804, p. 3.

[138] Douglas M. Arnold, *The Public Records of the State of Connecticut*, vol. 39 (Hartford, CT: The Office of the State Historian, 2007), 112, 118, 274.

blacks and whites could not peacefully and equally live under the same government and that the sectional compromises underlying the American project meant free people of color could not have been intentionally included within its terms.

Thomas Branagan, a former plantation overseer turned abolitionist, published in 1804 his *Preliminary Essay on the Oppression of the Exiled Sons of Africa*, denouncing the lie told by "the proprietors and managers of slaves" that "the poor Africans are not, strictly speaking, human beings" and concluding with a frank critique of Jefferson, "who cannot be supposed to be prejudiced in favour of the African race."[139]

But in his *Serious Remonstrances* a year later, Jefferson came in for elaborate praise for what Branagan now found to be a persuasive argument that black Americans needed to be removed from the country. He acknowledged that he had just recently defended the contrary argument, but claimed that this had been "done without due reflection." The entire essay shows its debt to Jefferson. In language very similar to the president's, Branagan implied that inherent racial differences would impede any intermixture, a claim that he had previously dismissed as self-evidently absurd, and that white prejudice and black Americans' anger was a bar to social equality: "every slave ship that arrives in Charleston, tends to obliterate that friendship." Just a year earlier, Branagan had called for America to be an "asylum for the oppressed of every country and complexion."[140] He now claimed it as an asylum for *Europeans* alone, and urged American citizens to organize the political and economic life of the country to the benefit of "our fathers, and our brothers in slavery in the old world." Blaming free blacks for undercutting the wages of the white working classes, for committing "horrid depredations, rapes, assassinations, robberies, thefts, &c.," and casting them as an internal enemy ready to betray the country to its enemies, Branagan endorsed Jefferson's argument entirely and demanded the removal of all persons of color.[141]

What had changed? Noel Ignatiev suggests that it was the campaign of Dessalines in Haiti against the white population, which Branagan thought

---

[139] Branagan, *Preliminary Essay*, 93, 230; Lewis Leary, "Thomas Branagan: Republican Rhetoric and Romanticism in America," *The Pennsylvania Magazine of History and Biography* 77, no. 3 (1953): 332–52.

[140] Branagan, *Preliminary Essay*, 228.

[141] Thomas Branagan, *Serious Remonstrances, Addressed to the Citizens of the Northern States* (Philadelphia: Thomas T. Stiles, 1805), 36, 103–7, 109–11, 118, 125–28.

was being reenacted in a series of Philadelphia race riots.[142] Beverly
Tomek suggests he was embittered when his self-appointed role as
a leader of the free black population was rebuffed.[143] But surely another
influence was Thomas Jefferson himself, who had read Branagan's earlier
work and sent a letter to Pennsylvania Senator George Logan with instructions to provide Branagan with financial and moral support, and who
would thereafter be his "most generous patron."[144]

The Second Missouri Crisis and Black Citizenship

Branagan was not the only antislavery Republican who had been listening
to the concerns of Southern Republicans. In February 1819, James
Tallmadge, Jr., introduced an amendment in Congress to a statehood
bill for Missouri, requiring it to adopt a policy of gradual abolition.
Tallmadge explained that he "was aware of the delicacy of the subject –
*and, that I had learned from southern gentlemen the difficulties and the
dangers of having free blacks intermingling with slaves.*" He conceded
everything that Southerners had been saying about "the danger of having
free blacks visible to slaves," and for this reason he had abandoned his
earlier hopes of abolishing slavery in the southwest territories. But
Missouri was remote, and abolition there could not pose a danger to the
South, freeing him to represent the "will of my constituents," to "proclaim their hatred to slavery in every shape."[145]

For the next year, Northern Republicans would provide the bulk of
support for restricting slavery, inflaming divisions within the party.
In New York, the James Monroe administration used its control over
patronage jobs and post offices to aid Martin Van Buren's political
machine in exchange for supporting a compromise. William Duane,
a supporter of labor rights and an advocate of further democratization
in Pennsylvania, threw his weight behind the effort to restrict slavery,
arguing that blacks and whites were "equal in nature, under the law, and

---

[142] Ignatiev, *How the Irish Became White*, 63, 66; Gary B. Nash, *The Forgotten Fifth:
African Americans in the Age of Revolution* (Cambridge, MA: Harvard University Press,
2006), 133.

[143] Tomek, "From Motives of Generosity, as Well as Self-Preservation," 132.

[144] Branagan, *Serious Remonstrances*, 107, 112, 118; Thomas Branagan, *The Guardian
Genius of the Federal Union; or, Patriotic Admonitions on the Signs of the Times, in
Relation to the Evil Spirit of Party, Arising from the Root of All Our Evils, Human
Slavery* (New York: Author, 1839), 20.

[145] *Rhode-Island American, and General Advertiser*, April 6, 1819, p. 1.

'in the eye of the creator.'" Monroe instead directed patronage to John Binns, who relied on favor with the administration, his influence with governors, and the support of local banks and large manufacturers to displace Duane's organization of Irish workers. Binns and Duane, who had both been United Irishmen in that country's failed rebellion, were vitally important in disseminating a language of radical democracy in early republican America. But as Christopher Malone notes, Binns's ascent coincided with his emergence as a "fervent supporter" of white republicanism, insisting that slavery and black citizenship should not be "mixed up with party politics," and providing space in his paper for opponents of antislavery.[146]

In March 1820, a compromise was arranged that allowed Missouri to enter the Union as a slave state but that excluded the institution from almost all of the remaining territory of the Louisiana Purchase. Maine was admitted as a free state, with the expectation that Missouri would soon follow.

But Republicans across the North were shocked when a Missouri convention drafted a constitution prohibiting the legislature from emancipating slaves and mandating laws to prevent the emigration of free black Americans. Hezekiah Niles had urged compromise during the first crisis, arguing that however much he hated slavery, he and other Northerners could not appreciate the threat of insurrection faced by white Southerners. In the name of national unity, he had urged that people concern themselves with "the peace and prosperity of the white population." But Missouri's racial exclusion clause went too far, and "may just as well apply to the exclusion of persons with black hair or blue eyes."[147] Another argued that black Americans were "Citizens and Subjects of every government where they may happen to reside," and could rightfully claim all the rights implied by the phrase that governments derive "their just powers from the consent of the governed."[148] One New York Republican argued

[146] *The American* (New York), October 21, 1820, p. 2, October 24, 1820, p. 2; *Daily National Intelligencer* (Washington, DC), November 2, 1820, p. 3; John Binns, *Recollections of the Life of John Binns* (Philadelphia: Author and Parry and M'Millan, 1854), 74, 197, 244; Nash, *Forgotten Fifth*, 154; Twomey, *Jacobins and Jeffersonians*, 201; Pasley, *The Tyranny of Printers*, 316; Wilson, *United Irishmen, United States*, 74; Robert Pierce Forbes, *The Missouri Compromise and its Aftermath: Slavery and the Meaning of America* (Chapel Hill: University of North Carolina Press, 2007), 89; Riley, *Slavery and the Democratic Conscience*, 71–79, 223, 236; Malone, *Between Freedom and Bondage*, 90.
[147] *Niles' Weekly Register*, December 23, 1820, 265–66.
[148] *Poulson's American Daily Advertiser* (Philadelphia, PA), November 8, 1820, p. 2.

that free blacks were "expressly recognized in our election laws" and thus clothed with "the distinguishing characteristic of a citizen, the elective franchise."[149]

Northern Republicans in Congress pressed the same themes, arguing that voting rights were proof of free blacks' citizenship and listing – to the surprise of Southerners – those states where free blacks were enfranchised. William Eustis recalled the services of black Americans during the Revolutionary War and asked who would have dared say to them after the war, "'You are not to participate in the rights secured by the struggle, or in the liberty for which you have been fighting'? Certainly no white man in Massachusetts."[150] (Of course, some white men in Massachusetts had dared to say this, but their effort to do so had been overturned and abandoned.) Rollin Mallary of Vermont argued that black suffrage and black citizenship had been intentionally recognized in his state, while David Morrill, from staunchly Republican New Hampshire, insisted that the "very definition of republicanism is a perfect equality among all the citizens." He asked of Southern legislators, "What is the man in his country who is neither a slave nor an alien? In mine he is a citizen."[151]

The Southern argument rested on a set of historical and social claims that would become vitally important to defining American peoplehood in the coming decades: that free blacks were nowhere recognized as fully equal members of the civil or political community and that the Southern states would never have agreed to a constitution in which they were to be considered part of the "the people." Philip Barbour argued that Southerners had long considered free blacks to be the population "most dangerous to the community that can possibly be conceived," the "primary cause" of insurrections, and "perpetual monuments of discontent and firebrands to the other class of their own color." Since the Constitution had been intended to protect the states, it could not be interpreted as requiring the recognition of black citizenship. "Indians, free negroes, mulattoes, slaves! Tell me not," he continued, "that the Constitution, when it speaks of *We, the people*, means these." The Constitution had been framed by the "European descendants of white men," in order to protect "the liberty and rights of white men," and "did not mean to meddle with" free blacks at all. "We, the white

[149] *Republican Advocate*, November 24, 1820; *The National Gazette and Literary Register* (Philadelphia, PA), December 2, 1820, p. 3.
[150] *Annals of Congress*, 16th Cong., 2nd sess., December 1820, 112, 636.
[151] Ibid., 633, 638; *North Star* (Danville, VT), February 8, 1821, 3.

people," he declared, "wanted, not merely to exist, but we formed a Constitution to condense the will of our fellow-citizens, and to borrow the arm of a mighty people for our protection."[152]

Louis M'Lane of Delaware argued that to be a citizen, one "must be a member of the *civil community*, and entitled as matter of right to equal advantages in that community." The reality was that free blacks held "their rights at the will of the local authority." The United States had been "settled, and the society formed, by a white population. It was essentially a white community," and this gave the lie to the "stale argument derived from the abstract doctrines announced in the Declaration of Independence, and the comprehensive expression of 'We the people.'" Broad as these declarations might appear, "every one knows they were limited."[153] Charles Pinckney claimed that by excluding free blacks, Missouri had acted not only "under the sanction of Congress, but I may almost be justified in saying under their recommendation." Congress's passage and acceptance of discriminatory laws in the territories had been an endorsement of repeated Southern warnings about the dangers of free blacks: members knew "the imminent danger there was in the Southern and Western States in admitting such persons, and, therefore, on every occasion where they were passed cheerfully acquiesced in them." He claimed to have personally drafted the Constitution's privileges and immunities clause and said that he had believed "that there did not then exist such a thing in the Union as a black or colored citizen, nor could I then have conceived it possible such a thing could ever have existed in it."[154]

The most detailed argument came from William Smith of South Carolina, who had earlier accused Northerners of having "sold off their stock of negroes, and vested the price in bank stock." He surveyed the laws and constitutions of the country to provide "a mass of evidence, which nobody could doubt but a sceptic, that free negroes and mulattoes have never been considered as a part of the body politic." He asked why, if the Declaration had been "for the blacks as well as the whites," Northerners had not emancipated "your slaves at once, and let them join you in the war." Of course, many black Americans had been emancipated and fought in the war, and all Northern states had by this point begun abolishing slavery. But Smith was engaged in a retelling of

---

[152] *Annals of Congress*, 16th Cong., 2nd sess., December 1820, 545–46, 549–51.
[153] Ibid., 613–18.
[154] *Annals of Congress*, 16th Cong., 2nd sess., February 1821, 1129–36.

American history that denied the reality of any and all emancipatory moments, and that insisted on an unwavering commitment of whites to an absolute supremacy.[155]

The argument that free blacks could not have been intended to be included in the ranks of citizens was now amplified by some Northern Republicans. Senator John Holmes of Maine, who corresponded with Monroe and Jefferson about the crises and asked for their guidance and encouragement in bringing them to a resolution, echoed Southerners' claims that the framers of the Constitution could never have envisioned black Americans as citizens, capable of being elected to national office: "gentlemen, with all their humanity, to be obliged to sit in this Senate by a black man, would consider their rights invaded."[156]

The irony of Holmes's stance was that during the drafting of Maine's constitution the year before, he had successfully opposed a motion to disenfranchise free blacks, arguing that they were "members of the body politic." "I know of no difference," he then had declared, "between the rights of the negro and the white man – God Almighty has made none. Our Declaration of Rights has made none. That declares 'all men' (without regard to colours) 'are born equally free and independent.'" This was a far cry from his new position that the exclusion of this "decrepit and vicious" population from any "agency in the formation or administration of the laws" was conclusive proof that they had been denied "the essential attributes of a citizen."[157]

What had changed for Holmes? Perhaps it was that when he defended black suffrage during the statehood convention, he had been expecting Maine to be quickly admitted to the Union without controversy; a year later, he was working on behalf of a compromise that he felt duty bound to defend. Rufus King was less charitable, dismissing Holmes as the "merest sycophant," more eager to serve the interests of Southern slaveholders than any other Northerner in Congress. Holmes was proof that there would always be a faction of Northern politicians whose "hopes of influence and distinction" depended on their "taking part in favor of the

[155] *Annals of Congress*, 15th Cong., 1st sess., March 1818, 231–39; 16th Cong., 2nd sess., December 1820, 57–58, 71; William Smith, "Speech of Mr. Smith, of South Carolina, on the Admission of Missouri" (Washington, DC, 1820); *Daily National Intelligencer*, January 18, 1821, p. 2.

[156] *Annals of Congress*, 16th Cong., 2nd sess., December 1820, 84–89; *Daily National Intelligencer*, January 25, 1821, p. 2.

[157] Charles Nash, *The Debates and Journal of the Constitutional Convention of the State of Maine, 1819–20* (Augusta: Maine Farmers' Almanac Press, 1894), 125–26.

slave States." These "peculiar friends of liberty, will keep alive & sustain a body considerably numerous, and who will have sufficient influence, to preserve to the slave States their disproportionate, I might say exclusive, dominance over the Union."[158]

Another Northern voice for the Southern position was offered by economist Tench Coxe, a Federalist turned Republican, erstwhile opponent of slavery and supporter of black citizenship, and an enthusiastic cotton booster. During the crisis, Coxe provided what Gary Nash has described as "a figurative road map that most white Americans followed in redefining citizenship and national identity." In thirteen essays, Coxe tried to persuade Congress and his fellow Northerners of the "southern view of black non-citizenship." He repeated Southern arguments that free blacks were not fit for citizenship, that postemancipation parties would inevitably be organized on racial lines, leading to extreme polarization and racial war, and that black Americans had not been party to the Constitution and that its republican commitments did not extend to them. As Gary Nash notes, "this assertion blatantly disavowed" what he had argued a few years before.[159]

In a letter to Madison, Coxe credited his argument as having been based on the exposition of the Southern case presented by William Smith. Coxe wrote that he was convinced that "the black & colored people" were not "parties to our social compacts (provincial or state)," and informed the president that "many here [in Pennsylvania] have been convinced" by the debates "that *fully enfranchised black and colored citizens* cannot be *created and maintained*." Like Branagan, Coxe had imbibed Southerners' warnings that blacks posed a unique threat to public order, a belief he suggested was increasingly shared among Pennsylvania's upper classes. All men, but "especially the active members of our city institutions," had come to believe this population posed a danger, and "the great question here now is, how and where can they be disposed of with justice and policy." And like Branagan, Coxe was tailoring his arguments to please a potential Southern patron: his essays were proffered in the explicit hope that Madison would help secure a government commission and were written after Madison had let Coxe know what line of

---

[158] Charles King, *The Life and Correspondence of Rufus King*, vol. 6 (New York: G. P. Putnam's Sons, 1900), 329; Matthew Mason, "The Maine and Missouri Crisis: Competing Priorities and Northern Slavery Politics in the Early Republic," *Journal of the Early Republic* 33, no. 4 (2013): 675–700.

[159] Nash, *Forgotten Fifth*, 125, 154–55, 162; *Delaware Gazette and Peninsula Advertiser*, December 15, 1820, p. 3; *Democratic Press*, December 25, 1820, p. 2.

argument would be most useful – Madison wanted a refutation of the
charge that the government was controlled by a "southern" rather than
a "Republican Ascendancy." For good measure, Coxe had requested the
essays be forwarded to Jefferson in the hopes he might supply monetary
support.[160]

The crisis ended when Henry Clay organized another compromise, requiring Missouri to resolve never to pass any law abridging the privileges and
immunities of any citizen while leaving open the question of whether free
blacks were citizens. One Northerner expressed a willingness to excuse the
irredeemable Southerners, who looked on free blacks "through a medium
which prejudice, habit and interest had filled with delusions." But they
warned Northern Republicans that they should not expect "the same char-
ity" if they voted with them.[161] When Thomas Ross, an Ohio Republican,
began to suspect that some of his co-partisans would vote with the South, he
accused them of acting "under the influence of improper motives."[162]

He was not far off: the Monroe administration relied heavily on
patronage to round up the needed votes – especially in Pennsylvania,
where the Second Bank of the United States pulled "out all the stops for
passage," using exactly the type of financial influence Republicans had
long warned would corrupt free government. The House voted eighty-
seven to eighty-one in favor of the compromise, with at least three votes
secured through the Bank's efforts and another gained by a promise that
a new tariff would be passed benefiting Pennsylvania's manufacturing
interests, to which this one representative "was deeply and dependently
in debt." While state caucuses in the North generally denied renomination
to Republicans who had voted with the South, the party's leaders "sought
to reward those Republicans who had backed the sub rosa party line and
punish those who had not."[163]

The Legacy of Missouri

The arguments that had received national attention during the Missouri
crises found a new hearing a few months later in the New York State

[160] David B. Mattern, J. C. A. Stagg, Mary Parke Johnson, and Katharine Harbury, ed.,
    The Papers of James Madison, Retirement Series: 1 February 1820 – 26 February 1823,
    vol. 2 (Charlottesville: University of Virginia Press, 2013), 142–43, 154–55, 162–63,
    193–195; Nash, *Forging Freedom*, 225.
[161] *Hampden Federalist and Public Journal* (Springfield, MA), December 27, 1820, p. 2.
[162] *Annals of Congress*, H. R. 16th Cong., 2nd sess., February 13, 1821, c. 1129.
[163] Forbes, *The Missouri Compromise and Its Aftermath*, 82, 118, 124.

Constitutional Convention of 1821, after a committee proposed extending the right to vote to persons who paid taxes or served in the militias but to restrict it to white men.

Erastus Root, who had voted for the state's gradual emancipation law, to enlist black men during the War of 1812, for black suffrage in Louisiana, who had championed an immediate emancipation bill, and had urged the state to put "the children of slaves upon the same footing as the children of free men," now explained that free blacks were not properly part of the social compact and that as voters they were the tools of the wealthy. "A few hundred free negroes of the city of New-York," he warned, "following the train of those who ride in their coaches, and whose boots and shoes they had often blacked, shall go to the polls of the election, and change the political condition of the whole state." Samuel Young was especially adamant that blacks needed to be excluded, claiming that respectable middle- and upper-class opinion was unanimous in rejecting equality. "No white man will stand shoulder to shoulder with a negro in the train band or jury-room. He will not invite him to a seat at his table, nor in his pew in the church. And yet he must be placed on a footing of equality in the right of voting, and no other occasion whatever, either civil or social." Jonathan Ross justified the disenfranchisement on the grounds that black New Yorkers did not share the burden of defending the state, even as he cited the battles in New Orleans and on Lake Erie – where free blacks had played vital roles – as examples where the white militiamen had earned their right to vote. Foreseeing where the debate would go, he preemptively declared that the exclusion had no "connection at all with the question of slavery."[164]

Federalist Peter Jay opened the attack. The state had only recently "taken high ground against slavery and all its degrading consequences and accompaniments.... Adopt the amendment now proposed, and you will hear a shout of triumph and a hiss of scorn from the southern part of the union, which I confess will mortify me – I shall shrink at the sound, because I fear it will be deserved." He rejected the claim of black inferiority as being "so completely refuted, and ... now so universally exploded, that I did not expect to have heard of it in an assembly so

[164] Jabez Hammond, *The History of Political Parties in the State of New York*, vol. 1 (Syracuse, NY: Halls, Mills, and Co., 1852), 581; Nathaniel Carter and William Stone, *Reports of the Proceedings and Debates of the Convention of 1821 Assembled for the Purpose of Amending the Constitution of the State of New-York* (Albany, NY: E. and E. Hosford, 1821), 180–81, 185–86, 190–92, 195, 199; *Albany Argus* (Albany, NY), February 17, 1846, p. 1.

enlightened as this." Still, he expressed a worry that Young's claim about white prejudices might sway delegates. He met this head on. "Why do we feel reluctant to associate with a black man? There is no such reluctance in Europe, nor in any country in which slavery is unknown. It arises from an association of ideas. Slavery, and a black skin, always present themselves together in our minds." It was slavery that preceded and caused white prejudice, and he hoped the convention would not "violate all those principles upon which our free institutions are founded, or contradict all the professions which we so profusely make, concerning the natural equality of all men, merely to gratify odious, and I hope, temporary prejudices." Federalist Abraham Van Vechten simply denied the relevance of white racism, asking whether "our prejudices against their colour destroy their rights as citizens." And he noted that efforts to cast doubts on black citizenship were palpably absurd in New York, resting on claims that had been unknown before Missouri: "We are precluded from denying their citizenship, *by our uniform recognition for more than forty years.*"[165]

While Federalists took the lead in denouncing disenfranchisement, many Republicans opposed it as well. Robert Clarke, a Republican aligned with the Tammany Hall "Bucktail" wing of the party, wanted to strike "white" because it was "repugnant to all the principles and notions of liberty, to which we have heretofore professed to adhere, and to our declaration of independence. . . .. The people of colour are capable of giving their consent, and ever since the formation of your government they have constituted a portion of the people."[166]

Martin Van Buren's political allies had walked a careful line during the Missouri crises, ostensibly supporting the antislavery position even as they absented themselves on key votes and worked closely with the national administration in support of a compromise. Their factional rival Republicans in the state – the Clintonians – accused them of having "thrown their weight into the scale with the negro holders of the south, for the two fold purpose of sharing the smiles and patronage of the general government, and obtaining its aid in building up their own party in this state."[167]

---

[165] Carter and Stone, *Reports of the Proceedings and Debates*, 183–84, 193–94, 201.
[166] Ibid., 187–88.
[167] *New York Columbian* (New York), February 24, 1821, p. 2; *Republican Advocate* (Batavia, NY), April 6, 1821, p. 2, November 24, 1820, April 4, 1821, p. 2; *New-York Statesman*, August 8, 1820, November 14, 1820; Donald Cole, *Martin Van Buren and the American System* (Princeton, NJ: Princeton University Press, 1984), 59, 69.

With Jay and others raising the specter of Missouri and implicitly threatening an antislavery campaign against the constitution, Van Buren's Bucktails watched their members waver. Few of them, and none of the country members, had pledged themselves on this issue, many had staked out strong positions during the Missouri crises in favor of free black citizenship, and they were all aware of the force of the recently aroused antislavery opinion in the state. When Jay moved to strike the word "white," it passed sixty-three to fifty-nine, with forty-four Republicans voting to strike and fifty-nine voting against; seventeen Federalists voted for black suffrage and five voted against. Worried the issue might lead to the constitution's rejection, even Van Buren voted with the majority to strike "white."[168] Root complained that the suffrage was "now extended to negroes; or in the polite language of the day, to *coloured people.*" But the debate moved on to the question of how far the franchise should be extended on class lines.[169]

Here, Bucktail Republicans were united in favor of removing property qualifications but divided over the question of just how far the expansion should go.[170] They successfully beat back an effort to require electors for the senate to own property in land or tenement, by a vote of 100 to 19. But they then watched as Federalists and Clintonians struck a clause enfranchising men who had performed public labor on the highways. And with the backing of some Clintonians, Bucktails now voted to add an alternative to the taxpaying requirement, enfranchising male citizens who had been resident for three years. This passed by a vote of sixty-three to fifty-five. The franchise had now been extended well beyond the "mechanics, professional men, and small landholders" that Van Buren had hoped to enfranchise. The party arranged for the suffrage clause to be sent to a new committee.[171]

As soon as the word "white" had been struck, voices in the party press began insisting that the question be reopened. Mordecai Noah, the racist editor of the *National Advocate,* warned that unless free men of color were disenfranchised, "we shall be inundated with blacks, who will crowd round our polls, pushing aside their white employers, to introduce their purchased votes." He appealed to party unity, urging the "country members" to listen to warnings that free black men's suffrage was, "particularly in the federal wards, a mere vendible article." Noah's argument

---

[168] See the discussion in *Extra Globe,* June 12, 1839, p. 86.
[169] Carter and Stone, *Reports of the Proceedings and Debates,* 202.
[170] Ibid., 185, 224, 239, 241, 257, 271–77.   [171] Ibid., 367.

mixed racist appeals to employers with the recently circulated tropes that black Americans had not been founding members of the people and that black citizenship posed a threat to the Union and Southern interests. "We have always considered the question of black rights and privileges a very dangerous one in this country," he wrote, "where a large portion of the union held slaves and could not get rid of them." There were men in the convention who would "delight in saying to the southern states – 'Look here: we will make you uneasy in your dwellings, and revenge your political influence, by *showing to your blacks that we can make them free*, and give them the entire rights and privileges of their masters.'" Noah repeated almost verbatim arguments that had been disseminated by Tench Coxe and others, asking, "Were the blacks ever a party to the original compact in this state? They were not." Implying that he had inside information about the intentions of the party leaders, the *Advocate* predicted that the vote would be revisited.[172]

He was right. The fix was in from the moment the new suffrage committee was named: of thirteen members, only four had voted with the majority in favor of black suffrage. Samuel Young promised that the next effort to disenfranchise free blacks would be in "no danger of another entanglement," and soon after he presented the committee's recommendation: every male citizen, resident one year in state, who had paid a state or county tax or been exempted from taxation, as well as every male citizen resident three years who had worked on the public highways, would be enfranchised, but with a proviso that black men would be entitled to vote only if they owned a freehold estate of $250, and would be excused from taxation if they did not. Near manhood suffrage was to be established for white men, while all but a tiny class of black New Yorkers were to be disenfranchised. Young accused supporters of black voting rights of failing to appreciate public sentiment on this issue, suggesting that the delegates "from the country ... know more about the feelings of the yeomanry, than those who, from their wealth, habits and official stations, do not mingle among the people." The question of black suffrage, unlike that of an expanded franchise, had not been agitated before the convention, and there is no evidence that this had been one of the reasons why voters in the state had supported a constitutional revision; moreover, it had been the country Republicans who had initially

---

[172] *National Advocate* (New York), September 24, 1821, October 2, 1821.

defeated disenfranchisement. Young was conjuring a silent majority and claiming the mantle of its representative.[173]

Republican Ezekiel Bacon continued to oppose disenfranchisement as a violation of republican principles that "recognize no distinct casts [sic] or orders of men, having distinct and fixed personal or political rights." Jay again took issue with racist arguments of black inferiority and pressed members to recognize the degree to which their prejudices clashed with their republican commitments and Christian beliefs.

But influential members from all parties now came out in support of the compromise. Federalist Chancellor Kent argued that allowing black men to vote only if they met a high property qualification would "alleviate the wrongs we had done them" and "make them more industrious and frugal." Briggs, an "ultra-democrat" and former mechanic, expressed his preference for including the word "white," so that there would be neither an odious property qualification nor black voting; but he noted that party leaders were urging him to drop it, and he withdrew his motion for an exclusively white democracy. James Tallmadge, who had introduced the Missouri resolution and who had opposed disenfranchisement earlier in the convention, accepted the discriminatory qualification as "a compromise of conflicting opinions." Van Buren now announced that the clause met with his approval, as "the right was not denied" on account of color but of wealth. And for good measure, Samuel Young let it be known that were the compromise to fail, he would again move to "insert the word *white* in the report and exclude them altogether." The threat was clear: pass this now, or the Bucktails would press their members to pass an absolute disenfranchisement. The vote on striking out the discriminatory provision failed by a vote of seventy-one to thirty-three.[174]

Both the disenfranchisement of black voters and enfranchisement of white voters were part of an effort to reconstruct the electorate in order to advantage a particular faction of the divided Republican Party. But while the latter had been a clear response to growing demands for reform from the western counties, with Bucktails throughout the state pledged to support an expansion, the only place where there had been any discussion before the convention of disenfranchising black men had been in

---

[173] Carter and Stone, *Reports of the Proceedings and Debates*, 288.

[174] Jabez Delano Hammond, *The History of Political Parties in the State of New York*, 4th edn., vol. 2 (Syracuse, NY: Hall, Mills, and Co., 1854), 10; Carter and Stone, *Reports of the Proceedings and Debates*, 285, 364–69, 374–77.

TABLE 3.3 *Voting in New York Constitutional Convention, 1821*

	Keep "White"	Strike "White"	Keep $250 Clause	Strike $250 Clause	Average Percent of Votes Cast for Black Voting Rights
Bucktail	58%	42%	85%	15%	39%
Clintonian	50%	50%	68%	32%	50%
Federalist	20%	80%	35%	65%	66%
For Manhood Suffrage	63%	37%	82%	18%	34%
Against Manhood Suffrage	34%	64%	65%	35%	56%
Oppose Property for Senate	53%	47%	83%	17%	40%
Require Property for Senate	32%	68%	32%	68%	68%

New York City, and that city's delegation had initially been divided on the question. With the party press and leaders urging a reconsideration, all of New York City's Tammany Hall delegates now voted for the discriminatory clause.[175] Still, both the Bucktails and their Clintonian rivals remained divided over the question of black disenfranchisement, although majorities of both factions rallied around the discriminatory property clause. As Table 3-3 shows, it was those most supportive of "manhood" suffrage who were also the most insistent on disenfranchising black American men, while those who were most committed to the existing property qualifications were the most steadfast in support of a racially neutral suffrage standard. The pattern that would define subsequent processes of democratization in antebellum America was now clearly set in place.

CONCLUSION

Black disenfranchisement in New York was the culmination of processes under way for two decades. Within the course of a generation, free blacks

[175] *Poughkeepsie Journal*, June 27, 1821, p. 3.

had been disenfranchised in Delaware, Kentucky, Ohio, New Jersey, Louisiana, and Connecticut, while a "white male" standard had been imposed in the territories and new states. Within a year, black voters would be disenfranchised in Rhode Island as well, when the Republican party finally came to power in the state: after years of promising to abolish the property qualification for voting, they disenfranchised black voters and left the property requirement untouched.

The results can be seen in Figure 3.2. The states and territory (Florida) in white disenfranchised either all or the vast majority of black voters through an explicit racial qualification of their own design – although often borrowed from others – while the states in gray continued to allow black men the right to vote. The states and territories marked by diagonal lines had a white male standard first imposed by Congress. By 1822, the upper South, mid-Atlantic, and lower New England states where the bulk of the free black population lived had almost all passed disenfranchising amendments. And as the lands of the Louisiana Purchase were organized over the next few decades, Congress would rely on a template for territorial government that extended the "white male" standard across the continent. The United States had become, in its institutions and increasingly in its public philosophy, a white man's republic.

This emergence of a pattern of "white democracy" – in institutional reforms, voting patterns, and political discourse – was not a straightforward product of American political culture, or "the ineluctable consequence of a white racist political ideology," or the "preordained outgrowth of a republic divided along lines of race."[176] Persons of African descent had long been subjected to racist ascription, with differences in color providing a marker of civic status and legal rights.[177] The turmoil of the Revolution, the War of 1812, continued violence along the frontier, and the revolution in Haiti led elites to further disseminate discursive frames presenting black Americans and the indigenous nations as "internal enemies," ready to attack white American homes and overthrow the republican project. The institutions and ideology of the white man's republic emerged within this cultural matrix, but they were not determined by it.

It was instead the organization of the Republican coalition that yoked egalitarian and inegalitarian positions together in institutional reforms,

---

[176] Polgar, "Whenever They Judge It Expedient," 17.
[177] See "Review of the Memoirs of the Life of Granville Sharp," *The African Repository, and Colonial Journal* 2, no. 7 (September 1826), 201.

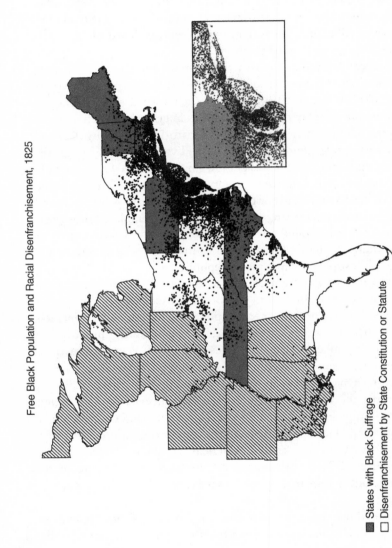

Free Black Population and Racial Disenfranchisement, 1825

■ States with Black Suffrage
☐ Disenfranchisement by State Constitution or Statute
▨ Disenfranchisement by Congress

Each dot is the approximate location of twenty persons. Population of Florida is unknown. Total population approximately 270,000.

FIGURE 3.2 Disenfranchising States and the Distribution of the Free Black Population, 1825

legislator positions, and eventually into a narrative of political community. From Jefferson onward, the "slave power of the South reached into the party councils of every state," shaping the policies that were adopted and the rhetoric that emanated from the party press. Their influence was so important "that they were not only tolerated by their northern allies, they were patronized, flattered, and allowed to dictate. After 1800 the management of party affairs was in the hands of slaveholders, and every northern politician came to terms with this fact of political life."[178]

The narrative of the white man's republic emerged out of this political configuration: still, its adoption was not a top-down imposition, but was worked out discursively by partisans at all levels as their egalitarian commitments collided with demands to defend slavery and deny black citizenship. The nationalization of politics produced by the Constitution and the parties, then, "provided the grounds for white racism's articulation, politicization, and institutionalization" in local and national politics.[179]

The contradiction of the white man's republic was not a natural product of how democracy was conceived, nor was it an invisible assumption or a consensus preference: almost everywhere disenfranchisement was resisted by substantial minorities, and politicians and writers remarked regularly on the contradiction that the cause of American democracy, the meaningful vision that Jeffersonians had adopted and disseminated to a new people, was to be limited to white men. As one satirist wrote, "it is a delicate matter on this point to reconcile our principles with our convenience.... Let us get over it as easily as we can," and get back to rejoicing in universal suffrage and American democracy. "What a glorious theme!"[180]

---

[178] McManus, *A History of Negro Slavery in New York*, 185.
[179] David Waldstreicher, "The Nationalization and Racialization of American Politics: Before, Beneath, and Between Parties," in *Contesting Democracy: Substance and Structure in American Political History, 1775–2000*, ed. Byron E. Shafer and Anthony J. Badger (Lawrence: University of Kansas Press, 2001), 55.
[180] *The Evening Post* (New York), November 30, 1821, p. 2.

4

The White Man's Republic

This is a nation of white people – its offices, honors, dignities and privileges, are alone open to, and to be enjoyed by, white people.
– James Bryan, 1835[1]

As the United States entered its fourth decade, the Republican Party dominated the country's politics. It was a political hegemony that would not last: over the course of the 1820s, the party descended into factional chaos.

The brief period of one-party dominance in America had been facilitated by institutions which allowed Republicans to adjudicate competition and policy conflicts between their ambitious politicians and associated interests and constituencies. Control over national and state patronage had provided a tool by which partisans across the country could be coaxed into compromise, while the caucus system for coordinating around a presidential nominee – in which the party's members in Congress would meet to select candidates for president and vice president – had repeatedly resolved potentially fractious questions of succession.[2]

The collapse of the Federalists, however, led to some of their most talented and ambitious politicians joining the Republican Party, and President Monroe began appointing them to national office and local patronage positions. This wreaked havoc with the calculations of state

[1] *Proceedings and Debates of the Convention of North Carolina, Called to Amend the Constitution of the State* (Raleigh, NC: Joseph Gales and Son, 1836), 67.
[2] *The Evening Post* (New York), April 1, 1824, p. 2.

parties and, combined with the decline of state-level Federalist parties, encouraged factionalism. Republicans now began attending to former Federalist constituencies and their priorities. The Second Bank of the United States was chartered in 1816 and was rescued by the Supreme Court from state-imposed taxes a few years later.[3] Nationalists such as Henry Clay and John C. Calhoun were calling on the federal government to bind "the republic together with a perfect system of roads and canals," and in 1824 Congress authorized a general survey for internal improvements.[4] That same year, a new protective tariff was passed over Southern opposition. These were the types of expansive readings of federal power that had long worried Southern Republicans, but their warnings that "if Congress can make banks, roads, and canals under the constitution, they can free any slave in the United State" seemed to carry less weight.[5] In early 1825, John Quincy Adams was elected president, the first non-Virginian in a quarter century. "Politically speaking," remarked one observer, "this might be called the age of splitting. The great national republican party [was] split into at least three parts."[6]

Behind the scenes, however, Martin Van Buren was working with Southern elites in an effort to reconstitute a national coalition. "Instead of the question being between a northern and Southern man," he wrote one Southerner, "it would be whether or not the ties, which have heretofore bound together a great party should be severed."

We must always have party distinctions and the old ones are the best of which the nature of the case admits. Political combinations between the inhabitants of the different states are unavoidable & the most natural & beneficial to the country is that between the planters of the South and the plain Republicans of the north.... If the [old party lines] are suppressed, Geographical divisions founded on local interests or, what is worse prejudices between free & slave holding states will inevitably take their place. Party attachment in former times furnished a complete antidote for sectional prejudices by producing counteracting feelings. It was not until that defense had been broken down that the clamor against Southern Influence and African Slavery could be made effectual in the North.... Formerly, attacks upon Southern Republicans were regarded by those of the north as assaults

---

[3] Charles S. Sydnor, *The Development of Southern Sectionalism, 1819–1848* (Baton Rouge: Louisiana State University Press, 1948), 136.

[4] John C. Calhoun, *The Works of John C. Calhoun*, vol. 2 (New York: D. Appleton, 1853), 190–91.

[5] Edwin Mood Wilson, *The Congressional Career of Nathanial Macon* (Chapel Hill: University of North Carolina Press, 1900), 46–47, 49, 72, 76.

[6] *Connecticut Courant*, April 1, 1823, p. 2.

upon their political brethren & resented accordingly. This all powerful sympathy has been much weakened. ... It can & ought to be revived.[7]

This was a well-calculated argument. An 1816 slave insurrection in Barbados had been followed by an apprehended rebellion in South Carolina, with free blacks and religious zealots held responsible.[8] The governor of South Carolina warned the state legislature in 1820 that the Missouri controversy had "given rise to the expression of opinions and doctrines ... which tend not only to diminish [the property value of enslaved persons], but also to threaten our safety," and called their attention to the fact that "free persons of colour have emigrated, and are daily emigrating to, and settling in this State."[9] The legislature responded by prohibiting all manumissions and stiffening penalties against free blacks entering into the state. Two years later came the Denmark Vesey scare and still more laws regulating free and enslaved persons of color.[10] In 1823 came the Demerara rebellion in Guyana, with correspondents describing how the British had impaled the heads of black insurgents on pikes and identifying the cause of the insurrection in the belief held by the free people of color that "they are deprived of the privileges that are the birthright of every Englishman."[11] Van Buren was offering white Southerners an ally and a form of relief.

The explicit promise of the Democratic Party was to draw on the rhetorical scripts of Jeffersonian Republicanism and persistent party loyalties to reinvigorate a system of political competition that ran *across* the fault line of slavery, creating an interlocking set of political interests that could be mobilized to suppress any attempt to organize politics along sectional lines. In doing so, it would preserve a constitutional order that many white Americans insisted was the hope for liberty and democracy in the world, a political project that offered its white citizens and immigrants opportunities for settler expansionism and that institutionalized in law

---

7 Forbes, *The Missouri Compromise and Its Aftermath*, 214.
8 *Missouri Gazette*, July 6, 1816, p. 1; *Raleigh Minerva*, August 2, 1816, p. 3.
9 *The National Gazette and Literary Register* (Philadelphia), December 9, 1820, p. 3.
10 Lacy Ford, *Deliver Us from Evil: The Slavery Question in the Old South* (New York: Oxford University Press, 2009), 207–98; Philip M. Hamer, "Great Britain, the United States, and the Negro Seamen Acts, 1822–1848," *Journal of Southern History* 1, no. 1 (1935): 3–28.
11 *The Torch Light and Public Advertiser* (Hagerstown, MD), January 27, 1824, p. 2; *The National Gazette* (Philadelphia), January 16, 1824, p. 2; *The Star* (Brooklyn, NY), January 29, 1824, p. 2; *The Republican Compiler* (Gettysburg, PA), February 18, 1824, p. 3.

and discourse, in the public philosophy that underlay the expanding
nation, the idea that the United States was the white man's republic.

* * *

As a discursive and institutional formulation, the "white man's republic"
had its origins in elite efforts to reconcile competing commitments and
preserve partisan (and with it, national) unity. But it also invited white
Americans into a valued political identity, as heirs to the Democratic
Republican project who were charged with preserving its foundational
commitments and extending its geographic scope. Insofar as this narrative
was expressed through the democratization of political institutions or the
subsidized acquisition of property, or was connected to the real and
imagined antagonisms of social life, the white man's republic could
become not just a dimension of elite ideology but a popular vision of
peoplehood, one whose resonance was anchored in the real opportunities
and meaningful identities the Republic enabled and affirmed.

But the white man's republic was never an unconsciously assumed
backdrop to political debate or a universally agreed set of principles
about how political life should be organized. It was a pragmatic way of
discursively reconciling republicanism with the country's substantial
investment in human servitude and the elaborate political, institutional,
and cultural infrastructure required to maintain it. Politicians eager to
advance within their party, or polemicists looking for patronage, saw in it
a script by which they could indicate their soundness on core commitments. Party leaders in turn helped cement an expectation that deviating
too much from its strictures would be costly. "What is the power that the
slaveholders exercise?" asked William Chandler in 1850. "It is the power
of combined Capital and Party Organization, working upon the cupidity
of Northern politicians."[12]

If its contested character meant that adherence to the white man's
republic had to be actively supervised and enforced, it also meant that
there was space for imagining different visions of political community.
And throughout the antebellum period, there were thousands of activists
and politicians organizing in pursuit of such alternatives. These conflicting
currents of a white man's republic and alternative visions advanced by
antislavery activists would produce a sharp polarization on issues of race
and slavery, while subjecting both of the national coalitions to intense

[12] Williston H. Lofton, "Abolition and Labor: Appeal of the Abolitionists to the Northern
Working Classes: Part I," *The Journal of Negro History* 33, no. 3 (1948): 249–61, 250.

internal pressures. The result would be the collapse of one party and the
fragmentation of the other, fracturing the Union they held together. And
as had occurred during the Revolution, the sharp break within the network of individuals and institutions that constituted the governing
regime, and the resulting need to turn to "the people" for political and
military support, created an opportunity to bring about a new and more
profoundly revolutionary democratization in America.

THE WHITE MAN'S REPUBLIC

The "white man's republic" was a story about the origins, purpose, and
boundaries of American political community. Its central theme was that
the United States was established by and for the white people, its founding
documents and commitments framed to protect and advance the interests
of this population alone. Free black Americans were neither citizens nor
part of the broader community whose interests and aspirations should
guide public policy. And they could not be admitted to equal standing
without undermining constitutive aspects of the nation's purpose: by
threatening the compromises necessary for its founding, by empowering
factions hostile to democratic government, and by deflecting the focus of
public policy away from the interests of the white people, who were the
intended beneficiaries of the national project. Black suffrage could operate
only "to deteriorate, corrupt, and wither our democratic institutions,"
and therefore was an unacceptable compromise of the nation's fundamental purpose.[13]

This narrative was repeated in numerous venues across the antebellum
period. The "free persons of color, including mulattoes, mustees, and
Indians, were not parties to our political compact," argued a resolution
against black suffrage in the Tennessee convention of 1834.[14] "It was
unquestionably true," argued one Whig delegate in Pennsylvania, "that
the people of the United States, assembled in convention, did not mean to
say that the coloured population of this Union, formed a portion of that
people, who were competent to frame a constitution. They did not mean
to include them as having participated in framing the constitution."[15]

[13] William Bishop and William Attree, *Report of the Debates and Proceedings of the
Convention for the Revision of the Constitution of the State of New York, 1846*
(Albany, NY: Evening Atlas, 1846), 1048.
[14] Caleb Perry Patterson, *The Negro in Tennessee, 1790–1865: A Study in Southern Politics*
(Austin: University of Texas, 1922), 170.
[15] Agg, *Proceedings and Debates ... Pennsylvania*, 10: 54.

"Free persons of color never were considered as citizens," declared Nathaniel Macon in 1835. "They made no part of the political family."[16] The argument of the white man's republic was frequently reworked to apply to a particular state. The people of Pennsylvania, argued John Sterigere, wanted to maintain the commonwealth as "it has always been, a political community of white persons."[17] "Ohio," declared James Loudon, "was a state for white men. The negroes were intruders among us."[18] "Who were the people of New York?" asked Benjamin Cornell in 1846. Citing the seventeenth-century jurist Samuel von Pufendorf, he argued that the "people" were the "primitive founders" of a community and those they had willingly incorporated, and he narrated a history of New York in which "negroes, whether of trans or cis-atlantic birth," had never been admitted to membership. Black Americans had been "an alien people on the day New York assumed existence as a sovereign state, and he denied that it could be shown that the state of New York had ever naturalized or consolidated into itself a single negro."[19] Debating Abraham Lincoln in 1858, Stephen Douglas declared that "I hold that this government is established on the white basis. It was established by white men, for the benefit of white men and their posterity forever, and should be administered by white men and none others."[20]

For some delegates, the white man's republic was the result of divine interposition: "These United States were designed by the God of Heaven to be governed and inhabited by the Anglo-Saxon race and by them alone."[21] More argued that the denial of black citizenship was a foundational principle of American constitutionalism, in "accordance with the spirit of the federal constitution, and the universal understanding and well known intention of the people of the States."[22] Some looked to state constitutions, whose embrace of a "white male citizen" standard in their organic laws affirmed a racially restricted vision of political community. Californian Winfield Sherwood, for instance, declared that he was

[16] *Proceedings and Debates ... North Carolina,* 69.

[17] Agg, *Proceedings and Debates ... Pennsylvania,* 9: 153.

[18] J. V. Smith, *Report of the Debates and Proceedings of the Convention for the Revision of the Constitution of the State of Ohio, 1850–51,* 2 vol. (Columbus, OH: S. Medary, 1851), 2:553.

[19] Bishop and Attree, *Debates and Proceedings ... New York,* 1047.

[20] *Chicago Tribune,* October 18, 1858, p. 1.

[21] Smith, *Debates and Proceedings ... Ohio,* 1:56; Bishop and Attree, *Debates and Proceedings ... New York,* 1034.

[22] Bishop and Attree, *Debates and Proceedings ... New York,* 1047.

"in favor of the distinct expression, 'every white male citizen' as used in the thirty different Constitutions of this Union."[23]

This narrative of community origins and boundaries provided a rhetorical script by which democratic commitments could be affirmed as defining the essential character of American peoplehood, even as their application to black Americans was denied. As an origin story, the white man's republic excised black Americans from the founding struggles and commitments. "Nothing," insisted Cornell, "could be claimed on account of their having been soldiers in our revolutionary and other wars."[24] "This is," declared one delegate, "a nation of white people, and the enjoyment of any civil or social rights by a distinct class of individuals, is merely permissive."[25] Free blacks were being rhetorically and institutionally consigned beyond the margins of the political community: "The people, strictly speaking, are all the white men, women and children, who are to be affected by the laws."[26] The fact of having been "born on our land, did not give them claims of country."[27] Black Americans, whether free or enslaved, were no more than "suffering strangers" who could be extended some hospitality but could never share in the authority of the political household.[28] "I cannot," declared one delegate, "consistently, with my sense of duty, vote for negroes to approach the ballot box, so long as I remember that we citizens are white men, and that we have acquired this country, (whether by fair, or foul means,) and it belongs to us."[29]

The historical argument that persons of color had not participated in the founding was never the only rationale given for excluding black men from voting rights. A desire to sustain partisan and national unity had first impelled the articulation of the white man's republic on a national scale, and when a new threat appeared in the form of the immediate abolition movement, free black rights were again attacked as a threat to the

[23] J. Ross Browne, *Report of the Debates in the Convention of California on the Formation of the State Constitution* (Washington, DC: John T. Towers, 1850), 72; Agg, *Proceedings and Debates . . . Pennsylvania*, 2:472, 3: 91.

[24] Bishop and Attree, *Debates and Proceedings . . . New York*, 1047.

[25] *Proceedings and Debates . . . North Carolina*, 62.

[26] Robert J. Ker, *Proceedings and Debates of the Convention of Louisiana* (New Orleans: Besancon, Ferguson and Co., 1845), 96.

[27] Bishop and Attree, *Debates and Proceedings . . . New York*, 1028.

[28] *Report of the Proceedings and Debates in the Convention to Revise the Constitution of the State of Michigan* (Lansing, MI: R. W. Ingalls, 1850), 294.

[29] Smith, *Debates and Proceedings . . . Ohio*, 2: 553.

Union.[30] Support for black suffrage, lawmakers repeatedly warned, would be interpreted in the South as "a sanction given to the anti-American doctrines of the abolitionists," proof that would be "carried to Congress to show how nearly this state was divided on the subject of abolition."[31] Advocates for black voting rights were accused of adopting "an attitude of defiance to the southern states, instead of doing all that lay in our power to quiet the apprehensions and alarm which the mad schemes and conduct of northern abolitionists had created among them!"[32] A number of delegates reflected on how they personally "looked to the south, and regarded her feelings, in every vote which he was disposed to give. We are part of the same family. Their interests are dear to us. Their interests cannot be injured."[33]

The concern for national unity led many to recast the US Constitution as mandating black disenfranchisement, a logical corollary to its implied protection of slavery and one that rested on a historical claim that Southerners would never have accepted a Union that recognized persons of color as founding members. "We are under a most solemn compact not to interfere in the domestic affairs of the people of the south," one delegate offered as an explanation for why black men should be disenfranchised in Pennsylvania.[34] Any extension of voting rights to men of color would "violate a sacred pledge given by this state to her sister states, at the adoption of the constitution of the United States," argued a delegate in New York, and "would be against the manifest spirit of the Federal Constitution."[35] "We keep not our faith," declared another, "if we receive negroes into our political family. Pledged and linked as we are, I see not how they can be made voters, without a total revolution – a radical remodelling of our whole federal system."[36] A Democrat in Michigan went so far as to argue that "our constitution is based on slavery," and reminded his colleagues that they were oath-bound to defend the Constitution on this basis: "Would it be well to take this class, considered as chattels in the constitution, and allow them to vote

---

[30] Nicholas Wood, "'A Sacrifice on the Altar of Slavery': Doughface Politics and Black Disenfranchisement in Pennsylvania, 1837–38," *Journal of the Early Republic* 31, no. 1 (2011): 75–106.

[31] Agg, *Proceedings and Debates ... Pennsylvania*, 10: 109.   [32] Ibid., 9: 392.

[33] Ibid., 10: 58, 9: 328; H. Fowler, *Report of the Debates and Proceedings of the Convention for the Revision of the Constitution of the State of Indiana, 1850* (Indianapolis, IN: A. H. Brown, 1850), 237.

[34] Agg, *Proceedings and Debates ... Pennsylvania*, 9: 353.

[35] Bishop and Attree, *Debates and Proceedings ... New York*, 1047.

[36] Agg, *Proceedings and Debates ... Pennsylvania*, 10:22, 23.

with us, and take them into our social circles? Would it not be a happy comment on our oath to support the Constitution of the United States?"[37]

Arguments mixing historical narratives and their implied constitutional commitments were important in resolving qualms about the historical justice or legal wrong of disenfranchising black men. But they were buttressed by others that claimed black Americans lacked independence and knowledge of public men and thus were "not fit to exercise the right of freemen."[38] In the early Republic, the most common form in which black inferiority was invoked was by referring to an ostensibly "degraded character," a consequence of slavery and the limits of freedom in a racist society. During that period, delegates had tended to claim that color was simply a rough proxy for distinguishing "between those who understand the worth of that privilege, and those who are degraded, dependent, and unfit to exercise it."[39] The worry they expressed was essentially the same expressed by many about white wage laborers, that their poverty and precarious terms of employment meant their "vote would be at the call of the richest purchaser."[40] As long as the free black voter remained impoverished, he would "be always ready to sell his vote," would "always be subject to the influence of the designing," and if admitted to the polls would always "be ready to go as they may be directed, influenced, and worked upon by some master of intrigue."[41]

The danger that the impoverished might become the tools of intriguers and adventurous demagogues was a longstanding theme in republican thought. It was common in republican discourse to argue that "in all civilized communities, the two extremes of society – the affluent and the breadless, the powerful and the impotent – come together and war upon the centre – the intermediate classes." Ely Moore – "labor's first congressman" – warned that the consequence of abolitionism and black suffrage would be to empower the wealthy aristocrats who wanted to "render the condition of the laboring classes of the north and east still more dependent and depressed."[42] Often described as a Lazzaroni, after the staunchly

---

[37] *Proceedings and Debates ... Michigan*, 291.
[38] Agg, *Proceedings and Debates ... Pennsylvania*, 9: 391.
[39] Carter and Stone, *Reports of the Proceedings and Debates ... New York, 1821*, 190, 198.
[40] Ibid., 190–91.
[41] Ibid., 198, 281, 364; Agg, *Proceedings and Debates ... Pennsylvania*, 3: 85, 5: 453, 10: 23, 90.
[42] Ely Moore, *Remarks of Ely Mr. Moore of New York, In the House of Representatives* (Washington, DC: n. p., 1839), 16; *Congressional Globe*, Appendix, 25th Cong., 3rd sess., February 1839, 241; George A. Stevens, "New York Typographical Union No. 6:

monarchist paupers of Naples, black Americans (and sometimes poor white Americans) were cast as a familiar type, the antirepublican allies of would-be oligarchs and monarchists.[43] Paradoxically, this casting was frequently paired with another: the worry that black voters would empower demagogic attacks on property. The inherent "brutishness" of black Americans, warned Clement Vallandigham, would make them the *"sans culotte"* of the United States, "who, led by the worst of white men, will make your revolutions and overturn your government." Or (what amounted to the same thing), black Americans would vote for antislavery candidates, transforming the Union from the defender of property to a threat against it.[44]

As the antebellum era progressed, claims that black men's supposed unfitness for republican citizenship rested on their poverty or the degradation supposedly wrought by slavery were increasingly displaced by those that claimed the authority of science and that cast people of African descent as inherently distinct and inferior. This was in part a manifestation of what historian James Brewer Stewart calls the emergence of "racial modernity," the embellishment of Jefferson's "suspicions" into an elaborate account of humanity's origins and an ascribed hierarchy between its branches.[45] Racist delegates could point to a growing body of scientific and ethnological literature, as well as their readings of history, to argue that the "vastly superior" "intellectual power of the white race" was a "'fixed fact' – not the mere conclusion of prejudice."[46] The "African race," argued a growing number, were "a people who never have from the time of the commencement of the world down to the present time with a single exception, exhibited sufficient energy of body or mind to assert their freedom," and this stood as proof of "the original and essential inferiority of the negro race."[47]

Study of a Modern Trade Union and its Predecessors," *Annual Report of the Bureau of Labor Statistics, State of New York*, 1912, no. 28 C., 184, 188.

[43] *The Washington Union*, November 4, 1858, p. 2.

[44] *Congressional Globe*, 35th Cong., 1st sess., p. 2320; Agg, *Proceedings and Debates … Pennsylvania*, 9:365, 10:23; *Macon Weekly Telegraph*, November 28, 1837, p. 2; Smith, *Debates and Proceedings … Ohio*, 2: 637; *Daily Iowa State Democrat*, June 27, 1858, p. 2; *Congressional Globe*, 30th Cong., 1st sess., Appendix, July 25, 1848, 1166.

[45] James Brewer Stewart, "The Emergence of Racial Modernity and the Rise of the White North, 1790–1840," *Journal of the Early Republic* 18, no. 2 (1998): 181–217, 182.

[46] Bishop and Attree, *Debates and Proceedings … New York*, 1018–19, 1027.

[47] Milo Milton Quaife, *The Convention of 1846* (Madison, WI: State Historical Society, 1919), 279; Browne, *Debates in the Convention of California*, 49, 62; Agg, *Proceedings and Debates … Pennsylvania*, 9: 328, 335; *Norwich Aurora* (Norwich, CT), July 25, 1859, p. 1; *Proceedings and Debates … Michigan*, 293.

Another common argument was that black enfranchisement would violate the prejudices and commitments of white voters to racial hierarchy. This claimed a democratic imprimatur for illiberal legislation, either because it was what the public wanted or because racial hierarchy in cases of extreme prejudice was necessary to sustain democratic government. Many legislators denied being personally prejudiced against people of color, but stated that they were bound by democratic principles to vote according to the racism of their constituents. Some, however, wore the badge of prejudice with pride, affirming it as a natural impulse or a marker of respectability and deducing from its existence dire consequences.[48]

These delegates argued that white prejudice would prevent what prevailing political theory took to be a fundamental prerequisite for democracy. Democracies, they claimed, required a broad equality of social and economic conditions in order to survive, as only through social intercourse on relatively equal terms could mutual interests be discovered and an embracing sympathy toward fellow citizens cultivated. The problem, highlighted earlier by slaveholders such as Jefferson, Tucker, Fairfax, and others, was that the strength of white prejudice precluded any free and equal "interchange of sentiments" between black and white Americans.[49] Whites would consequently have "no common interest with, no bond of union to that part of the community," while free black Americans, embittered by their exclusion, would forge new solidarities that were antagonistic to the security of the state.[50] Instead of a blending of sentiments into a subtly shaded public opinion, black Americans would be a group perpetually set apart, with ideas and aspirations in conflict with the social commitments and economic priorities of the white portion of the electorate.

George Washington Woodward provided one of the more nuanced articulations of this reasoning. "Political rights," he argued, "depend, for their preservation and right exercise, on social intercourse and equality":

Not that every man, must associate with every man in the community, but I hold there must be that free and unrestrained interchange of sentiments on public questions, which can only attend a state of general equality.... Every man, from

[48] Bishop and Attree, *Debates and Proceedings ... New York*, 1028.
[49] Agg, *Proceedings and Debates ... Pennsylvania*, 10: 22, 95.
[50] S. H. Laughlin and J. F. Henderson, *Journal of the Convention of the State of Tennessee, Convened for the Purpose of Revising and Amending the Constitution Thereof* (Nashville, TN: Banner and Whig Office, 1834), 92.

the highest to the lowest, has his sphere and his appropriate circle of friends, and in his daily intercourse with them, both in the business and the pleasures of life, opinions become formed and matured, which when all men come out on terms of exact equality to vote, manifest themselves and influence whatever decisions is to be made by the popular voice. And these separate circles or little societies which wealth or adventitious circumstances, and not our political institutions, have made distinct, have connecting links that extend the opinions thus formed by the contact of minds, from and to the extremities of the body politic, and keep up a sympathy between the whole and all its parts; and here is the foundation of the system of universal suffrage. For suffrage is only the expression of the opinions which are perpetually maturing under the influence of social intercourse and equality.[51]

But delegates regularly claimed that only among the most "degraded" whites and "fanatical" abolitionists was there anything resembling equal social intercourse across the color line; and among working-class whites, this intercourse was increasingly understood to be a marker of their own unequal status (free persons of color regularly complained about the racism and lack of equality in social intercourse from whites of all social classes, including dedicated abolitionists).[52] The cultivation of common opinions and mutual sympathy was ostensibly impeded, making black suffrage "dangerous to the harmony and peace of our commonwealth."[53]

This argument was not based primarily on inherent racial difference or hierarchy, although it was perfectly compatible with these. Rather, it was a social theory about the impossibility of democracy under conditions of social diversity: democracy required sympathy and a blending of sentiments, while persistent diversity produced polarization and racial contests for political power. Unless a perfect amalgamation of black and whites was accomplished – through equal social intercourse resulting in intermarriage – the country would be composed of "two distinct classes of people" who would "array themselves against each other, in perpetual hostility and mutual distrust."[54] "We should have nothing but the perpetual turmoil," warned one delegate, "which always existed when there were two races in the same country, antagonist to each other. One or the other must govern, and the struggle for superiority had kept all countries, where two such races existed, in constant turmoil and revolution."[55]

[51] Agg, *Proceedings and Debates ... Pennsylvania*, 10: 22, 95.
[52] Roediger, *Wages of Whiteness*, passim.
[53] Agg, *Proceedings and Debates ... Pennsylvania*, 10: 97.
[54] Laughlin and Henderson, *Journal of the Convention ... Tennessee*, 92.
[55] Bishop and Attree, *Debates and Proceedings ... New York*, 1034; Quaife, *Convention of 1846*, 242; Agg, *Proceedings and Debates ... Pennsylvania*, 10: 953.

By implication, if free blacks were to be recognized as political equals, statesmanship demanded that they be extended social equality as well. "You must," argued Joseph Konigmacher, "if you recognize them as citizens, place them on an equality with all other citizens, in social as well as political relations." Political equality without social equality would only "render their condition more unhappy; and, in my opinion, irritate the jealousy and prejudice, which after all is the only barrier between the races." Joseph Hopkinson insisted that if delegates were to end the political exclusion of black men but leave the social exclusion in "full force," it would be to "bring an irritated and bitter enemy into the body politic, who could never be reconciled by a vote for the insult to his feelings and pride, in his exclusion from your society."[56] Any extension of social equality, however, would require economic redistribution, integration of schools and other social institutions, and ultimately intermarriage, a prospect even many supporters of black suffrage believed to be "repugnant to the feelings of men and to the economy of divine providence."[57]

Central to this argument was the claim that white prejudice was, for all practical purposes, immutable. Whether "natural or acquired," argued one delegate, "this prejudice, if you will call it so – is so strongly rooted in our white population – nay, in their own hearts and bosoms – that there is no expectation – no hope, I may say no desire, that has been expressed here to remove it."[58] "The prejudices of the white man," argued one delegate, "must be respected – no matter how he came by them. He is the lord of the soil."[59] "We must legislate with a view to human nature," argued Woodward, "as human nature is constituted, nor expect any miraculous changes in its constitution, to suit a system that grossly violates all its principles and sympathies. Whilst this prejudice remains deep seated in the bosoms of the whites, I feel unwilling to disregard it, by making this which was formed a white government, a white and black government." He concluded that "we may love the virtues which they display, and we may sympathize in their sufferings, and alleviate their wants, but white men will not consent to the self-debasement, which political and social equality with them would imply. I stop not to inquire whether this be right or wrong, or whether it spring from the virtues or

[56] Agg, *Proceedings and Debates … Pennsylvania*, 10: 132–33, 95.
[57] Quaife, *Convention of 1846*, 242.
[58] Agg, *Proceedings and Debates … Pennsylvania*, 10: 94.
[59] Ibid., 10: 76; Bishop and Attree, *Debates and Proceedings … New York*, 1032.

vices of our nature – the fact is so, and it is the fact, immoveable and unchangeable as it is, on which I rest my argument."[60]

These different rationales for why blacks needed to be excluded from the bounds of the American people were not in conflict with each other, nor was there always a clear line separating one from the other. Speakers drew on multiple themes and combined them in creative ways. "They are not citizens," argued Joseph Carson, "and if they were, from their separate cast [*sic*], they could not be respected as such."[61] "Negroes were aliens," argued John Hunt, "not by mere accident of foreign birth – not because they spoke a different language – not from any petty distinction that a few years association might obliterate, but by the broad distinction of race."[62] White prejudice was the result of an "antipathy which nature had interposed between the races," and it was this which posed an "impassable barrier" against recognizing blacks as equal members of the American polity.[63] Starting from different premises, however, the conclusion was generally the same: black citizenship imperiled the Union, the cause of self-government, and the legitimate interests of the white population, the "true and primary proprietors of the state, and its political powers and rights – whose fortunes, and labor, and blood, have made it what it is."[64]

The basic argument of the white man's republic – that the "people" referred only to the white population, that the country was established for their benefit, and that black Americans were a distinct people not recognized as citizens by the founders, the Constitution, or the social behavior of white Americans – provided lawmakers and delegates to constitutional conventions with a compelling narrative by which they could sidestep the implications of republican commitments. It is impossible to fully recreate the social and intellectual context in which these debates took place, and so we can only imagine how compelling a particular line of reasoning might have been. But along with claims about inherent racial difference and inferiority, arguments that stressed a historical, constitutional, or sociological claim that black Americans could not be considered part of the American "people" were consistently the most common rationales

[60] Agg, *Proceedings and Debates . . . Pennsylvania*, 10: 23.
[61] *Proceedings and Debates . . . North Carolina*, 356.
[62] Bishop and Attree, *Debates and Proceedings . . . New York*, 1030.
[63] Fowler, *Debates and Proceedings . . . Indiana*, 233.
[64] Agg, *Proceedings and Debates . . . Pennsylvania*, 10: 95, 97.

given by legislators for their opposition to black suffrage in the post-Missouri era.

The White Man's Republic and Black Disenfranchisement

As an origins story, the white man's republic was untethered from either of the main national parties that emerged out of the factional chaos of the 1820s, both of which could claim to be the heirs of the old Republican Party. The wide circulation the narrative had gained during and after the Missouri crises – in part through the auspices of the American Colonization Society, which sought to bring the promise of the white man's republic into reality by removing free persons of color from the country[65] – ensured that it was a nationally available script for use by the opponents of black citizenship in a variety of political and legal disputes.[66]

Disenfranchisement in Tennessee
There had not been a racial qualification for voting in the constitutions of North Carolina in 1776 or Tennessee in 1796, and in both states, it was widely acknowledged that free black men could and did legally vote.[67] But

---

[65] George Washington Parke Custis, in an address to a colonizing society, noted that "some benevolent minds in the overflowings of their philanthropy ... say ... let the coloured class be freed, and remain among us as denizens of the Empire.... No, Sir, no.... What right, I demand, have the children of Africa to an homestead in the white man's country? ... Let this fair land, which the white man won by his chivalry ... be kept sacred for his descendants, untarnished by the foot print of him who hath even been a slave." *The Fourteenth Annual Report of the American Society for Colonizing the Free People of Colour of the United States* (Washington, DC: James C. Dunn, 1831), xxi; Lawrence J. Friedman, "Purifying the White Man's Country: The American Colonization Society Reconsidered, 1816–1840," *Societas* 6, no. 1 (1976): 1–24; *Race and Slavery Petitions Project*, Petition Analysis Record Number 10382701 (1827).

[66] A Kentucky court relied on the constitutional logic of the white man's republic to argue that persons of color were not citizens of the United States: "Free negroes and mulattoes are, almost everywhere, considered and treated as a degraded race of people; insomuch so, that, under *the constitution* and laws of the United States, they can not become citizens of the United States." *Amy (a Woman of Colour) v. Smith* 11 Ky. (1. Litt.), 326–37, 332–34 (Ky. 1822).

[67] Roger Wallace Shugg, "Negro Voting in the Antebellum South," *The Journal of Negro History* 21, no. 4 (1936): 357–64; Chase C. Mooney, "The Question of Slavery and the Free Negro in the Tennessee Constitutional Convention of 1834," *The Journal of Southern History* 12, no. 4 (1946): 487–509, 497n25; Stephen B. Weeks, "The History of Negro Suffrage in the South," *Political Science Quarterly* 9, no. 4 (1894): 671–703, 675; *National Banner and Daily Advertiser* (Nashville, TN), April 1, 1834, p. 2; Henry Thomas Shanks, ed., *The Papers of Willie Person Mangum*, vol. 1 (Raleigh, NC: State Department of Archives and History, 1950), 238; John Hope Franklin, *The Free Negro in*

there is little evidence of any groundswell of popular opposition to black suffrage. A few petitions to the Tennessee legislature in 1825 complained that the free people of color of Rutherford County could "control elections where they vote" and were generally "rude and insolent in their behavior."[68] And a petition from New Bern, North Carolina, complained that during elections, free black men were "courted and caressed by both parties and treated apparently with respect and attention," one way in which political equality might lead to the dreaded social equality.[69] But these were scattered complaints that did not prompt a quick response, and at least one North Carolinian noted that any proposal to disenfranchise black voters would be "of most questionable import." "If free at all," they argued, "they are entitled to the privileges of freemen. – This the Declaration of Rights, and the voice of unperverted reason, loudly proclaims."[70]

The Nat Turner insurrection in 1831, however, provoked a new panic about the threat free people of color posed to the region's security and racial hierarchy. The insurrection was blamed on Virginia's "permitting the free black and the slave to associate together," renewing worries that free blacks were, in the words of the Tennessee Supreme Court, "a very dangerous and most objectionable population where slaves are numerous," whose presence was only made worse in those states where they were included in the "body politic."[71] "Permitting free negroes to vote at elections," complained the prominent citizens of New Bern, "contributes to excite and cherish a spirit of discontent and disorder among the slaves," undermining "the barrier of opinion which alone keeps [the slave] in subjection."[72] Bartlett Yancey, a former member of Congress, was worried even before the insurrection that the "infernal spirit of emancipation,

---

North Carolina, 1790–1860 (Chapel Hill: University of North Carolina Press, 1943), 106–8.

[68] Other petitions had requested that the rights of certain individual free men of color be expanded. *Race and Slavery Petitions Project*, Petition Analysis Record Numbers 11482504, 11482515, 11481501, 11481927; Loren Schweninger, *The Southern Debate Over Slavery: Petitions to Southern Legislatures, 1778–1864* (Urbana: University of Illinois Press, 2001).

[69] *Race and Slavery Petitions Project*, Petition Analysis Record Number 11283108.

[70] Ford, *Deliver Us from Evil*, 419, 421, 428; *Raleigh Register* (Raleigh, NC), July 29, 1835, p. 3.

[71] Ford, *Deliver Us from Evil*, 392, 411; *National Banner and Daily Advertiser* (Nashville, TN), April 1, 1834, p. 2, August 14, 1835, p. 3; Mooney, "The Question of Slavery and the Free Negro in the Tennessee Constitutional Convention of 1834," 488.

[72] Franklin, *The Free Negro in North Carolina*, 108; Weeks, "The History of Negro Suffrage in the South," 676.

generated by Colonizing & emancipating societies, is greatly felt in this State, and so is the free negro suffrage." The implication Yancey drew from this was not that there was widespread hostility to black voting, but rather that racially egalitarian sentiment was *on the rise*, with voting a dangerous manifestation of a new assertiveness among free blacks. "If the people of this State are not more awake to their rights and interest on this subject," he warned, "a few years more will produce an influence here, greatly to be lamented & feared." Yancey was especially concerned to see the old Federalist John Stanly, a representative of New Bern and a favorite candidate among the free black population, support "the principle of the proposition of Mr. [Rufus] King" during the Missouri crisis, "declaring 'that negroes had the same God, & the same Redeemer the white has', which though literally true, serves to show you the *slang* employed on this question."[73]

The issue of black voting would come up during the Tennessee constitutional convention of 1834 in the context of the seeming growth of abolitionist sentiment in the state, after over a thousand petitioners called for a plan to gradually abolish slavery.[74] A committee chaired by the Whig delegate John McKinney gave several reasons why the convention should reject abolition, resting its objections primarily on the problem of freed blacks living in white society. White prejudice meant free black Tennesseans would be forever "denied the privileges of membership with the rest of the community," making their condition worse than slavery and ultimately pushing them to join with the slaves, "array themselves against" the whites, and reenact the "bloody scenes of St. Domingo." "Will not similar causes," asked McKinney, "always produce similar effects; would not the same horrible tragedy be acted over again in our own country, at our firesides, and in our bed chambers?"[75]

A number of delegates were shocked by the suggestion that freedom was worse than slavery, and entered a protest against the report on the grounds that its arguments were "subversive to the true principles of republicanism," provided an "apology for slavery," and flaunted "the

[73] Shanks, *The Papers of Willie Person Mangum* 1: 238.

[74] James W. Patton, "The Progress of Emancipation in Tennessee, 1796–1860," *Journal of Negro History* 17, no. 1 (1932): 67–102, 68, 70; Caitlin Fisk, "The Tennessee Antislavery Movement and the Market Revolution, 1815–1835," *Civil War History* 52, no. 1 (2006): 5–40; Mooney, "The Question of Slavery and the Free Negro in the Tennessee Constitutional Convention of 1834," 498.

[75] Laughlin and Henderson, *Journal of the Convention ... Tennessee*, 92.

public opinion of the state." To let the report stand unopposed would require delegates to "renounce the doctrine that 'all men are created equal, that they are endowed by their Creator with certain unalienable rights,'" and a committed minority refused to "assign to men their rights according to different shades of color."[76]

The convention then moved to disenfranchise black voters. Invoking the narrative of the white man's republic, Democrat G. W. L. Marr insisted that free people of color had not been "parties to the political compact" and explained that their inclusion in the 1796 constitution had been an oversight. This, however, was rebutted by Isaac Walton, the only delegate who had participated in the state's founding convention of 1796; he was quickly seconded by the other senior members of the convention. One delegate expressed his astonishment and regret at seeing "old members, yes, Mr. Chairman, old gray headed gentleman" defend black suffrage.[77]

After several days of tumultuous debate, the convention agreed to disenfranchise black voters but *retain* the voting rights of those free black men who had resided in the state six months and were over twenty-one when the new constitution was ratified. The majority in favor of grandfathering in black voters, however, was small and shallow. One member explained that while he did not want to disenfranchise existing voters, and was therefore opposed to including the word "white," he also did not want to explicitly recognize the voting rights of free men of color in the text of the constitution. The problem as he saw it was that the document would "be read where the circumstances attending the privileges here only intended to be continued, will not be fully understood, and it will be a fair conclusion to arrive at abroad, that the northern fanatics have made an impression amongst us."[78] Hardly a profile in courage, he was unwilling to disenfranchise existing voters, unwilling to allow other men of color the right to vote in the future, and unwilling to be seen doing one or the other.

Marr hoped to drive a wedge in this coalition. He introduced a series of resolutions, drafted by former governor Willie Blount, which he claimed would present "a true view of the relation or want of relation between the

[76] Ford, *Deliver Us from Evil*, 405; Laughlin and Henderson, *Journal of the Convention ... Tennessee*, 30, 72, 88, 92, 102–4, 126.

[77] *National Banner and Daily Advertiser* (Nashville, TN), July 15, 1834, p. 2; Ford, *Deliver Us from Evil*, 412; Mooney, "The Question of Slavery and the Free Negro in the Tennessee Constitutional Convention of 1834," 503.

[78] *Nashville Republican and State Gazette* (Nashville, TN), July 1, 1834, p. 2.

colored population of the country and its political institutions."[79] The resolutions were effectively a restatement of the white man's republic: "free persons of color, including mulattoes, mustees, and Indians were not parties to our political compact, nor were they represented in the Convention which formed the evidence of the compact" between the "free people" of Tennessee and the other states.[80] A Whig delegate, W. H. Loving, explained why the terms of the white man's republic were essential for slaveholding states but also for the Union itself. Free people of color, he argued, were the "corrupt link between the debased of our own color and the slave," and allowing them voting rights would provide an "evil example to our slaves" whose inevitable result would be to "awaken and excite feelings in the breasts of slaves, of a most delicate nature, embracing within their range, the overthrow or total extinction of the white race, one instance of which is yet fresh in our memory – that of the ill-fated Island of St. Domingo." For these reasons, it was "the true policy of all the States in the Union, and should be that of every free white American citizen, to keep their governments in their own hands to the total exclusion of all free persons of color."[81] "We, the people," Marr concluded, meant "we the free white people of the United States and the free white people only."[82]

Another delegate to the 1796 convention, observing the proceedings, was now asked whether it had been "the *intention*" of the founding convention to enfranchise free black men. Contradicting Walton's earlier claim, Charles McClung reported that while "he did not recollect that free persons of color were spoken of or thought of in prescribing the qualifications of electors," had they known that "the right would ever have been asserted, for the free colored population to vote for members of the General Assembly, the question would have been put to rest by *securing that right to the free white population only.*"[83]

The majority in favor of black voting rights collapsed after Marr's intervention. Two days later, the resolution retaining limited black suffrage was overturned.[84] A month later, the convention voted thirty-three

---

[79] *National Banner and Nashville Whig* (Nashville, TN), June 30, 1836, p. 2.
[80] Laughlin and Henderson, *Journal of the Convention ... Tennessee,* 107.
[81] *National Banner and Daily Advertiser* (Nashville, TN), July 15, 1834, p. 2.
[82] Ford, *Deliver Us From Evil,* 414, 416; *Nashville Republican and State Gazette* (Nashville, TN), July 15, 1834.
[83] *National Banner and Nashville Whig* (Nashville, TN), June 30, 1836, p. 3.
[84] A suffrage qualification enfranchising "every free man of the age of 21 years and upwards being a citizen of the United States" was passed, but it was recognized this was a placeholder. *Nashville Republican and State Gazette,* July 1, 1834, p. 3.

to twenty-three to insert the word "white," and then voted down a motion to continue voting rights for those who could exercise them under the old constitution (it did establish that no person would be disqualified from voting on account of color who was a competent witness against a white man under state law, which continued voting rights for men whose ancestry was one-sixteenth "black"). To mitigate the charge of denying republican commitments, amendments were passed "exempting" free men of color from militia service in peacetime and from paying a poll tax.[85] Black voting in Tennessee was over.

Disenfranchisement in North Carolina

Free black voting was more widespread in North Carolina than it had been in Tennessee.[86] When a convention was called in 1835, black suffrage was listed as one of the issues that could be considered for revision, although this was left to the discretion of the delegates. In any case, it had not been part of the broader set of complaints that motivated the proposed revisions, most of which stemmed from the legislature's malapportionment and the underrepresentation of the western counties and upon which the convention's hands had been effectively tied by the legislature.[87] When the convention did take up the issue, debate turned largely on the questions of what effect black suffrage had on slavery and whether free people of color were included within the American political community, with delegates offering competing proposals to retain voting rights for a subset of black men, to disenfranchise all, or to simply leave the qualifications as they were.

Joseph Daniel and John Branch, both Jacksonian Democrats from a county with nearly three hundred free black voters, suggested that black men who met a property qualification should be entitled to vote, reminding delegates that the British were abolishing slavery in the West Indies and that it would be wise policy to cultivate "a good understanding

---

[85] Laughlin and Henderson, *Journal of the Convention ... Tennessee*, 208–9.

[86] Other than the "Ten Mile Precinct" in Louisiana's Allen Parish, where a small community descended from North Carolina slaves successfully voted the Democratic ticket, as well as a few scattered reports from Kentucky, these states were the only instances of free black voting in the South after the disenfranchisement of black voters in Maryland. Shugg, "Negro Voting in the Antebellum South."

[87] Ford, *Deliver Us from Evil*, 428; North Carolina, *Acts Passed by the General Assembly of the State of North Carolina at the Session of 1834–35* (Raleigh, NC: Philo White, 1835), 4–5; North Carolina, *Journals of the Senate and House of Commons of the General Assembly of the State of North Carolina, 1834–1835* (Raleigh, NC: Philo White, 1835), 50, 73, 89, 97, 112, 123.

with the most respectable portion of our free persons of color, who might be very serviceable to us in case of any combination for evil purposes among their brethren in bondage."[88]

But delegates pounced when Daniel, responding to a concern that any disenfranchisement would violate the state constitution, conceded that "the Bill of Rights did not apply to men of colour. It embraced only free white men."[89] James Bryan, a Whig from an old Federalist family, now rose to demand the total disenfranchisement of black voters. The core of Bryan's argument was that black suffrage violated the precepts of the white man's republic. "This is," he declared, "a *nation of white people*," and the "nature of our Government and the institutions of the country, never contemplated that they should be placed upon an equality with the free white man."[90] Hugh McQueen, another Whig, asked whether free people of color were anywhere "recognized by public sentiment as constituting that class of people from which the political power of this country should flow in the whole, or even in part?" It was the "the white portion of the population of this country" who constituted "the proper depository of political power. They bled for it, they wrote for it, they spoke for it, they expended their treasure for it; their wisdom and valor has preserved."[91] The seventy-eight-year-old Nathanial Macon, now a Democratic supporter of Jackson and soon to be nominated as a presidential elector for Martin Van Buren, argued that "free persons of color never were considered as citizens." He acknowledged that he was more extreme in his opposition to black voting than many delegates, but he insisted that free blacks had not been required to take the revolutionary oath of allegiance and so could not be said to have participated in the founding of the country.[92]

After an extensive debate, the convention voted sixty-one to fifty-eight in committee, and sixty-six to sixty-one in full convention, in favor of a resolution that "free negroes and mulattoes, within four degrees, shall not in future be allowed to vote for members of the Senate or House of Commons."[93]

---

[88] *Proceedings and Debates ... North Carolina*, 60–61, 70, 72–73, 79.   [89] Ibid., 61.
[90] Ibid., 62–63.   [91] Ibid., 76–78.   [92] Ibid., 69–70.
[93] A resolution stating that that "by the existing Constitution of this State, free persons of color never have been considered as citizens, and therefore not entitled to vote; and that no privilege to vote for Senators or members of the House of Commons shall hereafter be extended to any free persons of color" was dropped when it was decided to be beyond the bounds of discussion allowed by the legislature. Ibid., 71.

But defenders of black suffrage were persistent and argued that the closeness of the vote suggested it merited reconsideration. The reason they gave was that supporters of disenfranchisement had been relying on a mistaken historical narrative, evidenced by Macon's claim that no person of color had ever taken the revolutionary oath of allegiance. Judge William Gaston now informed the convention that John Chavis, a free man of color, had since "handed to him a certificate of his having taken the Oath of Allegiance, dated Dec. 20, 1778, and signed James Anderson, Mecklenburg, Va."[94] Chavis took great pride in his service in the Revolutionary War, writing once "that if I am black, I am free born American & a revolutionary soldier & therefore ought not to be thrown entirely out of the scale of notice."[95] He now ensured that his own claim and the claims of other free black North Carolinians would be heard.

Democrat Owen Holmes was persuaded by Chavis's evidence and by similar cases brought to his attention from his own county. He entered the fray to argue that disenfranchisement was wrong and strategically unsound, pointing to the supposed exclusion of free black Haitians as provoking that country's revolution (the opposite of the usual story). Jacksonian Samuel King picked up the attack, arguing that free men of color had exercised their right to vote since 1778, one year after the state constitution and nine years before the US Constitution. In "neither of those instruments is to be found the term 'free white men,'" and it was inconceivable that this had been an oversight.[96]

The effort to expel black voters from the electorate had been defended by invoking a historical narrative that excised them also from the founding struggles. Recognizing the importance of this narrative, opponents of disenfranchisement made its refutation central to their counterefforts.[97] It was not enough, and the last effort to retain limited black suffrage was defeated sixty-four to fifty-five.

In both Tennessee and North Carolina, partisan affiliation was unrelated to positions on black suffrage; the most important predictor of how delegates voted was the proportion of the district population that was held in slavery. Figure 4.1 maps the proportion of the population composed of enslaved and free African Americans, with the counties in North Carolina and Tennessee shaded according to the level of support given for black

[94] *Proceedings and Debates . . . North Carolina*, 351.

[95] Edgar W. Knight, "Notes on John Chavis," *North Carolina Historical Review* 7, no. 3 (1930): 326–45, 327, 342, 344, 345.

[96] *Proceedings and Debates . . . North Carolina*, 352–54.   [97] Ibid., 355–56.

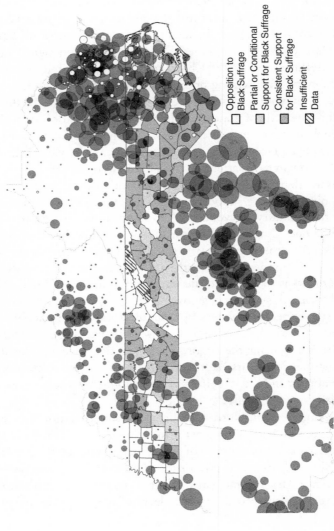

Black Population and Disenfranchisement
North Carolina and Tennessee, 1834–35

Opposition to
Black Suffrage

Partial or Conditional
Support for Black Suffrage

Consistent Support
for Black Suffrage

Insufficient
Data

Grey circles are the proportion of the county held in slavery, white circles the proportion free African American. Opposition to black suffrage was concentrated in the Northeast of North Carolina and in the Gulf Coastal Plains, Central Basin, and Cumberland Plateau regions of Tennessee. African American population of neighboring states shown for context.

FIGURE 4.1 Disenfranchisement and the Black American Population, Tennessee and North Carolina, 1834–35

suffrage: darker shades provided more consistent support for black voting rights, and lighter ones gave either partial support or total opposition.[98] While the size of the free black population was unassociated with legislator position, the size of the enslaved population was a strong negative predictor of opposition to black voting rights.

It had been the antislavery members of the Tennessee convention, and the western members of the North Carolina convention, that had taken the most consistently pro-suffrage positions. But as had been true in Maryland and New Jersey at the turn of the century, in New York in 1785, and in Congress when the question of black citizenship came on the agenda there, delegates with personal or constituent investments in human enslavement were adamantly opposed to recognizing black rights. Ironically, had the North Carolina convention been less grossly malapportioned, and the western part of the state fairly represented, black disenfranchisement would likely have been defeated.[99]

DEMOCRACY AGAINST ABOLITION

Opposition to black voting rights and reliance on the narrative of the white man's republic were equally common across party lines into the early 1840s. Over the course of the next two decades, however, the question of black suffrage would gradually map on to the partisan cleavage, so that by the 1850s, support for black suffrage had virtually disappeared among Northern Democrats, while Northern Whigs – about to disappear as a national party – were now more likely than not to support it. This process of issue polarization can be seen in Figure 4.2, which shows the probability that a legislator or delegate from a given party voted in favor of black suffrage, controlling for state, across the period 1834 to 1860.[100] Both parties had shown relatively equal levels of opposition to black suffrage in the 1830s, in the Southern states of Tennessee and North

---

[98] By estimating a logistic regression of party and the enslaved population on vote choice, the probability that a delegate would support black voting rights declines from 0.8 and 0.85, for Democrats and Whigs respectively, to 0.4 and 0.1 as the size of the enslaved population increased from zero to 65 percent of total.

[99] Had the convention been kept at 130 members, with each county receiving at least one member and the rest allocated by total population, white population, or "federal" population, and voting in the proportions that they did, the greater representation of the west would have defeated disenfranchisement. Henry Groves Connor, "The Convention of 1835," *The North Carolina Booklet* 8, no. 2 (1908): 89–110, 99.

[100] The results reflect a logistic regression of party on vote choice in two-year periods from 1834 to 1860.

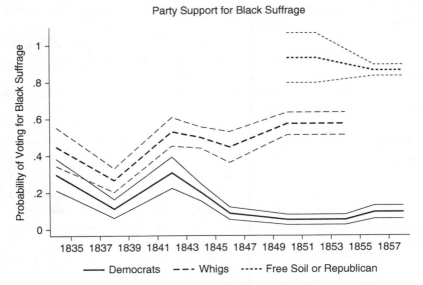

FIGURE 4.2 Probability of Voting for Black Disenfranchisement by Party

Carolina as well as in Michigan, Pennsylvania, and Connecticut, while the narrative of the white man's republic was invoked in equal measure by partisans on both sides. By the 1850s, however, Northern Whigs had become nearly as likely to support black suffrage as not, and while those who continued to oppose it still relied on the script of the white man's republic to do so, both this and opposition to black voting had become much more characteristic of the Democratic Party.

There were several reasons why the Democratic Party converged on opposing black voting rights while the Whigs became more supportive. The symbolism and policy that the Democrats offered potential constituents stressed egalitarian democracy as the country's defining feature, and so they were especially in need of a script that could confine this narrative to white men. This was not a logical unfolding of racially exclusionary implications of "democracy," but a pragmatic accommodation given the party's coalitional commitments. The party's embrace of white republicanism as its orienting principle was also a function of its relatively greater success and the responsibilities this entailed: the Whigs were less frequently in power, and so when abolitionist organizing was at its peak, it was the Democrats who felt more pressure to put it down. Finally, polarization on this issue was intensified by a dynamic process of conflict extension and representation. While Democratic constituencies and activists were possibly more racist to begin with – and most evidence suggests antiblack racism was ubiquitous among most groups of white Americans – they were soon subjected to a barrage of racist propaganda. Democrats began offering their voters a consistent message about the necessity of denying black rights, giving broader political meaning to existing racism, likely intensifying it and reinforcing an electoral constraint that already limited the degree to which legislators were willing to take racially egalitarian positions.

The positions of Whigs were shaped by similar dynamics, but these tended to work in the other direction. While they had their own cross-sectional coalition, they were relatively late in developing a national network of activists and a financial and organizational infrastructure to mobilize voters. They did not, for instance, cohere on a national ticket in 1836 but ran separate regional candidates, and more generally they tried to win national office by avoiding taking any "comprehensive stand on any issue."[101] And so while both parties felt obliged to oppose abolitionism, the Whigs maintained party unity less through the sticks and carrots of patronage and advancement but "by taking very different tacks" in different regions of the country.[102] This strategy was in some sense the luxury of defeat: they did not reliably hold the presidency except between 1849 and 1853, when the need to hold their own coalition together led the Millard Fillmore administration to aggressively enforce support for the 1850 compromise.[103] But for most of the antebellum era, the Whigs lacked the power and responsibility that came with the presidency, and enjoyed a flexibility that allowed many in its Northern wing the political space to support black suffrage. Finally, it would be the Whigs who were most pressed by the rise of the Liberty Party and the broader political activism of white and black Americans in the antislavery movement. Forced to respond to antislavery activism from below, and less constrained by their national coalition above, Northern Whigs could more flexibly support or oppose black suffrage based on their reading of the direction and intensity of local opinion. But for both Whigs and Democrats, the white man's republic provided a rhetorical script that seemed to make the denial of black suffrage an act of national conciliation.

[101] John M. McFaul, "Expediency vs. Morality: Jacksonian Politics and Slavery," *Journal of American History* 62, no. 1 (1975): 24–39, 33.

[102] Michael Holt, *The Rise and Fall of the American Whig Party: Jacksonian Politics and the Onset of the Civil War* (New York: Oxford University Press, 1999), 136, 236, 383; Vernon Volpe, "The Anti-Abolitionist Campaign of 1840," *Civil War History* 32, no. 4 (1986): 325–39.

[103] William Gienapp, "The Whig Party, the Compromise of 1850, and the Nomination of Winfield Scott," *Presidential Studies Quarterly* 14, no. 3 (1984): 399–415, 400.

The Party of White Democracy

During the first decades of the Republic, a story of the United States as a country dedicated to popular sovereignty and equality had become a crucial component of many Americans' civic identities. By the third decade of the nineteenth century, this story was under increasing strain. In 1819, the economy was sent into a deep recession from which it took almost a decade to fully recover. Preceded by a speculation and debt-fueled land boom, the recession laid bare the limits and contradictions of America's commercial empire: wages of unskilled workers and farm laborers would not reach the levels achieved in 1810 for another forty years, while physical stature among the white population – a common measure of well-being – began to drop precipitously.[104] In 1837, another speculation-fueled land boom came crashing down, leading to another prolonged recession and further stress on the working classes. Alongside these booms and busts came a profound reconfiguration of the country's industrial and commercial life, as skilled and independent artisans and mechanics were displaced by unskilled workers in large manufacturing complexes and agricultural communities experienced a disruption of relatively egalitarian distributions of wealth, as some lost their farms and others found themselves able to take advantage of the new market opportunities.[105]

The Democratic Party's response to these dislocations was to double down on the symbolic claims and policy priorities of the Jeffersonian Republican Party.[106] They argued that their party could alone uphold the civic status and material well-being of the white "producing classes," a vaguely defined composite that smoothed over potentially conflicting interests. They framed the United States as a country without distinction of rank, committed to equality in political relations and in social intercourse

---

[104] Robert Margo, *Wages and Labor Markets in the United States, 1820–1860* (Chicago: University of Chicago Press, 2000), 100–8; Richard H. Steckel, "Heights and Health in the United States, 1710–1950," in *Stature, Living Standards, and Economic Development: Essays in Anthropometric History*, ed. John Komlos (Chicago: University of Chicago Press, 1994), 153–70, 163–64.

[105] Melvyn Stokes and Stephen Conway, ed., *The Market Revolution in America: Social, Political, and Religious Expressions, 1800–1880* (Charlottesville: University of Virginia Press, 1996).

[106] There was a modest tendency for Democrats to win the support of communities left behind by the period's economic transformations and individuals who wanted to break up established networks of finance and commerce to pursue their own entrepreneurial projects. But the white working classes neither unanimously supported the party nor gave direction to its policy priorities. Sean Wilentz, "On Class and Politics in Jacksonian America," *Reviews in American History* 10, no. 4 (1982): 45–63, 57.

but under threat from would-be aristocrats, and narrated a story of civic worth contrasting the white producing classes with a Whig financial elite. On a policy level, the party tended to oppose state-established monopolies and high tariffs – which they cast as upward redistribution – and to support reduced government spending and taxes. Most famously, they opposed rechartering the Second Bank of the United States, highlighting the bank's role in first encouraging land speculation and later forcing the foreclosures of small farms and critiquing it as a private entity that enriched a small coterie of financiers at public expense. Finance capitalism itself, argued the most radical Democrats, constituted a new "antagonist" to human liberty, its arrival in the United States from England "the beginning of a counter revolution" that only Jackson and his partisan supporters could stop.[107]

Their most consequential policy response, however, was to intensify what had been bipartisan policy since the Revolution: expropriating territory from the indigenous nations in order to subsidize access to land on which white migrants could carve out an independent existence, take advantage of new opportunities for market-oriented agriculture, or accumulate capital through speculation.[108] A policy of removing the indigenous nations had begun under Monroe and Adams, but it would be dramatically escalated after the election of Andrew Jackson. The already-thin veneer of contract and treaty gave way to forced expulsions of the Cherokee in the Trail of Tears and of the Potawatomi in the Trail of Death. The Whigs, supportive of expansion but concerned that it not come at the expense of concentrated settlements in the East or old Northwest and Southwest, coalesced in opposition to some of these measures, making it an ideal issue upon which the Democrats could differentiate themselves. In 1844, Democrats sidelined Van Buren in favor of a candidate who supported the annexation of Texas and the aggressive resolution of the Oregon boundary; two years later, President James Polk

---

[107] *Congressional Globe,* 25th Cong., 2nd sess., Appendix, February 1838, 251–52; *Proceedings and Debates ... Michigan,* 487; John Ashworth, "The Jacksonian as Leveller," *Journal of American Studies* 14, no. 3 (1980): 407–21, 413; Moore, *Remarks of Ely Moore,* 16.

[108] With some exceptions, both parties supported territorial expansion westward, although the Democratic Party was the more aggressive of the two. But there were limits to what the Democratic Party could countenance: Southerners became increasingly opposed to expansion and homesteading as they began to worry it would create a "cordon" of free states, while a large majority of the party – with the support of a third of Whigs – insisted that it be restricted to whites. Frymer, *Building an American Empire,* 148–55; Stanley Legerbott, "The Demand for Land: The United States, 1820–1860," *Journal of Economic History* 45 no. 2 (1985): 181–212; D. Feller, *The Public Lands in Jacksonian Politics* (Madison: University of Wisconsin Press, 1984).

waged an aggressive war against Mexico in pursuit of even more new territory.[109]

The results of these policies can be seen in Figures 4.3 and 4.4, showing the distribution of the white (and after 1848, Mexican) and black population in 1820 and 1860. During the fight over Missouri, American settlement had only recently expanded into the Ohio River Valley, while its further expansion into the Northwest and southwestern states was blocked by the continued presence and unextinguished title of powerful indigenous nations. By 1860, American settlers had swept into almost all of the territory east of the Missouri River and south of the forty-third parallel, while the Mississippi delta and the old southwest had become the heartland of the empire of slavery. Territorial expansion redistributed land from the indigenous nations to white families, undergirding settler democracy while committing the country to ethnic expulsions, the further expansion of slavery, and the entrenchment of slaveholders' political power.

The removal of the indigenous nations and ongoing efforts to colonize free persons of color gave concrete meaning to the vision of a "white man's republic" as a country not only set aside for white men but actively being *cleared* of its original inhabitants. But as Paul Frymer demonstrates, each expansion brought under the country's dominion yet more persons of nonwhite status and increased the territory available for slavery, further diversifying the population, deepening the commitments of slaveholders, and rendering less feasible any prospect of whitening the country.[110]

The new territories and states that were created out of this land would have the most liberal voting qualifications in the world. Beginning in Michigan, Democrats pushed for an extension of the suffrage to recently arrived noncitizens who had declared their intent to naturalize: this would be later adopted in Indiana, Kansas, Minnesota, Nebraska, Oregon, Washington, and Wisconsin. In state and territorial conventions, they also pushed for an end to taxpaying qualifications for voting rights and for shortened residency requirements.

The combined impact of westward expansion and democratizing reforms on state enfranchisement rates was relatively modest. Still, in Rhode Island, a heavy property qualification combined with a racial exclusion disenfranchised approximately 55 percent of the adult male

[109] Richard Young and Jeffrey Meiser, "Race and the Dual State in the Early American Republic," in *Race and American Political Development*, ed. Joseph Lowndes, Julie Novkov, and Dorian Warren (New York: Routledge, 2008), 42.

[110] Frymer, *Building an American Empire*.

Distribution of American Settlements, 1820
Black Americans

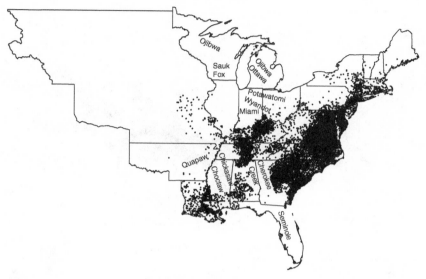

White Americans

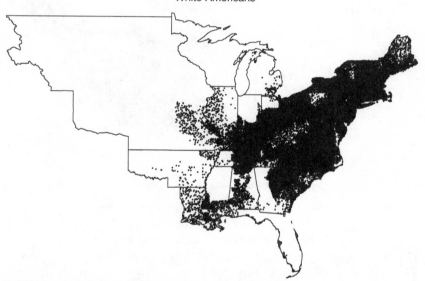

Each dot is the approximate location of one hundred persons. Florida population unknown.
Approximate location of select indigenous shown in top panel

FIGURE 4.3 Population Distribution in 1820

Distribution of American Settlements, 1860
Black Americans

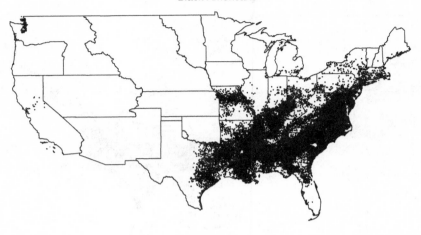

White and Mexican Americans

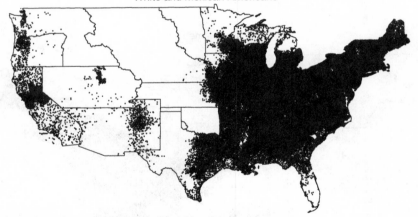

Each dot is the approximate location of one hundred persons.

FIGURE 4.4 Population Distribution in 1860

population until 1842, when the state's merchant and agricultural oligarchy was forced by the threat of civil war to open up the franchise –
although they retained a steep property qualification for the foreign-
born. In Louisiana, the constitution of 1845 substantially increased the
number of persons who could vote, as did reforms in Virginia in 1830 and
1851. Elsewhere, Democratic reforms stopped the rate from falling
despite increasing inequality.

Democratic Party support for liberalized voting rights was defended by reference to the purpose of America as a supposedly class-free society unburdened by "artificial distinctions." To single out property ownership, tax payments, or militia service as evidence of a contribution to the community was to erect aristocratic distinctions and embrace the "old antagonist principle of wealth against liberty." To make voting rights conditional on taxation was an "odious distinction" that could not be "sustained upon any ground of expediency or right" and that was "wholly inconsistent with the spirit of equality" that animated American democracy. It was nothing more than a relic of the property qualifications that the "privileged class" had always used as "a chain to bind and restrain the people." Democrats cast themselves as the defender of the "poor laboring man," whom they argued contributed at least as much to the community as the wealthy: "He, is, too, a producer in the community and both the wealthy and his country are reaping an advantage from his labor." And they rested their support for further democratizations on the basis of republican equality, natural rights, and the founding principles of the country. The suffrage was "a natural and inherent right," and its extension on terms of equality was required by the self-evident truths to which the United States was devoted. "Is it nothing to [the working man]," asked one delegate, "that he stands among men a man, equal to the highest and wealthiest?"[111]

Precisely because they most consistently invoked egalitarian principles, Democrats were especially in need of a script by which their application could be confined.[112] "This is not the home nor the country of the negro," argued a writer in the Democratic *New-York Globe*, in an explicit effort to reconcile black disenfranchisement with the "sacred principle, universal and world-wide in its application, that 'all men are born free and equal.'"[113] Benjamin Cornell found the narrative of the white man's republic helpful precisely because he believed that the right to vote was a "natural and inalienable right" and that the equality of man was "the fundamental basis of the true science of government, and civil society, and of American

---

[111] Agg, *Proceedings and Debates ... Pennsylvania*, 2: 473–74, 488, 490, 505, 537, 555, 3:113, 118–19; Virginia, *Proceedings and Debates of the Virginia State Convention of 1829–30* (Richmond, VA: Ritchie and Cook, 1830), 341, 410; Boston Daily Advertiser, *Journal of the Debates and Proceedings in the Convention of Delegates Chosen to Revise the Constitution of Massachusetts, 1820–1821* (Boston: Daily Advertiser, 1853), 254; Bishop and Attree, *Debates and Proceedings ... New York*, 467, 1036.

[112] Conservatives could simply justify exclusion on the grounds that the right to vote was a political concession rather than a natural right.

[113] *The Liberator*, January 8, 1847, p. 1.

constitutional law." How "could we exclude the negroes, or as gentlemen call them, our colored fellow citizens, without a gross violation of right and justice, by which we should forfeit all just claim to democracy or republicanism, and give to the negroes just cause and right revolution?" Only, he claimed, by denying black Americans' claim to be part of the people: they deserved the right to vote, but to do so in their own community and under their own government.[114]

Not all Democrats were convinced. A Wisconsin Democrat conceded that "the negro is not a white man" but nonetheless maintained that "he is here among us; he has been born here, brought here, speaks our language, and ours only; he knows no other country or government, is protected by our laws, and made subject to them, and is therefore to all intents and purposes a citizen of the country. It did therefore seem to him no very great stretch of what he understood to be true Democratic principles to allow him a voice in the election of officers who were to rule over him."[115] Samuel Denton, a Michigan Democrat, urged the state to drop its racial disenfranchisement on the grounds that it was a violation of the democratic republican principles to which the country "owed its being." The Democratic Party in particular was obligated to "carry out its principles," and it was an act of "unutterable littleness" to require a disenfranchised class to support the government: "There is not a member of the present legislature who has not in his pocket the money of the disfranchised, and politically degraded tax payer of color."[116] Many would leave the party altogether. Benjamin Gass, a Virginia-born operator on the Underground Railroad, noted during an Ohio Liberty Party convention that while he had always been a proud Democrat, he was "not a modern Democrat" and would have nothing to do with the "democracy, which teaches him that the sentiment, that all mankind are created free and equal, is like other abstractions, and has no actual existence."[117]

---

[114] See the attack on John O'Sullivan for his inconstancy in the *Tribune*, March 27, 1846, p. 2; Bishop and Attree, *Debates and Proceedings ... New York*, 1032, 1045–47; Smith, *Debates and Proceedings ... Ohio*, 2: 553, 1: 56; Agg, *Proceedings and Debates ... Pennsylvania*, 9: 349, 10: 101.

[115] Quaife, *Convention of 1846*, 240.

[116] Michigan, "Report of the Committee on State Affairs," *Documents Accompanying the Journal of the Senate and House of Representatives at the Annual Session of 1845* (Detroit, MI: Bagg and Harmon, 1845), no. 15, 6; Olbrich, *Development of Sentiment on Negro Suffrage*, 94–95.

[117] *Daily Ohio Statesman* (Columbus, OH), December 29, 1842, p. 3; Gerald Henig, "The Jacksonian Attitude toward Abolitionism in the 1830s," *Tennessee Historical Quarterly* 28, no. 1 (1969): 42–56, 50–51; *The Daily Louisville Democrat* (Louisville, KY), January 12, 1860, p. 1.

But for those Democrats who remained with the party, the need for a rationale that could confine the implications of egalitarian republicanism became more pronounced as an increasingly active abolitionist movement embraced the cause of black suffrage and began pressuring lawmakers to live up to their stated ideals. The choice to make black suffrage a centrally important part of the broader antislavery struggle was a result of the activism of black abolitionists, who insisted that the fight against Southern slavery needed to be accompanied by a more far-reaching battle against white prejudice.[118] This was one of the central themes of the subsequent National Conventions of the People of Color, held annually between 1830 and 1835 and again after 1843.[119] "Nearly all" of the conventions, notes Manisha Sinha, "focused on demanding the right to vote, civil rights, and equality before the law."[120] Equal rights were demanded both for their immediate practical benefits as well as for their symbolic value: legal distinctions were understood as part of the broader cultural infrastructure reinforcing white prejudice, which in turn undergirded slavery.[121] "Here, at least, our white friends will allow they may learn from us," wrote the *Colored American*. "The real battle ground between liberty and slavery is prejudice against color."[122]

The Colored Conventions, the antislavery movement, and their allies in state constitutional conventions and legislatures often embraced egalitarian rhetoric that was more commonly associated with the Democratic Party than with the Whigs. The Ohio Anti-Slavery Society demanded

---

[118] James Brewer Stewart, *Holy Warriors: The Abolitionists and American Slavery* (New York: Hill and Wang, 1997 [1976]), 110; Condit and Lucaites, *Crafting Equality*, 85.

[119] Some of the extraordinary work of the antebellum African American civil rights movement is being documented by the Colored Conventions Project, directed by P. Gabrielle Foreman, Jim Casey, and Sarah Lynn Patterson. Their work is transforming our understanding of black organizing in the nineteenth century (www.coloredconventions.org); Eve Kahn, "Colored Conventions, a Rallying Point for Black Americans Before the Civil War," *New York Times*, August 4, 2016; Howard H. Bell, "Free Negroes of the North 1830–1835: A Study in National Cooperation," *The Journal of Negro Education* 26, no. 4 (1957): 447–55; Howard H. Bell, ed., *Minutes and Proceedings of the National Negro Conventions, 1830–1864* (New York: Arno Press, 1969); John Wesley Cromwell, *The Early Negro Convention Movement* (Washington, DC: Academy, 1904).

[120] Sinha, *The Slave's Cause*, 325.

[121] William Yates, *Rights of Coloured Men to Suffrage, Citizenship and Trial by Jury* (Philadelphia: Merrihew and Gunn, 1838), iv; Hosea Easton, *A Treatise on the Intellectual Character, and Civil and Political Condition of the Colored People of the U. States; and the Prejudice Exercised Towards Them* (Boston: Isaac Knapp, 1837), 21, 31, 47.

[122] Sinha, *The Slave's Cause*, 306, 308.

"that all those statutes which discriminate between men, on account of color, be immediately repealed," casting these as "artificial distinctions in society, thus cultivating in the minds of the people monarchical and feudal notions."[123] The black abolitionist paper *The Weekly Advocate* staked out a traditionally Democratic position against "all Monopolies, which oppress the Poor and laboring classes of society," and insisted on manhood suffrage without distinction of color. Rather than treating suffrage as a political concession to which black Americans merited inclusion, abolitionists tended to insist – like the Democrats – that the suffrage was an inherent human right and that "all the civil and political disabilities of the colored people, are the effect of usurpation" against popular sovereignty.[124] A race qualification was an artificial distinction, "ridiculously absurd, and radically unjust." A Michigan Free Soiler threw Democratic doctrine back at the party, whose principles asserted that "'all political power is inherent in the people,' – not the white people, nor the black people, to the exclusion of the other class, but in all the people, including every individual of every color and condition."[125] Many would refer back to the Democratic Party's claimed founder, Jefferson: the "Declaration of our Nation's Independence boldly and unequivocally proclaims" that that all men are created equal, and in this "land of 'equal rights and equal privileges,'" any distinctions "in the exercise of the elective franchise, on account of color or complexion, [are] invidious and anti-republican."[126] A racial qualification for voting was "a violation of first principles, which we ourselves have acknowledged and established." Free Soilers, many of whom had once been Democrats, derisorily suggested instead that perhaps "Jefferson's rule should be amended so as to read 'equal and exact justice to all white men – or to all men except negroes.'" "I not only say," jabbed one, "but I believe that '*all* men are created equal.'"[127]

Denton urged his fellow partisans to recognize the justice of black men's claims and suggested that free blacks would cease organizing for

[123] Ohio Anti-Slavery Society, *Memorial of the Ohio Anti-Slavery Society to the General Assembly of the State of Ohio* (Cincinnati, OH: Pugh and Dodd, 1838), 3–4.
[124] Easton, *Treatise on the Intellectual Character, and Civil and Political Condition of the Colored People of the U. States*, 31; Sinha, *The Slave's Cause*, 299, 306, 324.
[125] *Proceedings and Debates ... Michigan*, 285–86, 289, 291; Smith, *Debates and Proceedings ... Ohio*, 2:552.
[126] Bishop and Attree, *Debates and Proceedings ... New York*, 1015–16.
[127] Smith, *Debates and Proceedings ... Ohio*, 2: 550, 554, 635; Quaife, *Convention of 1846*, 543–44.

the Liberty Party once Democrats joined in a defense of their rights, adding that most black voters could then be counted on to vote for the party that defended the interests of the common people.[128] Few of his co-partisans were persuaded, and by 1855 Denton was being denounced as a "traitor to the democratic party."[129]

More Democrats reconciled the inconsistency of their rhetorical commitments to equality and their political commitments to racial hierarchy and exclusion by doubling down on the vision of the white man's republic and endorsing the removal of black Americans from the country. Robert Dale Owen, an antislavery Jacksonian, former leader of the New York Working Men's Party, and a future Republican who would help draft the Fourteenth Amendment, argued in 1850 that black persons could "never obtain political rights here. They can never obtain social rights here. And for these reasons, I think, we ought not to have them amongst us. We ought not to have in our midst a race, daily increasing, who must of necessity remain disfranchised; a class of people to be taxed without being represented; on whom burdens are imposed, and who have no voice in deciding what these burdens shall be."[130] In order to render his opposition to black suffrage compatible with his adherence "to the motto of 'equal rights to all exclusive privileges to none,'" William Sawyer hoped "that the colored race should be colonized," so that the free black man could vote, be elected, and enjoy all the rights of citizens, "in his own place, and in his own order."[131] Colonization offered these Democrats hope that the country's founding principles could be made real, facilitating the eventual abolition of slavery and by making it no longer necessary to erect distinctions between men. "We might hope that our country would see the day," proclaimed one delegate, "when slavery on her soil would be extinct – her whole population white people, and this same government still enduring the glory of the world, and the fountain of infinite happiness."[132]

The departures of men such as Gass and Denton, and the reconciliation of equal rights with black exclusion through the narrative or promise of the white man's republic, contributed to a gradual partisan sorting on this issue: the most principled egalitarians left or were thrown out of the Democratic Party and – likely more common – Democrats who had

---

[128] Michigan, "Report of the Committee on State Affairs."
[129] *Detroit Free Press*, August 1, 1855, p. 2.
[130] Fowler, *Debates and Proceedings ... Indiana*, 231.
[131] Smith, *Debates and Proceedings ... Ohio*, 1: 56; 2: 553, 638.
[132] Agg, *Proceedings and Debates ... Pennsylvania*, 10: 24.

been willing to consider black political and civil rights changed their position to better reflect the increasingly clear stance of their party.

The Abolitionist Threat

Not only were Democrats in greater need of a script that could reconcile the claims of white supremacy and democratic equality, but their party also found itself in office when the abolitionist movement made its first and most dramatic foray into national politics. When the American Anti-Slavery Association began sending abolitionist newspapers and pamphlets to religious and civic leaders in the South and petitioning Northern members of Congress to abolish slavery in the District of Columbia, there was widespread outrage in the region and demands for a national response. With Democrats in the White House – and concerned about their prospects in the upcoming elections – responsibility fell primarily on their shoulders. As Gerald Henig has noted, while abolitionism was worrying to elites across the country, the Democrats "had a comparatively stronger national organization and were in control of the federal administration – a position which they were unwilling to jeopardize" by antagonizing the South.[133]

Ironically, however, it was the Whigs who first made support for black suffrage a line of partisan attack in the post-Missouri era. In the presidential election of 1836, they were running against Martin Van Buren and hoped to detach Southerners from the Democratic Party. Despite Van Buren's caginess during the Missouri crisis, he had taken positions necessary to advance in New York politics that were problematic for Southern slaveholders; in particular, he had voted in favor of black suffrage in the New York State constitutional convention. Whig meetings in the South were repeatedly told that his vote in favor of black suffrage revealed a "disposition" that was "totally irreconcilable with our views of policy or safety." "Upon this question of paramount importance to the South," charged one broadside, "he took ground, deliberately and advisedly, with the fanatics of the North," engrafting on to the constitution of New York "the odious principle of allowing negroes to vote." One Whig explained why Van Buren's vote was problematic: despite being "friends to the equal rights of man, we cannot so far forget our own social interests as to sanction the civil elevation of a class of men, who must always be to us dangerous political allies. Though the suffrage of the free negro may be exercised only in the State where he resides, still its influence will be felt throughout our country, and the time may come when

[133] Henig, "The Jacksonian Attitude toward Abolitionism," 48.

this distinct class of American population may contribute much to turn the scale of our political destinies."[134]

Amplifying Van Buren's sins was the fact that his vice presidential running mate, Richard Mentor Johnson, had lived in a "relationship" with enslaved women of color, introducing their daughters to society and even arranging marriages with white husbands. Northern Whigs made Johnson's "racial amalgamation" a central theme in their campaign, asking how it "would look in the eyes of civilized Europe" to have "yellow children" and a "wooly headed African wife" introduced to "the most fashionable and respectable society." Southern Whigs warned that Johnson's election would make it impossible to enforce norms of racial hierarchy, fearing that henceforth a man who admonished his son or complained to a neighbor for similar behavior would be met with the answer, "that 'the people' approve it." The prestige of the presidency would inaugurate a new "code of fashion" that would be incompatible with the "impassable barrier" needed to keep slaves in their place.[135]

Democrats excused Johnson's sexual relations – which were unquestionably coercive – as the sort of thing "most men have been equally criminal at some period of their lives."[136] And they explained Van Buren's votes as necessary to save the 1821 constitution from defeat at the hands of abolitionists. But they also insisted that "a majority of Van Buren's political friends" – Northern Democrats – had since come to recognize that free blacks were "unsafe repositories of the right of suffrage" and were now committed to opposing black voting rights.[137]

To prove his and his party's soundness on slavery and black citizenship, Van Buren released letters committing himself to oppose abolitionist priorities, hastily published in his campaign biography.[138] In a book intended to

[134] *National Banner and Nashville Whig* (Nashville, TN), May 29, 1835, p. 2; June 12, 1835, p. 3; James B. Latimer, "Martin Van Buren voted that every free negro be entitled to vote at the polls," August 11, 1836, http://mdhistory.net/msa_sc5807_oo/msa_s c5807_oo/pdf/msa_sc5807_oo-0131.pdf; William Shade, "'The Most Delicate and Exciting Topics': Martin Van Buren, Slavery and the Election of 1836," *Journal of the Early Republic* 18, no. 3 (1998): 459–84, 466–68.

[135] Thomas Brown, "The Miscegenation of Richard Mentor Johnson as an Issue in the National Election Campaign of 1835–1836," *Civil War History* 39, no. 1 (1993): 5–30, 5, 14.

[136] Ibid., 5, 18, 24.

[137] Shade, "The Most Delicate and Exciting Topics," 470; McFaul, "Expediency vs. Morality," 29.

[138] Shade, "The Most Delicate and Exciting Topics," 481; David J. Russo, "The Major Political Issues of the Jacksonian Period and the Development of Party Loyalty in Congress, 1830–1840," *Transactions of the American Philosophical Society* 62, no. 5 (1972): 351; William M. Holland, *The Life and Political Opinions of Martin Van Buren,*

help Van Buren's campaign, the prominent writer James K. Paulding –
a "very reliable pen for all things Democratic" – offered an exculpatory
history of slavery and the country's denial of black rights.[139] Paulding's
Slavery in the United States amounted to the "official statement of the
northern Democratic position on slavery and anti-slavery," according to
Alexander Saxton, one that fully embraced and further disseminated the
narrative tropes of the white man's republic.[140] "The government of the
United States, its institutions, and its privileges," wrote Paulding, "belong
of right wholly and exclusively to white men; for they were purchased, not
by the blood of the negroes, but by that of our fathers." People of African
descent, whether free or enslaved, "did not come within the scope and
meaning of the declaration of independence, which asserts the principle
'that all men are created equal.'" Paulding would be rewarded with the
position of secretary of the Navy.[141]

Van Buren won the presidency, but with considerably reduced
Southern support. Anxious to fortify their position in the region, party
leaders in Congress and the states pressed their members to support
a series of antiabolitionist resolutions. The leading Democrat in
Pennsylvania, Senator James Buchanan, endorsed resolutions offered by
John C. Calhoun as "a platform on which friends of the South in the
North could stand and defend themselves from the abolitionists."
The party's vote in favor was soon presented as evidence that
"Democrats, as a party, have repudiated the doctrines of the
Abolitionists." In July 1838, the Democratic members of Congress issued
an address in which they staked their reputation as a party on the defeat of
abolitionism and the threat it posed to the Union.[142]

Vice President of the United States, 2nd edn. (Hartford, CT: Belknap and Hamersley,
    1836), 352; Martin Van Buren, *Opinion of Martin Van Buren, Vice President of the
    United States, Upon the Powers and Duties of Congress, In Reference to the Abolition of
    Slavery Either in the Slave-Holding States or in the District of Columbia* (Washington,
    DC: n. p., 1836).
[139] Michael Black, "Review: James Kirk Paulding: Forgotten American," *New York History*
    88, no. 2 (2007): 207–13, 209; Ralph M. Aderman and Wayne R. Kime, *Advocate for
    America: The Life of James Kirke Paulding* (Selinsgrove, PA: Susquehanna State
    University Press, 2003).
[140] Saxton, *The Rise and Fall of the White Republic*, 151–52.
[141] James Kirke Paulding, *Slavery in the United States* (New York: Harper and Brothers,
    1836), 7–8, 42, 44, 93, 269.
[142] Russo, "The Major Political Issues of the Jacksonian Period," 18, 22; McFaul,
    "Expediency vs. Morality," 32; *Congressional Globe*, H. R., Appendix, 26th Cong.
    1st sess., January 16, 1840, 106; Henig, "The Jacksonian Attitude Toward
    Abolitionism," 48.

This was not simply the revelation of preexisting preferences among Democratic legislators. Politicians across the country were being made "aware of the larger implications of black suffrage," both to the Union and to their own careers.[143] Democratic leaders made clear that opposition to abolitionism and black citizenship would be a test of party regularity, and ambitious politicians responded by seeking to cultivate favor with the party leadership and the influential interests that supported it, taking extreme positions "in order to impress their political associates south of the Mason-Dixon line of their complete support and undiminishing friendship."[144] Levi Slamm, who was a leader of the Young Democracy movement that aggressively promoted American expansion as its "manifest destiny," announced that "we'll purge the Democratic party of the fanaticism which has been creeping into it for years, by separating the Negro suffrage fanatics from it, and drive them into the Federal [Whig] ranks where they belong.... The Democracy of Long Island, will not fraternize with any men or set of men who are in favor of Negro Suffrage or who blink the question." "Having glimpsed the specter of a schism between the North and South," writes historian Edward Widmer, "the Young Democracy poured all of its energy into allaying tensions with appeals to Americanism."[145]

Those who took a stance against slavery or in favor of black rights generally bore the costs. When the Democratic editor William Cullen Bryant endorsed giving free blacks the right to vote, he was accused of advancing doctrines "injurious to the best interests of the country," and he and his paper were effectively "excommunicated," denied a lucrative printing contract and ostracized by his former friends.[146] Thomas Morris, a Jacksonian Democrat from Ohio, had in the early 1830s endorsed colonization and written an article opposed to black suffrage in response to the Nat Turner rebellion. But in 1836, he introduced one of many petitions calling for the abolition of slavery in the District of Columbia.

---

[143] Wood, "A Sacrifice on the Altar of Slavery," 87.
[144] Henig, "The Jacksonian Attitude Toward Abolitionism," 48.
[145] *The Tribune*, January 12, 1846, p. 2; Edward L. Widmer, *Young America: The Flowering of Democracy in New York City* (New York: Oxford University Press, 1999), 48; Frederick Merk and Lois Bannister Merk, *Manifest Destiny and Mission in American History: A Reinterpretation* (Cambridge, MA: Harvard University Press, 1995 [1963]), 52–55.
[146] William Cullen Bryant II, *Power for Sanity: Selected Editorials of William Cullen Bryant, 1829–1861* (New York: Fordham University Press, 1994), xxi; William Cullen Bryant II and Thomas G. Voss, *The Letters of William Cullen Bryant, 1836–1849*, vol. 2 (New York: Fordham University Press, 1977), 7.

When attacked by Calhoun, Morris responded by accusing slaveholders of trying to gain control over the government for the purpose of expanding slavery. He was called to task by his state party, which demanded that he affirm his support for Democratic policies on banks, the independent Treasury, and its opposition to abolitionism. On the first two, he was a staunch Jacksonian, but while he noted his continued opposition to political and social equality for free people of color, he insisted that it was the duty of American citizens to seek the abolition of slavery. "If I am an abolitionist," he declared, "Jefferson made me so." In December 1838, Democrats in Ohio voted to replace the senator. Freed from party encumbrances, Morris chastised Northern Democrats for "throwing themselves into the arms of the Southern slave power," and insisted that if the "Declaration of Independence had said all men, but negroes, were created equal, Washington and La Fayette would never have lent their aid" to the revolutionary cause.[147]

The Ohio Democratic Convention of 1840 – which Morris denounced as the "Democratic proscriptive convention" for its reading of antislavery Democrats out of the party – defended slavery as recognized by the Constitution and declared that "the political action of anti slavery societies, is only a device for the overthrow of democracy."[148] This was a clear message to Democratic politicians in the state. The party nominee for governor, David Tod, had earlier in his career called for the repeal of the state's civil disabilities against people of color, but when this came to light he was called to task and forced to clarify that he "categorically denied any interest in 'Negro equality,'" and was adamantly opposed to black suffrage, to black men serving as jurors, and to black children attending common schools. His alienation of antislavery voters, however, likely cost him the election.[149]

In the Wisconsin territorial assembly in 1846, one Democrat proposed allowing black men to vote in a referendum on whether to seek statehood, only to be vigorously attacked by Moses M. Strong – who "commended himself to the favorable notice of many of the leaders of his party by his reckless and unscrupulous course as a partisan." Strong implored the

---

[147] Jonathan H. Earle, *Jacksonian Antislavery and the Politics of Free Soil, 1824–1854* (Chapel Hill: University of North Carolina Press, 2004), 37–46; *The Ohio Statesman* (Columbus, OH), October 5, 1838, p. 3, June 15, 1838, p. 3, January 23, 1841, p. 3; *Emancipator and Free Republican* (Boston), April 13, 1843, p. 196; *Congressional Globe*, 25th Cong., 3rd sess., Appendix, February 9, 1839, 168.

[148] *Emancipator and Free Republican*, Boston, April 13, 1843, p. 196; *The Ohio Statesman* (Columbus, OH), December 29, 1842, p. 3, January 10, 1840, p. 2.

[149] Middleton, *The Black Laws: Race and Legal Process in Ohio*, 135, 139.

assembly not to send a message to the South "that Wisconsin is favorably disposed to the abolition movement." In the ensuring statehood convention, he gave "a violent speech in opposition to negro suffrage," declaring that he "was in favor of no half-way measures with [abolitionists], but would give war – war to the knife, and the knife to the hilt!" A few years later, attempts to build antislavery coalitions of Democrats and Whigs in the state, pledged to "universal suffrage without invidious distinctions on account of religion, birth, or color," foundered when the Democrats withdrew, having been "warned they would be drummed out of the party if they persisted in their mutiny."[150]

During the New York State constitutional convention of 1846, Southern newspapers associated with the Polk administration hoped that the property qualification allowing wealthy African Americans to vote would be "stricken entirely off." "We call upon the N.Y. Democracy," wrote the *Richmond Enquirer*, "to stand their ground ... on this important point." Antislavery papers noted with disgust that were New York Democrats to refuse "this little chore for the Slave Power," they "would never get any more offices at the hands of Polk and the Land Pirate Democracy of the South. So down on your marrow bones, ye sturdy Sham Democrats of the Empire State! The SLAVE POWER speaks: *Do you hear?*"[151] During the convention, former New York governor William C. Bouck reported a draft suffrage clause that would have imposed a strict racial qualification. He was soon selected by national and state Democratic leaders "to fill the United States Office of Sub-Treasurer of the Revenues of the Republic collected at New York." The *Daily Tribune* remarked scornfully that "had he left out white would he have gotten that berth from a President who wages war against Mexico to restore Negro Slavery where it has been abolished?"[152] The full disenfranchisement was defeated, but so too was an effort to strike the word "white."

---

[150] Moses McCure Strong, *History of the Territory of Wisconsin from 1836 to 1848* (Madison, WI: Democrat Printing Co., 1885), 215, 558; Kenneth W. Duckett, "Moses M. Strong, A Story of Optimism and Failure in Early Wisconsin" (PhD diss., University of Wisconsin, Madison, 1951); Michael J. McManus, *Political Abolitionism in Wisconsin, 1840–1861* (Kent, OH: Kent State University Press, 1998), 21, 25; Silvana R. Siddalli, *Frontier Democracy: Constitutional Conventions in the Old Northwest* (Cambridge: Cambridge University Press, 2015), 57, 159; Quaife, *Convention of 1846*, 215; Olbrich, *Development of Sentiment on Negro Suffrage*, 88; Eugene W. Leach, "Marshall Mason Strong, Racine Pioneer," *Wisconsin Magazine of History* 5 (1921): 329–47.

[151] *Barre Patriot* (Barre, MA), January 2, 1846, p. 2.

[152] *New-York Tribune*, October 2, 1846, p. 4; Olbrich, *Development of Sentiment on Negro Suffrage*, 76.

The Boston *Emancipator and Free Republican* believed that there were many Democrats "in less conspicuous stations" than Morris who had been chastised for defending black rights. But they also complained that Northern Democratic cupidity had led fewer to do so than they expected, giving credence to the assertions of James Buchanan "that the peculiar institutions of the South have no other support beyond their own limits, except that which is afforded by the Democracy of the North." Antislavery activists denounced those who supported black disenfranchisement as "the bloodhounds of the South," who "for the sake of obtaining Southern favor and party promotion ... are willing to bay on the track of the poor colored man. These men know they have no valid reason for thus outraging human nature and human rights, the principles of Democracy and the rights of God. They do it to please the South and keep good their party."[153]

Conflict Extension and Representation

The Democratic Party's embrace of the white man's republic was also driven by a process of conflict extension and dynamic representation. Precisely because of the high stakes to their Union and party – and the material and psychological investments these entailed – lawmakers ratcheted up the intensity of antiblack rhetoric while casting opposition to abolition and black suffrage in emotionally charged terms, suggesting abolitionists wanted the desecration of the Union and the degradation of working-class whites through labor competition and interracial sexual intercourse. The rhetoric seems calculated to evoke anger against abolitionists and persons of color, and was perhaps especially likely to encourage white constituents to respond to racist rhetoric and to bring their racial prejudices to bear in evaluating candidates. This in turn would lead Democratic legislators in particular, whose constituents were especially subjected to racist discourse and whose more racist activists became more prominent as the party's antagonism to black Americans intensified, to be less willing to take positions that could be seen as supportive of racial egalitarianism.[154]

---

[153] *Emancipator and Free Republican* (Boston), April 13, 1843, p. 196; *Waukesha American Freeman* (Waukesha, WI), February 23, 1848.

[154] Conflict extension refers to the process by which elite-level conflict along a particular policy issue extends to encompass other issues, producing polarization not simply along the primary issue dimension separating the parties but along a series of other issues as well. As elites polarize, the cues they provide activists and, to a lesser degree, attentive publics are clarified, leading to shifts in attitudes for partisans. Geoffrey C. Layman and Thomas M. Carsey, "Party Polarization and 'Conflict Extension' in the American

In organizing opposition to abolitionism, Democrats framed the fight in terms they expected would resonate with the material interests, commitments to the Union, and civic statuses of their constituents. Party leaders regularly urged "moderate men" in their communities to counteract the growing "influence of sectional abolitionism," and in the 1830s they organized dozens of public meetings of prominent citizens and public officials in the hopes of reassuring Southerners and of giving a "moderating" influence to public opinion.[155]

Thousands of "moderate men" from all social classes responded to the call, some of them wielding influence in organizations whose membership could be educated in the dangers of abolitionism and black rights. Ely Moore of New York, the first president of the National Trades Union and an ambitious Democratic member of Congress, accused abolitionists of risking civil war and being willing to undermine the civic status and economic well-being of working-class whites.[156] The Irish Bishop of New York came out against abolitionism on the grounds that it threatened a Union in which his parishioners were deeply invested.[157] These frames were picked up by others, who sought to connect their own priorities to the expressed concerns of the country's political and religious elite. A meeting of Irish miners in Pottsville, Pennsylvania, repeated the bishop's criticisms verbatim and added that neither they nor "our wives and daughters" would look "upon the negroes as 'Brethren,'" as the Irish Liberator Daniel O'Connell had urged them to do.[158] The miners were about to engage in the first large-scale strike of the anthracite industry and needed powerful allies; they asked that the address be

Electorate," *American Journal of Political Science* 46, no. 4 (2002): 786–802; Geoffrey C. Layman et al., "Activists and Conflict Extension in American Party Politics," *American Political Science Review* 104, no. 2 (2010): 324–46. A similar dynamic is what Michael Tesler describes as the spillover of racialization, whereby racial considerations become more important to political evaluations across a range of issues. Michael Tesler, *Post-Racial or Most-Racial: Race and Politics in the Obama Era* (Chicago: University of Chicago Press, 2016). On the importance of anger in leading to racialized attitudes, see Antoine J. Banks, *Anger and Racial Politics: The Emotional Foundation of Racial Attitudes in America* (Cambridge: Cambridge University Press, 2014).

[155] Fowler, *Debates and Proceedings ... Indiana*, 237; Shade, "The Most Delicate and Exciting Topics," 473.

[156] Henig, "The Jacksonian Attitude toward Abolitionism," 44–45, 47; Moore, *Remarks of Ely Moore*.

[157] John R. G. Hassard, *Life of the Most Reverend John Hughes, D. D. First Archbishop of New York* (New York: D. Appleton and Co., 1866), 436.

[158] Angela F. Murphy, *American Slavery, Irish Freedom: Abolition, Immigrant Citizenship, and the Transatlantic Movement for Irish Repeal* (Baton Rouge: Louisiana State University Press, 2010), 89–90; Roediger, *Wages of Whiteness*, 136.

sent to papers throughout the country, and reached out to local Democratic politicians to negotiate with employers on their behalf. One of these in turn wrote an article praising the address and asking "Irishmen in America" whether they were prepared "to see this sacred fabric, cemented even by your own blood, mouldering in ruins from civil war?" William Lloyd Garrison noted worriedly that Southern Democratic slaveholders were, in return, giving monetary support to the Irish Repeal movement, hoping to win Irish support in opposing abolitionism.[159]

Another vitally important constituency of "moderate men" in the North were the businessmen and merchants engaged in the export and manufacture of cotton or conducting business in the South.[160] One prominent New York merchant made the stakes clear to an antislavery activist in 1835: "There are millions upon millions of dollars due from Southerners to the merchants and mechanics of this city alone, the payment of which would be jeopardized by any rupture between the North and the South. We cannot afford, sir, to let you and your associates succeed in your endeavor to overthrow slavery. It is not a matter of principle with us. It is a matter of business necessity." Already Southern storekeepers and merchants were organizing boycotts of Northern dry-goods dealers or any other good produced by a known supporter of abolitionism, and were threatening to start making most of their purchases in Philadelphia, where the residents, municipal, and state governments could be counted on to put down abolitionism by any means available.[161] "We mean, sir," the merchant concluded, "to put you Abolitionists down, – by fair means if we can, by foul means it we must." There would be several antiabolitionist riots in New York City and throughout the North that year.[162]

Antiblack and antiabolitionist rioting had occurred before, at the turn of the century and again in the 1820s, but there was a sharp increase in the

---

[159] *The Southron* (Jackson, MS), March 24, 1842, p. 2; *The Liberator*, August 5, 1842, p. 1; Grace Palladino, *Another Civil War: Labor, Capital, and the State in the Anthracite Regions of Pennsylvania, 1840–1868* (New York: Fordham University Press, 2006), 48–49.

[160] Cotton was a national enterprise, amounting to 67 percent of American exports in 1860, vital for New England's growing textile industry, and with New York City profiting immensely as the site of financial intermediation for its transportation and export. For a contemporary account of its national implications, see *New York Times*, 1861, "The Effect of Secession upon the Commercial Relations Between the North and South, and upon Each Section."

[161] Bertram Wyatt-Brown, "The Abolitionists' Postal Campaign of 1835," *Journal of Negro History* 50, no. 4 (1965): 227–38, 234–35.

[162] Samuel J. May, *Some Recollections of Our Anti-Slavery Conflict* (Boston: Fields, Osgood and Co., 1869), 128; Leo Hirsch, Jr., "New York and the National Slavery Problem," *Journal of Negro History* 16, no. 4 (1931): 454–73.

1830s as local antagonisms and white racism were refocused against the antislavery movement by Democratic politicians, the American Colonization Society – which saw financial contributions disappear in the face of antislavery criticism – and "gentlemen of property and standing" worried about relations with the South. When the Georgia-born Secretary of State John Forsyth wrote Van Buren in 1835 to warn that the antislavery movement was encouraging Southern separatism, he beseeched the vice president to "set the imps to work," to use his vast patronage network to defend Southern interests by encouraging violence against abolitionists.[163] In Cincinnati, "fears about the city's dependence on Southern commerce" led "the mayor, the party press, and Jacksonian officials" to organize mob action against the abolitionist editor James Birney.[164] Between 1830 and 1840, antiabolitionist and antiblack riots constituted approximately 30 percent of the country's total, and while local conflicts and antagonisms drove most of these, a considerable number were organized by political elites who warned of civil war but also of intermarriage and the social and economic degradation of whites.[165]

In their speeches and addresses, Democrats framed black suffrage in terms calculated to threaten whites' civic statuses, as aiming at the destruction of a Union in which they were psychologically invested and as an attempt by black Americans to intrude into the social spaces of respectable society. This process would begin at the polls, the legislature, and the jury box, and would radiate out from there to the home and family. If black men were allowed to

[163] He also suggested that "instead of mobbing the poor blacks, a little more mob discipline of the white incendiaries would be wholesome." Harriet Allen Butler, *A Retrospect of Forty Years, 1825–1865* (New York: Charles Scribner's Sons, 1911), 78–79.

[164] Stewart, "The Emergence of Racial Modernity and the Rise of the White North," 193; Leonard Richards, *Gentlemen of Property and Standing: Anti-Abolition Mobs in Jacksonian America* (New York: Oxford University Press, 1970), 31, 39; David Grimsted, *American Mobbing, 12828–1865: Toward Civil War* (New York: Oxford University Press, 1998), 10, 35, 58, 61; Carl E. Prince, "The Great 'Riot Year': Jacksonian Democracy and Patterns of Violence in 1834," *Journal of the Early Republic* 5, no. 1 (1985): 1–19, 13; Susan Wyly-Jones, "The 1835 Anti-Abolition Meetings in the South: A New Look at the Controversy over the Abolition Postal Campaign," *Civil War History* 47, no. 4 (2001): 289–309; John Runcie, "'Hunting the Nigs' in Philadelphia: The Race Riot of August 1834," *Pennsylvania History: A Journal of Mid-Atlantic Studies* 39, no. 2 (1972): 187–218; Linda Kerber, "Abolitionists and Amalgamators: The New York City Race Riots of 1834," *New York History* 48, no. 1 (1967): 28–39; Hirsch, "New York and the National Slavery Problem," 457–58.

[165] The riots, whether organized by elites or not, depended heavily on white racism both for their justification and for mobilizing the mobs. Sheldon G. Levy, *Political Violence in the United States, 1819–1968* (Ann Arbor, MI: Inter-University Consortium for Political and Social Research computer file, 1991).

vote, then "respectable citizens" would have no choice but to stay home: "such persons will not go to the polls and jostle with negroes," they would not deign to vote alongside "a posse of shoeblacks."[166] As the respectable classes withdrew, they would no longer be able to give direction to public opinion. The increasing importance of black voters would in turn require promises of local offices and patronage appointments. "What is the end of political power," asked John L. Carey in 1838, "except to secure social advantages?"[167] As soon as blacks were elected, the door would be opened "and you have them in your social circle. What man would like to see his daughter encircled by one of those sable gentlemen, breathing in her ear the soft accents of love?" Or to see a free black man act as a judge or juror, "deciding upon your *rights*, your *properties*, and *your lives*."[168]

Democrats were somewhat more likely than Whigs to argue that black Americans had to be denied political rights in order to protect the material interests of the white working classes. Cultivating the political support of black Americans would require government jobs, work on government-supported projects, employment in enterprises whose owners were aligned with one party or the other, or any of the numerous ways in which the parties and their wealthy backers might patronize a constituency. These jobs would then not be available to the brokers who distributed patronage to white constituencies, while the recognition given to black workers would invite more into the state, intensifying competition over employment. William Leggett, the Democratic editor of the *Evening Post*, initially opposed emancipation and black suffrage on the grounds that black workers who moved into the state would "throw the white workingman out of employment, or at least depreciate the value of labor to an extent that would be fatal to their prosperity."[169] A. G. Brown of Ohio warned that black suffrage would "have a tendency to degrade labor," while Ely Moore argued that capitalists would ally with abolitionists in order to suppress the wages of white workers.[170] "The capitalists will fill the land with these living machines,"

[166] Agg, *Proceedings and Debates ... Pennsylvania*, 9: 368, 2: 549.
[167] John L. Carey, *Some Thoughts Concerning Domestic Slavery* (Baltimore: Joseph Lewis, 1838), 83.
[168] Agg, *Proceedings and Debates ... Pennsylvania*, 3:88, 2:478, 9:328, 10:22–24, 114; *Proceedings and Debates ... Michigan*, 290.
[169] Henig, "The Jacksonian Attitude Toward Abolitionism," 54–55.
[170] Smith, *Debates and Proceedings ... Ohio*, 1:58; *Congressional Globe*, 24th Cong., 1st sess., Appendix, March 7, 1836, p. 16; 25th Cong., 3rd sess., Appendix, February 4, 1839, 241.

warned one California Democrat who opposed allowing free persons of color into the state. "Their labor will go to enrich the few, and impoverish the many: it will drive the poor and honest laborer from their field."[171]

The degradation they warned of was not narrowly economic. "If gentlemen were desirous to see the negroes on a level with whites," declared one delegate, "give these negroes the right of suffrage, and your sons and your daughters will, by and by, become waiters and cooks for them. Yes! For these black gentry – that will be the result of it."[172] The warning was not just that black men and women would take jobs reserved for whites but that they would invert the racial hierarchy. "Who was to be affected by" black suffrage, asked the Whig delegate Horatio Stow. "Men of high condition? The men of wealth, who were removed far from ordinary connection with labor, would feel it very little. It would extend mainly to those who labor day by day; it would reach that class of citizens and draw them down to give a doubtful elevation to another class."[173] This line of argument was also used to defend class-based voting restrictions for whites as well, with delegates insisting that abolition of a taxpaying qualification would degrade the "honest, industrious laborer" in order to benefit the poor white man: "*There* is where the distinction is to be produced, and not among the rich, because they are too far distant to feel it."[174] But the logic was the same in either case: the right to vote was a marker of civic status that enabled those who possessed it to claim the rank and prestige of citizenship, differentiating themselves from others within their communities.

Immigrant constituencies were reminded that the democratic character of the United States provided for a better life than they had in Europe and that it rested on a Union that abolitionism threatened. Paulding detailed the laws that oppressed the European peasantry, reminding his readers that America was a truly emancipatory project that needed to be preserved: "It is in the United States alone," he brazenly concluded his defense of slavery, "that labour claims and receives its adequate rewards."[175] American newspapers regularly described the "vast difference in favor of even the negro slaves of our happy country" over the "poor and laboring classes" of free-born Englishmen.[176] George Shellito

[171] Olbrich, *Development of Sentiment on Negro Suffrage*, 91; see also *Proceedings and Debates ... Michigan*, 292, 294; Fowler, *Debates and Proceedings ... Indiana*, 238.
[172] Agg, *Proceedings and Debates ... Pennsylvania*, 10: 114.
[173] Bishop and Attree, *Debates and Proceedings ... New York*, 1033.
[174] Agg, *Proceedings and Debates ... Pennsylvania*, 2: 518.
[175] Paulding, *Slavery in the United States*, 249–266.
[176] *Mississippi Free Trader* (Natchez, MS), July 19, 1843, p. 1.

attacked a delegate who had spoken positively about England as a country without racial discrimination, asking, "How many of her gallant soldiers, who had returned home, covered with wounds and glory, after fighting her battles, were permitted to vote? Let the gentleman answer that question, before he poured out his sympathy on these miserable blacks."[177] Lawmakers stressed that American democracy was a vulnerable experiment that European monarchs and local would-be aristocrats hoped would fail. "Abolitionists and the advocates of negro suffrage," they warned, were going to make a reality of the aristocratic prophecy that "'republicanism must be disgraced' – May they and all other enemies to the self-government of man, receive the pity and contempt they so richly merit, at the hands of a free people."[178] The Irish in particular were regularly implored not to "rashly ... *jeopardise the existence* and disturb the harmony of a country whose protection we have sought.... The high admiration [the Irish] feel for the *essential characteristics* of the American Constitution, is too deep and controlling *to allow them to engage in a question* which imperils the continuance of the only free government in the world."[179]

The status of "white" in America had long been defined by way of its antonym "black," the content of which signified that one was available for enslavement or under normal circumstances would be enslaved; "white" had thus long borne the implication of being "free." It was now receiving additional meaning, defined again by reference to blackness, as constituting the social basis of a democratic republican state, whose arms and efforts were needed to defend it: "the friends of the UNION – the friends of good order – and all those opposed to the demoralizing and disgusting tenets of abolitionism.... We have shown to our southern brethren that Pennsylvania can never be 'bowed to the dark spirit of abolitionism' – that she will stand fast by the sacred compact made by our fathers, and never endorse the doctrine ... as to its being either void or contrary to the Declaration of Independence."[180]

Abolitionists were accused of wanting to "elevate the negro to a full and complete equality of political rights," which had as its "necessary corollary" a social equality that would result in "amalgamation." This

---

[177] Agg, *Proceedings and Debates ... Pennsylvania*, 9: 114.
[178] Bishop and Attree, *Debates and Proceedings ... New York*, 1019; *The Keystone* (Harrisburg, PA), July 25, 1838, p. 3.
[179] *The Liberator*, February 25, 1842, p. 1.   [180] *The Liberator*, November 2, 1835, p. 2.

was repeatedly claimed as the end goal of abolitionists, who "would begin it with the laboring class" of whites, throwing them and black laborers into competition and – more dangerously – association and intercourse. "This morbid spirit of niggerology is the worst foe of American liberty."[181]

Democratic antiabolitionist rhetoric complemented and gave broader significance to changing racial formations among whites. As an extensive literature has shown, the dislocations and economic stress of the antebellum period deepened the racial divisions among the American working classes, as white men who had been raised in a republican tradition that equated freedom with economic independence were "driven to seek identifiable inferiors if only to guarantee themselves at least some status."[182] As one Pennsylvanian who supported black suffrage noted, "the only pre-eminence" that working class whites had over blacks was their color. "Take away that pre-eminence, and they possess no advantage over them, and have nothing to say. And there lies the cause of the jealousy, and of the mobs."[183]

This was now receiving an aggressive validation on the campaign, in public meetings, in the public addresses of the Democratic Party, and in its aligned newspapers and interests. As the *New York Tribune* noted, the "clamor against 'Niggers,' is naturally Loco Foco," i.e., Democratic: "hundreds of votes are won and retained by Loco Focoism, through its abuse of 'Niggers.'"[184] "Wherever in our state there is no pervading anti-slavery sentiment," it reported on another occasion, "there the loco-focos are red mouthed and vociferous against black suffrage at all hazards. Hostility to 'niggers' is their greeting card."[185]

The strength of racism had always acted as a constraint on legislators, who were aware that favoring black rights could leave them vulnerable to attacks from challengers. Still, it was elected representatives who had to decide whether to support black rights, and as we have seen many delegates and representatives did exactly this. But the intensifying racism

---

[181] Daily Iowa State Democrat (Davenport, IA), June 4, 1857, p. 2; B. F. Morris, *The Life of Thomas Morris* (Cincinnati, OH: Moore and Co., 1856), 158.

[182] Carl N. Degler, "Racism in the United States: An Essay Review," *The Journal of Southern History* 38, no. 1 (1972): 101–8, 103; George M. Frederickson, *White Supremacy: A Comparative Study in American and South African History* (New York: Oxford University Press, 1981), 155.

[183] Agg, *Proceedings and Debates ... Pennsylvania*, 10:90.

[184] *Richmond Enquirer* (Richmond, VA), October 5, 1847, p. 4.

[185] *New York Weekly Tribune*, April 8, 1846; Phyllis F. Field, *The Politics of Race in New York: The Struggle for Black Suffrage in the Civil War Era* (Ithaca, NY: Cornell University Press, 1982), 52.

likely strengthened the electoral constraint felt by many legislators. "The great body of our white voters," noted a New York Democrat, "feel that self-preservation itself, forbids [black suffrage]. And call it what you please, they are right."[186] "A very decided majority of the voters of Milwaukee" were opposed to black suffrage, noted a Democratic representative from that city; "believing as he did that a great majority of his constituents were opposed to the measure, he could not give it his vote."[187] It was a "duty I owe to my constituents and my own feelings," stated a Kansas Democrat, to do everything in his power to oppose "negro equality, negro emigration into this State, and to discourage the free negroes from here remaining."[188] With their party leadership and base strongly opposed, a declining portion of Democrats were willing to risk contravening the strictures of the white man's republic.

"BACKWARDS TOWARDS SLAVERY" – DISENFRANCHISEMENT IN PENNSYLVANIA

The dynamics of coalition maintenance, top-down pressure, and popular racism were revealed in the Pennsylvania convention of 1837–38. Despite the absence of an explicit racial qualification, free men of color faced considerable difficulty voting in Pennsylvania. In Philadelphia, tax officials would often refuse to assess the property of free black men, "exempting" them from taxes and in the process denying their right to vote; this was compounded by the threats of local residents, who warned of violence if black men were to approach the polls. Outside of Philadelphia, however, they could and did vote, and the question of black suffrage had not been debated during the years-long campaign for the convention; as one memorial from free black men would note, "There has been no general expression of the people demanding [disenfranchisement]; nothing has occurred to render it necessary."[189]

---

[186] Bishop and Attree, *Debates and Proceedings ... New York*, 1019.

[187] Quaife, *Convention of 1846*, 215, 227.

[188] Kansas, *Kansas Constitutional Convention: A Reprint of the Proceedings and Debates of the Convention which Framed the Constitution of Kansas at Wyandotte in July, 1859* (Topeka: Kansas State Printing Plant, 1920), 302; Agg, *Proceedings and Debates ... Pennsylvania*, 9:357; Fowler, *Debates and Proceedings ... Indiana*, 231, 77; Smith, *Debates and Proceedings ... Ohio*, 2:638; Wisconsin, *Journal of the Convention to Form a Constitution for the State of Wisconsin, With a Sketch of the Debates, Begun and Held at Madison, on the Fifteenth Day of December, Eighteen Hundred and Forty-Seven* (Madison, WI: Tenney, Smith and Holt, 1848), 181–82.

[189] Eric Ledell Smith, "The End of Black Voting Rights in Pennsylvania: African Americans and the Pennsylvania Constitutional Convention of 1837–1838," *Pennsylvania History:*

When the convention opened, many delegates expressed a reluctance to discuss the issue of black suffrage, which they expected would attract unwanted antislavery or Southern attention. While a few delegates moved to insert the word "white" in the proposed suffrage clause, party leaders in the convention repeatedly requested that they drop it. One Democrat withdrew his proposed racial disenfranchisement at the "request of some of his friends," while a Whig withdrew his own proposal when he too was persuaded that it would be better to leave a divisive issue "slumbering." But Democrat Benjamin Martin persisted. He acknowledged that "there was no disposition among members to enter into the discussion of this topic," but insisted that it was too important to be passed over: "The situation of the country, the fate and destiny of elections will, in future, depend pretty much on the fate of this amendment." Martin based his argument largely on the grounds that the African race was and would forever be inferior to "white citizens." "We are the descendants of Europe – some of us of English origin, others of Irish, Scotch, German, and Spanish. Our sires were the masters of the civilized world."[190]

Delegates of all parties urged Martin to withdraw the amendment, warning that it would "consume much time and produce great excitement," but also that antislavery sentiment in the state was currently so inflamed that "adoption of the amendment would, no doubt, prevent the people from accepting the Constitution." John Dickey, a former Democrat recently expelled from the party, accused Martin of violating the express instructions of his Philadelphia constituents by bringing up an issue they had not debated.[191] In any case, Martin's motion was *defeated* by a vote of sixty-one to forty-nine, the result of a complete "lack of public concern."[192] Nearly 20 percent of Democrats voted against it, while only one Whig and five Anti-Masons, a Northern party in coalition with the Whigs, voted in favor.

A few weeks later, a memorial from black activists in Pittsburgh opposed to disenfranchisement was introduced in the convention. Democrat Charles

A Journal of Mid-Atlantic Studies 65, no. 3 (1998): 279–99, 281–82, 284, 286; Malone, *Between Freedom and Bondage*, 81, 90–91; Julie Winch, *A Gentleman of Color: The Life of James Forten* (New York: Oxford University Press, 2002); David McBride, "Black Protest Against Racial Politics: Gardner, Hinton, and Their Memorial of 1838," *Pennsylvania History: A Journal of Mid-Atlantic Studies* 46, no. 2 (1979): 149–162, 160.

[190] Agg, *Proceedings and Debates . . . Pennsylvania*, 2: 357, 472, 479, 481, 484, 549, 561, 3: 30, 83–85.

[191] Agg, *Proceedings and Debates . . . Pennsylvania*, 3: 86–87, 89; Wood, "A Sacrifice on the Altar of Slavery," 96n28.

[192] Edward Price, "The Black Voting Rights Issue in Pennsylvania, 1780–1900," *The Pennsylvania Magazine of History and Biography* 100, no. 3 (1976): 356–73, 360.

Ingersoll, who had recently won praise from Southern Democratic leaders for a Fourth of July oration pledging the Democratic Party to the defense of slavery, moved that the memorial be sent to a special committee and, most importantly, not be printed. Black suffrage "involved questions of the utmost importance not only to the character of our deliberations, but to that of the State, and to the Union itself," and for this reason he implored the delegates to act with "the utmost circumspection."[193] Printing the memorial, warned James Porter, "would serve no purpose, but to circulate inflammatory ideas. If it was printed, it would, no doubt, be hailed in the abolition papers – which loaded our tables, and were furnished us, without our agency, and GOD knows, at whose expense – as a great triumph, and be proclaimed by the abolitionists, far and near, that this body was in favor of their views." He claimed to have once "believed, in the truth of the declaration, that 'all men are created equal,'" and as an election judge had even approved of black men as voters. But he interpreted his paramount priority as the preservation of the Union, which had led him to the position that black disenfranchisement was a "courtesy, due from us to our sister states." Still, the convention voted in favor of printing the memorial and then adjourned for the summer.[194]

The *Doylestown Democrat* in Bucks County now began warning that black suffrage would spell "doom" for the party in local elections, and their complaints were soon being reprinted in the South, where newspapers called black suffrage "a *black spot* upon the escutcheon of Pennsylvania" which they "would be pleased to see speedily eradicated."[195] The *Democrat*'s efforts gained new impetus when the party's candidates for state and local offices were defeated by "Anti-Mason/Whig or 'Anti-Van Buren'" nominees, and the paper loudly accused black men of coming to the polls armed and shouting warnings to shoot anyone who tried to deny their right to vote: "Is such conduct of negroes to be tolerated? Whoever heard of any white man going to the polls with his gun loaded, in order to shoot any person who should question his right to vote? Tolerate such inducements ... and they will make the very streets run with white man's blood."[196]

---

[193] Wood, "A Sacrifice on the Altar of Slavery," 87; *Washington Globe*, July 10, 1835; Shade, "The Most Delicate and Exciting Topics," 471; Agg, *Proceedings and Debates ... Pennsylvania*, 3: 683, 688.

[194] Agg, *Proceedings and Debates ... Pennsylvania*, 3: 693–96, 684–86.

[195] Wood, "A Sacrifice on the Altar of Slavery," 76, 90.

[196] Smith, "The End of Black Voting Rights," 289–90; Lyle Rosenberger, "Black Suffrage in Bucks County: The Election of 1837," *Bucks County Historical Society Journal* (Spring 1975): 28–36; Price, "The Black Voting Rights Issue in Pennsylvania," 358.

Local Democrats set out to organize an uproar. They called a series of public meetings where they alleged that their candidates had been defeated by illegal votes cast at the behest of abolitionists and British agents. These were thoroughly Democratic Party affairs. An initial meeting presided over by the soon-to-be Democratic member of Congress John Davis, and organized by Democratic officials and prominent Democratic attorneys, hired agents to organize a petition campaign and resolved to file a lawsuit contesting the election. At a subsequent meeting, "about six hundred people" discussed the memorial, including many German farmers and mechanics "who declared that they were as ready now to maintain and defend their sacred rights" as they had been during the Revolution. "The citizens unanimously approved resolutions opposing Negro voters, British influence, abolition, and to contest the previous election."[197]

One of the main organizers of the campaign was Samuel D. Ingham, the owner of the *Doylestown Democrat*, secretary of the treasury under Jackson, and Calhoun's "kingpin" in the state. Calhoun now urged Ingham to use his "best efforts to give proper direction to events," as he had done years earlier during the nullification crisis.[198] The election case would be heard by Judge John Fox, who had not only attended the Bucks County meeting but drafted the preamble to its memorial. Fox was also bankrolling Ingham's *Doylestown Democrat* and was "known as a very active politician" in the Democratic Party.[199]

In late December, Fox issued his opinion, which amounted to a straightforward recitation of the white man's republic: a free man of color could not be a "*citizen*, and a *freeman*" of Pennsylvania because the founding of the commonwealth had been accomplished by "*a community of white men exclusively.*" The state's revolutionary founders had acted "as if no such beings as negroes were in existence" – although these same founders passed an abolition law that intentionally did not disenfranchise persons of color – and only whites "*and their successors of the same caste*" could be considered members of the body politic. Nor were free people of

[197] Price, "The Black Voting Rights Issue in Pennsylvania," 358; Smith, "The End of Black Voting Rights," 290, 291; W. W. H. Davis, "Negro Suffrage in Pennsylvania in 1837," *The Era Magazine: An Illustrated Monthly* 12, no. 4 (1903): 384–87, 386; *The Keystone*, November 8, 1837, p. 3.

[198] During the nullification crisis, Ingham had tried to drum up popular support for South Carolina. Marguerite G. Bartlett, "The Chief Phases of Pennsylvania Politics in the Jacksonian Era" (PhD diss., University of Pennsylvania, 1919), 32; Wood, "A Sacrifice on the Altar of Slavery," 90.

[199] Agg, *Proceedings and Debates ... Pennsylvania*, 3: 700, 10: 48; Davis, "Negro Suffrage in Pennsylvania in 1837," 386.

color American citizens, for who could argue that the convention that
drafted the US Constitution, composed of so many slaveholders, could
have "contemplated that a negro was his equal in rights and privileges?"
Finally, free persons of color could not have been included within the
terms of the Declaration of Independence, as *"all the states whose delegates made that declaration were slave holding states."*[200]

Ambitious Democrats in the state, most notably Senator James
Buchanan, believed their aspirations to national office hinged on keeping
the state ranged against abolitionism. After Fox's decision, local
Democrats wrote Buchanan with the good news, and within a few months
both Fox and Ingham were invited to Washington to meet with John
Calhoun. Fox's decision would be praised in Southern and Democratic
newspapers as an "independent and righteous opinion" that "would do
honor to any Bench in America." "No State in the Union," wrote the
Calhoun-supported *Washington Chronicle*, "can boast of two more able
advocates of the old State Rights doctrine."[201]

When the convention reconvened in November, it was met with the
results of the Democratic petition campaign. Figure 4.5 shows the cumu-
lative number of petitions introduced in the convention, across four categories: against black suffrage, in defense of black suffrage, in support of
securing the right to a jury trial for black persons claimed to be fugitive
slaves, and in support of better securing free assembly from antiabolitionist
mobs. Tobias Sellers and John Sterigere, delegates from Montgomery
County – just south of Bucks and controlled by the Democrats – were
the most active in introducing antisuffrage petitions, for which the latter
was denounced as "the advocate of slavery doctrines."[202] Over 70 percent
of the pro-disenfranchisement petitions came from these two counties, in
addition to some from Philadelphia and a scattering from elsewhere.

Democratic organizers clearly framed the petitions in terms that were
meant to tap into and channel white racism. Many of them only obliquely
mentioned voting rights, demanding instead that the convention oppose

[200] *Opinion of the Hon. John Fox, President of the Judicial District Composed of the
Counties of Bucks and Montgomery, Against the Exercise of Negro Suffrage in
Pennsylvania* (Harrisburg, PA: Packer, Barrett, and Parke, 1838), 5, 7, 8, 9, 10,
11–12, 13.
[201] *Richmond Enquirer* (Richmond, VA), January 23, 1838, p. 2; *The Southern Patriot*
(Charleston, SC), January 15, 1838, p. 2; *The Daily Picayune* (New Orleans, LA),
January 20, 1838, p. 2; Wood, "A Sacrifice on the Altar of Slavery," 90–91;
Philadelphia National Enquirer, February 8, 1838, p. 88.
[202] Agg, *Proceedings and Debates … Pennsylvania*, 10: 48.

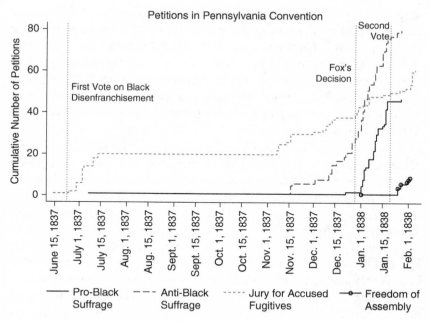

FIGURE 4.5 Petition Campaigns in Pennsylvania, 1837–38

"racial amalgamation," suggesting to the signatories that the convention was encouraging sexual intermixture. Local abolitionists, believing that no effort to disenfranchise black men would be seriously proposed, had earlier decided to devote their efforts to securing the right to trial by jury to black persons claimed as fugitive slaves. Only after Judge Fox's decision did they begin to redirect their efforts, and while they matched the pace of their opponents, they lagged by at least a month and were unable to catch up. Nor could they match the prominence of the signatories in favor of disenfranchisement: the unrecognized names on the petitions in favor of black suffrage were not held in equal esteem as the wealthy merchants of Philadelphia or the local officials of Bucks and Montgomery counties.[203]

In January 1838, the convention again picked up the draft of the proposed suffrage article. With state and national party leaders now paying close attention, the Democrats stood almost fully united.[204] In defending a new proposal to insert the word "white," delegates relied heavily on the

[203] Ibid., 1: 423–24, 10: 48–50, 12: 64.
[204] *The Pennsylvanian*, October 30, 1837, January 20, 1838; *York Gazette* (York, PA), January 30, 1838; *National Inquirer*, January 25, 1838; Price, "The Black Voting Rights Issue in Pennsylvania," 360; Wood, "A Sacrifice on the Altar of Slavery."

script of the white man's republic, which on the basis of Fox's decision and the ensuing petition campaign was now cast as both a legal interpretation and a popular belief in the boundaries of political community. "The people of the United states," one argued, "did not understand the black population to be citizens. They have never been recognized as such." The petitions against black suffrage meant there could be "no mistaking public opinion on this subject," that the people wanted to maintain the state as "a political community of white persons."[205]

It was George Washington Woodward, who earlier in the convention had eloquently defended abolishing the tax qualification for voting, who gave what would be described decades later as "the clearest, ablest, and most convincing vindication" of black disenfranchisement.[206] Woodward rested his argument on the grounds that the state had been "founded and reared by white freemen – it was a white government," and free people of color had no voice in its institutions, no share in its early struggles: "It was founded by white men and freemen, and they bequeathed it to us." And like his colleagues, he emphasized the national repercussions to the decision, urging the convention to demonstrate that "we mean not to disturb the foundations of our political fabric, but that we do mean to preserve them, where our revolutionary ancestors planted them." Woodward was then an "obscure and unknown lawyer from the north," but he caught the eye of James Buchanan, who would thereafter advance his career – including a failed nomination to the US Supreme Court – just as Woodward had advanced Buchanan's by helping keep Pennsylvania sound.[207]

Fox's decision also gave Whigs cause or cover to oppose black suffrage. One drew heavily on it to argue that "the framers of this constitution" had regarded people of color as "a degraded race, and therefore took no notice of them. Esteeming them neither citizens nor freemen, they left them where they had found them in the enjoyment of no political rights." Daniel Agnew agreed that Pennsylvania had been "settled exclusively by a nation of white men," and that "the history of Pennsylvania" proved that people of color "were not looked upon as being a part of the community at all, and consequently they could have no right to vote." He also urged the convention not to "meddle with a question which had so much reference to the

---

[205] Agg, *Proceedings and Debates . . . Pennsylvania*, 9: 357, 359, 367, 367, 385.
[206] George Brubaker Kulp, *Families of the Wyoming Valley: Biographical, Genealogical, and Historical. Sketches of the Bench and Bar*, vol. 3 (Wilke-Barre, PA: E. B. Yordy, 1890), 1153.
[207] Ibid.; Agg, *Proceedings and Debates . . . Pennsylvania*, 10: 20–21.

policy and action of many of our sister states." Former Federalist William Meredith had claimed to have not made up his mind about disenfranchisement. He now came out strongly in favor, fully convinced by Fox's decision that people of color had never been intentionally recognized as citizens and could not be so long as white prejudice denied the possibility of social equality. The right to vote "ought to be the privilege of white citizens alone," and legislators should pay greater attention to the English and German emigrants "from whom we ourselves have descended."[208]

Pro-suffrage delegates denounced the influence of the Democratic Party for detaching members from the country's founding commitments: disenfranchisement would never have passed "in the time of the revolution, or during the time that the men of the revolution held the government of the commonwealth." They emphasized the degree to which the Democratic Party, whose leaders had asserted that they were ready to punish anyone who voted against party principle, was strictly enforcing discipline on this issue: "The galling manacles of party slavery have been rattled within the walls of this convention – and the cry of traitor was shouted at the heels of a man, who, for a moment, lifted up his arm to work the freedom of truth." The lash had been "drawn, and the torture applied" to any Democrat who dared "to think that he was born free and equal, and to utter a sentiment that was at variance with the party plans and party discipline." It was obvious, suggested Emanuel Reigart, that it was the "slow, gradual, subtle policy of the past and present administrations of the general government [Jackson and Van Buren], towards affecting this darling object of the south, and to make it appear to be the work of the north. The lash of party has been unsparingly applied to the back of our northern politicians. Where that would not do, an occasional sop or a promise was given. When the work of degradation was complete, and when ... the faithful had testified their adhesion, the executive issues his edict, and these degraded sons of the north assist in registering it, and then openly proclaim their devotion to the dark spirit of slavery." The Democrats, they charged, wanted to "show to the south that their great leading principles on the subject of domestic slavery, have, after a lapse of more than half a century, been transplanted on the soil of a free state – cherished and nurtured by northern men."[209]

One delegate noted that had it not been for the "excitement which is known to exist at the south," the question of black suffrage would

---

[208] Agg, *Proceedings and Debates ... Pennsylvania*, 9: 221, 324–25, 328, 349–50, 353–55, 367, 369.
[209] Ibid., 9: 332, 374–77, 10:50, 74, 82.

never have come up. He listed the demands made in recent years by Southern governors and legislatures – to put down freedom of speech and of assembly, pass penal laws against abolitionists, hand over abolitionists for trial in the South, and the offering of rewards to kidnap abolitionists and send them South to be lynched – and suggested that disenfranchisement was just one more "high and imperious" demand, backed by party discipline, a common bond of nationality, capital investments, and the reward of higher office. In light of all this, he wondered, it might not be "a matter of any great astonishment, that most of the members of this convention should be found ready to minister to these bad desires."[210]

It was Thomas Earle, editor of the *Mechanics' Free Press and Reform Advocate* and a committed Jacksonian, who most passionately led the defense of black voting rights. "My democracy," he would often say, "is that which was advocated by Jefferson, my religion that of the New Testament."[211] Earle asked delegates to entertain the thought that "the declaration of independence meant what it said," and on this basis argued that disenfranchisement was unrepublican and would violate the principle that government must be founded on the consent of the governed. It would offend the "friends of free government in Europe," beleaguered democrats who looked to the United States for inspiration, and it could only be defended on the "horrible and despotic doctrine" that "no man had any natural right to enjoy political rights." Earle also attacked a central prop of the white man's republic, the claim that the United States had been founded as a racially exclusive community. He analyzed founding debates and documents to demonstrate that extending the "right of citizenship and political equality" had not only been intentional but also had been part of the "spirit of the age." The real commitment made by the founders was "to extirpate these distinctions, and establish the principle, that freedom and equality are the unalienable rights of all." The ultimate goal of the Constitution, the purpose of American nationality and the Union, was the abolition of slavery and the "establishment in practice, of the equality of rights which its framers advocated in theory."[212]

Earle also rejected the claim that white prejudice was any kind of compelling reason to deny free people of color their rights, denouncing it

[210] Ibid., 10: 39–42.
[211] Edwin B. Bronner, *Thomas Earle as a Reformer* (Philadelphia: International Printing Company, 1948), 11, 68.
[212] Agg, *Proceedings and Debates ... Pennsylvania*, 9: 335–36, 10: 31–37, 78.

as a "vile slander" against the people of Philadelphia "to say that they were so violent, so disorderly, that they would raise a mob, and even endanger the life of a negro, should he attempt to vote." There had been several race riots in Philadelphia in recent years, and there were more to come, but Earle pleaded that this did not reflect the mass of the people. He rejected the petitions as evidence of public opinion, noting that "you can frequently get up the names of more petitioners when the object in view is not good, than when it is; because you can procure the services of more active men to answer some political end." He did not believe that "the people, as a body, are bigotted, but a portion of the people are always so," and it was easy for the "aspiring politician, the demagogue" to gather their signatures and pass it off as the voice of the people. "We received some petitions praying that the right of suffrage might be limited to 'white' freemen," he conceded, "and gentlemen … said, no doubt conscientiously, that they were convinced that the people of the commonwealth required that this change should be made. Required, how? By the voice of ten thousand petitioners? Not at all. Did we get ten thousand petitioners? Nothing like it. We had only about fifteen hundred. We had nothing like a twentieth part of the taxable population even in Montgomery and Bucks; in which counties, as we know, that question was most agitated."[213]

On January 20, the convention voted seventy-seven to forty-five to insert the word "white." Seventeen members had switched their votes from supporting to opposing black suffrage, including seven Democrats, eight Anti-Masons, and two Whigs; an additional seventeen who had not voted on the first round, all but five of them Democrats, now cast their votes for disenfranchisement. While the Democratic Party had done most of the work and provided a majority of the votes, the expression of national anxieties and popular animosities pushed Anti-Masons and Whigs toward the white man's republic as well.

Black Pennsylvanians implored the convention not to give to white racism, already "of such wicked, and malignant influence, the additional strength it will derive from the influence of your high example, and sanction." But as the free African American Robert Purvis wrote in his *Appeal of Forty Thousand Citizens*, the "desire which is felt by political aspirants to gain the favor of the slaveholding States" had swayed delegates to do exactly this.[214]

---

[213] Ibid., 10: 37, 12: 81–82; *Pittsburgh Gazette*, January 25, 1838, p. 2.
[214] McBride, "Black Protest against Racial Politics," 156, 162; Robert Purvis, *Appeal of Forty Thousand Citizens, Threatened with Disfranchisement* (Philadelphia: Merriman and Gunn, 1838), 16.

After the convention had acted – but before the constitution had been ratified – the state supreme court rendered its verdict on a pending election case. They endorsed entirely the narrative of the white man's republic, noting that "our ancestors settled the province as a community of white men, and the blacks were introduced into it as a race of slaves." Because American citizenship was created through a compact with the South, it was inconceivable that free blacks could have been intentionally included within the "body politic" it established.[215]

Southern Democrats now trumpeted the convention's vote and the judicial opinions as evidence that "the Democrats of the North, as a party," were sound on the question of slavery. State Democrats praised themselves for a constitution that extended the right of suffrage to white men while putting "an end to the claim of those who are not entitled to political equality with white freemen."[216] Thomas Earle refused to sign the Democratic address, a stance that was said to have merited "the gratitude of the proscribed colored citizens of Pennsylvania." His fellow partisans were less impressed. Earle was drummed out of the Democratic Party, no longer welcome in the party whose "primary political principles" he had always supported.[217]

CONCLUSION

A few months after the vote to disenfranchise black men in Pennsylvania, the Connecticut state legislature considered the question from a different angle. In response to a petition by free men of color, the legislature considered an amendment to the state constitution that would *abolish* the racial qualification for voting. A sizeable majority of both parties voted 165 to 33 against striking the word "white."

The legislature had decided to debate the question only as the result of public interest, the culmination of an ongoing process of political organizing. As one correspondent noted, "the untiring efforts of the abolitionists out of doors," and the *"constant friction"* they had caused with their

[215] Frederick Watts, *Reports of Cases Argued and Determined in the Supreme Court of Pennsylvania*, vol. 6 (Philadelphia: Kay and Brother, 1880), 556, 560.

[216] *Daily National Intelligencer* (Washington, DC), September 28, 1838, p. 2; *Charleston Courier* (Charleston, SC), April 5, 1838, p. 2; *Extra Globe*, August 26, 1840, pp. 168–69; *The Sun* (Baltimore), January 23, 1838, p. 2; *Daily Picayune* (New Orleans, LA), January 30, 1838, p. 2; *Macon Georgia Telegraph*, March, 26, 1838, p. 2; *Richmond Enquirer* (Richmond, VA), November 16, 1838, p. 1; *Philadelphia National Enquirer*, March 15, 1838, p. 3; *Wyoming Republican and Farmer's Herald* (Kingston, PA), June 6, 1838, p. 2.

[217] *Pennsylvania Freeman*, March 15, 1838, p. 3; Bronner, *Thomas Earle as a Reformer*, 57.

lectures, had aroused public interest and encouraged at least a few politicians to take the floor in defense of black voting.[218] While the vote failed, it inaugurated a new period in the fight over black suffrage, as abolitionists embarked on a struggle against Northern legislation that imposed distinctions of race, sending thousands of petitions to state legislatures to demand the repeal of all laws that conditioned rights by race.

These campaigns occasioned a broader political activism, as activists and agents developed local contacts with people sympathetic to the cause of antislavery. This was made especially acute with the organization of the Liberty Party and later the Free Soil Party, which both drew on the petition campaigns and in many states pushed them forward on an even more aggressive path.[219] By the end of the antebellum period, in response to organized antislavery pressure, six states had asked the white electorate to decide themselves whether black men should be enfranchised.

The results were bruising defeats: only a quarter of New York voters and even fewer in Connecticut had supported black suffrage, while the results elsewhere were just as discouraging.[220] As the black abolitionist James McCune Smith noted, the white electorate harbored "a hate deeper than I had imagined."[221]

* * *

"The artificial bonds of interest, ambition, and political organization," worried the *Mississippian* in 1854, "so long used to curb the spirit of Abolitionism, is [*sic*] rapidly giving way. The tide is surging onward! It beats about the very bulwarks of the Constitution, and heaving higher and higher with every breath of fanaticism and passion, threatens to engulf all, in one common and universal ruin."[222] The political parties that had held the Union together were now in a state of severe crisis.

---

[218] *The Liberator*, June 8, 1838, p. 1; Olbrich, *Development of Sentiments on Black Suffrage*, 79.

[219] John W. Quist, "'The Great Majority of Our Subscribers Are Farmers': The Michigan Abolitionist Constituency of the 1840s," *Journal of the Early Republic* 14, no. 3 (1994): 325–58; Stewart, *Holy Warriors: The Abolitionists and American Slavery*, 93; Judith Wellman, *Grass Roots Reform in the Burned-Over District of New York* (New York: Routledge, 2000), chapter 5; Benjamin Quarles, *Black Abolitionists* (New York: Oxford University Press, 1969), 184–85.

[220] Rhode Island's referendum in 1842 was boycotted by opponents of the new constitution. That result, as well as one in Wisconsin in 1849, were the only successes for black suffrage. The latter, however, was invalidated on account of low turnout.

[221] Stewart, *Holy Warriors: The Abolitionists and American Slavery*, 112.

[222] Citing the *Semi-Weekly Mississippian, New York Times*, November 22, 1854, p. 3.

The Whigs, in office when the Compromise of 1850[223] was passed, were torn down the middle: the party ceased to exist in much of the South after 1852 and fragmented into new parties in the North in the years that followed. The Democrats were in better shape, but their ranks had been divided by the crisis over the Wilmot Proviso, an effort to exclude slavery from the territories conquered from Mexico (often referred to as the White Man's Proviso, on the grounds that it was intended to preserve the new territories for the white race alone).

In 1856, the Democratic Party turned for the third time in a row to a longtime champion of Southern interests, James Buchanan. He would do another service for the South, not his last. At the time of the presidential election, a case was pending before the Supreme Court over whether a man claimed as a slave, Dred Scott, could sue his ostensible owner for his freedom. Buchanan urged the Court to issue a broad decision that would serve as a final settlement of the issue.[224]

In early 1857, the Court did just that. While each member of the Court wrote their own opinion, it was the opinion of Roger Taney – whose father had supported reenfranchising freed black Marylanders at the turn of the century – that would have the most far-reaching consequences. "The words 'people of the United States' and 'citizens' are synonymous terms," Taney began, describing "the political body who, according to our republican institutions, form the sovereignty, and who hold the power and conduct the Government through their representatives." Former slaves and their descendants were "not included, and were not intended to be included, under the word 'citizens' in the Constitution." On the contrary, black Americans had been considered at the time of the framing "as a subordinate and inferior class of beings ... [who] had no rights or privileges but such as those who held the power and the Government might choose to grant them." This was straight out of Fox's opinion in Pennsylvania, but it could have come from any of dozens of debates that had touched on the question of black citizenship in the antebellum era.[225]

---

[223] The compromise included a more repressive fugitive slave law and allowed the new territories of New Mexico to decide whether they would be slave or free states.

[224] Michael Todd Landis, *Northern Men with Southern Loyalties: The Democratic Party and the Sectional Crisis* (Ithaca, NY: Cornell University Press, 2015), 166–71.

[225] Several state court decisions denied black citizenship, relying on the historical and constitutional claims of the white man's republic. *State v. Morris*, 2 Del. (2 Harr.) 534, 536 (1837); *Leech v. Cooley*, 14 Miss. 93, 99 (1846); *White v. Tax Collector*, 37 S. C. L. (3 Rich.) 136 (S. C. App. L. 1846); *Shaw v. Brown*, 35 Miss. 246, 316 (1858); *Heirn v. Bridault*, 37 Miss. 209, 233 (1859).

Taney insisted that neither freed slaves nor their descendants could have been recognized as full citizens of the states at the time of the Revolution and that the Constitution would not have been accepted had it implied black American citizenship. "It cannot be believed," he claimed, "that the large slaveholding States regarded them as included in the word citizens, or would have consented to a Constitution which might compel them to receive them in that character from another State." Being forced to recognize black Americans as citizens would have exempted them from "the special laws and from the police regulations which [white slaveholders] considered to be necessary for their own safety," giving them the right to enter the state, to travel "singly or in companies, without pass or passport, and without obstruction," to go wherever they liked "at every hour of the day or night without molestation." Recognizing black rights would have meant giving "them the full liberty of speech in public and in private upon all subjects upon which its own citizens might speak; to hold public meetings upon political affairs, and to keep and carry arms wherever they went." This, "in the face of the subject race of the same color," would "inevitably produc[e] discontent and insubordination among them . . . endangering the peace and safety of the State." The Constitution had been formed by the white citizens of the states, giving them powers that extended over the whole territory and placing them on an equal footing with each other. "It was formed by them," he wrote, "and for them and their posterity, but for no one else."

Taney used the language of the Declaration of Independence as a paradoxical confirmation that persons of color could not have been considered citizens. In response to its appropriation by abolitionists, many Southerners and Northern racists had begun denouncing the Declaration. Taney instead sought to rehabilitate the Declaration from the abolitionists. He quoted its introductory phrases and conceded that "the general words above quoted would seem to embrace the whole human family, *and if they were used in a similar instrument at this day would be so understood.*" "But it is too clear for dispute," he continued, "that the enslaved African race were not intended to be included, and formed no part of the people who framed and adopted this declaration."

Of course, as soon as it was drafted, the Declaration had been claimed by black persons for their own purposes, and even before the conclusion of the War of Independence many white republicans had agreed that it did apply to persons of color. The counterevidence to Taney's argument was the first wave of abolition that the Revolution had inaugurated. Taney simply denied its reality, arguing that the states that had abolished slavery had not been motivated by any egalitarian impulse but had made a simple business decision that slavery in northern climates was no longer profitable. Like William Smith during the Missouri crises, Taney was denying the existence of all racially emancipatory moments in American history: by re-reading history from this premise, he was able to deny the political possibilities raised by the abolitionists while preserving intact the myth of America's supposed commitment to republican and democratic ideals. While abolitionists insisted that Jefferson had meant what he said – that all men were created equal and that government derived its just powers from the consent of the governed – Taney asserted that what Jefferson had written had a clear meaning at the time that had only subsequently been lost. The founding generation "spoke and acted according to the then established doctrines and principles, and in the ordinary language of the day, and no one misunderstood them."[226]

The *Dred Scott* decision answered almost all the questions that had been raised in repeated controversies over slavery and black citizenship, overturned all the compromises, and provided a forthright and nationally encompassing denial of black citizenship. It was an authoritative affirmation of the white man's republic. And it would help destroy the Union, fracturing its political elite and opening up the possibility of a more profound and genuine democratization in America.

[226] *Dred Scott v. Sanford* 60 U.S. 393 (1857).

PART II

THE UNITED KINGDOM AND FRANCE

Introduction to Part II

I n February 2007, Prime Minister Gordon Brown gave a speech on the subject of "Britishness," where he described a "golden thread which runs through British history," a steady line that could be traced to that "long-ago day in Runnymede in 1215 when arbitrary power was fully challenged with the Magna Carta, on to the first bill of rights in 1689 where Britain became the first country where parliament asserted power over the king, to the democratic reform acts" of the nineteenth and twentieth centuries, and beyond to the present day.[1]

Brown's narrative of British history as a progressive movement toward expanded civil and religious liberty had a broader purpose: to offer his fellow Britons a vision of a meaningful political community that could serve as a response to resurgent nationalisms, to worries that immigration was fundamentally reworking the social heritage of the country, and to concerns over Britain's role in Europe.

This was not a new story. Since the nineteenth century, this history had been part of the "the common heritage of Englishmen," a broadly shared narrative of national identity that for decades had been closely associated with the particular party from which it gained its name.[2] The so-called Whig interpretation of British history emphasized the gradual expansion of liberty and political rights, framing a story of national exceptionalism

---

[1] "Full Text of Gordon Brown's Speech," *The Guardian*, February 27, 2007, https://www.theguardian.com/politics/2007/feb/27/immigrationpolicy.race.

[2] Herbert Butterfield, *The Englishman and His History* (Cambridge: Cambridge University Press, 1944), vii; Herbert Butterfield, *The Whig Interpretation of History* (London: G. Bell and Sons, 1931).

in which their "orderly extension" in Britain stood in "striking contrast to the revolutionary movements on the continent." "The British genius for peaceful popular reform," recited one example of the genre, "seemed to demonstrate a particular and significant ability on the part of the aristocracy, the middle classes and the people in harmonizing the institutions of an ancient kingdom with the advanced political ideas of the age."[3]

Many accounts of democratization in the United Kingdom still hew to this narrative, what Dietrich Rueschemeyer, Evelyn H. Stephens, and David Stephens refer to as a "classic (but not typical)" sequence in which political competition between elites was followed by the gradual extension of political rights "from the aristocracy to gentry to bourgeoisie, to petty bourgeoisie and upper working-class, to all male adults, and then to the whole population."[4] The "origins of democracy in Britain," argue Acemoglu and Robinson, are to be found in the "the creation of regular Parliaments that were a forum for the aristocracy to negotiate taxes and discuss policies with the king," an arrangement that was consolidated in the late seventeenth century. After this, the "first important move toward democracy in Britain was the First Reform Act of 1832," which began a process by which the right to vote was "gradually but inexorably" extended.[5] For Toke Aidt and Raphaël Franck, 1832 was "the pivotal event that got the snowball rolling."[6] While underscoring its gradual character, Daniel Ziblatt has recently recast our understanding of democratization's success in the United Kingdom as more contingent than often appreciated. It rested not on the moderating genius of the country's constitutional tradition, or on the presence of a large middle class that could safely be extended rights, but on the ability of the former elites to organize a professional conservative party that could animate non-class based lines of cleavage in British politics – in particular, empire and religion – while containing the antidemocratic forces that these new appeals brought forth.[7]

What is missing from these accounts, however, are the disenfranchisements that accompanied the foundational moments of democratization,

---

[3] Francis Herrick, "The Second Reform Movement in Britain, 1850–1865," *Journal of the History of Ideas* 9, no. 2 (1948): 174–92, 174.

[4] Rueschemeyer, Stephens, and Stephens, *Capitalist Development and Democracy*, 62.

[5] Acemoglu and Robinson, *Economic Origins of Dictatorship and Democracy*, 1–2.

[6] Toke Aidt and Raphaël Franck, "How to Get the Snowball Rolling and Extend the Franchise: Voting on the Great Reform Act of 1832," *Public Choice* 155, no. 3–4 (2012): 2.

[7] Ziblatt, *Conservative Parties and the Birth of Democracy*, 82–138.

which rested on the reorganization and suppression of conflict along lines of religion, empire, and social class in order to allow a new hegemonic coalition to define the British state and its politics on its own terms. The defining feature of the Glorious Revolution – parliamentary supremacy – was a weapon in the fight for Anglican ascendancy and against Catholic "subversion". The restrictions on Catholics and non-Anglican Protestants would be lifted in 1828 and 1829, when reformers provoked a series of crises that brought the Whigs to office for the first time in a generation, but only after Catholic emancipation had been accompanied by the disenfranchisement of Irish farmers, newly activated as a political force and threatening to thrust the national and land questions to the center or British politics. When in 1832 the Whigs set out to enfranchise hundreds of thousands of middle-class voters, reapportioning representation to the north of England and its large dissenting and industrial population, they accompanied this democratization with a new *disenfranchisement* of tens of thousands of working-class voters, whose support for the Tories had been a bulwark of the old order, while reaffirming the recent exclusion of the Irish peasantry.

The electorate of the Reform Act undergirded a substantial transformation in the institutions, policies, and public philosophy of the country. Even though the Whigs could never count on being entirely dominant afterward, the reforms raised to power what Matthew Arnold called "middle-class liberalism, which had for its cardinal points of its belief the Reform Bill of 1832, and local self-government, in politics; in the social sphere, free-trade, unrestricted competition, and the making of large industrial fortunes; in the religious sphere, the Dissidence of Dissent and the Protestantism of the Protestant religion," with an Established Church whose prerogatives were gradually reduced.[8]

In France, a different pattern of democratization unfolded. For generations after the Revolution, republicans drew inspiration from the uprisings of the late eighteenth century, the moment when "the people" supposedly reclaimed their rightful sovereignty. And generations of monarchists and Catholics saw in the Revolution nearly unparalleled sin, a revolt against Christ and the desecration of his church. Nineteenth-century French political development was torn between competing efforts to instantiate these different visions, whipsawing between unstable republics and monarchical or imperial regimes, the former resting on or moving

---

[8] Matthew Arnold, *Culture and Anarchy and Other Writings*, ed. Stefan Collini (Cambridge: Cambridge University Press, 1993 [1867]), 73.

toward near–manhood suffrage and overthrown in part because of elite fears about the electoral power of millions of peasants and urban workers.

There was nothing inevitable, given this history, about the establishment of the Third Republic in the 1870s. That it organized an electoral system resting on manhood suffrage was perhaps even more surprising. The republican regime was won by a single vote, and the disenfranchisement of large portions of the French working classes only narrowly defeated. And yet while "le suffrage universel" would be emblazoned as the essential principle of the Third Republic, there were always far more adult French nationals without the right to vote than with it.

* * *

I argued in Chapter 1 that understanding the association between democratization and disenfranchisement requires thinking about democratizing projects as efforts to reconfigure governing authority by recomposing the social basis of the state, shifting influence and representation toward some groups and away from others. I suggested that disenfranchisement and democratization would go together when: (1) the institutional context brings those with an interest in expanding political rights into a coalition with those interested in sustaining or erecting new exclusions; (2) when these groups are able to work out a joint project by which these potentially divergent projects can be reconciled; and (3) when their appeals are popular enough to secure sufficient political support to sustain their project and neutralize, if needed, the to-be-disenfranchised.

Democratization in the United Kingdom was not primarily a process of mass revolt and elite response, but a political effort to redefine the sectarian and social character of the state. The institutional context of the pre-1832 regime united aristocratic Whigs, political reformers, Protestant dissenters, and, more contentiously, Irish Catholics, into a loose oppositional coalition that aimed at reconfiguring the country's civil and political institutions. These groups were suspicious of each other, but the most important groups gradually cohered on a narrative of political community and purpose that helped reconcile some of their differences. The result was the successful displacement of the Tories, and the passage of reforms that liberalized the sectarian state and opened up channels of influence and government employment to Catholics, dissenters, and the broad middle classes. The adherence of the middle classes to the new regime this coalition established likely helped the country avert revolution in 1848, but the positive affect they held toward the postreform regime rested on the vision of political community that had been forged during the earlier struggle.

In France, the question is why the democratizing juncture of 1870 to 1875 was *not* accompanied by a mass disenfranchisement of the working classes, and why republicans would be so adamantly *opposed* to further extension of voting rights in the decades that followed. The context here was the strong association of "universal suffrage" with the Second Empire, which led many republicans to join liberal and conservative monarchists in being suspicious if not hostile toward the principle. In struggling to put together a coalition capable of founding the Republic, French republicans developed a narrative of French history that simultaneously praised the Revolution and insisted that the direct participation of "the people" in politics was a thing of the past. In doing so, they rehabilitated the idea of manhood suffrage, now characterized as a fundamentally conservative, antirevolutionary, and very limited exercise of sovereignty. By gradually persuading liberal monarchists of its conservative character, and of the danger of its repeal given the deep divisions within the country, the republicans secured the new regime. But the deep and widespread opposition to the Republic, strongest among devout Catholics, meant they could never rest easy. Until the "people" had been fully republicanized, true universal suffrage would have to wait.

5

The Fall of the Protestant Constitution

It is of the very essence of the truth of God to make distinctions. God put a difference between the fruits of Eden: Satan said there was none. Liberalism is the very principle of Satan in action at the present day.
– "A Tory of the Old School"[1]

Democratization in the United Kingdom began as an effort to redefine the sectarian character of the British state.[2] There were three prongs to this project: the repeal of the Test and Corporation Acts that excluded non-Anglican dissenting Protestants from local offices, passage of a Catholic relief or emancipation law that would allow Catholics to sit in Parliament and hold public offices and commissions, and passage of what would become the Reform Act of 1832, which reapportioned seats in Parliament and revised the qualifications for voting rights. Together, this amounted to a radical reconfiguration of the United Kingdom's constitutional order, one that brought about the political ascendancy of the middle classes and set the stage for the country's subsequent process of iterative democratizations.

These three distinct goals, *repeal of the Test and Corporation Acts, the relief of Catholics from the penal laws,* and *the reform of Parliament,* appear today as natural companions, each an implication of liberalism's

---

[1] Henry Drummond, *A Letter to the King Against the Repeal of the Test Act* (London: J. Ridgway, 1828), 28.

[2] J. C. D. Clark, *English Society 1688–1832: Ideology, Social Structure and Political Practice During the Ancien Regime* (Cambridge: Cambridge University Press, 1985); see the contributions to *Albion: A Quarterly Journal Concerned with British Studies* 21, no. 3 (Autumn 1989): 361–474; Linda Colley, "Britishness and Otherness: An Argument," *Journal of British Studies* 31, no. 4 (1992): 309–29.

emphases on religious liberty and limited popular self-government. At the time, however, there was little reason to believe that these would occur alongside each other, let alone be associated politically. In fact, there was good reason to believe otherwise. The adherents to the dissenting Protestant churches were often extremely anti-Catholic, the Catholic rights movement had traditionally been led by aristocrats opposed to political reform, and Catholics – especially the Irish – were viewed with suspicion and animosity among the working- and middle-class English and Scots who expected to be the primary beneficiaries of electoral reform.[3]

By 1832, these projects had been successfully bundled together as the foundational achievements of nineteenth-century British political liberalism. And for decades afterward, they would be celebrated by Whigs and Liberals as embodying the essence of the country's ostensibly progressive and reformist constitution. This narrative, much like the American story of progressive democracy, continues to be invoked by British politicians as defining the country's essential and particular character. And much like America's own historical amnesia, the British story of progressive liberalism generally omits the fact that it rested on a new set of exclusions.

This chapter reexamines this pivotal period of democratization in the United Kingdom, focusing on how reform of Parliament and relief from religious disabilities came to be associated with each other and with the disenfranchisement of Irish farmers and English working-class voters.

Why were these projects yoked together? One self-professed "Tory of the Old School" believed the answer was obvious: both Catholic relief and repeal of the Test Act shared "the same root of infidelity," the principle that "there is no difference, and that there ought to be none made, 'between him that feareth God, and him that feareth him not.'" It was liberalism – "the very principle of Satan in action at the present day," as he called it – that was to blame for the growing support for repeal and relief. But this Tory was shocked to find even the despotic "papists" embracing a broader principle, "the absurd sentiment, that the people are the source of legitimate power." This alliance suggested to him a deeper and more sinister design, that Catholics and dissenters sought to empower the "people" as a stepping stone to their ultimate goal: the overthrow of the

---

[3] "Dissenters" refers to Protestants who did not adhere to the Church of England or the Church of Ireland. Scots Presbyterians are not included in the ranks of the dissenters but are members of the established church in Scotland.

Anglican state and the unmooring of the state and people from an adherence to God.[4]

The "Old-School Tory" was wrong to believe that the association between these different causes was a logical unfolding of liberal premises. But while the Whigs did not want to overthrow the country's religious establishment, they did seek to reconstitute "the people" as represented in Parliament and privileged in the laws of the state. In doing so, they established a foundation for their continued rule and created institutions that would sustain a different set of interests, priorities, and politicians in power. Very much as this Tory feared, they remade the state and the people in line with a new set of collective aspirations, radically altering the identity of the British state and "the people" that were crafted in its image.

THE PROTESTANT CONSTITUTION

Understanding the origins of British democratization in the first half of the nineteenth century requires us to understand the political system and regime that this old-school Tory believed was under threat: the complex system of religious exclusions, civil and political privileges, and political malapportionment that ensured the continued ascendancy of the landed aristocracy and Anglican gentry.

The dominant understanding of political community in Britain in the late eighteenth and early nineteenth centuries was what contemporaries called the Protestant Constitution. "King, Parliament, Electors, Army, Revenue, Benches of Justice, Hierarchy, in all their branches," must be "Protestant," the "*lives and fortunes*" of the Anglican population pledged to defend this principle.[5] This provided both an historical narrative as well as a vision of purpose and community, and had at its core the belief that the constitution had attained a "peculiar excellence" with the Glorious Revolution of 1688 only after a "long, painful struggle with Popery."[6]

The Glorious Revolution is often praised for securing parliamentary supremacy, English civil liberties, and the rights of property. Each of these, however, was understood during the eighteenth and early nineteenth centuries as inseparable from the Protestant character of the

---

[4] Drummond, *A Letter to the King*, 28–29.
[5] National Archives, Public Record Office, HO 42/216/ff.4.
[6] G. F. A. Best, "The Protestant Constitution and its Supporters, 1800–1829," *Transactions of the Royal Historical Society* 8 (1958):105–27, 109.

state. Parliamentary supremacy had been defined through its authority to determine the conditions for succession to the throne – ensuring that the monarch could never again be Catholic – and through its claim to be the legislative body for the established Churches of England and Ireland. The 1689 Bill of Rights guaranteed Protestants the right to bear arms, necessary for the suppression of Catholic or Jacobite rebellions, and nullified the King's "pretended power" to not execute the laws, ensuring that a sympathetic monarch could never again set aside the laws against Catholics and dissenters. The variety of Penal Laws that followed the revolution were justified as needed to check the subversive tendencies of Catholicism and dissenting Protestantism.

In England and Ireland, especially in the latter, the penal laws also worked to protect the property redistributions that had accompanied the religious conflicts of the previous centuries while facilitating new redistributions that would more firmly vest economic and political power in the hands of Anglicans, transferring to churchmen "those holdings which had, despite the seventeenth century confiscations, remained in Catholic hands."[7] The prohibition against Irish Catholics' purchasing land in freehold or taking a lease exceeding thirty-one years made it easier for Protestants to acquire productive land. Restrictions throughout the United Kingdom against Catholics and dissenters holding the "little offices of the revenue, and little military commissions" denied them access to public offices that were of vital importance to many middle-class families.[8] Other penal laws allowed the Protestant relatives of Catholics to claim the property of their diseased kin, prohibited Catholics' inheriting or purchasing property, prohibited priests from conducting mass or sending children to be educated by Catholics abroad, required Catholic property to be registered – increasing the cost of transactions – or imposed additional taxes on "papists." These were not always strictly enforced, although they were more stringently applied in Ireland and raised the cost for Catholics to acquire property in both countries. But combined with outright confiscations, these restrictions transferred wealth from Catholics and encouraged them to convert, their numbers in England

---

[7] Thomas O'Neill, "The Irish Land Question, 1830–1850," *Studies: An Irish Quarterly Review* 44, no. 175 (1955): 325–36.

[8] Enid Campbell, "Oaths and Affirmations of Public Office under English Law: An Historical Retrospect," *Journal of Legal History* 21, no. 3 (2000): 1–32, 16; Charles F. Mullett, "The Legal Position of English Protestant Dissenters, 1689–1767," *Virginia Law Review* 23, no. 4 (1937): 389–418; Edmund Burke, *The Works of Edmund Burke* (Boston: C. C. Little, 1839), 538.

falling from approximately 115,000 to an estimated 80,000 persons between 1720 and 1770 and the property of the Catholic majority in Ireland declining from 14 percent of the country's total in 1703 to 5 percent by 1780.[9]

In short, the Glorious Revolution and its aftermath had limited the power of the Crown and secured parliamentary sovereignty precisely in order to affirm the Protestant character of the state and its "people," securing "liberty" and Protestant property.[10] Given this history, it was considered by many a "self-evident absurdity to allow Roman Catholics any share" in parliamentary sovereignty.[11] After all, the last time Catholics had been allowed to sit in the Irish Parliament, under James II, they had used their majority to return confiscated land to the descendants of the original Irish owners. By the end of the eighteenth century, the threat of large-scale reparations was perhaps less important, outside of Ireland at least, but the tithing and rate-levying authority of the established churches constituted vested property rights that privileged tens of thousands of church officials and their congregations. These would undoubtedly be at risk were any substantial number of Catholics and dissenters elected to Parliament.

It was never just property that was at stake. The constant juxtaposition of British liberties against Catholic despotism, declared from the pulpit, in "political catechisms," and in the meetings and addresses of hundreds of chartered corporations, was a crucial ingredient in forging a "British" identity in the eighteenth century. The narrative retelling of Catholic tyranny, the honor roll of martyrs to Catholic despotism, and the association of these evils with a recognizable outgroup within the country (and two powerful geopolitical rivals, France and Spain) was crucial in creating a sense of a meaningful, cross-national, and even cross-class political community in the eighteenth and early nineteenth centuries.[12] As one government file noted, "the perfidy of Papists ... should not be told ye

---

[9] That conversion was an effort to remake the people is suggested by Robert E. Burns, "The Irish Popery Laws: A Study of Eighteenth-Century Legislation and Behavior," *The Review of Politics* 24, no. 4 (1962): 485–508; Nigel Yates, *Eighteenth Century Britain: Religion and Politics, 1714–1815* (London: Routledge, 2008), 38; Roy F. Foster, *Modern Ireland, 1600–1972* (London: Penguin Books, 1989), 155; Louis Cullen, "Catholics Under the Penal Laws," *Eighteenth-Century Ireland/Iris an dá chultúr* 1 (1986):23–36, 24–25.

[10] Anonymous, *The Case of the Revolution Truly Stated* (London: J. F. for A. Dodd, 1746); *British Magazine*, March 1832, p. 40.

[11] Best, "The Protestant Constitution and its Supporters, 1800–1829," 109.

[12] Linda Colley, *Britons*, 2nd edn. (New Haven, CT: Yale University Press, 2005).

people often, but very often, to make an undecaying impression on their minds." After the succession of the Hanoverians to the throne in 1715 – and the Jacobite rebellion that followed – "the administration and its supporters conceived anti-Papist propaganda as of the utmost value in helping to unite the population behind" the new dynasty.[13]

Paradoxically, this virulent anti-Catholicism was seen as perfectly consistent with another feature of the Protestant Constitution: religious toleration of nonconforming Protestant churches. In fact, it was the principle of toleration that was perhaps most often invoked to justify the exclusion of Catholics. Horace Walpole wrote that "I have ever been averse to toleration of an intolerant religion."[14] The poet Robert Southey prided himself on his liberalism, and was all "for abolishing [the penal laws] with regard to every other sect – Jews and all – but not to the Catholics. They *will not tolerate*: the proof is in their whole history."[15] "I should justly render suspect my pretension to the character of a Briton and a Protestant," wrote one Englishman, "if I wished to have confided to them a *legislative authority* which their principles would oblige them to use for the suppression of *heresy*, that is in their language *Protestantism*, and the establishment of the Papal faith and influence over the British dominions."[16] Catholics were supposedly under the control of the priesthood, and thus "not masters of their own consciences, their own opinions, and their own conduct." And they were incapable of allegiance to the English Crown, both because there was a line of Jacobite Pretenders to whom they supposedly clung but also because their primary allegiance was to the Pope.[17] Lord Molesworth, an influential defender of religious toleration, excepted Catholics from its ambit, not because they were of a different religion but "because popery sets up *a foreign jurisdiction*

[13] Colin Haydon, *Anti-Catholicism in Eighteenth Century England, c. 1714–80: A Political and Social Study* (Manchester, UK: Manchester University Press, 1993), 91.

[14] Horace Walpole, *Letters of Horace Walpole, Earl of Orford, to Horace Mann, His Britannic Majesty's Resident at the County of Florence, from 1760 – 1785*, vol. 4 (London: Rich Bentley, 1844), 197.

[15] Charles Southey, *The Life and Correspondence of Robert Southey* (New York: Harper and Brothers, 1855), 217.

[16] George Pellew, *The Life and Correspondence of the Right Honourable Henry Addington*, vol. 3 (London: John Murray, 1847), 349, 495.

[17] Eamonn Ó Ciardha, *Ireland and the Jacobite Cause, 1685–1766: A Fatal Attachment* (Dublin: Four Courts Press, 2004); Anonymous, *The Admission of the Catholics into the Legislature Inconsistent with Constitutional Principles, and of Advantage to None but the Priesthood* (London: J. Hatchard, 1827), 7–8.

paramount to our laws. So that a *real* Papist can neither be a true *governor* of a Protestant *country*, nor a true *subject.*"[18]

The place of Protestants who did not adhere to the Church of England was more ambiguous. Dissenters were not considered intolerant, nor were they bound in allegiance to a foreign power. They could accordingly be afforded more rights. Indeed, the Test and Corporation Acts excluding dissenters from public office in municipalities and local corporations were usually exempted on an annual basis by repeatedly passed Indemnity Acts.[19] There was nonetheless strong opposition to extending them an official equality with adherents of the established church: indemnity was one thing, but repeal of the Test and Corporation Acts would sever the connection between state and church, send a signal to the population that religious noncommunion was acceptable, and embolden them to demand exemption from tithing or rate collections imposed by the Church.

And insofar as the idea of the Protestant Constitution was implanted in popular identities and associated with the country itself, dissent could bear the stigma of disloyalty.[20] This was especially true during the American Revolution, when it became apparent that dissenters were more supportive of the colonial cause.[21] The Anglican clergy, by contrast, was "the most consistently pro-government body in the nation," nearly unanimous in supporting coercion in the name of "a deep conviction that the government in church and state was genuinely a Christian government, guided by a Christian sovereign, on Christian principles."[22] Even Edmund Burke, who had sympathized with the Americans and supported measures of Catholic relief, would later come out against repeal of the

---

[18] Robert Molesworth, "Translator's Preface," *Franco-Gallia*, 2nd edn. (London: Edward Valentine, 1721).

[19] This was costly, uncertain, and required the dissenters to take an oath and receive the sacrament according to the rituals of the Church of England within a year. *The Test-Act Reporter* 1 (January 1828), 26; Thomas Bennett, "Hallam and the Indemnity Acts," *Law Quarterly Review* 26 (October 1910): 400–7; Campbell, "Oaths and Affirmations of Public Office under English Law," 16.

[20] Dissenters had been loyal supporters of the Hanoverian dynasty after 1715, and before the American Revolution were often seen as especially loyal to the old Whig ministries that governed during this period.

[21] James E. Bradley, *Religion, Revolution, and English Radicalism: Nonconformity in Eighteenth Century Politics and Society* (Cambridge: Cambridge University Press, 1990).

[22] James E. Bradley, "The Anglican Pulpit, the Social Order, and the Resurgence of Toryism During the American Revolution," *Albion: A Quarterly Journal Concerned with British Studies* 21, no. 3 (1989): 361–88, 363, 376.

Test Acts and denounce the "rising race of Dissenters" for their radicalism and antagonism to the established churches.[23]

The Unreformed Electorate, Bulwark of the Protestant Constitution

Because Parliament was the bulwark of the Anglican ascendancy, it followed that its membership should be closely regulated to ensure that only those who could "be cordial friends to the *entire* constitution of this realm, *with perfect consistency of principle*" could be admitted.[24] This was accomplished through reinforcing religious disabilities, voting qualifications, and electoral practices. Sitting in Parliament required an oath whose terms excluded Catholics, while the right to vote in many districts was extended only to members in closed city corporations from which dissenters and Catholics were generally excluded. The Anglican universities of Cambridge and Oxford were given separate representation, allowing its graduates – a network of clergy that encompassed the entire country – to cast additional votes. Offices of the Anglican Church – primarily clergymen, but sometimes including the chorister, bell-ringer, organ-blower, and others – were deemed to confer the property qualification for voting on those who held them. And the bishops of the Church of England sat in the House of Lords, where they added their own independent voices to those of the country's aristocracy. Backing up these sectarian privileges was an extensive system of corruption, elite collusion, and intimidation through which the primarily Anglican aristocracy and gentry could secure a numerical preponderance in the House of Commons. The unreformed electoral system provided the institutional foundations of the Protestant Constitution.

Voting rights in the United Kingdom were a complicated tangle of medieval franchises. The franchise in the English and Welsh counties was conferred on male subjects who held freehold land whose rent value was assessed at forty shillings (£2) a year, above all encumbrances, and

---

[23] *Parliamentary Debates*, H. C., March 2, 1790, vol. 27, 182; see also Richard Woodward, *The Present State of the Church of Ireland*, 7th edn. (Dublin: T. Cadell, 1787), 14–15; Jacqueline Hill, "The Meaning and Significance of 'Protestant Ascendancy,' 1787–1840," in *Ireland after the Union: Proceedings of the Second Joint Meeting of the Royal Irish Academy and the British Academy, London* (Oxford, UK: Oxford University Press, 1989), 1–22; David Rice, "Combine Against the Devil: The Anglican Church and the French Refugee Clergy in the French Revolution," *Historical Magazine of the Protestant Episcopal Church* 50, no. 3 (1981): 271–81, 276.

[24] William Campbell, *A Vindication of the Principles and Character of the Presbyterians of Ireland, Addressed to the Bishop of Cloyne* (Dublin: P. Byrne, 1787).

had paid taxes. In Scotland, voting rights in the counties required ownership of land that had been valued at forty shillings *before 1681*, which controlled for inflation and excluded all of the lands that had been subsequently opened for freehold ownership; as a result, the country was left without even "a vestige of popular representation."[25] A forty-shilling freehold franchise existed in Ireland, supplemented by franchises for owners of freehold property worth twenty or fifty pounds per year. Forty-shilling freeholders had to obtain a voting certificate at least one year before an election, which they had to renew every eight years. Since there was no way of accounting for when certificate holders died or moved away, and nothing to prevent freeholders from acquiring multiple certificates for the same property, they could be bought by election brokers and distributed as needed.[26]

The large majority of seats in Parliament were borough constituencies: towns, cities, and the occasional uninhabited hill that had been extended a franchise to elect representatives. The voting qualifications for the boroughs varied enormously, producing electorates that ranged from those which "approach[ed] universal suffrage" to the rotten borough of Old Sarum (thirteen voters and twelve residents, none of them the same) or the closed corporation of Belfast (thirteen voters and forty thousand residents). The most common franchise qualification in the boroughs extended the right to vote to the town freemen, men who had by service or membership in certain guilds or by invitation of the corporation been admitted to the freemanship. In the large and mid-sized freeman boroughs, between one-quarter and one-third of all adult males had the right to vote, although these numbers are inflated by the fact that brokers often

---

[25] *Hansard*, March 1, 1831, 3rd series, vol. 2, cc. 1078–79.

[26] Edward Porritt and Annie Porritt, *The Unreformed House of Commons: Parliamentary Representation Before 1832, England and Wales* (Cambridge: Cambridge University Press, 1903), 20; Edward Porritt and Annie Porritt, *The Unreformed House of Commons: Parliamentary Representation Before 1832, Scotland and Ireland* (Cambridge: Cambridge University Press, 1903), 80; Charles Seymour, *Electoral Reform in England and Wales: The Development and Operation of the Parliamentary Franchise, 1832–1885* (New Haven, CT: Yale University Press, 1915), 11–12, 106; John Carmont, "Old Extent," *The Scottish Historical Review* 26, no. 102 (1947): 178–88, 180; Arthur Cleary, *The Franchises and the Registration of Parliamentary Voters in Ireland* (Dublin: E. Ponsonby, 1886), 3; Stephen Farrell, "Ireland," in *The House of Commons, 1820–1832*, ed. D. R. Fisher (Cambridge: Cambridge University Press, 2009); K. Hoppen, *Elections, Politics, and Society in Ireland, 1832–1885* (Oxford: Clarendon Press, 1984), 6.

arranged for the admission of nonresident men.[27] In Ireland, the freemanship was effectively restricted to Anglicans, with a tiny number of Catholics and not many more Presbyterians. Across the different nations, the freemen were the most widely disparaged class of voter: radical supporters of parliamentary reform attacked them for selling their votes, while supporters of the Protestant Constitution complained that they extracted an excessive remuneration.[28]

Scot-and-lot boroughs extended voting rights to householders who had paid a local tax, and while these constituencies often had relatively high enfranchisement rates, they tended to have very small electorates in which bribery (or payment of the tax) by election brokers was both more affordable and easier to surveil. Larger scot-and-lot boroughs such as Westminster and Southwark, however, had a lively and relatively independent political life, approaching manhood suffrage. Potwalloper boroughs enfranchised the adult male head of a household with a hearth large enough to boil a cauldron: these tended to have high rates of enfranchisement and were generally less subject to elite influence. Freeholder boroughs, which existed primarily in Ireland, enfranchised those who owned a forty-shilling freehold property within the borough. The large landlords of the freeholder boroughs generally had sufficient influence here that they were recognized as nearly in full control over the parliamentary representation. Two other types of boroughs – corporation and burgage boroughs – had almost no other function than representing the interests of wealthy patrons. The former allowed only a dozen or so town councilors and the mayor to vote, and they generally placed themselves under the patronage of some aristocratic family. The burgage boroughs vested the right to vote in ownership of specific properties, so that owning property rights in the salt water arising from a pit in Droitwich, or certain pigeon lofts in Richmond, entitled the male owner to vote. Ownership could be quickly acquired as an election approached, allowing brokers to purchase and distribute these as needed.[29]

---

[27] Frank O'Gorman, *Voters, Patrons, and Parties: The Unreformed Electoral System of Hanoverian England, 1734–1832* (Oxford, UK: Clarendon Press, 1989), 180–81, 192.

[28] Hoppen, *Elections, Politics, and Society in Ireland*, 3, 5; R. G. Thorne, *The House of Commons, 1790–1820* (London: Secker and Warburg, 1986), 103.

[29] Thorne, *House of Commons, 1790–1820*, 30, 31, 77, 103–104; O'Gorman, *Voters, Patrons, and Parties*, 181, 240; Porritt and Porritt, *Unreformed House of Commons, England and Wales*, 31, 36, 55; John A. Cannon, *Parliamentary Reform: 1640–1832* (Cambridge: Cambridge University Press, 1973), 29.

Figure 5.1 shows the distribution of parliamentary seats by the size of their electorate. Across all constituencies, the median electorate size was around five hundred voters, most of whom would not actually go to the polls unless a close competition drove up the price for votes. In the boroughs, the median electorate size was around two hundred voters, while in the counties electorates ranged from Yorkshire, with its fifty thousand potential voters – a nightmare for the local gentry, who could not bribe or monitor such a large number – to the sixteen voters of Clackmannan, Scotland.[30]

Through the support of influential patrons and bribery by the British treasury, the government could generally count on the boroughs to provide them with a majority in the Commons and to secure the quick election of potential cabinet members.[31] They had proliferated in part for this reason, so that by the nineteenth century they constituted 70 percent of parliamentary seats – and 85 percent of English seats – despite having at most 20 percent of the population. Small electorates and a proliferation of government offices, argued Christopher Wyvill, had allowed the Crown "to influence or command Elections in many sea-ports [boroughs]," where customs offices were located, while elsewhere, the aristocracy, "by creating fraudulent and fictitious votes, has destroyed the Right of Election, and acquired the absolute power of nomination."[32] This system figured prominently in the development of transatlantic republican thought: as James Madison noted in the American Constitutional Convention of 1787, "It was in the boroughs and cities, rather than the counties, that

---

[30] Before 1832, the numbers reflect the range of scholarly estimates of the total number of electors per constituency; after 1832, the counts are of registered voters. Derek Beales, "The Electorate Before and After 1932: The Right to Vote, and the Opportunity," *Parliamentary History* 11, no. 1 (1992): 139–50; Frank O'Gorman, "The Electorate Before and After 1832," *Parliamentary History* 12, no. 2 (1993): 171–83. The estimated electorates in the counties and boroughs for the prereform period were taken from the volumes of the *History of Parliament: House of Commons* series and are very rough approximations based on their classifications. Thorne, *House of Commons, 1790–1820*; Lewis B. Napier, *The House of Commons, 1754–1790* (London: Secker and Warburg, 1985); D. R. Fisher, ed., *The House of Commons, 1820–1832* (Cambridge: Cambridge University Press, 2009).

[31] George Burges, *Sixty-Eight Reasons for Opposing the Reform Bill Now Pending in Parliament* (London: J. G. and F. Rivington, 1832), 9.

[32] Christopher Wyvill, *Political Papers, Chiefly Respect the Attempt of the County of York, and other Considerable Districts, to Effect a Reformation of the Parliament of Great-Britain*, vol. 3 (York, UK: W. Blanchard, 1794), 15.

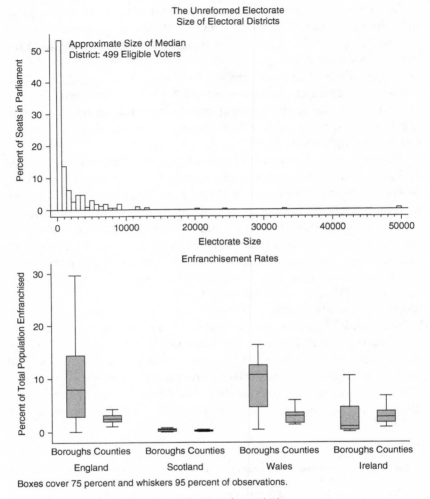

FIGURE 5.1 The Unreformed Electorate

bribery most prevailed, and the influence of the Crown on elections was most dangerously exerted."[33]

In the counties, the problem was less bribery than elite collusion and intimidation, a "deference" to elite preferences that rested on the ability of large landlords to make the lives of residents difficult. In Ireland, where

[33] E. H. Scott, *Journal of the Constitutional Convention, Kept by James Madison* (Chicago: Scott, Forman, and Co., 1893), 470.

the Protestant Constitution was nakedly extractive, it was common for even short-term leaseholders to be treated as freeholders, leading the patriot Wolfe Tone to float the possibility as early as 1790 of disenfranchising this "wretched tribe ... whom we see driven to their octennial market, by their landlords, as much their property as the sheep or the bullocks which they brand with their names."[34] But freeholders too lived under the threat of the "numberless means which always reside in magistracy and influence to oppress."[35]

The county districts were never as securely under the thumb as the aristocracy and gentry might have liked. There was always a worry that the excitement and competing inducements offered during contested elections could fracture "the connection between the gentry and their dependents."[36] To avoid this, local elite often negotiated agreements allowing a county's representation to be divided equally between dominant families or to be passed back and forth with every election. As a result, from 1754 to 1830, an average of only 22 percent of county seats were contested in any general election; only 13 percent had been contested before the American Revolution, which had spurred on more political competition in Great Britain.[37]

Large landowners and wealthy patrons, including a number of "middle-class" industrialists, could never act with total impunity: while they regularly spoke of "controlling" or having an interest in a district, this often required them to cultivate support through community service and even a measure of policy representation. When there was a seriously contested election, "the opinions and feelings of the voters had, in the last analysis, to be consulted." This was particularly true when the election turned on certain "long-term issues, such as the war in America, Catholic emancipation, slavery, the Corn Laws, and parliamentary reform."[38] Still, representation was fundamentally shaped by the unequal power relationship between wealthy patrons and landlords and the borough electors and vulnerable freeholders.[39]

---

[34] Wolfe Tone, *An Argument on Behalf of the Catholics of Ireland* (Dublin: P. Byrne, 1791), 43–44.

[35] Burke, *The Works of Edmund Burke*, 466.

[36] O'Gorman, *Voters, Patrons, and Parties*, 60.

[37] Farrell, "Ireland"; Seymour, *Electoral Reform in England and Wales*, 11; J. G. Simms, "Irish Catholics and the Parliamentary Franchise, 1692–1728," *Irish Historical Studies* 12, no. 45 (1960): 28–37, 37.

[38] O'Gorman, *Voters, Patrons, and Parties*, 53.

[39] Cullen, "Catholics Under the Penal Laws," 27.

Catholic exclusion, the Test and Corporation Acts, and the unreformed electoral system reinforced the political power of the Anglican establishment and the landed nobility. Not including Scottish Presbyterians – the Established Church of Scotland – only 2 percent of the members of Parliament elected between 1715 and 1820 were dissenters from the Church of England or Ireland, despite the fact that this group comprised about 20 percent of the total population of England and Wales and was growing rapidly.[40] None were Catholics, despite their constituting over a quarter of the UK population in 1800. And with the exception of a small minority, most legislators were strongly supportive of the Protestant Constitution, the allocation of material benefits that it sustained, and the vision of English nationality that it affirmed.

The Years of Crisis and the Sectarian Basis of Popular Loyalism

The war in American quickly led to pressures for reform in Britain and Ireland. As British troops were withdrawn from Ireland to fight abroad, the landed gentry helped organize local militias – called Volunteers – to protect against a French invasion or agrarian insurrections. To secure the loyalty of Catholics, the government in 1778 passed a series of relief laws in Britain and Ireland, repealing portions of the penal laws persecuting priests and Catholic teachers and allowing Catholics who took an oath of allegiance to inherit land.[41] These modest steps were met with the Gordon Riots targeting Catholics in England and Scotland, often treated as the first major instance of cross-national working-class collaboration in Britain.[42]

Further concessions were soon given to Irish Protestant reformers, as the Volunteer militias now became the site for political organizing in favor of liberalized trade and a measure of independence from Britain. The civil

[40] Bradley, *Religion, Revolution, and English Radicalism*, 98.
[41] R. K. Donovan, "The Military Origins of the Roman Catholic Relief Programme of 1778," *The Historical Journal* 28, no. 1 (1985): 79–102.
[42] G. I. T. Machin, "Resistance to Repeal of the Test and Corporation Acts, 1828," *The Historical Journal* 22, no. 1 (1979): 115–13; Colley, *Britons*, 23; Eugene Charlton Black, "The Tumultuous Petitioners: The Protestant Association in Scotland, 1778-1780," *The Review of Politics* 25, no. 2 (1963): 183–211, 199; George Rudé, "The Gordon Riots: A Study of the Rioters and their Victims," *Transactions of the Royal Historical Society*, 6 (1956): 93–114, 111–12; J. H. Hexter, "The Protestant Revival and the Catholic Question in England, 1778–1829," *Journal of Modern History* 8, no. 3 (1936): 297–319; Haydon, *Anti-Catholicism in Eighteenth-Century England*, 223–29.

disabilities against Irish Presbyterians were removed in 1780, and in 1782 the British granted the Irish Parliament its independence for the first time since the late seventeenth century.

The Volunteers soon turned their attention to parliamentary reform, a cause that was receiving increasingly vocal support in England as well.[43] In February 1780, the Nottingham Committee of Association "resolved that the legislature's independence from the executive could best be secured by manhood suffrage in the counties and the boroughs, equal-sized constituencies, the secret ballot, and annual parliaments," a program that was embraced and expanded upon by the Westminster Committee of Association a few months later.[44] Support for expanding the right to vote now received some support from influential quarters. In June 1780, the Duke of Richmond presented a bill for manhood suffrage declaring that "EVERY MAN of the commonalty (excepting infants, insane persons, and criminals) is of common right, and by the laws of God, a FREE MAN, and entitled to the full enjoyment of *liberty*."[45]

William Pitt, a rising political star, was both worried by the growth of radical sentiment and looking to divide a government headed by rivals Lord North and Charles James Fox, a brilliant orator who was becoming increasingly influential under the tutelage of Burke. In 1782, Pitt presented a very modest reform proposal, and while the bill was defeated, it divided the ministerial ranks and contributed to its subsequent defeat; the twenty-four-year-old Pitt was asked to form a government the next year. Pitt's attention was immediately drawn to Ireland, where the growth of radicalism in Dublin and Ulster threatened a possible insurrection. He pressed the Irish government to reform that country's parliament, with the explicit hope that a limited reform might satisfy moderate Protestants, detach them from the radicals, and buttress the Protestant Constitution. He encouraged the lord lieutenant to adopt a *"prudent and temperate reform of Parliament"* that could "unite the Protestant interest in *excluding the Catholics from any share in the representation* or the government of the country." Pitt calculated that a large number of "the Protestant reformers

[43] Porritt and Porritt, *The Unreformed House of Commons, Scotland and Ireland*, 240.

[44] Stephen Conway, *The British Isles and the War of American Independence* (Oxford, UK: Oxford University Press, 2000), 222.

[45] "House of Lords Journal Volume 36: June 1780 1–10," in *Journal of the House of Lords Volume 36, 1779–1783* (London: His Majesty's Stationery Office, 1779–1783), 139–45; Charles Lennox, *The Bill of the Late Duke of Richmond for Universal Suffrage and Annual Parliaments* (London: W. Hone, 1817).

are alarmed at the pretensions of the Catholics, and for that very reason would stop very short of the extreme speculative notions of universal suffrage."[46]

The French Revolution brought a new urgency to the situation in Ireland, where the threat that a French invasion might be welcomed by the majority of the native Irish was a deep cause of concern. It was the need to secure Catholic loyalty that ultimately led the British ministry to take the drastic step of enfranchising Irish Catholic freeholders.[47] Threatened by the prospect of war and the danger that Irish Catholics might desert the army, throw their support behind Presbyterian revolutionaries, or welcome the French, the ministers felt that they had no choice. "Under the present circumstances of this country and of Europe," wrote the British secretary for Ireland, "it is particularly desirable, if it be possible, to avoid any occasion which might lead those who are in general attached to order and regular government to join themselves with persons of opposite principles. It seems, there, to be of the utmost consequence not to lose the assistance of the Catholics in support of the established Constitution."[48] In 1792, the secretary informed the lord lieutenant that war was at hand and that the right to vote would have to be extended. With the support of Irish members of Parliament (MPs) – paid off by the British treasury – a bill allowing Catholics to vote was passed. Still, the Irish executive and Commons, with the support of the British, insisted that no Catholic be eligible to sit in Parliament.[49]

While some English radicals had supported Catholic enfranchisement, many insisted this should only be done if coupled with a higher property qualification, lest enfranchisement amount to a "transfer of the power of the protestants, a transfer of the constitution into [Catholic] hands." Irish Protestants generally agreed, with Henry Grattan secretly urging the government to limit enfranchisement to only the wealthiest Catholic freeholders – numbering about one thousand in the whole country.[50]

---

[46] Thorne, *The House of Commons, 1790–1820*, 102; Conway, *The British Isles and the War of American Independence*, 140–41; John Rutland, *Correspondence between the Right Honourable William Pitt and Charles, Duke of Rutland, 1781–1787* (Edinburgh: W. Blackwood, 1890), 43–44, 46.

[47] Simms, "Irish Catholics and the Parliamentary Franchise"; Eamon O'Flaherty, "The Catholic Convention and Anglo-Irish Politics, 1791–3," *Archivium Hibernicum* 40 (1985): 14–34, 20–22.

[48] William E. H. Lecky, *A History of England in the Eighteenth Century*, vol. 6 (London: Longmans and Co., 1891), 556.

[49] Porritt and Porritt, *The Unreformed House of Commons, Scotland and Ireland*, 276, 282.

[50] James Kelly, "The Parliamentary Reform Movement of the 1780s and the Catholic Question," *Archivium Hibernicum* 43 (1988): 95–117, 97, 98.

The ministry refused, in part because they wanted to avoid antagonizing the Catholic population but likely also because they recognized the possibility that enfranchising the forty-shilling farmers was likely to have the paradoxical effect of empowering the Anglo-Irish landlords.

The grant of voting rights to the Irish Catholics foreclosed the possibility of reforming Ireland's parliamentary representation. With Catholics now a potential electoral force, the Irish government was now more dependent than ever on its control over the "rotten" and "pocket" boroughs.

The opportunity for political reform was closing across the Irish Sea as well. With the French Revolution embracing manhood suffrage, the government decided that even a modest reform would be an "opening for those principles which aim at nothing less than a total annihilation of the constitution."[51] Outside of Parliament, the paid and unpaid supporters of the government cast parliamentary reform as subversion and treason. Newly organized loyalist associations disseminated a vision of political community that was essentially a "statement of commitment to the principal features" of the Protestant Constitution.[52] The author of the *Englishman's Political Catechism* educated Englishmen that reform was "the foundation, the step, on which those enemies of the community want to mount, who, instead of the present form of government, wish to have us under the dominion of the mob."[53] In Ireland, moderates proposed a meager reform in 1793, only to find even the more liberal landlords unwilling to support it – lest they be seen as "associat[ing] themselves with the United Irishmen," largely Presbyterian radicals – and conservatives absolutely opposed on the grounds that it would strengthen the power of the Catholics.[54]

---

[51] William Pitt, *The Speeches of William Pitt, in the House of Commons*, 2 vols. (London: Longman, Hurst, Rees, Orme, and Brown, 1817), 2:300, 1:448.

[52] Jennifer Mori, *Britain in the Age of the French Revolution* (London: Longman, 2000), 81; Jennifer Mori, "Languages of Loyalism: Patriotism, Nationhood, and the State in the 1790s," *English Historical Review* 118, no. 475 (2003): 33–58, 38, 45; Conway, *The British Isles and the War of American Independence*, 251; Haydon, *Anti-Catholicism in Eighteenth-Century England*, 264; Nicholas Rogers, *Crowds, Culture, and Politics in Georgian Britain* (Oxford: Oxford University Press, 1998), 77; Rice, "Combine Against the Devil," 271; Robert Hole, "English Sermons and Tracts as Media of Debate on the French Revolution, 1789–99," in *The French Revolution and British Popular Politics*, ed. Mark Philip (Cambridge: Cambridge University Press, 1991), 45.

[53] Anonymous, *Englishman's Political Catechism* (Exeter: R. Trewman, 1797), 8.

[54] Denis Kennedy, "The Irish Opposition, Parliamentary Reform, and Public Opinion, 1793–1794," *Eighteenth-Century Ireland/Iris an dá chultúr* 7 (1992): 95–114, 113.

The opposition party that was beginning to crystallize around Charles James Fox now came under enormous pressure to denounce the causes of suffrage reform, and to reaffirm their support for the Protestant Constitution.[55] When Charles Grey, a young Foxite Whig, proposed a reform bill, it was defeated 256 to 91, prompting most of Fox's supporters to walk out of Parliament and stay away.[56] A similar fate was meted out to the cause of the dissenters. Edmund Burke argued that "the majority of the people of England" considered the church establishment as "the foundation of their whole constitution," that "Church and State are ideas inseparable in their minds, and scarcely is the one ever mentioned without mentioning the other."[57] Repeal of the Test Act, warned Pitt, would create an equality between dissenters who wanted "to subvert the establishment" and churchmen, which "indispensable necessity" precluded.[58] The ministerial party backing Pitt repulsed the effort to repeal the discriminatory laws, further consolidating their authority and legitimacy among the Anglican electorate.

Rebellion would eventually break out in Ireland, giving the defenders of the Protestant Constitution a new opportunity to highlight the subversive danger of both dissenters and Catholics. The British and Irish governments had been worried by Presbyterian radicalism in Ulster since the American war. "The leveling system, under the mask of reform, is spreading furiously," wrote the secretary to the viceroy in Ireland, and the "source of all the mischief is the town of Belfast. The merchants of that town are the persons principally at the bottom of it."[59] British policy had long been explicitly premised on the belief that Irish Presbyterians and Catholics were "naturally jealous of each other from principle," and that the government should foster this distrust. "The dissenters," wrote the Lord Lieutenant Rutland, "seek for such an alteration of the constitution as will throw more power into their hands for bringing the government

[55] Michael S. Smith, "Anti-Radicalism and Popular Politics in an Age of Revolution," in *Partisan Politics, Principle and Reform in Parliament and the Constituencies, 1689–1880: Essays in Memory of John A. Phillips*, ed. Clyve Jones, Philip Salmon, and Richard W. Davis (Edinburgh: Edinburgh University Press, 2005), 82.

[56] Eric J. Evans, *Political Parties in Britain, 1783–1867* (London: Methuen and Co., 1985), 16–17.

[57] Edmund Burke, *Reflections on the Revolution in France* (Boston: C. C. Little and J. Brown, 1839), 123.

[58] *Parliamentary Debates*, March 2, 1790, vol. 27, 156.

[59] Lecky, *A History of England in the Eighteenth Century*, 557; H. C. M. Lyte, *The Manuscripts of His Grace the Duke of Rutland*, vol. 3 (London: Eyre and Spottiswood, 1894), 163.

nearer to that of a republic," while the Catholics were so numerous as to "speedily give them the upper hand if they were admitted to a participation in the Legislature." So long as there was not "some bond of union, [the] different parties will keep each other from encroaching upon the Government; but once united, they will become formidable." The situation in the country, however, presented the terrifying specter of an alliance between these two oppressed classes: "Such a union may, I fear, occur on the present occasion." This fear, which he had raised in 1785, would materialize briefly during the rebellion of 1798.[60]

After the rebellion was suppressed, commentators framed it as a nearly fatal moment of dissenter and Catholic unity. Lord Castlereagh blamed the rebellion on a "Jacobinical conspiracy" organized by dissenters that pursued "its object with Popish instruments." Richard Musgrave's *Memoirs of the Different Rebellions in Ireland*, which surpassed even Burke's *Reflections on the Revolution in France* as defining "the nineteenth-century British Right," argued instead that the Catholic Committee had been the real force behind the rebellion.[61] Pitt came down in the middle, deciding that "Jacobin principles were the foundation of the rebellion," and that while "the influence of the priests themselves, tainted with Jacobin principles," had aggravated the problem, "they were not the cause of it."[62]

From the moment that Catholic enfranchisement had passed in 1793, some Anglo-Irish MPs had argued that only through union with Britain could the Protestant Constitution in Ireland be maintained, as the ability of the landlords, wealthy patrons, and closed corporations to control Catholic electors or impede a popular majority was not infinite.[63] The rebellion confirmed their worst fears. In 1800, the Act of Union joined the countries in the United Kingdom, consolidated the Churches of

---

[60] Porritt and Porritt, *The Unreformed House of Commons, Scotland and Ireland*, 325; Nancy J. Curtin, "The Transformation of the Society of United Irishmen into a Mass-Based Revolutionary Organisation, 1794–6," *Irish Historical Studies* 24, no. 96 (1985): 432–92.

[61] Jim Smyth, "Anti-Catholicism, Conservatism, and Conspiracy: Sir Richard Musgrave's Memoirs of the Different Rebellions in Ireland," *Eighteenth-Century Life* 22, no. 3 (1998): 62–73, 71; James J. Sack, *From Jacobite to Conservative: Reaction and Orthodoxy in Britain* (Cambridge: Cambridge University Press, 1993), 96.

[62] Pitt, *Speeches of William Pitt*, vol. 3, 424; James Patterson, "Continued Presbyterian Resistance in the Aftermath of the Rebellion of 1798 in Antrim and Down," *Eighteenth-Century Life* 22, no. 3 (1998): 45–61, 57.

[63] Parliament of Ireland, *Parliamentary Register, Fourth Session of the Fifth Parliament* (Dublin: P. Byrne, 1793), 324; Kennedy, "The Irish Opposition, Parliamentary Reform, and Public Opinion," 99.

England and Ireland, and declared their continued establishment as "an essential and fundamental part of the union." The new United Kingdom was an explicit reaffirmation of the Protestant Constitution, intended to provide an overwhelming force to counter the possibility of Catholic political power.

The reinforced support for the Protestant Constitution would define the politics of the next several decades. The years of crisis had scrambled existing factional alliances, drawing new party lines that separated what would eventually be identified as a new "Tory" party organized around Pitt from the "Whigs" organized around Fox. The organization of loyalist and patriotic associations, supported in part by government funding, provided a basis for the defense of the "values and institutions of the country." "True Blue Clubs," "King and Constitution Clubs," "Loyal Briton Societies," and "Pitt Clubs" – "dedicated to counteracting the 'principles disseminated by the partisans of the French Revolution" and memorializing Pitt as an opponent to parliamentary reform and Catholic emancipation – helped build a mass base, stretching down into the minor gentry and middle classes, for the Tories.[64] These would provide the infrastructure for the later formation of the Brunswick Clubs, whose declared purpose was "the *support of our protestant constitution.*"[65] In periodicals such as the *Antijacobin Review and True Churchman's Magazine*, the Protestant Constitution was regularly reaffirmed and mobilized in support of Tory politicians.[66]

When a Whig ministry briefly came to power in 1807 and proposed a modest Catholic relief bill – as well as prohibiting the slave trade – this network of activists organized an extensive "No Popery!" campaign: "Support the King and the Protestant Constitution!" they urged. The Whigs were decimated in the general elections. For the next two decades, popular anti-Catholicism gave the Protestant Constitution an electoral strength that persuaded many MPs that relief was not worth pursuing. "As an English question," wrote Willoughby Gordon in 1811, Catholic relief "is decidedly unpopular." He warned that "unless the temper of the people is very much changed, there is nothing which

---

[64] O'Gorman, "English Loyalism Revisited," 227; James Sack, "The Memory of Burke and the Memory of Pitt: English Conservatism Confronts Its Past," *The Historical Journal* 30, no. 3 (1987):623–40, 635, 637.

[65] *The Protestant Warder* 1, no. 4 (February 14, 1829): 74.

[66] Mori, "Languages of Loyalism," 39, 56.

would be more likely to create a popular ferment, if handled by designing knaves, (of which there is never a scarcity) than a Catholic concession."[67]

The reaction that had set in with the outbreak of the French Revolution did not end with the defeat of Napoleon. Instead, it was buttressed by harsh measures intended to repress organized support for political and constitutional reforms. On August 16, 1819, a mass meeting in support of parliamentary reform in Manchester was violently dispersed by cavalry. The government responded with the Six Acts, toughening penalties for "blasphemous libels" against the established church, requiring magistrates' permission for any large meeting that dealt with matters connected with the church or state, and raising the duties required of newspapers. Ultra-Protestant Lord Sidmouth explained that the country faced a conspiracy "for the subversion of the constitution and of the rights of property," one "intended to subvert the fabric of the constitution in church and state." What parliamentary reform threatened, and what the new network of Tory activists was defending, was the sectarian state, the established church, and the property claims this enabled.[68]

BUILDING AN ALTERNATIVE TO THE PROTESTANT CONSTITUTION

After the "No Popery" campaign of 1807, the dominance of the Tories was secured for a generation. Their political strength, however, brought with it new complications, as aspiring politicians, including many liberals, decided that adherence to Tory ranks was a prerequisite to public office. The consequences of the Act of Union continued to play out, as persistent violence in Ireland pushed some ministers to consider ways in which they could win the quiescence of the Catholic population. Military officers in particular noted that Catholics were a very large share of the armed forces but were impeded from advancing in the ranks or holding high commissions.[69] A growing minority of potential ministers now supported

---

[67] Hexter, "The Protestant Revival and the Catholic Question in England, 1778–1829," 297–319, 201; Michael Roberts, "The Fall of the Talents, March 1807," *English Historical Review* 50, no. 197 (1935): 61–77, 65; *Hansard*, April 14, 1825, 2nd series, vol. 12, cc. 1336.

[68] *Hansard*, November 29, 1819, 1st series, vol. 41, cc. 344; Pellew, *The Life and Correspondence of the Right Honourable Henry Addington*, 278.

[69] W. R. Brock, *Lord Liverpool and Liberal Toryism, 1820–1827*, 2nd edn. (Hamden, CT: Archon Books, 1967); John Bew, *Castlereagh: A Life* (New York: Oxford University Press, 2012), 301.

some measure of Catholic relief, which remained anathema to most of the leadership and the party's base in the landed gentry and the Anglican clergy. As a result, it was increasingly difficult to form a government unless the prime minister could promise his colleagues that any legislation concerning Catholics would not be made a matter of collective responsibility.[70]

The growing divisions in the Tory ranks were mirrored in the dilemmas facing a fractious and divided opposition. Some connections between the aristocratic Whigs, religious dissenters, and middle-class radicals had been established during the Fox years, but there was little in the way of organizational or ideological unity among them; there was even less with the growing number of middle-class Irish Catholics demanding emancipation from the penal laws. Dissenters were clearly split on the question of Catholic emancipation, with many church leaders supporting it but much of the membership and constituents opposed. When a bill for Catholic relief was debated in 1825, hostile petitions were submitted by various dissenters, which were in turn condemned by the Unitarian Association, the dissenter members of the House, and by the General Body of Protestant Dissenting Ministers. "Intolerant Protestantism," writes Linda Colley, also "served as a powerful cement between the English, the Welsh and the Scots, particularly lower down the social scale."[71] As with white racism in America, anti-Catholicism has been identified by historians as a central part of popular political traditions, "closely linked with abiding memories of 'the Good Old Cause,'" the republican Commonwealth of 1649. Knowledge of popular prejudice and the memory of the riots that had accompanied earlier Catholic relief bills only confirmed many liberals in their opposition to parliamentary reform.[72] The antagonism between aristocratic liberals and parliamentary reformers intensified after the victory over Napoleon, as radicals among the working classes renewed their agitations for reform and were met with intensified repression. While many Whigs opposed the severity of the Six Acts, "they felt and expressed so much aristocratic aversion to the Radicals, even while they were defending their liberties, that union of

[70] A. Aspinall, *The Letters of King George IV, 1812–1830* (Cambridge: Cambridge University Press, 1938), 94; Sack, *From Jacobite to Conservative*, 20.

[71] Colley, *Britons*, 23.

[72] Machin, "Resistance to Repeal of the Test and Corporation Acts"; Rudé, "The Gordon Riots," 112–13; Colin Haydon, "Parliament and Popery in England, 1700–1780," *Parliamentary History* 19, no. 1 (2000):49–63, 55; Cannon, *Parliamentary Reform*, 186–87.

action between the Whigs and the mass of the people was rendered impossible." Reform was still "inscribed on [the Whigs'] banner, but not as their chief and most immediate object," and the party was so divided on the extent to which any reform should go that its leaders proposed little more than vague references to what Fox and Grey had supported twenty years earlier.[73]

The problems confronting these different groups were how to persuade a largely hostile electorate to support their policy proposals, and how to forge a united front when they shared little in the way of a common policy program or sense of ideological purpose. The divisions separating these disparate groups were never quite reconciled, especially between the British and Irish factions. But gradually they were able to work out a rhetorical script of British community around which they could frame their different objectives, with formal organizational unity coming only – and for the Irish Catholic movement only briefly and contentiously – after the goals of repeal, relief, and reform had been accomplished, and with the Whigs assuming the mantle of political leadership.

Opposition Rationales for Reform

Drawing on existing strands of British political rhetoric, reformers proclaimed that the cause of Britain was "civil and religious liberty, all over the world" and that the true genius of the British constitution was its progressive character, which, properly understood, demanded judicious reforms to accommodate changed circumstances and expand the scope of liberty. This counternarrative to the fixity of the Protestant Constitution could encompass repeal of the Test Acts, Catholic emancipation, and parliamentary reform, as well as a foreign policy dedicated to liberty and the abolition of the slave trade and slavery. These disparate causes could thereby be defended from the charge that they were opposed to England's national character and purpose: indeed, they could be claimed as the realization of the constitution's progressive reformist objectives.

Catholic relief was the central commitment of the Whigs. As one friendly historian has written, "their obstinate fidelity" to this cause was "one of the main reasons for their failure to obtain office," alienating them from the king and from the restricted electorate.[74] Since 1807, Whigs had

---

[73] G. M. Trevelyan, *Lord Grey of the Reform Bill: Being the Life of Charles, Earl of Grey* (London: Longmans, Green and Co., 1920), 182.

[74] Michael Roberts, *The Whig Party: 1807–1812* (New York: Macmillan and Co., 1939), 2.

been grasping for rhetorical framings that would allow them to support relief without incurring the wrath of the electorate. One tactic was to argue that Catholics were no longer the threat they had been. When Lord Calthorpe made this argument, however, he was met with a flood of angry letters, forcing him to quickly clarify his position: while Catholicism, the great enemy of the English people, remained unchanged, the influence of the clergy had diminished.[75]

This was hardly a compelling argument, as even if it were true, the clergy might yet regain influence. Until there was "a considerable change in the principles and character of the church of Rome," the laws were necessary as security for "the Protestant constitution of this country." Any effort to show that Catholics had changed amounted to the "the hood-winking of poor John Bull" and betrayed an ignorance of the history of England, which time and again showed that "the church of Rome is not merely unchanged, but unchangeable."[76] Moreover, whether Catholics had changed was irrelevant to the central question of whether the Protestant Constitution was right and should be maintained. As Lord Eldon argued, "The times, it is said, are changed and the Catholics, it is said, are changed; be it so; but such change does not affect the soundness of the principles, upon which this kingdom has established itself as a 'Protestant kingdom' with the powers of the state in Protestant hands, and with a Protestant church establishment, and toleration, – toleration from time to time enlarged to the utmost extent the public welfare will admit; but toleration only, for those who dissent from it."[77]

Another line of argument was that Catholic disabilities had become the root cause of Irish instability. Arthur Young's popular *A Tour in Ireland* had detailed the oppressions of the Irish laboring classes by "the little country gentlemen, or rather vermin of the kingdom," who could "scarcely invent an order which a servant, labourer, or cottar dares to refuse to execute" and who would be satisfied by nothing "but an unlimited submission." As we have seen in the United States, settler societies are often associated with deep commitments to hierarchy, as the status and material well-being of the settlers depend upon the specific ideas and institutional

---

[75] *Hansard*, April 14, 1825, 2nd series, vol. 12, cc. 1272–73.

[76] *Hansard*, May 10, 1825, 2nd series, vol. 13, c. 489; February 28, 1821, vol. 4, cc. 997–98; E. A. Kendall, *Letters to a Friend on the State of Ireland, the Roman Catholic Question, and the Merits of Constitutional Religious Distinctions*, 2nd part (London: James Carpenter, 1826), 328, 514–15; "Constitutional Questions," *The Edinburgh Annual Register for 1821*, vol. 14, chap. 4 (Edinburgh: John Ballantyne, 1823), 133.

[77] *Hansard*, April 17, 1821, 2nd series, vol. 5, c. 317.

arrangements that can justify and organize the expropriation and suppression of the indigenous population.[78] This was certainly evident in Ireland: Young blamed the exactions and arrogance of the "gentlemen of Ireland" for Irish instability, but argued that these settlers were enabled by the "ill-judged laws" that sustained the "abominable distinction of religion." The English laws establishing a civic hierarchy, the choices the English state had made in establishing its settler society, were now sustaining antagonisms along religious lines that – Young suggested – should have been eradicated by time. The only "cure of insurrection," he wrote, lay in removal of the "religious persecution" that "has divided the kingdom against itself."[79]

This would become one of the more resonant themes offered by reformers, promising a reduction in violence in the country and greater geopolitical security. Lord Grey noted that French conquests on the continent meant Napoleon would soon possess "a point, from which the most formidable attack may be directed against the shores of Ireland. Let us then, my Lords, before it be too late, provide for it that best security, that chief defence, more impregnable than fortifications and navies. – I mean the cordial attachment and combined energies of its whole people."[80] When Henry Grattan introduced petitions for Catholic emancipation, he likewise argued that this would "give strength to the Protestant church, to the act of Settlement, and to the Protestant succession to the crown," by uniting the people with the government and preserving "tranquility at home, and security and respectability abroad."[81]

Robert Peel denied that this would bring peace. To believe religious discrimination was the cause of violence was a fatal misunderstanding: it was instead a "gallant struggle for mastery" between settlers and natives, one that had involved "perpetual transfers of power" and "repeated confiscations of property," from the Irish to the English and Scots settlers, from Catholics to the Anglican aristocracy, clergy, and landed gentry. It was not prejudice or religious bigotry that was at issue, but the property

---

[78] Rana, *Two Faces of American Freedom*.

[79] Arthur Young, *A Tour in Ireland, 1776–1779* (London: Cassell and Co., 1897 [1780]), 165–69.

[80] T. C. Hansard, *The Parliamentary Debates from the Year 1803 to the Present Time*, vol. 17 (London: Longman, Hurst, Rees, Orme, and Brown, 1812), cc. 553–54.

[81] *Hansard*, May 3, 1819, 1st series, vol. 40, cc. 6–7; O'Ferrall, *Catholic Emancipation*, 26–27; James Loughlin, *The British Monarchy and Ireland: 1800 to the Present* (Cambridge: Cambridge University Press, 2007), 18.

of the Church of Ireland, the plantation of Ulster, and the large and small incomes in Ireland and Great Britain that these produced.[82]

Whigs and other advocates of Catholic rights also developed a reinterpretation of the British constitutional tradition, one that placed civil and religious liberty – and not mere toleration – at its core. This reinterpretation cast as the defining characteristic of the British Constitution its ability to be gradually adapted to achieve this central purpose and to accommodate changed circumstances. For example, in his 1821 *An Essay on the History of the English Government and Constitution*, future Whig prime minister John Russell argued that while the revolutionaries of 1688 had done all they could have been expected to do to establish "religious liberty" in the country, "by their maxims [they had] laid the foundation of much more."[83] Reformers such as Russell argued that instead of having been a final constitutional settlement, 1688 had established instead a set of principles whose realization required the regular adaptation of governing institutions: English political development had long relied on the "practical wisdom of our ancestors" who knew when "to alter and vary the form of our institutions" in order "to suit them to the circumstances of the time, and reform them according to the dictates of experience." This art of reform, he regretted, "is now seldom used."[84]

The language of progressive reform was most clearly and effectively invoked on the subjects of Catholic emancipation and parliamentary reform, the two issues most in need of rhetorical cover against the "trembling anxiety for the immutability of the laws of our ancestors" and the "antijacobin clamor against innovation."[85] As early as 1792, Charles Grey had argued that reform was needed to secure the "the genuine principles of our Constitution," which time and corruption had subverted. "We wish to reform the Constitution," he argued then, "because

[82] *Hansard*, February 28, 1821, 2nd series, vol. 4, cc. 1001; Fergus O'Ferrall, *Catholic Emancipation: Daniel O'Connell and the Birth of Irish Democracy, 1820–30* (Dublin: Gill and Macmillan, 1985), 6.

[83] John Russell, *An Essay on the History of the English Government and Constitution* (London: Longman, Hurst, Rees, Orme, and Brown, 1821), 13–15, 105, 239–73.

[84] Reformers likewise drew on the new language of historical progress – "scientific Whiggism" – that owed much to the Scottish Enlightenment. Gordon Pentland, *Radicalism, Reform, and National Identity in Scotland, 1820–1833* (Rochester, UK: Boydell and Brewer, 2008), 12–13; Hansard, *The Parliamentary Debates*, vol. 17, cc. 562–64.

[85] William Smith [Protestant Dissenter], *An Appeal to the Protestant Dissenters of Great Britain, to United with Their Catholic Brethren* (London: A. J. Valpy, 1813), 2.

we wish to preserve it."[86] This phrase, repeated by Whigs whenever reform was debated between the 1790s and the 1830s, became a touchstone for their understanding of their own political purpose and the principles of the British constitution. The constitution was progressive, and it was the responsibility of enlightened statesmanship to offer judicious reforms as needed to accommodate the improvement of the country and advance the sphere of civil and religious liberty.

The claim that the inclusion of Catholics in Parliament was consistent with the country's constitutional tradition provided cover for liberal Tories, while the narrative of an adaptable constitution with the promise of civil and religious liberty at its core served as an umbrella under which Catholic relief, repeal of the Test Acts, and parliamentary reform could be treated as implications of a common project.[87]

"Civil and Religious Liberty, All Over the World!"

These rhetorical strategies would establish a set of common principles upon which activists associated with the different reform movements could advance their distinct policy goals. Dissenters worked to muster an often suspicious constituency behind the standard of religious liberty for all, arguing that "if the Dissenter deserts the standard of religious freedom, his consistency is lost forever. To stand trembling is to be destroyed; to unite is to conquer."[88] William Smith, the Unitarian MP for Norwich, advanced this argument at length in his pamphlet, "An Appeal to the Protestant Dissenters of Great Britain, to unite with their Catholic brethren, for the removal of the disqualifications by which they are oppressed."[89]

Catholic reformers reached out to dissenters on the same principle. The Catholic Association of Birmingham issued a public expression of its "anxious wish to join the Dissenters of this town and neighbourhood in common exertions to obtain the full enjoyment of their constitutional rights," and proposed the formation of a common society whose sole object would be to obtain the "unconditional repeal of every law which imposes any religious test oath or declaration other than a simple oath of

---

[86] Hansard, *The Parliamentary Debates*, vol. 17, c. 564; see also *Hansard*, October 7, 1831, 3rd series, vol. 8, cc. 313–14.
[87] Brock, *Lord Liverpool and Liberal Toryism*; O'Ferrall, *Catholic Emancipation*, 26–7.
[88] Hexter, "The Protestant Revival and the Catholic Question in England," 304.
[89] Smith, *Appeal to the Protestant Dissenters*.

civil allegiance to the Government of the country as a qualification for holding office." The association invited "Dissenters of every denomination, Catholics, and those most numerous, liberal, and respectable Protestants of the established church" to "wipe off the foul blot of religious intolerance." White the meeting's agenda was limited to the topic of religious reform, representatives of the working classes and advocates of parliamentary reform were also invited, with toasts praising the "Mechanics of Birmingham" for exemplifying the steady softening of the working classes' religious intolerance.[90]

In Ireland, a more broad-based Catholic Association was being organized, but here too there were repeated efforts to forge a common sympathy and project with dissenters. Daniel O'Connell, a young Irish Catholic lawyer, often repeated the framing offered by English Whigs of an English constitution that was intended to secure religious liberty for all. When the Catholic Association moved to organize a petition campaign for "the liberty of conscience," O'Connell proposed to have "one prepared praying Parliament that the Protestant Dissenters of England may be put on the same footing as those of Ireland."[91] He frequently reminded his audiences that "every additional Protestant who joined was an accession of strength as the principle they acted upon was one of universal liberty of conscience."[92]

The narrative of common purpose that was being worked out was embedded in a motto that would become the defining slogan of the post-Fox Whig party. John Russell, reflecting later in life, noted that as a member of "the Whig party, the aim of that party has always been my aim – 'The cause of civil and religious liberty all over the world.'"[93] Charles Grey toasted the same cause in the 1790s and in 1829 wrote that he had always been "a friend, in the words of the old Whig toast, to 'the cause of liberty all over the world.'"[94] *The Manchester Guardian*, launched in 1821 as a liberal weekly with a dissenting readership, promised in its prospectus to "zealously enforce the principles of civil and

[90] Midland Catholic Association, *Report of the Proceedings of the Midland Catholic Association* (London: W. E. Andrews, 1826), 13.

[91] Minutes of the RCA, National Archives, HO100/213/ff.269, HO100/213/ff.108.

[92] John O'Connell, *The Select Speeches of Daniel O'Connell, M. P.* (Dublin: Duffy, 1867), 322.

[93] John Russell, *Recollections and Suggestions, 1813–1873* (London: Longmans, Green, and Co., 1875), 213.

[94] F. A. R. Russell, *Early Correspondence of Lord John Russell, 1805–40* (London: T. F. Unwin, 1913), 299.

religious liberty" and to "warmly advocate the cause of reform."[95] This motto was a regular toast at political and religious meetings, where it was generally received with hearty applause, and was described as "a sentiment which should be warmly cherished by every Dissenter."[96]

While it seems to have initially been seen as a Protestant toast – for the principal enemy of liberty in Europe was supposed to be the Catholic Church – reformers in the late eighteenth and early nineteenth centuries began to expand its purview.[97] At the meeting of the Birmingham Catholic Association, a toast was offered to "the cause [of] Civil and Religious Liberty all over the World!" This shocked the representative of the city's mechanics, who rose to describe the "warm interest I feel in the toast you have recently drank. . . . I had never heard a Catholic speak on the subject of Catholic Emancipation, and now that, for the first time in my life, I have the honour of sitting down with a Catholic body, my ears are greeted with the great and glorious toast – 'Civil and Religious Liberty all over the world!'"[98] At an 1817 meeting of political reformers in London, a series of Whig toasts were given that called for reform and praised the cause of civil and religious liberty. A liberal Irish lawyer, John Philpot Curran, was moved by the last, and was hopeful that the toast's coverage might be universal:

You have been pleased, however, to give one toast – the cause of civil and religious liberty all over the world. When you drank that toast, I felt my heart embrace the negro – I felt also that it sympathised with my own poor country. Ireland, if it heard that toast, would bless that generous prospect of yours, from which alone can grow our human existence – (applause).

"You will not find them unworthy coadjutors in the vineyard of liberty," he promised.[99] At a feast in Ireland for the Friends of Religious Liberty,

[95] Archibald Prentice, *Historical Sketches and Personal Recollections of Manchester* (London: Charles Gilpin, 1851), 206.

[96] *The Monthly Repository (and Review)*, April 1817, p. 248; for a sample of the toasts, see *The Times* (London), June 10, 1811, p. 3; January 26, 1820, p. 3; June 5, 1820, p. 3; January 22, 1821, p. 3; *The Irishman* (Belfast), June 29, 1821, p. 1; *The Manchester Guardian*, October 13, 1821, p. 2. Abraham Kriegel, "Liberty and Whiggery in Early Nineteenth-Century England," *Journal of Modern History* 52, no. 2 (1980): 253–78, 262.

[97] Protestant Advocate, "Prospectus," *The Protestant Advocate* 1 (October 1812):1–2, 1; Kendall, *Letters to a Friend on the State of Ireland*, 542; the first appearance I can find of the full toast is in *Morning Chronicle* (London), December 10, 1792, p. 3.

[98] Midland Catholic Association, *Report of the Proceedings of the Midland Catholic Association*, 19.

[99] *Niles' Weekly Register*, March 29, 1817, p. 76.

Catholic attendees toasted "civil and religious liberty all over the world," and called for a moment of silence for "the glorious and immortal memory of Charles James Fox." The *Protestant Advocate*, reporting on the meeting, remarked that "the candid reader must acknowledge that Papists can hardly be comprehended in the toast." But this was precisely the point.[100] The *Irishman* of Belfast, denouncing the suppression of English liberties after the Peterloo Massacre – and noting that when this had earlier been done to Ireland, England had "laughed at the wounds and suffering of our country" – declared its belief that "the [parliamentary] Reformers of England are the real, honest and sincere friends of the Liberty of our Country, and as such we feel it our duty to embrace the cause they so boldly and honestly advocate." Only with a reform of Parliament, after all, could the "Irishman, be he Protestant or Catholic," hope to receive justice: the unreformed "Parliament cannot act as a free agent; it must obey the Minister or the Boroughmonger [i.e., election brokers], or rather, both must obey the Established Church, and that church will never tolerate civil and religious liberty."[101]

The reformers were advancing an understanding of British political community in which the principle of civil and religious liberty, encompassing Catholics, was read into the heart of the British constitutional tradition. And as John Russell and others insisted, securing civil and religious liberty required political liberty: the "right of the people to control their government, or to take a share in it" was "the only efficient remedy against oppression."[102] After toasting "the cause of civil and religious liberty, all over the world" at a dinner honoring reformer Joseph Hume, one gentleman rose to state, "I despair of seeing this country prosperous, or its people happy and free, without a reform in Parliament; I therefore propose – 'A full and fair representation of the people in the British House of Commons.'" This was met with "great applause."[103] Similar scenes were repeated across the country in the 1820s, as toasts connecting the cause of civil and religious liberty to reform became a mainstay of "Fox Dinners," Whig meetings, and any gathering of reformers.

The mantra was invoked precisely because it allowed the projects of repeal, relief, and reform to appear as shared implications of a common

[100] "Waterford Feast of Religious Liberty," *The Protestant Advocate* 1 (April 1813): 369–71.
[101] *The Irishman* (Belfast), October 8, 1819, p. 2; December 19, 1824, p. 2; December 24, 1824, p. 2.
[102] Russell, *Essay on the History of the English Government and Constitution*, 86, 115, 148; *Manchester Guardian*, May 31, 1823, p. 4.
[103] *The Times* (London), October 1, 1822, p. 3.

cause. The vision of collective purpose and constitutional narratives that this implied would be central to the efforts of Whigs to build support for their policies and election. By cheering on progressive reforms to better advance the cause of civil and religious liberty, they offered potential constituents and committed activists a vison of political purpose that was both the cause of a party and, they claimed, the cause of the British people.

THE CATHOLIC REVOLT

Catholic emancipation was ultimately forced on the English government by the successful efforts of the Catholic Association in Ireland. It came at a steep price: the disenfranchisement of the forty-shilling freeholders in the Irish counties.

The Catholic Association was an important moment in the development of mass contentious politics in the United Kingdom, organizing a social movement across class – and at times even sectarian lines – while remaining entirely within the narrow bounds of what the British state considered legal, in order to pressure a government that was actively hostile to its professed objectives. Its most important innovation was the Catholic Rent, which required all Irish Catholics, no matter how poor or rich, to give money each month, scaled according to wealth. The money paid for petition drives, a permanent lobbyist in Westminster, legal representation for victims of Orange Order violence, support for a liberal press in Dublin, and eventually for helping tenant farmers evicted by their landlords for voting for liberal candidates. But the funds had a broader purpose as well, as the number and diversity of people willing to pay and the amount the association was able to raise provided concrete measures of the breadth of the association's base of support. In short, it allowed the association to claim to "represent the public voice and guide the public opinion," and raised the fear of the British government that a counterpower was being raised in its most insurrectionary province.[104]

Before the Rent, emancipation bills had been regularly defeated in Parliament. One liberal Whig, William Plunket, presented a petition for Catholic relief in 1824, but he also told O'Connell that no legislative action would be forthcoming. "The [supportive] English Representatives," he reported, "will not vote, or attend when the subject

[104] O'Ferrall, *Catholic Emancipation*, xiv, 51, 53–54.

is merely discussion."[105] The next year, however, the scale of support
indicated by the Rent had given these English members a bit more
spine, and the Whigs decided to press the issue in the Commons.
The Tory government in the Commons was headed by a liberal who
was supportive of Catholic emancipation but opposed to repeal of the
Test Acts and parliamentary reform. George Canning was willing to
allow a vote on relief, but he demanded that it be preceded by the
repression of the association, which he described as an unconstitutional "*imperium in imperio*" and denounced as "self-elected – self-
constructed – self assembled – self-adjourned." Robert Peel reminded
the Commons that "there were many persons who considered the
representation of the people in parliament to be so bad and imperfect,
that a large portion of the people were deprived of their rights," and
warned that if the association was not repressed, "why might not the
country expect an Association for the purpose of obtaining parliamentary reform?" This was met with loud approval from the Whig
benches.[106] A repression bill passed 226 to 96, outlawing the Catholic
Association.

Francis Burdett then moved that the House form a committee to consider Catholic emancipation. He warned that tranquility would not continue "until full and ample justice be done." He acknowledged that in past
centuries, the Catholics really had been dangerous and the penal laws
justified. He said circumstances had changed, that the papacy was no
longer a threat, and that the "public mind of this country" had changed
and become less bigoted. He declared his loyalty to the Church of
England. And finally, he hoisted the standard of religious and civil liberty
as a constitutive principle of the country. "I have further to remember
what the constitution of my country teaches me," he declared. "*I contend,
that, so far from this being a Catholic question, the Catholics themselves
stand upon a Protestant principle; and that I am now maintaining their
claims, upon the very principles which assured the security of England. ...*
The Catholics are asking for nothing more than what the Protestants first
desired – namely, that we should deal out to them the principle of constitutional and religious freedom [hear, hear!]." Another argued that in
advocating this principle they were not "fighting the battle of the
Catholics but his own battle – the battle of all the Dissenters – the battle

---

[105] Minutes of the RCA, National Archives, HO100/213/ff.131.
[106] *Hansard*, February 10, 1825, 2nd series, vol. 12, cc. 248; February 15, 1825, vol. 12, cc.
465; February 25, 1825, vol. 12, cc. 719.

of civil and religious liberty."[107] Whigs were arguing that the British constitution, properly understood, *mandated* emancipation. Burdett's motion to form a committee was passed by a vote of 247 to 234; a few months later, a relief bill passed the House of Commons 268 to 241.

These were relatively narrow victories, possible only because the leader of the government was a supporter of emancipation, because the Catholic Association had been repressed, and because two accompanying bills would secure "inviolate the Protestant Episcopal Church of England and Ireland" by providing a government veto over the appointments of the Catholic clergy and their direct payment by the treasury – so they would be dependent on the government – and disenfranchising the mass of Catholic voters.

In an effort to not alienate liberal Tories, the association had carefully avoided taking a position on parliamentary reform, although it supported repeal of the Test Acts. Still, English political reformers had been impressed by the organizing success of the association and had hoped that O'Connell might use his new prestige to come out in favor of reform. But to the disillusionment of many political reformers and leading members of the Catholic Association, O'Connell not only maintained his silence on reform but also indicated his contingent support for Irish disenfranchisement.[108] If O'Connell was willing to sacrifice the Irish franchise, asked the reformer William Cobbett (whom we last saw as a Federalist writer in Philadelphia), what reason was there to think he would support the middle classes of England?[109] One Whig member of Parliament worried that "if a forty-shilling qualification were considered as too small for an elector in Ireland, what was to prevent its being considered as too small for an elector in England?"[110] Lord Grey opposed disenfranchisement on the grounds that it conflicted with the Whig stance on parliamentary reform and was "quite untenable either in policy or principle."[111]

Most Whigs, however, eager to pass emancipation and many distrustful of Irish voters, were willing to go along. Burdett insisted that Irish disenfranchisement was entirely separate from the cause of expanding voting rights in England, and urged members to seize the opportunity to

[107] *Hansard*, March 1, 1825, 2nd series, vol. 12, cc. 764–85; February 15, 1825, vol. 12, c. 429.
[108] *Hansard*, May 12, 1825, 2nd series, vol. 13, c. 566–68.
[109] William Cobbett, "To the Freeholders of Ireland," *Weekly Register* 53, no. 12 (1825): 705–48.
[110] *Hansard*, March 28, 1825, 2nd series, vol. 12, cc. 1249–50.
[111] G. I. T. Machin, "The Catholic Emancipation Crisis of 1825," *English Historical Review* 78, no. 308 (1963): 458–82, 463, 473.

achieve emancipation and establish peace in Ireland on "the solid basis of civil and religious liberty." Thomas Spring Rice suggested that disenfranchisement was acceptable precisely because it would not diminish "the strength of popular principles among the peasantry and the small land-owners of Ireland." Because the freeholders of Ireland were under the thumb of their landlords, their disenfranchisement "would be a most wise, salutary, and popular reform of the constituent body."[112] Lord Althorp likewise argued that the forty-shilling voters of Ireland were not independent, and insisted that it was not only compatible with his support for parliamentary reform but very much in the same spirit, which aimed to "deprive of the right of voting those who had no independent vote." Henry Parnell defended disenfranchisement and quoted Fox as supporting the principle of "includ[ing] the greatest number of independent electors, and exclud[ing] the greatest number of those who are necessarily by their condition dependent."[113]

Repression passed the Commons, emancipation passed the Commons, and disenfranchisement would have passed as well. The House of Lords, however, stood for the Protestant Constitution. The Tory Lords insisted that the Irish "would be content with nothing short of Catholic ascendancy." They could not, as a matter of principle, "be admitted to a participation with Protestants of certain civil rights and political power in a free Protestant country," and so emancipation would necessarily entail "the sacrifice of some essential principles of our Protestant constitution and government."[114] After two days of debate, the Lords rejected the bill by a majority of forty-eight votes, more than even the more pessimistic supporters of relief had feared.[115]

The Tory Duke of Wellington had worried that the government might not be able to mount a successful anti-Catholic campaign, that the force of bigotry had waned in the English population. In the general election that followed, however, the Tories and their network of loyalist and Protestant clubs again rose to the occasion, winning on a "No Popery!" campaign that seemed to confirm the depth of anti-Catholic sentiment. The anti-Catholic numbers increased by approximately a dozen members, and Tories interpreted the results as "decidedly friendly to Ministers, and particularly to

---

[112] *Hansard*, April 26, 1825, 2nd series, vol. 13, cc. 239–40, 243; March 28, 1825, vol. 12, c. 1248.

[113] *Hansard*, April 22, 1825, 2nd series, vol. 13, c. 127, 132; April 26, 1825, vol. 13, c. 176, 178, 231.

[114] *Hansard*, May 17, 1825, 2nd series, vol. 13, c. 676, 688, 694.

[115] O'Ferrall, *Catholic Emancipation*, 101.

Protestants. The Whigs have been beaten, wherever there have been popular contests," and "the radicals have not met with much better success."[116]

In Ireland, however, the election campaign revealed the potency of the Catholic movement, which had now reorganized itself into a "New Catholic Association" that narrowly complied with the repression law.[117] During the election, Thomas Wyse – a member of the Catholic gentry – led an effort to defeat one of the Beresfords, an aristocratic family considered a pillar of the Protestant ascendancy. Each elector was entitled to cast a vote for both of the two county seats, and Beresford – following a relatively common practice – demanded that his tenants cast one for him while allowing them to cast the other for a candidate of their choice (he let it be known that liberal Protestant Richard Power would be acceptable). The final result, however, saw Power with 1,424 votes, 1,357 for Henry Villiers Stuart, another liberal Protestant who had the support of Wyse and the Catholic movement, and a humiliating 527 for Beresford. Exercising the prerogative of his class, Beresford evicted tenants who voted against him. Elsewhere, the aristocratic families who controlled most of the county seats had generally decided that an election contest would be too dangerous, and so colluded to ensure none took place. Still, in eight contested counties, the Catholic Association had endorsed a candidate and were successful in six.[118]

The election led to a proliferation of "Liberal Clubs" across Ireland, intended to organize support for liberal candidates and to protect Catholic freeholders from the inevitable landlord reprisals. The clubs were to provide "a uniform, universal, permanent, system of enlightened and energetic co-operation," linking local concerns with the national New Catholic Association and the cross-national cause of an emerging "liberal-ism." "The Catholic, or rather independent constituency of Ireland," announced Wyse, would through the clubs "be completely disciplined, and will not need any application of extraordinary stimulants to rouse them to a sense of their constitutional duty."[119] The possibility of inde-pendent Catholic political organizing led one Protestant to write to Peel

[116] Richard Davis, "Wellington and the 'Open Question': The Issue of Catholic Emancipation, 1821–1829," *Albion: A Quarterly Journal Concerned with British Studies* 29, no. 1 (1997): 39–55, 45; O'Ferrall, *Catholic Emancipation*, 147; http://www.historyofparliamentonline.org/volume/1820–1832/parliament/1826–0.

[117] Thomas Wyse, *Historical Sketch of the Late Catholic Association of Ireland*, vol. 1 (London: Henry Colburn, 1829), xl, app. 15.

[118] O'Ferrall, *Catholic Emancipation*, 132, 143–44.

[119] Wyse, *Historical Sketch of the Late Catholic Association*, cxlv, cliv.

that "a *bellum servile*" – a slave or servant war – "would ensue all over Ireland."[120]

Opening the Floodgates

Throughout his life, King George III had insisted that Catholic emancipation would be a violation of his coronation oath, and his religious devotion was such that few believed he could be swayed. His death in 1820 brought his son to power. George IV had no religious scruples, and no one believed his oath would be an obstacle to anything.[121] But his younger brother – the Duke of York – carried considerable influence with him and was a notorious bigot. The prime minister, moreover, was Lord Liverpool, who had argued that emancipation would lead the country to "revert to a state of ignorance," and had warned his colleagues that when "the *crisis does come*, the *Protestants* must go to the wall."[122]

Things started to look better for the Catholic cause when the Duke of York died; even better prospects seemed to follow a debilitating stroke that ended Liverpool's career. His replacement was Canning, who remained opposed to repeal of the Test Acts against dissenters and parliamentary reform but in favor of Catholic emancipation. Still, the king agreed to Canning forming a government only after another Catholic relief measure was defeated, suggesting that the measure was doomed for the immediate future. Even then, Peel, Wellington, and anti-Catholic cabinet officers either resigned or turned down Canning's invitation to join the government. Canning was next to die, bringing Peel and Wellington – whose influence rested on a combination of their talent, service to their country, and vehement opposition to any reform of the fundamental principles of the constitution – into office. The cause of civil and religious liberty had not looked so bleak since 1807.

In 1828, however, John Russell moved that the Test and Corporation Acts against dissenters be repealed, and against the vigorous opposition of a surprised government, it passed the Commons. The success of repeal has often been said to have improved the chances of Catholic emancipation, by undermining the "principle that the State and the established Church were

[120] O'Ferrall, *Catholic Emancipation*, 151.
[121] Hexter, "The Protestant Revival and the Catholic Question in England," 302.
[122] Brock, *Lord Liverpool and Liberal Toryism*, 269.

co-extensive."[123] Many contemporaries, however, believed the exact opposite: that repeal would undermine the prospects for emancipation by driv-
ing a wedge between reformers, passing the more popular measure and
leaving the Catholics isolated. The United Committee of Dissenters, for
instance, announced that year that they would no longer work with the
Catholics, in the hopes of winning the support of the anti-Catholic
Protestant Association. A number of dissenters had long argued that supporting both repeal and relief was a mistake, that while there was no
principled reason why they should not "make common cause," the measures should be kept distinct so as to make it easier to secure repeal: "I think
it can never be deemed a want of liberality in Protestant Dissenters, if they
should wish to disjoin their cause from the Catholics, against whom
a prejudice exists, that retards the accomplishment of their most earnest
and reasonable hopes. . . . [M]any no doubt might be disposed to listen to
the application for relief from Protestant Dissenters, whose honest and
conscientious scruples would indispose them to make any further concessions to the believers in the religion of the Church of Rome."[124] Even some
of the Tory "Ultras" – the most vitriolic defenders of the Protestant
Constitution – had begun to waver on the question of repeal, believing
that they needed to detach dissenters from the Catholic cause and promote
a more genuinely "Protestant" political project. It was the Ultras, in fact,
who provided the surprising margin of victory for repeal.

The ideological and coalitional work of the last several decades now
paid off: despite efforts to separate the two issues of repeal and relief, one
historian has noted that this "distinction could not be complete because
the whigs did not believe in such a severance. As positive supporters of
catholic emancipation, they saw the two causes as fundamentally linked in
their policy of civil liberty."[125] The Whigs had repeatedly committed
themselves to "the cause of civil and religious liberty all over the
world," they had strenuously argued that this included Catholics, and
their representatives insisted that it would be on the basis of the "one great
principle of universal, undistinguishing right to religious liberty, and on

---

[123] Machin, "Resistance to Repeal of the Test and Corporation Acts," 118–19;
Thomas Ertman, "The Great Reform Act of 1832 and British Democratization,"
Comparative Political Studies 43, no. 8–9 (2010): 1000–1022; O'Ferrall, *Catholic
Emancipation*, 180.
[124] Civis, *A Letter to Lord John Russell on the Necessity of Parliamentary Reform* (London:
R. Hunter, 1819), 36.
[125] Machin, "Resistance to Repeal of the Test and Corporation Acts," 119.

that alone," that they would vote.[126] While Whig leaders worried that they might lose some dissenter support, they also believed that "to gain the principle established by repeal would, of itself, be of more use to the Catholics than the votes of the Dissenters they may lose."[127] They worked carefully behind the scenes to keep dissenting members from abandoning the Catholic cause, and they marshaled the leadership of the dissenting denominations to publicly reaffirm their commitment to emancipation. Daniel O'Connell drew up a petition that announced the absolute support of the Irish Catholic population for repeal, which passed unanimously in the Catholic Association and was presented to Parliament with 80,000 signatures. He then issued an *Address of the Catholic Association to the Protestant Dissenters of England*, reminding them of their common cause and urging them to not desert the standard of religious liberty.[128]

When the crucial division on repeal came, there was "a perfect whip" among the Whigs.[129] Almost all of them would then support a resolution in favor of Catholic emancipation offered a week later. Only thirty-nine members of the Commons voted for repeal and against emancipation, the large majority of them Ultra Tories; only twenty-three MPs, most of them liberal Tories and cabinet members, voted against repeal and for emancipation.

Peel and Wellington were left with no options but to resign, oppose the bill in the House of Lords, or offer it their support. The first was unpalatable, the second would lead to a political crisis that they did not believe they could withstand, and so for lack of any better option, they chose the third. Repeal of the Test and Corporation Acts passed the Lords soon after.

Russell, responding to an inquiry about his health, remarked that "my constitution is not quite so improved as the Constitution of the country by late events, but the joy of it will soon revive me. It is really a gratifying thing to force the enemy to give up his first line – that none but Churchmen are worthy to serve the State; I trust we shall soon make him give up the second, that none but Protestants are."[130] The repeal of the Test Acts did provide a new boost to the Catholic movement, but this reflected the

---

[126] *Hansard*, February 26, 1828, 2nd series, vol. 18, cc. 738.
[127] Edward Law, *A Political Diary, 1828–1830*, vol. 1 (London: Richard Bentley and Son, 1881), 44.
[128] Daniel O'Connell, *A Full and Revised Report of the Three Days' Discussion in the Corporation of Dublin on the Repeal of the Union* (Dublin: J. Duffy, 1843), 63.
[129] Machin, "Resistance to Repeal of the Test and Corporation Acts," 123.
[130] S. J. Reid, *Lord John Russell* (London: Sampson, Low, Martson, and Co., 1895), 58.

ideological work undertaken over the previous two decades, which had helped constitute a broadly shared interest among reformers in affirming the common principle of civil and religious liberty.

A few weeks later, an Irish MP – William Vesey-Fitzgerald – joined the Wellington ministry and resigned his seat to stand for reelection.[131] The Catholic Association was pledged to oppose all supporters of the Wellington government, and after failing to find a suitable liberal Protestant, they selected Daniel O'Connell himself as their candidate. While O'Connell could not sit in Parliament without taking the proscriptive oath, there was no law to stop him from running.

It was a bitter election, with Catholic Association and Liberal Club organizers canvassing the county and liberal Protestants desperately warning the voters that "the county would not be fit for a gentleman to live in if the result ... were to show that property had lost its influence." O'Connell, attacked for having accepted the disenfranchisement proposal in 1825, declared that he had done so because he had been "of the opinion that it would be impossible to free [the forty-shilling freeholders] from the influence of their landlords. I now want to know whether the forty-shilling freeholders of Clare are the slaves of their landlords. Are they, like the negroes, to be lashed by their torturers to the slave mart and sold to the highest bidder? This experiment I am about to make.. ... It was a fault in me to have consented to their disfranchisement; but I have made full and ample reparation, and sooner now would I shed the last drop of my blood than consent to their disfranchisement."[132] Fitzgerald carried "all the gentry and all the £50 freeholders – the gentry to a man." But the forty-shilling voters broke against their landlords despite promises of evictions. O'Connell won, 2,057 to 982.[133]

It was a political earthquake, and Peel foresaw violent aftershocks. The "instrument of political power" that had maintained the Protestant ascendancy in Ireland had been "shivered to atoms in the county of Clare," and no one should delude themselves into thinking it "could still be wielded with effect in Cork or Galway." It had been "the force of local and personal attachments" – i.e., landlord intimidation and tenant dependency – that had maintained Protestant and landlord control over elections. These had now been decisively displaced by the organized

---

[131] It was customary upon entering the cabinet to resign and seek reelection.

[132] Michael MacDonagh, *The Life of Daniel O'Connell* (London: Cassell and Co., 1903), 157.

[133] O'Ferrall, *Catholic Emancipation*, 96, 199.

counterforce of the Catholic Association. "What was the evil to be apprehended," he asked. "Not force – not violence – not any act of which law could take cognizance. The real danger was in the peaceable and legitimate exercise of a franchise according to the will and conscience of the holder," which he described as being a "novel exercise" of the right to vote. The forty-shilling franchise, which had secured landlord dominance, now threatened the "Protestant Constitution in Church and State." It was a "transfer of political power," from the Protestant landlords to the Catholic tenants. Even more dangerous was the prospect that there would be a "repetition in each county," with the gentry voting "one way, their alienated tenantry another," leaving the "agitator and the priest laughing to scorn the baffled landlord." Genuinely contested elections would occasion violence and polarization, ending in the eventual breakdown of British rule: "The local heavings and throes of society on every casual vacancy in a county – the universal convulsion at a General Election – this was the danger to be apprehended."[134]

The immediate worry for the government, however, was both what to do with O'Connell and what to do if a large body of Catholic members were elected and refused entry to Parliament: they could sit as a separate "popish Parliament," as Sinn Féin would do ninety years later. O'Connell insisted on his peaceful desire to enter Parliament, but also reminded the government that the British state was heavily reliant on Irish Catholics: in a public comment to the Duke of Wellington, he offered "one whisper to your ear. 300 soldiers threw up their caps for me since I left Ennis."[135]

John Leslie Foster, a hardline anti-Catholic Anglo-Irish MP, wrote Peel that it was now absolutely necessary that the Irish tenants be disenfranchised.[136] The function of the franchise before "the rebellion of the freeholders [was] to enable a few great proprietors to nominate the county Members," and while Foster regretted that disenfranchisement might reduce the influence of the "great proprietors," transferring "much of the real power" to the "minor gentry, the [Protestant] clergy, and the more opulent farmers," he saw this as preferable to the continued influence of the Association. If disenfranchisement was "an evil," he asked, "can we help it?"

---

[134] O'Ferrall, *Catholic Emancipation*, 202; Philip Stanhope, *Memoirs by the Right Honourable Sir Robert Peel: Part 1, the Roman Catholic Question* (London: John Murray, 1856), 117.

[135] O'Ferrall, *Catholic Emancipation*, 200; Virginia Crossman, *Politics, Law and Order in Nineteenth Century Ireland* (New York: St. Martin's Press, 1996), 10–11.

[136] Charles Parker, *Sir Robert Peel: From His Private Papers*, 2nd edn. (London: J. Murray, 1899), 423.

The influence of the aristocracy is annihilated. The priests and the demagogues are in their place. The practical question seems to be whether we should not now aim at placing the power in the hands of that middle class as the best course within our reach. The minor gentry of Ireland are essentially Tory rather than Whig. Very little of what is radical enters into their composition. They are also essentially Protestant.

The Protestant Constitution in Ireland had relied on the ability of the aristocracy to control the forty-shilling voters, and now that this was shaken there was no alternative but to empower the minor gentry – Protestant but more Presbyterian and middle class than the government would have liked. If the Protestant Constitution was to be preserved, the government needed to take "the business of elections out of the hands of the lower classes."[137]

In the summer of 1828, Wellington informed the king that "we have a rebellion impending over us in Ireland," that they could not dissolve Parliament lest Catholics win the Irish county seats, and that a majority of the Commons supported emancipation and would not support the needed repressive legislation unless this was coupled with relief. The king gave him permission to consider emancipation, although when later presented with their plans, he sputtered, "Damn it, you mean to let them into Parliament." The very day before the emancipation bill was to be introduced, he drunkenly told Wellington and Peel that he would not accept changes to the "ancient Oath of Supremacy" and dared them to resign. Upon sobering up, he was advised that no other ministry could be formed: he wrote to Wellington, asking him to stay on and acknowledging that emancipation would have to be conceded.[138]

O'Connell was sounded out, and it was found that his support could be gotten "quite cheap." He was willing to accept the payment and "management of the priests," but noted that disenfranchisement was going to be more difficult, as the Association could not "all at once give them up." Still, O'Connell indicated as he had in 1826 – and despite his pledge on the hustings – that he could accept the disenfranchisement of the forty-shilling voters.[139]

The government now proposed to establish near civil and political equality for Catholics, coupled with the disenfranchisement of the forty-shilling voters. Peel defended the government's radically changed position in the Commons. He reminded MPs that since 1800, not a single year had

---

[137] Peel Papers, Department of Manuscripts at the British Library, add. 40397, ff. 384–94; *Hansard*, May 9, 1828, 2nd series, vol. 19, cc. 538–39.
[138] Ibid., 238, 245. [139] O'Ferrall, *Catholic Emancipation*, 203.

passed in which Ireland been governed by regular laws without a suspension of habeas corpus or emergency legislation, and that such disturbances would only grow now that the Catholics had organized a force through which voters could exercise the "tremendous power" of the franchise. He considered the possibility that an election could be held and an anti-Catholic majority returned after a "No Popery" campaign, but was forced to reject it: you could not hold elections in Great Britain "without making a simultaneous appeal to the elective body of Ireland – that body exercising the present franchise, under every circumstance of superadded mistrust, apprehension, and excitement." The result would be to sever the last ties between tenant and landlord, to confirm the power of the priests "in political matters," and the permanent unification of "Roman Catholic wealth, intelligence, numbers, and religion" in a "dangerous, but not illegal, exercise of a great constitutional right."

The only solution he could see was concession combined with disenfranchisement and repression. The "landlord has been disarmed by the priest," and that "weapon which he has forged with so much care, and has heretofore wielded with such success, has broke short in his hand. ... To the Protestant I would say, 'We restore to you your just weight in the representation – you are now overborne by a herd of voters, *the voice of each of whom is equal to yours* – you are foremost in that industrious, honest, and independent class, whose influence will be mainly increased by the disfranchisement of poverty and ignorance.'" Peel framed his motivation as the "anxious desire to provide for the maintenance of Protestant Interests; and for the security of Protestant establishments. This is my defence – this is my consolation – this shall be my revenge."

Peel moved that the House go into committee to consider relief, which was followed by "loud and protracted cheering." When the Commons voted to resolve itself into committee, the vote was 348 to 160, a determined majority but with the Tory party evenly divided.[140]

A reaction was brewing in the country, organized by "Brunswick Clubs" and the Anglican bishops. Over fourteen thousand inhabitants of Leeds – "including most of the respectable and influential persons" – signed a petition stating that the "strongest objections to any further Concession of Political Power to Roman Catholics prevails throughout a vast majority of all classes."[141] Similar petitions were organized across the country, and "the number of anti-catholic

---

[140] *Hansard*, March 5, 1829, 2nd series, vol. 20, c. 738, 746, 764, 772, 777, 779–80.
[141] National Archives, Ho 44/18/ff. 256.

petitions far outran the pro-catholic."[142] Having so radically changed course on emancipation, Peel felt obliged to stand for reelection in his University of Oxford constituency. In a shocking result, he was defeated, as the country's Anglican clergy and Oxford graduates punished his apostasy from the Protestant Constitution. He was quickly reelected in one of the pocket boroughs that the government commanded.

In the House of Lords, Wellington tried to defend emancipation as consistent with the Glorious Revolution: "In the Bill of Rights, there are some things permanently enacted, which I sincerely hope will be permanent; – those are, the liberties of the people; the security for the Protestantism of the person on the throne of these kingdoms, and that he shall not be married to a papist."[143] But the "principles of 1688" did not mandate Catholic exclusion; they only required this as a security for property and privileges of the Church establishment. Acquiescing in part to the Whig interpretation of Britain's constitution, he argued that if Catholic exclusion was not a permanent feature of the constitution, then it could be done away with. In April 1829, the emancipation bill passed the Lords by a vote of 213 to 109. Despite the frantic efforts of Church of Ireland bishops, the king signed the law on April 13, 1829.

Soon after came disenfranchisement: the forty-shilling franchise was abolished, and a new £10 freehold qualification imposed (in reality, £20 given that the law also changed the way in which freeholds were valued): it passed second reading with only seventeen votes against, at least six of which were from hardline anti-Catholics who refused to take any part in dismantling the sectarian pillars of the Constitution.[144] Most Whigs and reformers either abstained or cast their votes for it. Even the Radical MP Joseph Hume, who voted against second reading, explained that he would not oppose it too strenuously "lest he might thwart, the great measure of emancipation." Disenfranchisement decimated the Irish electorate: the number of voters in the countryside collapsed from more than two hundred thousand registered voters to fewer than forty thousand.[145]

---

[142] G. I. T. Machin, "The No-Popery Movement in Britain in 1828–9," *The Historical Journal* 6, no. 2 (1963): 193–211, 205.

[143] *Hansard*, April 2, 1829, 2nd series, vol. 21, cc. 48–51.

[144] *Hansard*, March 19, 1829, 2nd series, vol. 20, c. 1363; Farrell, "Ireland."

[145] Machin, "The No-Popery Movement in Britain," 195; Hoppen, *Elections, Politics, and Society in Ireland*, 1; *Hansard*, March 26, 1829, 2nd series, vol. 20, c. 1478.

"THE ONLY STRUGGLE REALLY WORTH MAKING"

Repeal and emancipation delivered "a hefty blow to the Tory concept of an inviolable Protestant constitution" and marked a fundamental change in the constitution of the country.[146] It also split the Tory Party open wide, its more active partisans unwilling to forgive Wellington and Peel. Posters defending "Our Protestant Constitution and the Ancient Institutions of My Country for ever!" were posted throughout Cambridge declaring that the Tory leaders "are our enemies.... Impeach them."[147]

Many of the Protestant Ultras believed the government had been able to pass emancipation only because of their control over pocket boroughs, ironically leading some to embrace the cause of parliamentary reform. The Marquis of Blanford introduced a bill calling for a general taxpaying franchise and the abolition of rotten boroughs, believing that the middle and upper working classes were more anti-Catholic than the aristocracy and more reliable than the placeseeking officeholders in Parliament. A Commons that "was not faithful to the exclusive principle of a Protestant king and Protestant parliament" needed to be replaced by a body that would "represent the anti-catholic sentiments of the people."[148] Blanford's proposal was supported in the House by Hume but also by O'Connell. No longer needing to reassure liberal Tories and moderate Whigs, O'Connell now outed himself as a "radical reformer" and defended the principle "that all who paid taxes directly or indirectly were entitled to a vote in the election of the Representatives," and appealed "to the great principle of democratic liberty which made England" great.[149]

One of the major impediments to building a broad movement in support of parliamentary reform had been the differing currents of opinion separating radicals from more modest reformers. The *Manchester Guardian*, for instance, wanted reform so that members of Parliament could be elected who were "intimately and practically connected with the cotton manufacture" – a booming industry that was

---

[146] Pentland, *Radicalism, Reform, and National Identity in Scotland*, 50.
[147] National Archives, HO 44/19/ff. 112
[148] Sack, *From Jacobite to Conservative*, 152–53; Blandford, *Hansard*, March 6, 1829, 2nd series, vol. 20, cc. 854–55; Asa Briggs, "The Background of the Parliamentary Reform Movement in Three English Cities (1830–2)," *Cambridge Historical Journal* 10, no. 3 (1952): 293–317.
[149] *Hansard*, February 18, 1830, 2nd series, vol. 22, cc. 720.

expanding slavery in America and building fortunes in England – and hoped the franchise would be set "on a basis so broad as to secure its being popular, but at the same time" subjected to "such limitations as might tend to prevent the exercise of a decisive influence on the result of elections by that class which, from want of education, and from penury, is least likely to use it with honesty and independence."[150] Others wanted reform in order to represent "acknowledged seat[s] of wealth, industry and commercial enterprise," such as Manchester and Birmingham.[151]

The example provided by the Irish gave parliamentary reformers a model to unify religious and political reformers around similar themes and patterns of action across the United Kingdom. Thomas Attwood – a proponent of expansionary monetary economics who largely distrusted the working classes but believed their expanded representation was needed to force Parliament to agree to currency reforms – organized the Birmingham Political Union.[152] Attwood believed that "there were materials of discontent enough" in the population, but that "the only difficulty was in making them harmonize and unite in some common remedy." What was needed, he declared, was "Union – such as the Irish exhibited."[153] William Biggs of the Leicester Political Union praised the Catholic Association as "a lesson to us" and a model for future action. William Cobbett joined with Henry Hunt and other members of the Friends of Civil and Religious Liberty clubs – which had pushed for Catholic emancipation and repeal of the Test Acts – to form the Friends of Radical Reform.[154] O'Connell now began consulting with and even chairing meetings of the political unions.[155]

---

[150] *Manchester Guardian*, May 19, 1827.
[151] Briggs, "Background of Parliamentary Reform Movement," 297.
[152] Ibid., 298–300; David Moss, *Thomas Attwood: The Biography of a Radical* (Montreal: McGill-Queen's Press, 1990), 162–65.
[153] Briggs, "Background of Parliamentary Reform Movement," 297; Nancy LoPatin, *Political Unions, Popular Politics, and the Great Reform Act of 1832* (London: Macmillan, 1999), 7.
[154] Charles Tilly, *Popular Contention in Great Britain, 1758–1834* (Cambridge, MA: Harvard University Press, 1998), 322.
[155] Philip Salmon, "'Reform Should Begin at Home': English Municipal and Parliamentary Reform, 1818–32," in Jones, Salmon, and Davis, *Partisan Politics, Principle and Reform in Parliament and the Constituencies, 1689–1880*, 106; Carlos Flick, *The Birmingham Political Union and the Movements for Reform in Britain, 1830–1839* (Hamden, CT: Archon Books, 1978); Pentland, *Radicalism, Reform, and National Identity in Scotland*, 50; O'Ferrall, *Catholic Emancipation*, 95; Cannon, *Parliamentary Reform*, 194.

The changing language of British political liberalism infused the political reform movements of each of the different countries, each of which appealed "to a history of British liberty" and its progressive constitution.[156] Wyse described the purpose of the Irish Liberal clubs as the cause of civil and religious liberty: "we call ourselves *Liberal* – and are what we profess to be – We abhor exclusions, monopolies and oppressions of all kinds, but none more than those created or continued by religious ignorance and intolerance. We are foes to all Ascendancies, whether Catholic or Protestant, which set up the false interests of the few at the expense of the just interests of the many." They had won an important victory in the right to "worship God according to the dictates of his conscience," and now were redoubling their efforts to secure the "*Right* to the advantages and honours of the State" for the citizen who contributes to its burdens.[157]

For Whigs, "the only struggle really worth making was reform of parliament."[158] As John Russell recollected later, reform would provide them with their only opportunity for dislodging the "Tory supremacy which had for sixty years, with little interruption, ruled England."[159] Or as one contemporary recalled, all the Whigs wanted to talk about was how they needed to "cook" the boroughs and "expel as much as possible all local interests belonging to Tories."[160]

The death of the king in 1830 triggered a general election. The Whigs increased their seat share, although the Tories could still count on a majority. But in a closely watched contest, Henry Brougham, a reforming political activist, was elected in the enormous county of Yorkshire. Precisely because of Yorkshire's size, the local elite desperately sought to avoid electoral contests, aware that they did not have the resources to court enough voters to control the election.[161] Drawing on the county's extensive antislavery network, however, Brougham built

---

[156] Pentland, *Radicalism, Reform, and National Identity in Scotland*, 154.

[157] O'Ferrall, *Catholic Emancipation*, 221.

[158] Edward Pearce, *Reform! The Fight for the 1832 Reform Act* (London: Jonathan Cape, 2003), 53.

[159] Russell, *Recollections and Suggestions*, 60.

[160] J. H. H. Malmesbury, *Memoirs of an Ex-Minister* (London: Longmans, Green, and Co., 1884), 37.

[161] In the last century, Yorkshire had seen only four contested elections. The previous one had been in 1807, when the antislavery movement propelled William Wilberforce to victory.

a funding operation that could defray the massive costs of the campaign. Wellington and the Earl of Ellenborough were left to lament that "no gentleman could bear the expense. The middle classes had it all to themselves."[162] Brougham's election was widely interpreted as a sign that public opinion supported reform.[163] Elsewhere, contemporaries noted a "collapse of the traditional electoral influence of the ruling elite," with the "one great feature" of the county elections being "that the small gentlemen and the independent farmers separate themselves from the aristocracy, and usually oppose the government candidates."[164]

The mood seemed hospitable to at least a modest reform, and many calculated that the Tories would offer some small measure that might attract moderate Whigs turned off by the radicalism of the political unions. It thus came as a genuine surprise when in the House of Lords Wellington launched into a defense of the unreformed system, whose virtue was that it "contained a large body of the property of the country, and in which the landed interests had a preponderating influence." He insisted that not only would he not bring forward any reform proposal, "but he would at once declare that as far as he was concerned, as long as he held any station in the government of the country, he should always feel it his duty to resist such measures when proposed by others."[165]

There was an immediate sensation: everyone but Wellington seemed to recognize that he had gone too far, uniting the Whigs, upsetting those Tories who wanted modest reform, and giving the anti-Catholic Ultras their opportunity to exact revenge. In less than a week, the government was defeated on a confidence vote, and Lord Grey was asked to form a government.[166]

---

[162] F. M. L. Thompson, "Whigs and Liberals in the West Riding, 1830–1860," *English Historical Review* 74, no. 291 (1959): 214–39, 218–19.

[163] Henry Brougham, *The Results of the General Election*, 4th edn. (London: James Ridgway, 1830), 20.

[164] Pearce, *Reform!*, 57, 64; Pentland, *Radicalism, Reform, and National Identity in Scotland*, 29–30; Law, *A Political Diary*, vol. 1, 329; Trevelyan, *Lord Grey of the Reform Bill*, 219; T. G. Baring, *Journals and Correspondence from 1808 to 1852 of Francis Thornhill Baring*, vol. 1 (Winchester, UK: Warren and Son, 1905), 66; http://www.historyofparliamentonline.org/volume/1820-1832/survey/v-general-elections-1820-1831.

[165] *Hansard*, November 2, 1830, 3rd series, vol. 1, c. 53.

[166] Reid, *Lord John Russell*, 61.

Reform, Not Revolution

When the reform bill was introduced in 1831, it was far more extensive than almost anyone had expected. Of 658 parliamentary seats, 168 were to be abolished or redistributed, all of them in England. Scotland and Ireland would each gain five seats – hardly equality, but an improvement on Ireland's extreme underrepresentation. More than thirty new borough districts were to be created, enfranchising towns such as Manchester and Birmingham. And the right to vote was to be extended, through the creation of a number of new qualifications enfranchising distinct classes of men.[167]

In introducing the bill, Russell declared that "the principle on which I mean to act is neither more nor less than that of reforming to preserve, and not to overthrow." He was not referring to the immediate political context, but was placing the bill within a discursive frame that reformers had been developing for forty years, one that Fox and Grey had outlined in the 1790s and that Russell had recalled in the early 1820s.[168]

Central to the bill's purpose was the creation of not just an enlarged electorate but also a respectable one. And this meant that in addition to the new voting rights the reform bill would introduce, many of the qualifications that had given some working-class men the right to vote would be abolished. Nonresident freemen in the boroughs were to be disenfranchised immediately, as were voters in the abolished boroughs unless they could meet the new county qualifications. Those whose right to vote rested on the scot-and-lot, freehold, burgage, and potwalloper franchises were to retain the right to vote only so long as they lived within seven miles of the borough where the right originated, and no new electors would ever be qualified under these franchises. Many of the taxpaying franchises were altered to require payment by July of each year, or else the voter would be permanently struck from the lists; and only householders who paid the tax themselves were to be counted as taxpayers.[169] The explicit intent was that the classes enfranchised under these qualifications would gradually diminish as a proportion of the electorate.[170]

---

[167] Pearce, *Reform!*, 72.   [168] *Hansard*, November 22, 1830, 3rd series, vol. 1, c. 613.

[169] A widely used system allowed taxes to be paid to a landlord who then paid a reduced rate to the local government. The system was to continue but no longer count as payment of a tax for voting purposes.

[170] Philip Salmon, "Electoral Reform and the Political Modernization of England, 1832–1841," *Parliaments, Estates, and Representation* 23, no. 1 (2003): 49–67, 59; Seymour, *Electoral Reform in England and Wales*, 150.

Finally, a new system of annual voter registrations was to be established that would impose severe obstacles to securing the right to vote (while opening the opportunity for an intense politicization of the process).

In defending the disenfranchisements, Russell narrated a history in which the vote had gone from being the right of a broad class of property holders to one held by either closed oligarchies or liberally granted to "householders of all kinds, down to the lowest degree, and even sometimes beyond." It was this process by which the lower classes had gradually been enfranchised, he claimed, that had led to the "great evil" of nomination, in which a small number of mostly Tory patrons were able to control elections through their ability to bribe and intimidate poor electors. By contemporary estimates, there were approximately two hundred seats "in the hands of what may be called the Tory aristocracy," while Whig patrons only controlled seventy-three; the remainder were either open boroughs, the seats of particular families, or were in the pocket of the treasury. Only Tories and the most extreme radicals, argued Russell, "contend for a very low franchise," the first hoping "to swindle the poor and ignorant out of their votes by beer and bribery," and the second counting on using the working classes to come to power, "by false representations of public abuses, and by promising remedies which neither this nor any other Reform can ever give." By simultaneously expanding the right to vote and constricting it, the reform bill was intended to limit the power of nomination, especially among Tories, by "placing the franchise as much as possible in the hands of the middle classes" and disenfranchising most of the laboring classes.[171]

The movement for parliamentary reform had long been divided between radicals and moderates. While the Whigs offered a far-reaching proposal, covering much greater territory and creating more liberal franchise provisions than anticipated, their support for disenfranchisement and emphasis on incorporating wealth and industry made clear where their priorities lay. Indeed, for many Whigs the disenfranchisements were one of the chief virtues of reform, ensuring "that wealthy and respectable men would be let into the right of voting" and that the current electors who "were neither rich nor noble" would be excluded.[172] George Wilbraham "did not see any evil likely to arise from taking the franchise

---

[171] Trevelyan, *Lord Grey of the Reform Bill*, 223n2; *Hansard*, March 1, 1831, 3rd series, vol. 2, c. 1069, 1070, 1139–41; December 17, 1831, 3rd series, vol. 9, c. 497.

[172] *Hansard*, March 24, 1831, 3rd series, vol. 3, cc. 895–96; Cannon, *Parliamentary Reform*, 257.

from the lowest classes, because they were too often made the tools of the higher classes."[173] Russell bragged about the exclusion of the working classes, comparing the "quarters of the town chiefly inhabited by the working classes," where only one in every fifty households would have the vote, to the "principal streets for shops" where "almost every house-holder will have a vote."[174] The disenfranchisement of poor voters was also necessary to comfort moderate Whigs, and Grey was tasked with reassuring a skeptical king that "in truth, the right of voting, taken generally, will be found much less popular than the old one."[175]

The proposed disenfranchisements were more concerning to the few radicals in Parliament. Henry Hunt presented a petition with three thousand signatories "praying that the franchise rights which they at present possessed might not be interfered with." He was proud for having always "advocated, both outside of the walls of that House and within them, the principle of an equality of political rights," that "taxation and Representation should go hand in hand." He asked whether "in taking away from that 'rabble'" – Thomas Macaulay's term for the to-be-disenfranchised voters – "the right of choosing Representatives, he was also willing to exempt them from the payment of the taxes – from serving in the Militia, or from being called on to fight the battles of their country?" Throughout the months of debate, Hunt would repeatedly denounce the bill's exclusion of the working classes. But he was anxious not to sink the bill and so decided "to give up a great deal."[176]

This left the Tories in the paradoxical position of being the most vocal opponents of disenfranchisement, which many of them cast as "an unjust attempt to reduce the power of the aristocracy as well as of the lower classes." Many Tories defended the limited working-class franchises because they empowered the landed aristocracy, but a number also defended the electoral system for including "property and wealth" as well as "the very lowest contributors." Lord Ellenborough noted fearfully in his diary that were the disenfranchisements to pass, "in ten years the

[173] *Hansard*, April 19, 1831, 3rd series, vol. 3, c. 1616.
[174] *Hansard*, December 17, 1831, 3rd series, vol. 9, cc. 497, 498.
[175] *Hansard*, March 3, 1831, 3rd series, vol. 2, cc. 1321, 1324; H. G. Grey, *The Reform Act, 1832: The Correspondence of the Late Earl Grey with His Majesty King William IV* (London: J. Murray, 1867), 456.
[176] *Hansard*, March 2, 1831, 3rd series, vol. 2, c. 1212; June 23, 1831, 3rd series, vol. 4, cc. 277–280; August 25, 1831, 3rd series, vol. 6, c. 554.

poorest class will be unrepresented & then we shall have a servile war or universal suffrage."[177]

Central to both parties' calculations was the pitched contest for political advantage, for determining which vision of political community and which set of associated priorities would be empowered. Tories opposed the disenfranchisement of the working-class voters as the abolition of a right derived "from their being freemen," who, while liable to "the temptation of bribery," at least possessed "an inalienable right of voting, not acquired by, and in no way dependent on, the will of the aristocracy."[178] A proposal by the Tory Marquess of Chandos to extend the right to vote to tenants-at-will who paid £50 rent passed against the opposition of the Whig leadership, who argued that a tenant-at-will standard, the basis for the new franchises in the boroughs, was inappropriate in the counties, where it was in "the power of the landlord of the farmer to do his tenant a greater injury than the landlord of the householder."[179] This would ultimately prove to be one of the most enfranchising provisions of the bill, with "Chandos electors" amounting to around 20 percent of the aggregate post-reform county electorate and over a third in at least twenty-three counties.[180] The freemen in the small boroughs and the Chandos electors in the counties both had the advantage of being disproportionately supportive of Tory candidates.

For the most part, however, the Tories opposed the bill on the same grounds they had opposed repeal and emancipation: it was an overturning of the constitution and the "ancient institutions" of the country. The measure was "unprincipled, tyrannical, revolutionary, introducing a new Constitution," with an electorate no longer responsive to the Anglican aristocracy and gentry. The unreformed system had enabled these classes to return a majority of the Commons, giving them and the Anglican bishops in the House of Lords a disproportionate influence over the nation's policy. The reform bill proposed to abolish many of the pocket boroughs, increase the number of seats from the dissenting areas of northern England, and make bribery and intimidation more difficult by

---

[177] *Hansard*, March 4, 1831, 3rd series, vol. 3, c. 53, 89; May 7, 1832, 3rd series, vol. 12, c. 730; Pearce, *Reform!*, 276.

[178] *Hansard*, March 3, 1831, 3rd series, vol. 2, c. 1348.

[179] *Hansard*, August 18, 1831, 3rd series, vol. 6, c. 281.

[180] Hoppen, *Elections, Politics, and Society in Ireland*, 205; Seymour, *Electoral Reform in England and Wales*, 79.

expanding the number of voters in most constituencies. This would make the House of Commons "the slave of public opinion," and especially of dissenter public opinion.[181] Wynford predicted that after reform, "the Church would be first attacked," anticipating that the first act of a post-reform Parliament would be to "vote at once for getting rid of tithes" and for doing "away with the property of the Church."[182] Tories warned that dissenters in the political unions saw "Parliamentary Reform, chiefly as a step to the abolition of tithes," while reformers were accused of wanting "the Church to be despoiled of its property."[183] Even liberal Tories argued that the bill was a "revolutionary measure" that provided "no moorings or anchorage-ground for the Constitution."[184]

Party strength in the Commons was fluid, with many members absent and with a good number holding their seats as personal fiefdoms. To pass the bill would require the Whigs to secure the support of as many floating MPs as they could. The government now brought enormous pressure to bear on them. They were, according to one Tory, "moving *hell* and *earth* ... tampering even with the *little* household officers."[185] The ministers had informed every MP with a government sinecure, of which there were a great many, that these would be lost if they did not vote for passage.

The government also took the unusual step of intervening to delay the prosecution of Daniel O'Connell, who had been arrested for a speech urging a run on the banks to force reform. His presence in the Commons was absolutely essential to rally the liberal Irish members. The alliance between the Whigs and the Irish Liberals was already difficult, and would only become more so.

On March 22, 1831, in the most attended vote in British history, the bill passed second reading by a vote of 302 to 301. Even though the government made good on its threat to strip members of the sinecures, the majority of the English, Welsh, and Scottish MPs voted against. It passed only through the support of the liberal Irish, and the vote of

---

[181] *Hansard*, March 4, 1831, 3rd series, vol. 3, c. 32, 38.
[182] *Hansard*, October 7, 1831, 3rd series, vol. 8, cc. 200–1.
[183] *Hansard*, March 4, 1831, 3rd series, vol. 3, c. 86; LoPatin, *Political Unions, Popular Politics, and the Great Reform Act*, 58, 61, 83, 108–9.
[184] *Hansard*, March 7, 1831, 3rd series, vol. 3, c. 161–63, 138; October 6, 1831, 3rd series, vol. 8, c. 106.
[185] Louis Jennings, *The Croker Papers: The Correspondence and Diaries of the Late Right Honourable John Wilson Croker*, 2nd edn. (London: J. Murray, 1885), 112.

a man who had just been released from police custody and who was generally detested by the Whig leadership.

In what would become a recurring strategy of a reconfigured Conservative party in the post-reform era, the Tory leaders decided to recover the lost ground by appealing to anti-Catholic and anti-Irish sentiment: they introduced an amendment that would entirely foreclose the modest redistribution of seats to Ireland and Scotland. It was a naked attempt by the Tories "to excite English prejudices," declared O'Connell, and he urged the ministers to hold fast: "the country was with them – Ireland was with them. . . . [The Catholics] had won their civil rights, and they would wear them thus – by, on all occasions, supporting the principles of civil and religious liberty." Russell made clear that this would be a vote of no confidence in the government. By a vote of 299–291, the amendment passed, and the ministers asked the king to call an election.[186]

The election was a massive victory for reformers, who could now command a 140-vote majority. The Tories were defeated in almost all of the districts where even some semblance of an open vote was held. The result, writes one historian, was "a referendum – not so much on the bill under discussion . . . but on the abstract principle of reform (and opposition to slavery)."[187] This was not a disenfranchised mass demanding the right to vote from a narrow elite: it was the enfranchised themselves, including large numbers of the working-class freemen and farmers who had long negotiated the sale of their vote to brokers or followed the dictates of patrons or landlords, demanding the suffrage be extended to others. A new reform bill was introduced that was broadly similar to the first and after months of delay, the bill passed the Commons by a vote of 346 to 237.

The Protestant Constitution, however, still had its inner ramparts. In October 1831, the bill was defeated in the House of Lords. Riots immediately broke out in Nottingham and Derby, although the government did not believe these were a serious threat.[188] The Bristol riots a few weeks later were more alarming, lasting three days and suppressed only by the army. Instead of making MPs more willing to reform, however, the unrest hardened "the anti-reform stance of the Tory MPs and of their

---

[186] *Hansard*, March 21, 1831, 3rd series, vol. 3, c. 690; April 19, 1831, vol. 3, c. 1664, 1687.
[187] LoPatin, *Political Unions, Popular Politics, and the Great Reform Act*, 73–81; Pearce, *Reform!*, 149; J. J. Parry, *The Rise and Fall of Liberal Government in Victorian Britain* (New Haven, CT: Yale University Press, 1993), 96.
[188] LoPatin, *Political Unions, Popular Politics, and the Great Reform Act*, 92.

patrons."[189] The violence confirmed in Tories the belief that reformers were Jacobins who would not stop until there were no more
"King, no Lords, no inequalities in the social system; all will be
leveled to the plane of the petty shopkeepers and small farmers."
Were it to pass, England would live under "a *different* form of
constitution," warned John Wilson Croker.[190] But for the Whigs,
the violence only made the intransigence of the Lords more galling,
and further ennobled their sense of purpose. Catholic emancipation
had been passed only under the threat of civil war, and Whigs'
understanding of statesmanship – anchored in a belief in
a progressive and reformist constitution – demanded that reforms
be offered in an expedient manner as needed to accommodate changed conditions. It was the Tories' refusal to see the true genius of the
British constitution that had threatened the country in 1828, and
that would threaten it again if reform were passed not as a grant but
as a reluctant concession.

The Whigs had earlier persuaded the king to agree to create as many
peers as needed to push the bill through. When the time came, however,
the king denied the request, leaving the Whigs with little choice but to
resign. This was the beginning of a sustained political crisis, the Days
of May.

"Modern historians," notes John Beckett, "no longer think of the 1831
riots as heralding revolution."[191] The Days of May perhaps came closer,
a profound constitutional crisis that divided the elite and opened the
possibility for extralegal action by the various groups organized in recent
years. And yet the most important of these were the political unions,
which were generally intent on keeping the peace. While the Tories were
accusing the unions of plotting violent revolution and the overthrow of
the church, the Whig government believed they were essential allies in
maintaining public order. The unions sent addresses to the king proclaim-
ing their loyalty and affection, the Home Office issued a report – intended
to reassure the king – showing that the unions had helped secure order,
and the prime minister and other cabinet members sustained an ongoing

---

[189] Aidt and Franck, "How to Get the Snowball Rolling and Extend the Franchise,"
229–50, 242.
[190] Jennings, *The Croker Papers*, 113.
[191] John Beckett, "The Nottingham Reform Bill Riots of 1831," in Jones, Salmon, and
Davis, *Partisan Politics, Principle, and Reform in Parliament and the Constituencies,
1689–1880*, 114.

and direct communication with the unions, coordinating their efforts behind an insistent demand for reform.[192]

The political unions were also working with the government in pursuit of a shared objective. Since at least 1820, Grey had realized that reform would require the extensive mobilization and demonstration of public opinion: if reform were to be pursued against the hostility of the landed gentry and aristocracy, he had written then, with the certainty of being "ultimately betrayed and sacrificed by the Court on the first favourable opportunity," then Whigs would need to be able to point to public opinion, given deliberate form and an insistent voice, in order to persuade the unelected branches to accept it.[193] This was the reason they had decided on such a far-reaching bill, as no modest reform could hope to win the support of the public. And it was in part why the bill was so generous to the middle classes, as it would give this constituency – better able to organize visible expressions of "respectable" public opinion – a stake in the outcome, while its exclusions would dampen worries of excessive popular influence. Shortly after the bill had passed the Commons, Grey met with the leadership of the political unions, asked them how they would respond to a possible defeat of the bill in the Lords, and hinted *"against too much quiet"* were it rejected.[194] Now that the unions were rapidly proliferating, Grey could point to them in his presentation to the king "as proof of public support for the Bill."[195]

Grey and other Whigs sincerely believed that absent reform, a revolution would occur, but it was an eventuality that had no set timeline and that they at least did not see as likely during the crisis itself. But Grey had decided that a demonstration of public opinion would be needed to "force the Court before it is too late to carry this or any other measures."[196] To make sure that the king and Lords were aware of this, the Whigs made the prospect of revolution central to their rhetoric, just as they had been doing for the last forty years.[197] And they actively encouraged the unions to be forceful but not too aggressive. In a model of elite

[192] Pearce, *Reform!*, 208, 226, 276; *Hansard*, October 6, 1831, 3rd series, vol. 8, c. 106; LoPatin, *Political Unions, Popular Politics, and the Great Reform Act*, 88, 99–101; Grey, *The Reform Act*, 473; Cannon, *Parliamentary Reform*, 227.
[193] Trevelyan, *Lord Grey of the Reform Bill*, 370–71.   [194] Pearce, *Reform!*, 165.
[195] Trevelyan, *Lord Grey of the Reform Bill*, 370–71; LoPatin, *Political Unions, Popular Politics, and the Great Reform Act*, 101.
[196] Trevelyan, *Lord Grey of the Reform Bill*, 373.
[197] Brougham, *The Results of the General Election*, 28; *Hansard*, March 2, 1831, 3rd series, vol. 2, c. 1193.

versus masses, with democratization as a forced concession, this was largely a preemptive gambit.

Some of the political unions now began moving toward more direct forms of political action, such as the nonpayment of taxes or an organized run on Tory-owned banks and the Bank of England (sparing the provincial banks whose directors were more likely to be Whigs and often members of the Unions). Withdrawals of 1.5 million pounds were made from reserves of 4 million.[198]

But while this heightened the drama, it did not change the underlying calculation. The king was reluctant to create peers, but he did want a reform bill passed. And a large majority in the Commons had voted not to sustain any government that did not keep all the essential provisions of the Whig bill intact.[199] When the Tories suggested that a Wellington ministry might pass the bill, it was attacked on all sides: Robert Inglis, speaking for the far right, said that it would be "one of the most fatal violations of public confidence which could be inflicted."[200] Only Grey could muster the support of the Commons, and only the king could move the House of Lords.

On May 15, the Duke of Wellington informed the king he could not form a government. Three days later, the Whigs were back in power, with a guarantee that the king would create however many peers were needed. In the end, this was not necessary: the Tory Lords simply walked out, allowing the bill to pass with only twenty-one votes against. The Lords conceded because the king preferred extensive reform to no reform and had the power to create new peers at will. Public agitation was important, but it was not directed against the government so much as it was in support of the government. Throughout the crisis, Grey continued to coordinate with the unions, helping to direct their activities while urging them to avoid action that might weaken the Whigs. He remarked during this period that their conduct had "been praiseworthy," and he expressed his belief that "if things can only be kept quiet I have not the least doubt of

---

[198] LoPatin, *Political Unions, Popular Politics, and the Great Reform Act*, 150; Pearce, *Reform!*, 298. Bond yields had shot up after the collapse of the Wellington government, the introduction of the first bill, its defeat, and the ensuing election campaign. They stabilized after the Whigs were returned and did not increase during the Days of May. Aditya Dasgupta and Daniel Ziblatt, "How Did Britain Democratize? Views from the Sovereign Bond Market," *Journal of Economic History* 75, no. 1 (2015): 1–29.

[199] See the Ebrington resolution, *Hansard*, May 10, 1832, 3rd series, vol. 12, c. 788.

[200] *Hansard*, May 14, 1832, 3rd series, vol. 12, c. 947, 913, 922, 958, 975–76; Cannon, *Parliamentary Reform*, 235.

being able in a very few days, to set everything right again."[201] He was proven entirely correct.

The king, however, felt that he had been left with no choice: despite Grey's entreaties, he refused to sign the bill in person, and on June 7, 1832, the bill received assent without his signature.

A Middle-Class People Without Religious Distinction

This was not only the inauguration of a new constitutional order. It was the institutionalization of a new vision of the boundaries and basis of political community. Whigs repeated the constitutional narrative that they and other reformers had been advancing for decades, arguing that reform was not a betrayal of the constitutional tradition but rather its embodiment. Public agitation was a manifestation of the underlying problem, that changes in society had not been accommodated by changed political institutions. The political unions and the Catholic Association, like the Irish Volunteers and the American Revolutionaries, were the product of "Justice denied – rights withheld – wrongs perpetrated – the force which common injuries lend to millions." Chief among these was "the idiotcy of treating Englishmen like the children of the South Sea Islands – the frenzy of believing, or making believe, that the adults of the nineteenth century can be led like children, or driven like barbarians!" As with Catholic emancipation, the progressive principles supposedly embedded in the British constitution required, when necessary, statesmen "to alter, adapt, and enlarge [governing] institutions, in order to accommodate the continually increasing number of intelligent and independent citizens who are entitled to share in their benefits."[202]

Thomas Macaulay laid out what was becoming the central theme of Whig statesmanship and history: the enlightened accommodation of institutions to progress. History was the story of revolution and reform, driven forward when "a portion of the community which had been of no account, expands and becomes strong," and demands a status and rights suited "to its present power. If this is granted, all is well. If this is refused, then comes the struggle between the young energy of one class, and the

---

[201] Had an election been called, the intensity of the fight would have only further frayed elite influence in the electorate while almost certainly returning a Whig majority. LoPatin, *Political Unions, Popular Politics, and the Great Reform Act*, 155; Grey, *The Reform Act*, 460–69.

[202] *Hansard*, October 7, 1831, 3rd series, vol. 8, c. 263, 269; March 4, 1831, 3rd series, vol. 3, c. 62.

ancient privileges of another." This was the story of the American and French revolutions. But it was also the story of "the struggle which the Catholics of Ireland maintained against the aristocracy of creed," and the ongoing story of "the struggle which the free people of colour in Jamaica are now maintaining against the aristocracy of skin." And it is "the struggle which, the middle classes in England are maintaining against an aristocracy of mere locality – against an aristocracy, *the principle of which is to invest one hundred drunken, potwallopers in one place, or the owner of a ruined hovel in another, with powers which are withheld from cities renowned to the furthest ends of the earth, for the marvels of their wealth and of their industry.*" Macaulay was implicating the struggles of Ireland, America, France, and of free blacks in Jamaica in the cause of civil and religious liberty. He was outlining the purpose of British liberalism as the struggle against odious distinctions.[203]

And he was circumscribing its liberality. The Protestant Constitution rested on the ability of the upper classes and landed gentry to intimidate and bribe the working classes. It was the franchise, seemingly vested in the laboring classes but in reality exercised by the Anglican elite, that had to be reformed. But this did not mean that the right of the working classes to vote should be reestablished on surer foundations. Manhood suffrage might exist in the United States without "very frightful consequences," although as a few members noted, the "boundless extent of unoccupied land in the United States" and the resulting "different distribution of property" made it a poor example. But the working class of England was poor, and in distress they might look for "immediate relief." Still, if "the labourers of England were [ever] in that state in which I, from my soul, wish to see them, – if employment were always plentiful, wages always high, food always cheap," then the "principal objections to Universal Suffrage would, I think, be removed." The implication was that future reforms should depend on the material and intellectual progress of the working classes, embedding the promise of progressive reform as well as the basis for legitimate exclusions into what was becoming the governing philosophy of the Whigs and the broad liberal coalition that they sought to lead.[204]

Throughout the debates the Whigs returned to the theme of "the people," whose reconstitution was necessary to recover the progressive purpose of the British constitution. The Commons was supposed to

[203] *Hansard*, March 2, 1831, 3rd series, vol. 2, c. 1196.
[204] *Hansard*, March 2, 1831, 3rd series, vol. 2, c. 1192, 1352.

represent "the knowledge and spirit" of the people, but the overweighted influence of the laboring classes had allowed the aristocracy to gain control.[205] A new "people" was needed to restore balance to the constitution. This new people were the middle classes: "the people – and by the people, I repeat – I mean *the middle classes, the wealth and intelligence of the country, the glory of the British name.*"[206] The measure promised "to the people of England an overpowering influence in the choice of Representatives," with the people being "the great majority of the respectable middle classes of the country."[207] "The middle classes – those hundreds of thousands of respectable persons – the most numerous, and by far the most wealthy order in the community," were distinguished from the "populace," who could only "look up to them as their kind and natural protectors."[208]

They would need protectors, for after reform the working classes would be even less represented than before. The right to vote in the unreformed open boroughs had "reached quite far down the social scale, beneath the artisanate and into the labouring classes to an extent that the Great Reform Act could not emulate."[209] As the "ancient right" voters died, moved, or missed paying taxes, the working-class proportion of the electorate would gradually decline. Of the 1,200 enfranchised freemen of Boston, only some 300 were able to register after 1832, and thirty years later only 150 remained. In Honiton, there were 450 registered electors in 1837, the large majority of them potwallopers; thirty years later, only 53 remained, and the overall electorate had declined to only around 300 persons, despite population growth.[210] While the English county electorate increased from around 220,000 to nearly 350,000 – most of these brought in against the government's wishes – the impact in the boroughs was more mixed. The overall increase was from 160,000 to 270,000, largely due to the creation of new boroughs such as Manchester and Birmingham. In boroughs that existed before 1832, however, the increase was only twenty thousand. Across all the

[205] *Hansard*, March 24, 1831, 3rd series, vol. 3, c. 898.
[206] *Hansard*, October 7, 1831, 3rd series, vol. 8, cc. 264–65.
[207] *Hansard*, March 1, 1831, 3rd series, vol. 2, cc. 1143–44.
[208] *Hansard*, October 7, 1831, 3rd series, vol. 8, cc. 252–53, 308–9.
[209] O'Gorman, *Voters, Patrons, and Parties*, 216.
[210] James Vernon, *Politics and the People: A Study in English Political Culture, 1815–1867* (Cambridge: Cambridge University Press, 1993), 38; T. A. Jenkins, "Honiton," in *The House of Commons, 1820–1832*, ed. D. R. Fisher (Cambridge: Cambridge University Press, 2009).

English boroughs, the enfranchisement rate declined from 7 percent in 1832 to 6 percent in 1851, a drop that was most severe in the boroughs that had formerly approached manhood suffrage.

Figure 5.2 shows the approximate change in English constituencies between 1831, immediately before the Reform Act, and 1851, after most of the "ancient right" voters had been disenfranchised. While most constituencies saw a modest increase in the enfranchisement rate, a considerable number showed substantial declines; in many of these, the actual number of electors declined over the period, despite population growth.

Figure 5.3 compares the occupational structure in the English boroughs before and after reform. In places such as Boston and Lewes, retailers, craftsmen, and unskilled laborers had "accounted for 80 per cent or more" of the electorate, and in some of the open Irish boroughs, the freemanship included large numbers of Protestant bricklayers, cutlers, joiners, shoemakers, carpenters, smiths, as well as merchants.[211] After reform, semi- and unskilled labor were now less influential relative to retailers, merchants, manufacturers, gentlemen, and professionals. As the author of the most thorough study of the impact of the Reform Act on the electorate notes, "There seems no escape from the conclusion that the 1832 Reform Act diminished the penetration of the electorate down the social scale."[212] Curtailing this base had been as central to the reform project as expanding the electorate.[213]

The inclusion of a disproportionately dissenter middle class was another blow to the sectarian character of the state. Reflecting on the change in 1833, Wellington remarked that "the revolution is made," the "power is transferred from one class of society, the gentlemen of England, professing the faith of the Church of England, to another class of society, the shopkeepers, being dissenters from the Church." Property continued to have its influence, and in the counties the "gentry have as many followers and influence as many voters at elections as they ever did." But a "new democratic influence" had been introduced, who were all

---

[211] Vernon, *Politics and the People: A Study in English Political Culture*, 34.

[212] Nossiter includes the categories of "Drink" (9 percent) – allocated here between the Merchants/Manufacturers and the Retailers – and "Other" (6 percent), which O'Gorman treats as comparable to the Semi/Unskilled Laborers. O'Gorman, *Voters, Patrons, and Parties*, 217, tables 4.12–4.16; T. J. Nossiter, *Influence, Opinion, and Political Idioms in Reformed England: Case Studies from the North-East, 1832–74* (Hassocks: Harvester Press, 1975), 166.

[213] Seymour, *Electoral Reform in England and Wales*, 116; Salmon, "Electoral Reform and the Political Modernization of England," 54, 59.

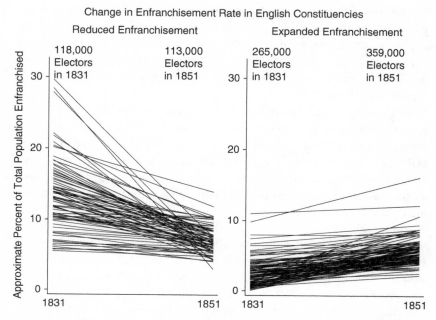

FIGURE 5.2 Approximate Change in Enfranchisement in English Constituencies

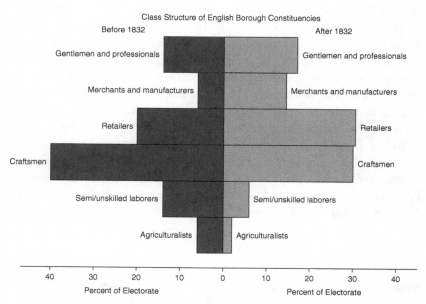

FIGURE 5.3 Class Structure of English Borough Constituencies

"Dissenters from the Church, and are everywhere a formidable active party against the aristocratic influence of the Landed Gentry." "There are Dissenters in every village in the country; they are the blacksmith, the carpenter, the mason, &c. &c. The new influence established in the towns has drawn these to their party; and it is curious to see to what a degree it is a Dissenting interest."[214]

And "the people" being defined were not just English. Scotland got a representative system for the first time since 1701 – its prereform system being entirely unrepresentative – and the passage of the Scottish Reform Bill was fairly straightforward. The bill for Ireland was more controversial. Russell remarked that the Irish "have suffered the greatest inconvenience and injury from the political rights being in the hands of a few," but also made clear that there would be no revision of the 1829 disenfranchisement.[215]

Using language that would become commonplace in Liberal rhetoric for the next several decades – especially when the Whigs were out of power – the chief secretary for Ireland, Edward Smith-Stanley, proposed "to assimilate the practice in England and Ireland." He dared members "to contend, that what was true with respect to England was false when applied to Ireland – unless there were hon. Members prepared to maintain, that the reality of Representation should apply to England while only the mockery should be continued in Ireland."[216]

This was a dare the Tories eagerly accepted, seeing in the English MPs' antipathy toward the new Irish Catholic representatives a final chance for splitting the reform coalition. The Bishop of Exeter, in a speech and widely reprinted pamphlet, reminded the Lords that the Protestant Constitution in Ireland had depended on the closed boroughs, that the electoral system was "avowedly unequal" as it had been "formed for a small band of Englishmen settled in the midst of a hostile population." Opening up the closed boroughs to Catholic electors would undermine their central function, to maintain the Anglican character of the state. Power was to be "taken from the Protestant influence and conferred upon the Roman Catholic Population. Can your lordships conceive a greater change – a more

---

[214] Jennings, *The Croker Papers*, 205–6.
[215] *Hansard*, March 1, 1831, 3rd series, vol. 2, cc. 1081–82.
[216] Stanley would later break with the Whigs when they sought to reform the Church of Ireland, and would go on to be a Conservative Party prime minister. *Hansard*, March 24, 1831, 3rd series, vol. 3, c. 866; January 19, 1832, 3rd series, vol. 9, c. 595.

important change – a more fearful change?"[217] Ultra-Tory Robert Inglis inquired, "bigot as he might be thought for asking, whether this country had not prospered exactly in proportion as it had maintained its Protestant character, and had defended Protestant interests every where?" Anthony Lefroy insisted that reform of the Irish boroughs meant the fall of the Church of Ireland, and with it, the Church of England. O'Connell delighted in mocking members who insisted that their "Protestantism will be destroyed, that it will be for ever annihilated, if you destroy thirteen rotten boroughs! The gallant Member's Protestantism is not 'built upon a rock,' but upon thirteen rotten boroughs."[218]

"All religious distinctions," claimed Stanley, "with their kindred rancour and strife, had been done away in Ireland." Now that the necessity for reform was admitted, and that Parliament had erased the major distinction "between the Church of England and the Catholics, or between the Church of England and the Dissenters, he asked upon what ground they could turn round and say, that they would not extend the right of returning Members to Parliament because the Catholics must participate in the extension? They might as well object to Reform in England, because the Dissenters would share its benefits." Of course, this was exactly what many Tories had been saying.[219]

O'Connell and the Liberal Irish initially expressed satisfaction with the bill and told the Whigs that it "would contribute to make a perpetual and irreversible union of the two countries."[220] This conciliatory language disappeared as the bill was modified and as new information on its expected impact became available, showing only a modest opening of the Irish boroughs and almost no compensation in the counties for the previous disenfranchisement.[221] The Whigs rejected O'Connell's

---

[217] Henry Phillpot, *Speech of the Bishop of Exeter in the House of Lords* (London: J. Murray, 1832), 12–14; see also R. H. Froude, *Remains of the Late Reverend Richard Hurrell Froude: Part II*, vol. 1 (Derby: Henry Mozley and Sons, 1839), 212.

[218] *Hansard*, January 19, 1832, 3rd series, vol. 9, c. 618; May 25, 1832, 3rd series, vol. 13, c. 126, 146.

[219] *Hansard*, January 19, 1832, 3rd series, vol. 9, cc. 603–4; May 25, 1832, 3rd series, vol. 13, c. 121.

[220] *Hansard*, March 24, 1831, 3rd series, vol. 3, cc. 868, 872.

[221] A report had estimated that the Irish borough electorate would go from 22,603 to 45,598, but this was shown to be off by around 16,000. *Hansard*, June 18, 1832, 3rd series, cc. 764–819; House of Commons, *Parliamentary representation, Ireland. Further returns to an order of the Honourable House of Commons, dated 8th May 1832*. H. R. Parl. Papers (219) XLIII.1; Farrell, "Ireland."

proposal to reinstate the forty-shilling freehold qualification and to lower the property requirement, and instead included some of the English bill's disenfranchisement of ancient right voters, provided less liberal versions of the new English franchises, and left out altogether any equivalent to the "Chandos" franchise.

By the spring of 1832, O'Connell was denouncing the government's proposal, mocking the ministers' claims that they were assimilating the qualifications of Ireland and England for always being "used when the constituency was to be decreased, but it was never applied for the opposite purpose."[222] In O'Connell's letters *To the Reformers of Great Britain*, he asked "for the people of Ireland the same measure of Reform which the people of England receive," that there should be "as complete an equality of Reform in both countries as possible." The rhetorical value of giving to Ireland as was given to England even led him to embrace a measure that was clearly against his political interests: continuing the franchise of the ultra-Protestant and notoriously corrupt Irish freemen. O'Connell, looking to buttress his claim that he opposed any disenfranchisement and supported the same qualifications in England as in Ireland, demanded that the freemen still be allowed to vote; the Tories threw him their support, and the Irish freemen franchise was continued.[223] No other meaningful concession was given to the Irish Catholics whose votes had ensured the advance of English reform.

Figure 5.4 shows the change in the enfranchisement rate across Irish constituencies, from 1828 to 1829 and then again from 1831 to 1832, with the boroughs shown in gray and the counties in black. The Irish had gained a substantial electorate, albeit a narrow and heavily manipulated one, with Catholic enfranchisement in 1792 – going from approximately 1 percent of the total population to 3.5 percent – only to lose this with the disenfranchisement of 1829, which pushed the enfranchisement rate back down to 1 percent. This was only partially undone by reform. The median Irish borough went from having two hundred to five hundred voters, with all of the closed corporations opened up to the middle classes. The counties saw a very modest increase, although a loophole allowed landlords who were uncertain

[222] Grey, *The Reform Act*, 27; Hansard, June 18, 1832, 3rd series, vol. 13, c. 775, 795.

[223] M. F. Cusack, *The Speeches and Public Letters of the Liberator: With Preface and Historical Notes*, vol. 2 (Dublin: McGlashan and Gill, 1875), 458–59, 461; Hansard, January 19, 1832, 3rd series, vol. 9, c. 605–6; July 2, 1832, 3rd series, vol. 13, c. 1263; July 23, 1832, 3rd series, vol. 14, c. 628–30; Hoppen, *Elections, Politics, and Society in Ireland*, 3.

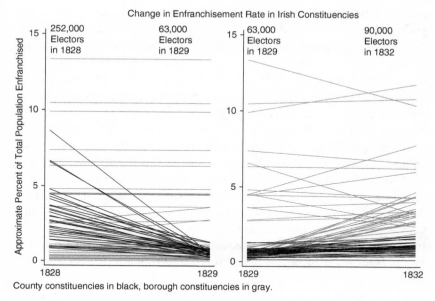

Change in Enfranchisement Rate in Irish Constituencies

County constituencies in black, borough constituencies in gray.

FIGURE 5.4 Approximate Change in Irish Constituencies

about their leaseholders' politics to restrict the right to vote, so much so that in some counties, the "real electorate was halved between 1832 and 1841."[224]

The disenfranchisement of the Irish freeholders had resulted in power being "transferred from the serfs of the great landed proprietors to the merchants and traders of Belfast." The Tories had preferred this to either civil war or Catholic electoral influence, but the Whigs' Irish Reform Act furthered this process even as it empowered a new class of Catholic merchants and professionals, modestly opening up the political system to middle-class voters without religious distinction.[225]

CONCLUSION

The impact of the Reform Act of 1832 was important, but "scarcely the stuff of which political revolutions are made." It did not end bribery or displace the aristocracy entirely in favor of dissenters and the industrial

---

[224] Hoppen, *Elections, Politics, and Society in Ireland*, 8.
[225] Suzanne Kingon, "Ulster Counties in the Age of Emancipation and Reform," in *Politics and Political Culture in Britain and Ireland, 1750–1850*, ed. Allan Blackstock, Eoin Magennis, and Suzanne Kingon (Belfast: Ulster Historical Association, 2007), 11.

middle classes. But it facilitated the gradual emergence of organized political parties connected to mass constituencies through partisan attachments rooted in social identities, public policy, and contrasting framings of ideological purpose.[226] It did not "cook" the Tories, as some had hoped, but it did cause them to begin the process of reorganizing themselves as the Conservative Party, not yet a professional party but expanding their base beyond the Anglican gentry. Given their continued control over many boroughs and counties, the gradual disenfranchisement of "ancient right" voters, and the organizational infrastructure, dispersed as it was, connecting them with the remaining working-class electors as well as middle-class "Chandos" electors in the counties, they would remain a force to be reckoned with. Explicit acceptance of the Reform Act, moderation toward dissenters, and a renewed appeal to anti-Catholicism became the central ways in which the party tried to sustain itself in the new environment. As one conservative operative put it in 1839, "Our great force has been Protestantism, we began the re-action with it; every step of success has been founded on it."[227]

It was not the expansion of the electorate that was most important about the Reform Act, but rather its recomposition – the extension of voting rights to the middle classes, the disenfranchisement of the working classes of the boroughs, the increased size of the constituency electorate, and the redistribution of seats to the growing cities, centers of religious dissent, liberal economics, and reformist politics. And while the disenfranchisement of the forty-shilling freeholders was not a demand of the Catholic Association or of the parliamentary reformers in England – and in this sense contrasts with the United States – they acquiesced in it and the Whigs would not do much to undo it.[228] A new type of political order was being created, and the new electors were expected to shape the

---

[226] O'Gorman, *Voters, Patrons, and Parties*, 179, 182; John Phillips and Philip Salmon, "England's 'Other' Ballot Question: The Unnoticed Political Revolution of 1835," in Jones, Salmon, and Davis, *Partisan Politics, Principle, and Reform in Parliament and the Constituencies, 1689–1880*, 139; Derek Beales, "The Electorate Before and After 1832: The Right to Vote, and the Opportunity," *Parliamentary History* 11, no. 1 (1992): 139–50; John Phillips and Charles Wetherell, "The Great Reform Act and the Political Modernization of England," *American Historical Review* 100, no. 2 (1995): 411–36.

[227] Ian Newbould, "Sir Robert Peel and the Conservative Party, 1832–1841: A Study in Failure?" *English Historical Review* 98, no. 388 (1983): 529–57; *Morning Chronicle* (London), April 30, 1835, p. 4.

[228] They would modify it to end some of its more extreme sectarian implications, first in 1832 and then with the rebuilding of the electorate in 1850 after the devastation of the Famine.

constitution to reflect their beliefs and interests. And by insisting that the essential purpose of the constitution was to achieve perfect civil and religious liberty, through judicious reforms to accommodate changed circumstances, the Whigs embedded a vision of gradual but limited reform into their governing philosophy, one that would help define the next fifty years of British political life. Peel saw what was coming, and mocked those who insisted that their reform was going to be final: other parties will "outbid you, not now, but at no remote period – they will offer votes and power to a million of men, will quote your precedent for the concession, and will carry your principles to their legitimate and natural consequences."[229]

By 1867, a small but influential number of Conservatives had become convinced that "a steady, well-to-do working man, if he only keep himself free from the bondage of Trades-unions, is far more likely to vote as we could wish him to do, than an arrogant, Church-hating, and democratic £10 Dissenter." That year, Peel's protégé Benjamin Disraeli would preside over a massive expansion of the electorate in England, Scotland, and Wales, and barely at all in Ireland.[230] Seventeen years later, Disraeli's Liberal rival – William Gladstone – would finally provide what O'Connell had asked for a half-century earlier, establishing an equality in electoral rights between Ireland and Great Britain and extending the qualifications established in 1867 across the four nations. This new electorate would again redefine the contours of British politics, cementing the electoral strength of Irish nationalists, splitting the Liberals on the issue of Irish Home Rule, and raising the Conservatives to political ascendancy on a platform of "popular Anglicanism, the fostering of anti-Irish sentiment," and Empire.[231]

---

[229] *Hansard*, March 3, 1831, 3rd series, vol. 2, c. 1353.
[230] G. R. Gleig, "Clause III and Mr. Lowe," *Blackwood's Edinburgh Magazine* 101 (June 1867): 770–77, 772–73, 777.
[231] E. H. H. Green, *The Crisis of Conservatism: The Politics, Economics and Ideology of the British Conservative Party, 1880–1914* (London: Routledge, 1995), 117; Ziblatt, *Conservative Parties and the Birth of Democracy*, 141.

6

The Republic Through the Side Door

We must not permit Napoleon, either in history or in his descendants, to benefit from this admirable conquest of the soil that we owe to the Revolution. We must break with this tradition. We must prove to the peasant, rather, that it is to the democracy, to the Republic, to our predecessors that he owes not only his land, but his right; for it is by the Revolution alone that he became a property owner and a citizen.

– Léon Gambetta[1]

On July 19, 1870, imperial France declared war on Prussia. By September, Louis-Napoleon and his army had surrendered. A republican provisional government was formed, an armistice was declared, and elections were held to a National Assembly in February 1871. It was a triumph for the far right, with a large majority of delegates committed to the restoration of the monarchy. The rival royalist factions, each with its own pretender to the throne, began working out the rough terms of a compromise: the Bourbon, Légitimist claimant – the childless Count de Chambord – would take the throne, and upon his death, it would pass to Louis-Philippe of the House of Orléans.

In the end, the dreams of monarchical restoration were dashed. Chambord stubbornly insisted that he would not accept the throne unless the Tricolor was replaced with the white flag of the Bourbons. President Patrice de Mac-Mahon – the descendant of an Irish family that had fled to France in 1689 – warned him that this would cause a revolt in the army, and Pope Pius IX urged him to reconsider. The count was steadfast, and

[1] Joseph Reinach, *Discours et plaidoyers politiques de M. Gambetta*, vol. 2, part 2 (Paris: G. Charpentier, 1880), 29–34.

his refusal to do so was a major setback to the monarchist cause. Still, royalists hoped to prevent the recognition of a republic in the new constitution, and they defeated repeated attempts to do so.[2]

On January 30, 1875, however, a Catholic deputy – Henri Wallon – proposed that the first article of the constitution read, "The President of the Republic is elected by the absolute majority of suffrages by the Senate and the Chamber of Deputies." It was a brilliant coup: by establishing a senate, the amendment went against the republican position that there should be a single chamber; but by including the term "President of the Republic," it explicitly acknowledged that the new regime would be a republican one. After intense debate, it passed 353 to 352.[3]

The Third Republic, then, "slipped in by the side door," the result of parliamentary compromise, the royalists' failure to unite around a common banner, the unity of the republicans, and, as many would note in later years, the votes of overseas deputies who owed their election not to "universal suffrage" but to a highly restricted franchise that included only a tiny minority of their local population. It was certainly not what many republicans had envisioned when they thought of themselves as the inheritors of the revolutionary tradition, organized, as Victor Hugo had written, into radiant battalions, blessed by the people, passing through the high azure gate of the dazzling future.[4]

* * *

The Second Empire of Louis-Napoleon inaugurated a form of rule that has come to be known as electoral authoritarianism.[5] The Bonapartist

---

[2] Stephen Hanson, "The Founding of the French Third Republic," *Comparative Political Studies* 43, no. 8–9 (2010): 1023–58, 1038, 1041.

[3] Jacques Kayser, *Les grandes batailles du radicalism: des origines aux portes du pouvoir, 1820–1901* (Paris: M. Rivière, 1962), 89; "Foreign History," *The Annual Register: A Review of Public Events at Home and Abroad for the Year 1875* (London: Rivingtons, 1876), 154, 157.

[4] J. P. T. Bury, *Gambetta and the Making of the Third Republic* (London: Longmans, 1973), 220, 226.

[5] Levitsky and Way distinguish between competitive and electoral authoritarianism, with the former offering genuine if constricted opportunities for the opposition to come to power and the latter merely legitimating autocratic rule. The Second Empire was more of the latter, although gradual liberalizations gave its elections a more genuinely competitive character by the 1860s. Steven Levitsky and Lucan Way, "The Rise of Competitive Authoritarianism," *Journal of Democracy* 13, no. 2 (2002): 51–66; Nicolas van de Walle, "Africa's Range of Regimes," *Journal of Democracy* 13, no. 2 (2002): 66–88; Andreas Schedler, ed., *Electoral Authoritarianism: The Dynamics of Unfree Competition* (Boulder, CO: Lynne Rienner, 2006); Marina Ottaway, *Democracy Challenged: The Rise*

regime aggressively promoted itself as the defender of universal suffrage, holding elections that, while heavily manipulated, were not entirely a sham, and resting the regime's legitimacy on national plebiscites. That a despot could repeatedly win in elections held by manhood citizen suffrage deeply undermined republican faith in the "people" long extolled by the revolutionary tradition.

And yet beginning under the Empire, a new generation of self-identified radical republicans gradually converged on a narrative of French political community that reinterpreted and reaffirmed republicans' commitment to popular sovereignty and universal suffrage. They argued that the revolution had regenerated France by redistributing property, creating a pantheon of heroes and a new political iconography, and establishing the sovereignty of the people as the defining feature of the nation. But in a break with earlier republican traditions, this new generation insisted that the direct action of the people was no longer appropriate to modern conditions. Instead, the people must look to universal suffrage as the only appropriate manifestation of their sovereignty; and only under the Republic could universal suffrage be given its appropriate freedom and force. The people were to be sovereign but constrained, and "universal suffrage" was defended as the radical but conservative mechanism of reconciling democracy with political order.

This retelling of French history, republican purpose, and popular sovereignty would eventually prove crucial in reassuring liberal monarchists and conservative republicans that manhood suffrage could be retained without threatening property. It became a central pillar of radical republicans' efforts to connect with growing middle-class constituencies outside of Paris while winning over some working-class voters for both the promise to defend voting rights and the suggestion of new social reforms to follow. And it would ultimately come to define a new national mission for the Republic and political program for what would eventually become the Radical Republican party: to wed social reforms with a conservative defense of property, to advance the cause of secular education, and to defend the Republic against the dangers of

of *Semi-Authoritarianism* (Washington, DC: Carnegie Endowment for International Peace, 2003); Daniel Brumberg, "The Trap of Liberalized Autocracy," *Journal of Democracy* 13, no. 4 (2002): 56–68; Brownless, *Authoritarianism in an Age of Democratization*; Yonatan L. Morse, "The Era of Electoral Authoritarianism," *World Politics* 64, no. 1 (2012): 161–98.

Catholic clericalism by gradually molding the French into a nation of republican citizens.

The founding of the Third Republic did not, for the most part, result in the curtailment of manhood suffrage, a puzzling outcome given the suspicions of liberals and many republicans and the fierce opposition of most monarchists. Instead, "universal suffrage" was inscribed as the fundamental principle of the new regime. But this regime rested on both the inclusion of particular groups, which provided it with a popular social base, but also on exclusions that would define the fight over democracy in France for the next seventy years.

DISENFRANCHISEMENT AND REVOLUTION

Mass elections were viewed with particular anxiety in nineteenth-century France. Elections to the Estates-General had kicked off the revolution, as representatives of the Third Estate abolished feudalism and issued the Declaration of the Rights of Man and of the Citizen. In the decades after the restoration, every electoral surprise in which a more radical candidate than could be countenanced was elected was met with reaction in the form of a revised electoral law, either establishing hierarchical and indirect elections or culling the electorate through disenfranchisement. When the aging republican Abbé Grégoire was elected, for example, the monarchist legislature refused to seat him and passed legislation restricting the right to vote and giving the richest quarter of voters an additional vote in a new college that would return half the representatives. A decade later, when a royalist legislature voted no confidence in the government and was sustained in the subsequent elections, the king responded with the July Ordinances, which would have severely diminished the electorate from 0.3 percent – ninety thousand voters in a country of thirty-two million – to 0.07 percent of the population.

This was a disenfranchisement too far: the Bourse ceased making loans, newly disenfranchised manufacturers closed their shops and laid off their workers, and the discharged men joined the swelling ranks of the unemployed in manning the barricades that began to go up around the city. In short order, the government fell, the king fled, and the Duke of Orléans was installed in his place. A new electoral law modestly expanded the right to vote, although the enfranchisement rate was still less than 1 percent of the total population.

Just as the Protestant Constitution in the United Kingdom rested on corrupt electoral practices in the small boroughs, the so-called July Monarchy rested on bribery and intimidation in 459 single member constituencies.[6] By the 1840s, the link between the restricted right to vote and the endemic corruption of the regime had become "one of the major themes of republican literature."[7]

But if there was broad agreement that ministerial corruption depended on the restricted electoral system, there was less agreement as to what should be done.[8] A small number of left-wing republicans embraced manhood suffrage, which had been promised by the never-enacted 1793 constitution. They argued that manhood suffrage alone could "render corruption impossible" by substituting "compact masses for those bourgeois cliques, for these privileged minorities."[9] Publications such as the *New Republican Catechism*, intended to disseminate republican principles among a suspicious population, listed as the first principle of republican government that "sovereignty resides in the universality of the citizens."[10]

But these were a distinct minority, and most liberals and republicans opposed manhood suffrage as likely to enfranchise a dangerous population that would threaten private property. A central committee of reform organized a petition campaign in 1839 and 1840, gathering hundreds of thousands of signatures in support of the principle that "Every citizen having the right to serve in the national guard should be an elector!" More common were modest proposals to extend the franchise to those eligible to serve on juries. Adolphe Thiers, minister of commerce and of public works, ridiculed these, by pointing out that if it were a "gross oppression, to govern 32 million persons with only 240,000 voters," then surely the evil would not be eliminated by the inclusion of 20,000 or 500,000 more electors.[11] Even many socialists opposed too quick an embrace of universal suffrage,

---

[6] By 1846, only 61 of 459 districts had more than 800 electors, while 172 had fewer than 400 electors. Raymond Huard, *Le suffrage universel en France, 1848–1946* (Paris: Aubiér, 1994), 23. Electing legislators at the departmental level had been associated with support for the Bourbon Right under the restoration electoral laws. Thomas D. Beck, *French Legislators, 1800–1834: A Study in Quantitative History* (Berkeley: University of California Press, 1974), 76.

[7] Pierre Rosanvallon, *Le sacre du citoyen: histoire du suffrage universel en France* (Paris: Editions Gallimard, 1992), 278.

[8] Huard, *Le suffrage universel en France*, 24–30.

[9] Rosanvallon, *Le sacre du citoyen*, 278.

[10] Un Prolétaire, *Nouveau catéchisme Républicain* (Lyon: La Glaneuse, 1833), 46–47.

[11] *Archives parlementaires de 1781 à 1860*, 2nd series, vol. 85, January 4, 1834, 447.

warning that "for thirty years, the counter-revolution alone has spoken in France," that the "education of the masses has been done only by oral instruction, which has always belonged and belongs still to the enemies of the Republic," namely the priests and local aristocrats. "The people" were simultaneously too radical for some and too conservative for others.[12]

The Second Republic and the Dangers of Universal Suffrage

When liberal reformers, inspired by the success of the anti–Corn Law agitation in Britain, began holding banquets to get around the laws prohibiting political meetings, they asked only for modest extensions of suffrage, which prime minister François Guizot dismissed as inopportune. Given the opposition of the governing Orléanists, the banquet organizers were forced to reach out to republicans, repulsing liberal monarchists.[13]

The banquets were banned in February 1848 during a prolonged economic depression. By the end of the month, a new revolution had occurred, a provisional government had been formed, and a decree had been issued announcing elections for a constituent assembly.

Despite the anxieties of many republicans and almost all liberals, the elections to a National Assembly were to be held by "direct and universal" suffrage: all French males aged twenty-one years, resident in their commune for six months, not deprived of their rights for a felony conviction, bankruptcy, or some other offense to the state or morality were extended the right to vote. This included male citizens in Algeria and other colonies, as well as those who were enrolled in the army or navy. The number of electors increased from approximately 246,000 to nearly 10,000,000 – from less than 1 percent of the population to over 27 percent, and likely over 90 percent of the adult male population.[14] The electoral process was also radically redesigned: instead of the earlier practice of having all eligible voters assemble in the administrative capital of the department to elect deputies after a period of deliberation, votes were to be cast by ballots deposited in the canton and counted in the departmental capital. From this point on, remarks Raymond Huard, "it is the simple counting of votes cast successively and independently of each other that tends to become the essence of the election."[15]

---

[12] Huard, *Le suffrage universel en France*, 5.
[13] Christopher Guyver, *The Second French Republic: A Political Reinterpretation, 1848–1852* (London: Palgrave Macmillan, 2016), 45–48.
[14] Huard, *Le suffrage universel en France*, 43.   [15] Ibid., 34.

The new constitution maintained the commitment to near–manhood suffrage, its first article declaring that "sovereignty resides in the universality of French citizens. – It is inalienable and indefeasible. – No individual, no fraction of the people can claim to exercise it." Just as important, there would be no complicated system of electoral colleges to dampen their influence. The provisional government passed a decree abolishing slavery, and the constitutional convention declared that those "colonies purified of servitude and the Indian possessions will be represented in the National Assembly."[16] Freed men were declared citizens, with supposedly equal legal standing as male citizens in the metropole, including the right to vote, and Louisy Mathieu, a former slave, was elected representative of Guadeloupe to the National Assembly in 1848, where he sat with the extreme left.[17] In Senegal, however, the abolition of slavery created an unexpected situation: newly freed men were able to claim status as French citizens and be inscribed on the electoral lists, but the indigenous Muslim population – whose legal status placed them under the authority of a colonial-enforced Muslim law rather than the Civil Code – could not. Given that this latter population included much of the commercial elite of the colony, an exception was made, and noncitizen indigenous inhabitants of Senegal and the French colonies in India who could prove a residence of more than five years were excused from having to prove their status as French citizens. An electoral law passed on March 15, 1849, would have led to a purge of "all *indigenes* who were of the Muslim religion [and who] were not subject to the rule of French civil law for that which concerned their personal status." But events in the interim intervened, and the law was never proclaimed in the colonies, a fact that would be of lasting significance in the Third Republic.[18]

---

[16] J-B Duvergier, *Collection complète des lois, décrets, ordonnances, réglements, et avis du Conseil d'Etat*, vol. 48 (Paris: Directeur de l'administration, 1848), 194; Raymond Betts, *Assimilation and Association in French Colonial Theory: 1890–1914*, 2nd edn. (Lincoln: University of Nebraska Press, 2005), 13.

[17] In fact, local labor laws were established that limited freedom of association, movement, and employment. Oruno D. Lara, *La liberté assassinée. Guadeloupe, Guyane, Martinique et La Réunion, 1848–1856* (Paris: Editions L'Harmattan, 2005); Oruno D. Lara, *Suffrage universel et colonisation, 1848–1852* (Paris: Editions L'Harmattan, 2007).

[18] A man of mixed ancestry, Durand-Barthélemy Valantin, was elected from Senegal. Lara, *Suffrage universel et colonization*, 237–39; Bernard Moleur, "L'indigène aux urnes: le droit de suffrage et la citoyenneté dans la colonie du Sénégal," in *Les droits de l'homme et le suffrage universel*, ed. Jean-Luc Chabot (Paris: Editions L'Harmattan, 2000), 70–74.

While freed men and some indigenous noncitizen men were being enfranchised, there was also some debate over whether women should be extended the right to vote. Instead, the provisional government insisted that it alone could not break with the precedent[19] of limiting voting rights to men; and the Constituent Assembly, which did have such authority, instead affirmed the exclusion of women, which would be repeated in the electoral law of March 15, 1849. While the cause of woman suffrage could count on some vocal support from the far left in the assembly, a proposal to allow women to vote was defeated with only one vote in favor.[20]

The decision to turn to manhood suffrage during the early days of the revolution had been a product of contingent circumstance: the left-wing republicans who were most committed to it, such as Alphonse de Lamartine and Alexandre Ledru-Rollin, were more involved in the revolutionary events in Paris and consequently exercised an influence in the early decisions well beyond their numbers.

Anxieties over manhood suffrage persisted, however, and became more pronounced as the revolution seemed to take a more socialistic bent. The provisional government had established a series of National Workshops – employment centers supported at public expense – that became crucibles for radicalizing the working classes and organizing them into a coherent political force.[21] In June 1848, the Executive Committee ordered that the National Workshops be closed and that all unemployed persons in Paris either leave the city immediately or, if under twenty-five, join the army. The barricades went up, and in a few days the insurrection had been suppressed, with thousands dead or shipped off to Algeria.[22]

---

[19] Noble and ecclesiastical women could vote at times for the Estates-General. Armand Brette, *Recueil de documents relatifs á la convocation des Etats généraux de 1789*, vol. 1 (Paris: Imprimerie nationale, 1894), 71–75; Lynn Hunt, *The French Revolution and Human Rights: A Brief Documentary History* (New York: St. Martin's Press, 1996), 60–63; Karen Offen, *The Woman Question in France, 1400–1870* (Cambridge: Cambridge University Press, 2017), 73–90; Steven C. Hause and Anne R. Kenney, *Women's Suffrage and Social Politics in the French Third Republic* (Princeton, NJ: Princeton University Press, 1984), 3–4.

[20] Claire Goldberg Moses, *French Feminism in the 19th Century* (Albany: State University of New York Press, 1984), 136, 142.

[21] Roger V. Gould, *Insurgent Identities: Class, Community, and Protest in Paris from 1848 to the Commune* (Chicago: University of Chicago Press, 1995).

[22] Judith F. Stone, *Sons of the Revolution: Radical Democrats in France, 1862–1914* (Baton Rouge: Louisiana State University Press, 1996), 27.

In December 1848, Louis-Napoleon Bonaparte – a nephew of the despot, whose adulthood had been spent organizing poorly executed putsches – was elected president of the Second Republic, winning nearly three-quarters of the vote by appealing to order, promising vaguely defined social reforms, and capitalizing on his name recognition. In the next year's legislative elections, the conservative Party of Order – combining Bourbon Légitimists, liberal Orléanists, and some conservative republicans – won a commanding majority. Responding to Catholic complaints that the existing educational system was controlled by secular and anticlerical teachers, the Party of Order passed legislation simultaneously expanding education – extending it to girls – while giving the Catholic Church a much greater role, including allowing clergy and nuns to teach without being qualified by the state-run university system.

The right wing was empowered, and the center was collapsing: moderate republicans were elected in small numbers, while the new Democratic Socialists – the "Montagnards" – made impressive inroads in the interior of the country and in the major cities. A series of special elections only confirmed the rising influence of the Democratic Socialists, with the party's candidates – including some who had been exiled after June 1848 – defeating moderate and conservative opponents.

As if on cue, the Orléanist Adolphe Thiers proposed the soon-to-be-infamous Electoral Law of May 31, 1850. The law raised residency requirements, imposed new burdens on registration, and expanded the number of offenses for which an elector could be disenfranchised, to include proscribed political activities – such as distributing pamphlets – outrages against public morality or religion, questioning the principle of property or the family, vagabondage, or interference with army recruitment. Residence for voting purposes could be established by three years' inscription on the list of taxpayers, which automatically included an elector on the voting rolls. For nontaxpayers, the procedures were more burdensome and expressly designed to facilitate intimidation by employers. "We excluded from the ballot a few well-intentioned and sober workers," noted one member of the Party of Order, "but on the other hand, we forbade the assemblies to all the vagabonds, the ex-convicts, the citizens without domicile and without confession, the formidable recruits and fanatical henchmen of the social Republic. Could we hesitate before this alternative? We think not."[23]

---

[23] Huard, *Le suffrage universel en France*, 58.

Effect of the Disenfranchisement Law by Department

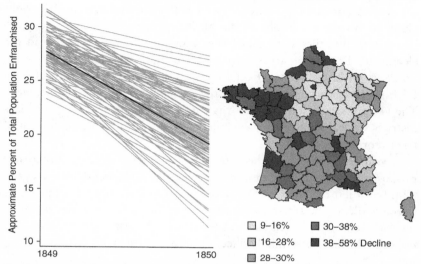

Grey lines represent Departments, and the black line represents the national total.

FIGURE 6.1 The Disenfranchisement of May 1850

Republican activists organized a massive petition campaign in opposition, with over 7,000 petitions and 527,000 signatures sent to the assembly. The majority referenced the constitution's declaration that "sovereignty resides in the universality of French citizens." They described the disenfranchisement as "a violation of the constitution," as "threatening the foundations of the Republic, the most sacred right." The new suffrage regime, they argued, would replace a "common right of all the people by a privilege instituted for a fraction of the people." "The right of suffrage," declared one petition, was "inseparable from the right of sovereignty" and was a right "anterior and superior to the positive law." This was a veiled threat of revolution, justified by the assembly's attempt to divide "citizens into two classes: one that makes the law, and another that must obey it."[24]

The result would be among the largest single disenfranchisements by an otherwise democratic regime in world history. Of an electorate of approximately ten million, almost three million were disenfranchised.

---

[24] François Jarrige, "Une 'barricade de papiers': le pétitionnement contre la restriction du suffrage universel masculin en mai 1850," *Revue d'histoire du XIXe siècle* 29, no. 2 (2004): 4, 9; Huard, *Le suffrage universel en France*, 53–54, 62; see the collection in the Archives Nationale, C//2300 to C//2313 AN.

The left panel of Figure 6.1 shows the decline in the enfranchisement rate
for every department in France, as well as the national average. The right
panel shows the geography of disenfranchisement, dividing the departments into quintiles with the darker regions showing a decline in the
electorate. The major areas affected were the industrial regions of the
north, the Rhône, centered on Lyons, and the poor agricultural (and
Légitimist) regions of Brittany and the Pays-de-la-Loire in the northwest.
The voting population of Paris was cut in half, and some working-class
districts were almost entirely excluded; the city of Lille lost 80 percent of
its electorate.[25]

A year later, posing as the defender of universal suffrage, Bonaparte
proposed the repeal of the disenfranchising law. This was defeated 355 to
348, but it left the Party of Order isolated. On December 2, 1851, came
the coup d'état, the arrest of thousands of republicans, uprisings throughout the country, and its bloody suppression by the army and police, whose
upper ranks had been quietly filled with Bonaparte loyalists.

The Empire of Universal Suffrage

Under the July Monarchy, many republicans – ranging from moderate
liberals to radicals and socialists – had been skeptical about whether the
"people" could be trusted with manhood suffrage. Their anxieties were
intensified under the Second Republic, as the June insurrections had been
directed against the republic itself, demanding not the liberty of the middle-class and bourgeois republicans but a right to work. The election of
Louis-Napoleon and a conservative National Assembly had deeply dis-
turbed their belief that the will of the nation was for the republic. Under
the empire, their worst suspicions were confirmed.[26]

To justify the coup, Bonaparte issued an "Appel au peuple" in which he
based his authority on the "six millions votes" he had received in the
election to the presidency. He argued that by restricting the suffrage, the
conservative government had violated the constitution and threatened the
republic. The "people," he declared, "were the only sovereign
I recognize." In the decree dissolving the National Assembly, he

---

[25] Jarrige, "Une 'barricade de papiers,'" 4; Jacques Bouillon, "Les Démocrates-socialistes
Aux élections de 1849," *Revue française de science politique* 6, no. 1 (1956): 70–95;
Huard, *Le suffrage universel en France*, 57.
[26] Philip G. Nord, *The Republican Moment: The Struggle for Democracy in Nineteenth-
Century France* (Cambridge, MA: Harvard University Press, 1995), 1–5.

announced that "universal suffrage is reestablished," consolidating his self-presentation as the defender of popular sovereignty.[27] He then called for a referendum to approve his coup, and with local officials warning that the names of any man who voted against him would be published, 7.4 million voters voted in his favor, 640,000 voted against, and 1.7 million abstained. While intimidation, the banning of opposition publications, and martial law pushed the margin upward, it was clear that a majority of the population had voted in favor.

The self-proclaimed defender of universal suffrage, the constitution, and the republic then abolished the republic, declared himself emperor, and established an electoral regime with a broad but meaningless right to vote. The new constitution was approved with 97 percent of votes cast in favor. So important was the idea of "universal suffrage" to the regime's legitimacy that it even allowed Abd al-Qadir – a leader of the anti-colonial struggle in France – and his retinue to vote in Amboise, where they had just recently been released from prison (Figure 6.2).[28]

Elections in the Second Empire were tightly controlled, although like modern electoral authoritarianisms there were more or less real competitions in many districts. Districts to the legislative body were gerrymandered every five years, "official candidates" were generously subsidized, local officials threatened reprisals against those who voted for their opponents, and election committees were outlawed until the mid-1860s. Algeria and the other colonies, with their black or settler electorates, were denied representation in the legislature, while soldiers were denied the right to vote. In any case, the elections were for a relatively toothless assembly.

The regime's favored candidates won a majority in every legislative election under the empire, and in 1870 a plebiscite held to approve reforms to the constitution passed easily, with a "yes" vote clearly framed as "a national ratification of the empire." Only the republican strongholds of Seine and Bouches-du-Rhône, along with Algeria – whose French citizens were allowed to vote in national referenda and who were

---

[27] Louis-Napoléon Bonaparte, *Discours et proclamations de Louis-Napoléon Bonaparte, depuis son retour en France jusqu'au 1er janvier 1852, années 1849, 1850 et 1851* (Paris: Typographie Plon Frères, 1852), 201, 203.

[28] In the plebiscite of 1851, Algeria had been only narrowly in favor of Bonaparte; by 1852, the votes of the colons lined up with those of mainland France in favor of the Empire. Bertrand Jalla, "Les colons d'Algérie à la lumière du coup d'état de 1851," *Afrique & histoire* 1, no. 1 (2003): 123–37; *The Illustrated London News*, December 4, 1852, p. 495.

FIGURE 6.2 Abd al-Qadir Voting for the French Empire, from the *The Illustrated London News*

increasingly opposed to the empire after Napoleon's declaration that Algeria constituted an "Arab kingdom" – voted against the proposal.[29]

Universal suffrage was absolutely central to the regime's legitimacy. To celebrate the plebiscite of 1851, the number of "yes" votes was emblazoned on the façade of Notre-Dame cathedral. Medals were struck commemorating Louis-Napoleon's "acclamation," giving prominent place to the exact number of votes cast for him. A series of prints was issued celebrating "Louis-Napoleon Bonaparte, elected, by virtue of 5,434,226 votes" – the number of votes he received in 1848. Within a few years, it was the 7,500,000 votes in favor of the empire being emblazoned on documents and stamped on medals. Another series was prepared commemorating "Louis-Napoleon Bonaparte re-establishing universal suffrage, December 2 1851."[30]

Bonapartists were unanimous in their praise of universal suffrage: it served as their answer to every critique, and its repeated invocation was

[29] Alistair Cole and Peter Campbell, *French Electoral Systems and Elections Since 1789* (Brookfield, VT: Gower, 1989), 5; Roger Price, *The French Second Empire: An Anatomy of Political Power* (Cambridge: Cambridge University Press, 2001), 111–18.
[30] Matthew N. Truesdell, *Spectacular Politics: Louis-Napoleon Bonaparte and the Fête Impériale, 1849–1870* (New York: Oxford University Press, 1997), 8.

intended to assimilate the image of Bonaparte and his supporters with the singular and unanimous voice of the people. When Henri d'Orléans, one of the pretenders to the throne, denounced Bonaparte, his supporters responded that "the best argument that we have to oppose you is *universal suffrage*, of which you lose sight, about which you do not even want to discuss, and with good reason." Napoleon's "power rests entirely on this national manifestation."[31] Another asked if the empire had merited the support of the people: "the answer is the 8 million votes that once founded it and to which it owes its legitimacy."[32] The number of votes creeped upward.

Doubting Republicans

The close ideological association of the regime with manhood suffrage gave republicans and royalists ample reason to denounce the idea of an equal voice among citizens in national affairs. And many of them did. Most of the royalist right had never supported it, and neither did most liberals, whose tolerance for it under the empire rested on its being contained. Ernest Renan – a self-styled "mere liberal" rather than a "republican a priori" – believed that universal suffrage had made France mediocre, "without originality or boldness."[33] "Universal suffrage," reported one address to the legislature, "appears to us today as a pupil held in tutelage by the government – a benevolent tutelage, an honest protection, a necessary guidance." But the tutor, they insisted, should never be "elected by the pupil," and only once the citizenry had been educated in liberal principles could they be allowed an unfettered voice in public affairs. Until then, free manhood suffrage would be "a social danger, a pretext to anarchy."[34] A rector confessed that free manhood suffrage "frightens me as it frightens every honest man. It carries within it the seeds of catastrophe, of a social revolution which will break out one day, if we persist with it." Electoral manipulation was absolutely necessary, and anything else would "be suicidal." A procurer-general in Dijon believed in "the instability of the people's sentiments," and feared reawakening "its belief in its own sovereignty." The people were "not

[31] Anonymous, *Lettre d'un français à M. Henri d'Orléans* (Paris: n. p., 1861), 8.
[32] Auguste Davons, *Napoléon III devant le suffrage universel* (Paris: A. Davons, 1869), 5.
[33] Ernest Renan, *La réforme intellectuelle et morale* (Paris: Michel Lévy frères, 1871), 26; Ernest Renan, *Discours et Conférences* (Paris: Calmann Lévy, 1887), 243.
[34] Charles Talboscq and F-H Hippolyte, *Le suffrage universel et l'instruction primaire: à MM. les deputes de 1864* (Paris: Chex les Auteurs, 1864), 9, 36.

incapable of reason and good sense, but they are neither sufficiently enlightened nor wise enough to intervene regularly in affairs of state."[35]

Most conservative republicans seem to have opposed it as well. The National Workshops, the June insurrections, and the elections of the Democratic Socialists had heralded the arrival of socialism as a political force. The rural masses had shown that they were neither particularly sympathetic to the urban working class – alienating socialists and other left republicans – nor particularly attached to the republic, alienating the rest. Prominent republicans now asked why something as vital as the republic should be left in the hands of an ill-informed and superstitious popular sovereignty. If Louis-Napoleon based the legitimacy of his overturning the republic and his empire on the authority of "universal suffrage," these republicans claimed that the "Republic was above universal suffrage." Since at least 1792, the republican tradition had associated the republic with "the people," its iconography steeped in recollections of the National Assembly, the revolutionary crowds, and the "levée en masse" that had repulsed foreign invaders. They were now questioning this tradition, and arguing that the republic was right not because it was an expression of popular sovereignty; it was right regardless of what the people wanted.

Louis Gensoul, for instance, argued that the republic was necessitated by "invariable law" of social organization, and that universal suffrage was an "improper" arbiter of regime type, "as ridiculous as asking [the people] about the movement of the earth or sun." Universal suffrage must "abdicate before science," and republicans were called on to recognize "that the voice of the people, like the voice of god, is nothing but the voice of ignorance."[36] The positive philosopher Emile Littré, an important influence among republicans, continued to defend male citizen suffrage but argued that it was a function more than a right, whose operation should be confined to the simple act of electing representatives under a republican regime, and its use fortified and purified by education.[37] The voice of the

---

[35] Price, The French Second Empire, 105.

[36] Louis Gensoul, La République au-dessus du suffrage universel: étude demonstrative de philosophie et de politique positives (Paris: A. Lacroix Verboeckhoven et Cie., 1871), 9, 13, 40, 42, 48.

[37] Emile Littré, "Du suffrage universel en France, considéré comme une experience sociologique," La Philosophie Positiviste 4 (Janvier 1869): 31–51; Emile Littré, Conservation, Révolution, et Positivisme (Paris: Librarie Philosophique de Ladrange, 1852), xviii; Emile Littré, "Variétés," La Philosophie Positiviste 2 (Juin 1868): 463–66; Sudhir Hazareesingh, Intellectual Founders of the Republic: Five Studies in Nineteenth-

people should be no more than a choice between established candidates committed to the republic, and must not be used in referenda on issues where the people were not competent to decide. Universal suffrage, wrote Edgar Quinet, a republican who now lived in exile in Switzerland, had been taken up by the enemies of liberty, "a new weapon that they seized when all the others had been wasted." "If France could perish," he wrote, "it would be by a false idea of universal suffrage and the power of assemblies."[38] Republican attitudes were increasingly well characterized by one of their Bonapartist critics: unable to accept the empire, they rejected manhood suffrage with it, "putting the Republic above universal suffrage, above the will of the French, above the sovereignty of the nation."[39]

It was not just popular sovereignty; the entire revolutionary tradition had been thrown into doubt. Victor Hugo attacked the National Workshops as a dangerous threat to the principles of the republic, and summarized how republicans understood the proper relationship between themselves and the French working classes: "the liberty of '89, the republic of '92, July 1830, February 1848; these great things, who is it who accomplishes them? The thinkers of Paris who prepare them, and the workers of Paris who execute them." The workers of Paris should have remembered their place.[40] Hugo, who perhaps more than anyone else glorified and helped disseminate the heroic revolutionary stories of popular uprisings, believed that June 1848 had been illegitimate, and as a member of the National Assembly he had supported its suppression. "At its core, what was June 1848?" he would ask in *Les Misérables*. It was "a revolt of the people against itself." What did the barricades "attack in the name of the Revolution? The Revolution itself. That barricade – danger, chance, disorder, terror, misunderstanding, the unknown – had facing it the Constituent Assembly, the sovereignty of the people, universal suffrage, the nation, the republic." It had been the insurrections, republicans argued, that had provoked a conservative backlash in the countryside, the election of Louis-Napoleon, an emboldened Party of

Century French Republican Political Thought (Oxford: Oxford University Press, 2001), 57–58.

[38] Edgar Quinet, *La République, conditions de la régénération de la France* (Paris: Dentu, 1872), 13, 19.

[39] A. L. I. de Saint-Amand, *Le règne de Napoléon III, 1861* (Paris: Dentu, 1899), 214.

[40] Guyver, *The Second French Republic*, 2; Félix M. Wouters, *Histoire parlémentaire de l'Assemblée nationale, précédée du récit de la revolution de Paris* (Bruxelles: Bureaux de l'association des ouvriers typographes, 1848), 372.

Order, the disenfranchisement of 1850, and ultimately the loss of the republic.[41]

The historian François Furet has identified and celebrated an important shift in how the revolutionary tradition was perceived in French republican thought, as the demoralized republicans of 1848 began to reinterpret this tradition in light of their own experiences. Of particular importance was Edgar Quinet's 1865 *La Révolution*, which denounced the Jacobin legacy and placed the blame for the coup not only on the socialist insurrectionaries but on the republican tradition itself. Its publication resulted in heated critiques by Jules Michelet – the foremost republican historian – and others, but it found a receptive audience among a younger generation.[42]

This new generation would, in the coming decades, disseminate a new account of French history and republican purpose, and how these related to the revolutionary tradition. The vision of political community that they articulated continued to emphasize the central importance of the French Revolution. But instead of being portrayed as a model of direct popular participation, worthy of emulation and with the uprising of the people given center stage, the importance of the revolution was reframed as a great work of national rejuvenation whose purpose had been largely, but not entirely, fulfilled. It had created a new iconography for a new nation, one that rested on a new class of propertied landholders, petit bourgeois shopkeepers and merchants in towns and cities throughout the country.[43]

Drawing on Quinet and others, this new generation of republicans argued that the revolution had so profoundly changed the French national character that the republic alone was adapted to its mores. The republic, then, stood above the nation, above popular sovereignty: the fact that a monarch or emperor had been overturned seven times since the beginning of the century simply proved as a scientific fact that only the republican form of government was compatible with modern France. The revolution's purpose had largely been accomplished, in the form of a new and distinctive national character and a supporting pattern of property relations. What remained to be completed were the installation

---

[41] Victor Hugo, *Les Misérables*, vol. 3 (London: Hurst and Blackett, 1862), 159, 161.

[42] François Furet, *La gauche et la révolution au milieu de XIXe siècle: Edgar Quinet et la question du jacobinisme, 1865–1870: suivi de Le pieces du débat* (Paris: Hachette, 1986), 72; Nord, *The Republican Moment*, 14–30.

[43] Furet, *La gauche et la revolution*, 83; Stone, *Sons of the Revolution*, 34.

and consolidation of the only form of government compatible with this changed and rejuvenated nation, a republic, whose achievement had been interrupted by a succession of Napoleons.

Instead of leading them to reject universal suffrage, however, republicans used the primacy of the republic to reappropriate suffrage from the Bonapartist regime and emplace it as the centerpiece of their own story of French community. The republic was "in principle above decision," but it was also necessitated by universal suffrage, for only under a republican form of government could universal suffrage continue to have a real existence.[44] "Universal suffrage itself can do nothing against the republic," argued Louis Blanc, a socialist who remained close to self-styled radical republicans, "because the present generation cannot confiscate the right of future generations.... If universal suffrage established a monarchy, a hereditary monarchy – which supposes immutability – universal suffrage would commit suicide and would lose, by this very act, its very reason for existence."[45] Instead of the republic being above universal suffrage, Sigismond Vainberg argued that "universal suffrage is the Republic." Only under a republican form of government could universal suffrage not lose its universal and sovereign character, by abdicating on one question and thus losing itself forever. In a republic, new leaders could be chosen and old ones displaced, while in a monarchy or empire, this act could only be done through revolution, of which republicans "want no more."[46]

Perhaps the most striking fact about republicanism as it emerged under the Second Empire was that its political posture was "at once radical and conservative," promising future civic, political, and social reforms that could equalize social relations even as they offered reassurances that property and social order would not be disrupted. Once universal suffrage was understood as a simple mechanism for arbitrating decisions, the self-styled radical republicans promised that it would become a central means (complemented by education) by which the country's endemic class conflict could be resolved: universal suffrage would require statesmen to appeal to broad constituencies and devise solutions that could be acceptable to both capital and labor. Their policy proposals mixed promises of

---

[44] Charles Pajot, *La république est-elle au-dessus du suffrage universel? Lettre au rédacteur de l'Opinion nationale* (Paris: n. p., 1871), 8.

[45] *Annales de l'Assemblée Nationale* 1 (February 17, 1871): 64.

[46] Sigismond Vainberg, *Le suffrage universel est la République* (Paris: E. Leroux, 1873), 105–6.

social reform with explicit opposition to property redistribution, and they repeatedly insisted that their program meant "not the equalization of wealth, but only of narrowing the gap by assuring to all the means of escaping misery, and placing a modest comfort within the reach of the greatest number."[47]

Following Quinet, republicans began, hesitatingly at first, to explicitly reject the Jacobinical tradition.[48] Jules Ferry, who would be one of the founding statesmen of the Third Republic and a key figure in defining republicanism after 1877, argued that "Jacobinism was no longer a weapon but a peril," whose dangers had been revealed by 1848.[49] Vainberg went further than many in arguing that universal suffrage had "the right to pronounce on all questions, a right that it cannot renounce," but he likewise insisted that "it must never have recourse to violent methods, to change the situation that it has made; rather, it must wait with patience the hour of the vote to make a new situation."[50] Henri Allain-Targé argued that under a "government of free universal suffrage," the country would experience a material prosperity that it had never known, allowing for the resolution of social and class conflict; the people had reflected "on the ideas born in 1848. They have abandoned utopias, empiricism, fantasies" and had instead become "perfectly convinced" of universal suffrage's "moderation and power." Universal suffrage promised to merge "the classes and reunite men of all origins and all creeds under the same flag, in a single goal: liberty, the doctrine of which has definitively conquered the primitive socialist theory, that is to say, the communist and dictatorial principle."[51]

The purpose of radical republicanism was to carry the revolution through to its logical conclusion, a parliamentary republican regime, elected by universal suffrage, in which direct expressions of popular sovereignty would no longer be justified, electoral politics would be the only appropriate form of popular political participation, and accommodation among parliamentary representatives would be the only legitimate

---

[47] Léonce Ribert, *La Gauche, la situation, le programme démocratique* (Paris: Le Chevalier, 1869), 73.

[48] James Lehning, *To Be a Citizen: The Political Culture of the Early French Third Republic* (Ithaca, NY: Cornell University Press, 2001), 31; Stone, *Sons of the Revolution*, 34.

[49] Furet, *La gauche et la revolution*, 78–79.

[50] Vainberg, *Le suffrage universel est la République*, 106.

[51] François Allain-Targé, *Les déficits, 1852–1868* (Paris: Le Chevalier, 1868), 27; Sanford Elwitt, *The Making of the Third Republic: Class and Politics in France, 1868–1884* (Baton Rouge: Louisiana State University Press, 1975), 21.

source of public policy. The revolutionary tradition was being confined to the past, and universal suffrage – as a symbol, an idea, and a rhetorical trope – was the means by which it would be buried.

Republicans were not so much trying to persuade themselves that their doubts about "the people" were invalid. They instead were arguing that a republic could *create* a people that would accept the republic as a scientific fact, provided it undertook the types of reforms that they desired and that they believed they alone could accomplish. To reconcile popular participation with stability required not only piecemeal social reforms, but also the transformation of the citizenry, wresting them from the ideological grasp of the *ancien régime* and the priesthood who sustained it. The threat posed by organized Catholicism was "one of the principal barriers to their vision of republican citizens."[52] It was also the most insidious, as the priesthood claimed a unique access to the innermost circles of the family.

This was not a new theme. In the 1840s, Michelet had famously complained that "our wives and our daughters are being raised, are being governed, *by our enemies*," while Quinet in 1850 argued that the "the institutions and mores of France" should ensure the absolute "separation of the domain of secular society from the domain of particular religious dogma."[53] In order to reassure themselves that resting a new regime on universal suffrage would not mean sacrificing it to the supposed prejudices and superstitions – in short, the Catholicism – of the rural population, republicans insisted that as its essential corollary "universal suffrage demands the diffusion of public education."[54] This was a central commitment of the League for Instruction, for example, which clandestinely circulated the 1789 Declaration of the Rights of Man and the Citizen and believed compulsory, and absolutely secular, primary education was the "indispensable corollary" to universal suffrage. This would be a vitally important group in disseminating a changed republican discourse during the late empire and early years of the Third Republic.[55] Edouard Laboulaye insisted that republican radicalism would be the "vaccine to communism, socialism, Jacobinism and the whole scourge of *isms* that have afflicted us for seventy-

---

[52] Lehning, *To Be a Citizen*, 36.
[53] Jules Michelet, *Du Prêtre, de la femme, de la famille* (Paris: Paulin, 1845), 3; Edgar Quinet, *L'enseignement du Peuple* (Paris: Chamerot, 1850), 228.
[54] Ribert, *La Gauche, la situation, le programme démocratique*, 51–52.
[55] Katherine Auspitz, *The Radical Bourgeoisie: The Ligue de L'enseignement and the Origins of the Third Republic, 1866–1885* (Cambridge: Cambridge University Press, 1982), 60.

years," and sought to discourage liberals from attacking universal suffrage: "Far from trying to weaken [universal suffrage], it needs to be strengthened, by enlightening it," by providing for an extensive system of education that would attach the citizenry to republican principles and detach them from the Catholic Church.[56] Republicans' renewed faith in universal suffrage went hand in hand with their faith that they could and would be able to claim control of the state, establish a compulsory and public system of secular education, and remake the people in their own image.

* * *

In 1869, a young lawyer name Léon Gambetta was invited by local republicans to stand for election in Marseilles and a working-class district of Paris known for its political radicalism, Belleville. It was in the latter that Gambetta gave the speech that would raise him to national prominence, denouncing the regime and fully embracing the Belleville republicans' demands for the most "radical application of universal suffrage." "As with you," he told the working-class electors, "I think that there is no other sovereign but the people, and that universal suffrage, the instrument of this sovereignty, has no value and basis and carries no obligation, unless it be radically free." The first goal of radical republicans, then, "must therefore be to free universal suffrage from every tutelage, every shackle, every pressure, every corruption." "Universal suffrage," he concluded, "once made the master, would suffice to sweep away all the things which your program demands, and to establish all the freedoms, all the institutions which we are seeking to bring about." It alone could "complete the French Revolution and found for all time real order, absolute justice, full liberty, and genuine equality," realizing the social reforms that the Belleville committee desired and that radicals such as Gambetta were assimilating to their own program. A republic supported by universal suffrage promised "the moral and material emancipation of the greatest number, and best ensures social equality in laws, actions, and customs."[57]

He quickly shot to prominence as an uncompromising member of a new generation of republicans, winning both districts and coming in ahead of Adolphe Thiers in Marseilles. In a politically astute move,

---

[56] Edouard Laboulaye, *Le parti liberal, son programme et son avenir* (Paris: Charpentier, 1863), xiii, 145, 150.

[57] A. Tourneur, *Pages d'histoire. Gambetta en 1869. Belleville et Marseille. Lettres et documents inédits* (Lille: A. Devos, 1904), 41, 88, 94.

however, he chose to sit for Marseilles, where he would be less subject to the extreme demands of the Belleville workers.[58]

FOUNDING A NEW REPUBLIC

With Bonaparte's surrender, the imperial edifice quickly collapsed, giving republicans an opportunity they could not pass up. With a crowd bursting into meetings of the Legislative Corps, republican deputies convinced their colleagues that the empire was lost, proceeded to Paris's Hotel de Ville, declared the republic, and organized a Government of National Defense. In its popular acclamation by a Parisian crowd, it was very much in line with the revolutionary tradition. Still, Gambetta was careful to provide a veneer of legality to the actions, pleading with the amassing crowd not to hint at violence or disorder: "Paris, at the moment, holds in its hands not only the salvation of the country, but the salvation of the French Revolution," he told them. "I will rejoin my colleagues and I swear that the night will not pass, or mid-day tomorrow, without us having undertaken energetic measures, worthy of the people. But we must not appear to be deliberating under pressure from outside!"[59] The decision to establish a republic, he insisted, had to look as though it were the product of the independent judgment of the Legislative Corps. Gambetta was quickly named minister of the interior.

After initially calling for national elections in October 1870, a divided provisional government decided to postpone these, leaving the government without much popular support outside of Paris – where it was increasingly pressed by socialists and organized working-class constituents – and the cities of Lyons, Marseilles, and Nimes. A delegation headed by Adolphe Crémieux, an aging republican who had long defended liberal ideals, was sent from Paris to Tours to organize the government in the provinces. It was soon decided that more energetic leadership was required. After most candidates had refused, Gambetta agreed to go to Tours and take over. On October 7, 1870, Gambetta escaped a now-surrounded Paris by hot air balloon.

From Tours, Gambetta would direct the war effort with near-dictatorial authority, insisting on "war to the utmost" even after most of the political elite of the country had decided that surrender was the best

---

[58] Kayser, *Les grandes batailles du radicalism*, 38, 43.
[59] Joseph Reinach, *Discours et plaidoyers politiques de M. Gambetta*, vol. 1, part 1 (Paris: G. Charpentier, 1880), 396.

option. When a French army of 133,000 men surrendered at Metz, Gambetta denounced what he called "treason by officer": the officers had delivered the soldiers to the Prussian army and then been left to return home unguarded, while the commanding French general met secretly with the local paymaster to collect his salaries as a senator and marshal of France and under cover of darkness slipped behind Prussian lines. The willingness of the top echelons of the French army to surrender to invading armies rather than sustain a republic that they hated would be a recurring worry for republican statesmen in the Third Republic. The immediate problem, however, was that almost the entire pre-war French army had been captured and many of its officers bitterly resented Gambetta for his criticism and for continuing a fight they believed to be lost.[60]

Gambetta had seized the opportunity of the war to advance a position he had maintained for a while, that republicans should "spread our principles, our doctrines, your aspirations, among the populations of the countryside." Acting with untrammeled authority, he reinstituted elections to municipal and departmental councils: the appointed councils, he argued, had been "the worst assemblies of the Empire, the home of all bonapartist conspiracy," and their reorganization and recomposition with republicans was necessary to give satisfaction "both to the rights of universal suffrage and to republican opinion."[61] He also replaced nearly the entire prefectorial personnel in the departments, naming 136 prefects and subprefects, the vast majority of whom were known republicans. And he requested the newly installed republican prefects to prepare lists of functionaries and teachers who were "gravely compromised in the fallen regime," giving them full authority to replace them with loyal republicans. In November, as the army was surrendering at Metz, Gambetta announced the establishment of the Bulletin of the French Republic, which was to aid in the instruction of the people in republican principles: every Sunday, and additional days if possible, the instructor of each commune was tasked with discussing the contents of the bulletin with the assembled residents, focusing "particularly on raising awareness of articles on doctrine or history, which have as their object the

---

[60] Geoffrey Wawro, *The Franco-Prussian War: The German Conquest of France in 1870–1871* (Cambridge: Cambridge University Press, 2003), 251; Jacques Chastenet, *Gambetta* (Paris: Fayard, 1968), 147, 155; Wolfgang Schivelbusch, *The Culture of Defeat: On National Trauma, Mourning, and Recovery* (New York: Picador, 2003), 9.

[61] Jean Marie Mayeur, *Léon Gambetta: La Patrie et La République* (Paris: Fayard, 2008), 83.

enlightenment of the spirit of the people, to teach them in their political and social rights as well as the corollary duties, and to demonstrate that essential truth that the Republic alone can assure by its institutions the liberty, greatness, and future of France."[62]

The government in Tours would also issue what would become known as the Crémieux Decree, declaring the indigenous Jewish population of French-occupied Algeria to be French citizens with equal civil and political rights.[63] This would become one of its most controversial acts, and the source of anti-Semitic organizing among settlers and mainland French for generations.[64] Other decrees confirmed the French nationality but non-citizenship status of Muslims, rolled back the *bureaux arabes* – military offices hated by the settlers for their supposed sympathy toward the Muslim population (by, for instance, representing Muslims in disputes with settlers) – and repealed recent changes providing a measure of indigenous voting and representation in municipal and departmental councils.[65] The republican government largely sided with the settlers, rejected even a limited representation of the indigenous Muslims as "a political threat to colonization and its political economy,"[66] and enfranchised 35,000 new indigenous citizens expected to defend the republic.[67]

Gambetta's actions under the Government of National Defense helped create a national political infrastructure for republican organizing, but

[62] Ibid., 106–7, 110–11.

[63] An imperial decree had accorded indigenous Algerians – Jews and Muslims – French nationality but severed this from citizenship. Laure Blévis, "En marge du décret Crémieux: Les Juifs naturalisés français en Algérie (1865–1919)," *Les Belles lettres* 45, no. 2 (2012): 47–67; Z. Szajkowski, "Socialists and Radicals in the Development of Antisemitism in Algeria (1884–1900)," *Jewish Social Studies* 10, no. 3 (1948): 257–80; Azzedine Haddour, *Colonial Myths: History and Narrative* (Manchester: Manchester University Press, 2000), 5; Sophie B. Roberts, *Citizenship and Antisemitism in French Colonial Algeria, 1870–1962* (Cambridge: Cambridge University Press, 2017).

[64] When the subsequent Thiers ministry considered abrogating the decree, Crémieux denounced its opponents as "hateful and retrograde in spirit, who do not want to understand that there will be from now on, in Algeria, forming part of the French nation, French Jews, as there are French Protestants, and French Catholics." Adolphe Crémieux, *À l'Assemblée nationale* (Paris: Imprimeri de Schiller, 1871), 4.

[65] In 1870, departmental councils had been reorganized so that they would be composed of elected representatives of Jews, Muslims, non-French settlers, and French citizen settlers, with steep voting qualifications for the first three groups. The new republican government claimed this violated French legal principles by conferring the right to vote to noncitizens. Gouvernement Général de l'Algérie, *Bulletin officiel du gouvernement général de l'Algérie* (Alger: A. Bouyer, 1871), 156–86; Robert Estoublon, *Jurisprudence algérienne de 1830 à 1876* (Alger: Adolphe Jourdan, 1891), 125–26.

[66] Haddour, *Colonial Myths*, 5.

[67] Roberts, *Citizenship and Antisemitism in French Colonial Algeria*, 20.

they also gave credence to the denunciations of him as an unreconstructed Jacobin. His efforts to displace local authority, to continue the war at all costs, and to use the opportunity of a wartime emergency to instill republican principles were the sort of radicalism that made the republic anathema to many liberals and monarchists.[68] In January 1871, after a failed attempt to break the German siege and a subsequent insurrection by the far left, the government in Paris decided to agree to an armistice.

After months of delay, they now turned to the task of organizing elections to a National Assembly charged with creating a government that could negotiate a peace treaty. Royalists won approximately two-thirds of the seats. The results were an absolute repudiation of Gambetta's wartime policies and "of all that he had stood for," and led republicans to worry that the assembly would now take on the role of a constituent body and draft a new constitution. The former Orléanist and conservative minister Adolphe Thiers was elected in eighty-six departments, and was quickly installed as the "head of the executive power of the Republic," although only after royalists made clear they would accept the hated term "republic" as a temporary measure. The former prime minister of the July Monarchy, architect of the mass disenfranchisement of the French working classes, and leader of the monarchist forces in the imperial Legislative Corps would govern the country for the next two years.[69]

The peace treaty had allowed the National Guard in Paris to retain its weapons to provide order in the city. The guard, however, was itself increasingly radicalized and in March 1871, it rejected the authority of the arrondissement mayors and organized elections to the Commune. After it had embarked on an extensive program of social reforms, Thiers sent in the army, massacring somewhere between six thousand and ten thousand persons in the course of a week.

For radical republicans such as Gambetta and Georges Clemenceau – recently returned from chronicling Reconstruction in the United States – the commune nearly extinguished their flickering hopes for a republic.[70] Gambetta's friend and adviser Eugène Spuller summed up what many of them feared, that the republic had "perhaps received her death blow and

---

[68] Chastenet, *Gambetta*, 178; J. P. T. Bury, *Gambetta and the National Defence: A Republican Dictatorship in France* (Westport, CT: Greenwood Press, 1971), passim.

[69] Chastenet, *Gambetta*, 179; Bury, *Gambetta and the Making of the Third Republic*, 9.

[70] Georges Lecomte, *Georges Clemenceau: The Tiger of France*, trans. Donald Clive Stuart (New York: D. Appleton and Co., 1919), 27.

we shall have to spend our lives bringing up a new generation capable of founding it after having for a moment hoped to found it ourselves."[71]

The "Republican O'Connell"

In taking office, Thiers warned the different parties not to presume that they uniquely represented the will of the people. "You are divided," he told the deputies, "and do you know why? Because the country is." But Thiers gave a special warning to the republicans. There were some, he noted, who believed that as long as the republic existed in constitutional form, it remained the republic, regardless of which party was in power. But there were also those who would "not admit the existence of the Republic except when it is in their hands." He reminded them all that the republic existed, that a peace would be negotiated and the foundations of a new government established under its authority. "Now don't come to us and say, 'don't sacrifice the Republic!'" "Do not lose it yourselves! The Republic is in your hands, and will be the prize of your wisdom and nothing else." If radical republicans raised "inopportune questions" or appeared to be the accomplices of "men of disorder," they would provoke a reaction that would consolidate elite opinion behind the royalist option. "In accepting the appearance of complicity ... you will hit the Republic with the most violent blow that she could receive." Thiers was announcing the cost of conservative and liberal support for the republic, the repudiation of the revolutionary tradition, of class conflict, and of questioning the distribution of property.[72]

Thiers's advice resonated with many republicans. Radicals, organized in a parliamentary group called the Union Républicaine, continued to offer a moderate and often explicitly conservative tone in their public addresses. They reasserted their commitment to universal suffrage but framed it as fundamentally conservative and argued that it and the republic were the established institutions of the country. Were the assembly to constrict the right to vote or try and establish a monarchy, it would be overturning the existing order and provoking instability.

The Union Républicaine now turned to the task of disseminating republican ideology to the countryside. On June 26, 1871, after a months-long absence from the political scene, Gambetta announced his return

---

[71] Bury, *Gambetta and the Making of the Third Republic*, 21.
[72] *Annales de l'Assemblee Nationale* 1 (March 10, 1871): 286–87; Bury, *Gambetta and the Making of the Third Republic*, 20.

with a rousing speech in Bordeaux. He referenced Thiers's speech, in which the President had said the future would go to the wisest, to the most worthy. "Perfect!" Gambetta declared. "It is a bet that we must accept." He urged republicans to prove their worth by producing "republican solutions" to every question that arose, focusing always on discrete policy questions rather than broad social critiques. The aim was to show the electors of France that "we are a party of government capable of directing the country's affairs, the party of intelligence and reason, and that it is among men adhering to our principles that we will truly find the guarantees of science, of disinterestedness, and of order." He underscored the radical republicans' break with the revolutionary republican tradition, announcing that the "heroic, chivalric" age of the republicans had passed. The French Revolution must be completed, but he took pains to stress that by "revolution" he meant only "the diffusion of the principles of justice and reason by which it was inspired and I entirely reject its identification by our enemies with violent enterprises." Now that the republic had been established, the responsibility of the opposition was to "press and regulate, it must not destroy." This was an explicit effort to instruct republicans, and especially the self-styled radicals, in the form of opposition that could secure republican cooperation. "Thanks to the union of the diverse nuances of republican opinion, we can give to France the sight of a disciplined party, firm in its principles, hard-working, vigilant, and absolutely resolute to convince France of its ability to ability to govern." "We will now," he remarked a few months later, "found a moderate and rational Republic which will save France."[73]

Spuller had advised Gambetta to be "a Republican O'Connell, touring the countryside, travelling from town to town, constantly orating, making the public aware of him, aware of a Republican programme and of a Republican party as an active progressive force, rallying the scattered troops of Republicanism throughout France."[74] He would spend the next several years doing exactly this, repeating in town after town the narrative that radical republicans had fashioned during the 1860s. He was, in the contemptuous words of one opponent, a "traveler and salesman for the democracy." Given that his appeals were directed in large part to the shopkeepers, instructors, and the petit bourgeoisie of the countryside, it

---

[73] Reinach, *Discours et plaidoyers politiques de M. Gambetta*, vol. 2, pt. 2, 19, 21, 261; Bury, *Gambetta and the Making of the Third Republic*, 28.
[74] Bury, *Gambetta and the Making of the Third Republic*, 65.

was a label he wore with pride, repeating it at meetings to thunderous applause.[75]

By the summer of 1871, republican societies were being organized throughout the country. These societies constituted a network of local activists who were being educated in the republican message and who could help disseminate its principles more broadly: as one historian has remarked, the "importance of these Republican committees in the provinces can hardly be overestimated."[76] There was a steady insistence on organizing as broad a coalition as possible. For Gambetta, this included some who had formerly supported the empire or royalists. The "proven leaders of monarchist intrigues and plots, all those who were the servants of the pretenders, who were the agents of anti-patriotic disorder," needed to be excluded. But it was important to "distinguish between the leaders and those who followed them, because these might be of good faith, they might just be lost! ... You see, sirs, that my idea is this: separate the leaders from their supposed army; the army can enter into the ranks of the democratic party."[77]

In a speech meant to appeal to his radical base, Gambetta asked the large bourgeoisie – whose interests had been central to French national policy since 1830 – whether they had truly "reflected on what is happening." Had this class, who generally supported liberal royalists as the surest safeguard of property, not seen the rise of a new generation?

Have we not seen appear, all across the country, – and I want very much to highlight this new generation of the democracy, – a new political candidate, a new personnel of universal suffrage? Have we not seen the workers of the cities and the countryside, the working world to which the future belongs, make its entrance into political affairs? Is this not the characteristic warning that the country, – after having tried so many forms of government, – wants finally to turn to another social stratum [couche sociale] to experiment with the republican form?

The line met with prolonged applause. "Yes!" he continued, "I suspect, I feel, I announce the arrival and the presence, in politics, of a new social stratum that has been busy for almost nineteen months, and which is certainly far from being the inferior of its predecessors." In the assembly, Gambetta explained that these social strata had been "created by the

---

[75] Reinach, *Discours et plaidoyers politiques de M. Gambetta*, vol. 2, pt. 2, 261; Lehning, *To Be a Citizen*, 26.

[76] Ibid., 51.

[77] Mayeur, *Léon Gambetta*, 153; Gambetta, *Voyage et discours de M. Gambetta dans la Savoie et le Dauphiné*, 54.

French Revolution, favored in their development by the application of the ideas, the theories, and the laws of the French Revolution," and that they had become conscious of their existence thanks to the universal suffrage secured by the Second Republic. To this new social strata, the inheritors of the French Revolution, belonged the future of the republic. This would subsequently be "quoted in innumerable speeches and books" throughout the remainder of the Third Republic, and the radicals would repeat it ceaselessly during campaigns across the country in the 1870s. Gambetta was deliberately identifying the republican "people" with the country's broadening middle class.[78]

Conservatives – monarchist and republican – were incensed at what seemed to be an invitation to class divisions. One liberal rejected Gambetta's distinction of "two Frances," insisting that "we are all French and equal; there are whigs and torys [sic], but there are not two Frances."[79] Thiers castigated Gambetta for "provoking class war." But the statement was a continuation of the vision of the people that radical republicans had been advancing for years. They had talked incessantly of "the people, petits bourgeois, workers and peasants," who every day had "a clearer perception of the connection between their affairs and politics," who wished "to have their own representatives."[80] Led by the *Ligue de L'enseignement*, radicals had been insisting that education alone, "obligatory, free, and ... *absolutely secular*," could "unite the classes, because despite the law there are still classes, no matter what anyone says."[81] Jules Simon, in *La Politique radicale*, had noted that "when we speak of the re-establishment of classes, you are indignant. You should be. When we speak of the rich and the poor, and we say that there are rights for the rich that do not exist for the poor, you are indignant. Again, you should be."[82] The radical program promised to "equalize the classes, to dissipate the so-called antagonism between the cities and the countryside," not through the redistribution of property but through education, and "by the diffusion of science for all, return to the country its moral and political vigor."[83]

---

[78] Bury, *Gambetta and the Making of the Third Republic*, 114; Joseph Reinach, *Discours et plaidoyers politiques de M. Gambetta*, vol. 3, pt. 2 (Paris: G. Charpentier, 1880), 101; Joseph Reinach, *Discours et plaidoyers politiques de M. Gambetta*, vol. 4, pt. 3 (Paris: G. Charpentier, 1880), 42; *Annales de l'Assemblée Nationale* 19 (July 12, 1873): 141–44.

[79] *Annales de l'Assemblée Nationale* 19 (July 12, 1873): 141–44.

[80] Bury, *Gambetta and the Making of the Third Republic*, 48, 117.

[81] Reinach, *Discours et plaidoyers politiques de M. Gambetta*, vol. 2, pt. 2, 174.

[82] Jules Simon, *La politique radicale* (Paris: A. Lacroix, 1868), 246.

[83] Reinach, *Discours et plaidoyers politiques de M. Gambetta*, vol. 2, pt. 2, 39.

This vision of the people was now informed by the experience of organizing, of corresponding with republicans across the country, and of seeing their reaction to public speeches. Activists in the Union Républicaine were now convinced that the people were for the republic and could now point to new victories to prove it. In a series of special elections in July 1871, the radicals had picked up an addition thirty-five seats, with thirty-eight going to moderate republicans. Only twelve monarchists had been elected.

Back in February 1871, it had been sufficient for royalists to build a local "coalition among the notables." By July, the cost of election campaigns had increased thirty-fold, requiring the renting of public halls, the publication of pamphlets, posters, and ballots, the payment of electoral agents, and the provision of meals and drinks for the electors. Electioneering was proceeding "at an intensity never previously experienced," engaging a far-flung network of activists relying on mass appeals. The republicans were far more adept at this new style. Between July 1871 and September 1874, the combined republican vote in by-elections was 5.7 million, against 2.5 million for the monarchists and 700,000 for the Bonapartists. Royalists were increasingly worried that their chance to found a monarchy was going to be lost.[84]

REACTION AND THE PROMISE OF DISENFRANCHISEMENT

Even before the convening of the National Assembly, conservatives, liberals, and monarchists had begun debating various schemes to restrict "universal suffrage." H. Druon, for instance, asked whether a taxpaying qualification might be desirable: "Sure, a taxpaying electoral corps displeases us as much as anyone. But come on, to ask that every citizen, to be admitted to the right to vote, pay a direct contribution, no matter how small, would this be too rigorous?"[85] "The religion of universal suffrage," wrote another, "still has its devotees who profit from it, but I no longer see any believers who defend it.... In the same way that certain republicans, run out of arguments, invented the republic above universal suffrage, the theorists of universal suffrage avoid the embarrassment of defending it by

---

[84] Robert R. Locke, *French Legitimists and the Politics of Moral Order* (Princeton, NJ: Princeton University Press, 1974), 224; Henri Salles, *L'avènement de la république affrmé par des chiffres, ou L'assemblée nationale de février 1871 devant le suffrage universel: mouvement des esprits en France depuis 1870* (Paris: Le Chevalier, 1874).

[85] H. Druon, *Le Suffrage Universel et La Loi électoral* (Paris: Charles Duoniol et Cie, 1871), 8.

denying anyone the liberty of attacking it."[86] The Bourbon pretender declared that France must have "a universal suffrage honestly practiced," which meant a restricted franchise with multiple stages of indirect elections or with more votes for wealth and heads of families.[87] The Orléanists, lacking the Bourbons' faith in the religiosity of the peasantry, were especially adamant that "universal suffrage" needed to be curtailed. "The electoral law," wrote the Catholic journalist Henri Lasserre, "is the entire Constitution."[88]

After the defeats to republicans in the special elections, royalists and liberals modified the recruitment law to disenfranchise soldiers on active duty, who had been reenfranchised by the return to the pre-1850 voting qualifications. Because vote-splitting among the royalists had helped republicans and Bonapartists, they also changed the electoral law to require a majority rather than a plurality of votes, which conservatives and liberals insisted was necessary: in order that "universal suffrage is not the victim of a surprise.... we must organize a sort of right of appeal against the first ballot."[89]

But true to historical form, it was the election of a radical deputy from Paris that would provoke a more substantial effort at disenfranchisement. Adolphe Thiers had decided that the only unelected member of his government, Charles de Rémusat, a close confidant and former minister in the July Monarchy, should be elected in a Parisian district, believing that the control the army and police had asserted over the city since the commune assured his election. The Union Républicaine was committed to opposing all nonrepublican candidates, but Gambetta wavered, worried about incurring Thiers's wrath. The local republican committees, however, were decided: they nominated Désiré Barodet, a former mayor of Lyons who had been deposed by the national government for replacing church schools with secular ones.

When a close friend of Gambetta's insisted at a dinner party that the republican leader would never back Barodet, a "young man raised his head and quietly asserted that Gambetta would change his mind. He held to this opinion despite our protests ... and told us that the man whom

---

[86] Antonin Rondelet, *Les limites du suffrage universel* (Paris: H. Plon, 1871), 7–8.

[87] Huard, *Le suffrage universel en France*, 108.

[88] Henri Lasserre, *De la réforme et de l'organisation normale du suffrage universel* (Paris: V. Palmé, 1873), 1.

[89] Cole and Campbell, *French Electoral Systems and Elections since 1789*, 49; J. B. Duvergier, *Collection complète des lois, décrets, ordonnances, réglements, et avis du Conseil d'Etat* (Paris: A. Guyot et Scribe, 1873), 31.

Paris would elect would be M. Barodet." The young man in question was Edouard Portalis, the editor of a radical newspaper and recently returned from the United States, where he had cheered the election of Ulysses S. Grant as the repudiation of an aristocracy of race.[90] Gambetta and other republicans were coming under intense pressure from "obscure clubs and committees ... from freemasons and pressure from all those among whom 'the old leaven of the Commune' was said to be working." Much as Portalis had predicted, Gambetta came out in support of Barodet.[91]

The Paris radicals campaigned on a three-part program, calling for the absolute integrity of universal suffrage, the immediate dissolution of the Versailles Assembly, and the election of a new assembly with full authority to draft a new constitution.[92] But it was "universal suffrage" that "most viscerally gripped Radical opinion" and became the central issue on which the election was fought. "The vote to which Parisians are called must have a decisive meaning and influence," declared Portalis, "their vote must save the Republic and universal suffrage from the perils that threaten them."[93]

Rémusat, who had voted in favor of the disenfranchisement of 1850, was now forced to announce his support for universal suffrage, recognizing that failure to do so would cost him the election. This, however, estranged monarchists and split a possible conservative coalition. "M. Barodet," remarked *The Economist*, "can count on the votes of three-fourths of the [Republican] party. An alliance between the moderate Republicans and the Conservatives might have returned Count de Rémusat, but he has estranged many of these latter by his address, in which he promises to maintain the Republic and to preserve universal suffrage intact."[94]

---

[90] Édouard Portalis, *Les États-Unis, le self-government et le césarisme* (Paris: Le Chevalier, 1869).

[91] Bury, *Gambetta and the Making of the Third Republic*, 140–41; Jean-Claude Wartelle, "L'élection Barodet (Avril 1873)," *Revue d'histoire moderne et contemporaine* 27 no. 4 (1980): 601–30, 606–7.

[92] Republicans claimed that the elections of February 1871 had been to establish a government that could negotiate a peace treaty.

[93] Wartelle, "L'élection Barodet (Avril 1873)," 605, 613; Édouard Portalis, "Une Protestation," *Le Corsaire*, April 6, 1873; Bury, *Gambetta and the Making of the Third Republic*, 144.

[94] "Foreign Correspondence," *The Economist*, Saturday April 19, 1873; Wartelle, "L'élection Barodet (Avril 1873)," 601.

Barodet defeated the chosen candidate of the president on the first ballot, 52 to 39 percent, throwing upper-class Parisians, conservatives across the country, and the deputies sitting in Versailles into a "veritable stupor," terrified that they were watching "the resurrection of the Commune." The prefect of police was appalled that Paris could have elected "a man who represented the defeated doctrines of the month of May 1871." Even more worrying was that Rémusat had been supported by many prominent liberals and moderate republicans, including Emile Littré. The liberal *Revue des Deux Mondes* noted that "for some time, the radicals are accustomed to strange victories. Radicalism wants to show its force." To preempt this and maintain a "genuinely, essentially conservative" government, a new electoral law would have to be prepared.[95]

The Government of Moral Order

Less than a month after Barodet's election, Jules Dufaure, a close associate of Thiers, introduced a measure to restrict the franchise by requiring two years' residence and increasing the list of crimes that would result in the loss of political rights. This was not enough to placate conservative worries. With a peace treaty signed and German troops withdrawn from the country, royalists no longer needed Thiers. Supported by terrified liberals, they rushed through a nonconfidence motion in the president's cabinet in May 1873, claiming that it could no longer fight the advance of radicalism. The Légitimist general Patrice Mac-Mahon was named president with only one vote against (and most republicans abstaining) and the Orléanist Albert de Broglie was named prime minister in a Government of Moral Order, committed to suppressing radicalism and restoring the monarchy.[96]

In 1871, one conservative had asked skeptically whether "twenty-years of practice with universal suffrage" had done anything to raise the country's "moral and political level." In the aftermath of the commune, the "great argument of the educative virtue of universal suffrage resembles a bloody irony."[97] Hostility toward universal suffrage characterized

[95] Kayser, *Les grandes batailles du radicalisme*, 72; Wartelle, "L'élection Barodet (Avril 1873)," 602; Rosanvallon, *Le sacre du citoyen*, 316; Charles De Mazade, "Chronique de la quinzaine," *Revue des deux mondes* 105 (Mai–Juin 1873): 950–66, 962.

[96] Rosanvallon, *Le sacre du citoyen*, 316.

[97] Paul L. I. Devaux, *Du suffrage universel et de l'abaissement du cens electoral* (Bruxelles: Librairie de l'Offce de Publicité, 1871), 21.

a large portion of the writing produced during a remarkable period of public debate. Hundreds of pamphlets, books, and newspaper articles advocated a dizzying array of schemes by which the suffrage could be decreased or reorganized to purge or discipline the electorate. Most authors proposed diminishing the influence of "numbers," either by reducing the electorate through restrictive qualifications, mediating a broad suffrage through indirect elections, or giving certain classes of voters additional ballots or greater weight through separate representation. As Louis Blanc noted, ever since the republicans had begun making inroads in the countryside – since the "villages voted like the cities" – the right had "thought of nothing else but to construct barriers between itself and this great sea that rises: universal suffrage." To this, one conservative deputy shouted out his response: "Yes, the Red Sea."[98]

The new conservative government had quickly moved to sack republican officials and teachers, suspend newspapers, and further restrict meetings and civic funerals, which republicans used as occasions to demonstrate a commitment to secularism. They were setting the stage for a monarchical restoration: in August, the Orléanist and Bourbon pretenders publicly reconciled and confirmed an arrangement in which the latter would come to power while the former would accede to the throne upon his death. The Ultras among the Bourbon Légitimists suggested that the restoration of the Bourbons to the throne would "end the perversion of 1789," including parliamentary government and even aspects of the country's property settlement (as Gambetta noted, "we are not yet under the fleur-de-lis, [and] a proposal has been introduced in the Assembly to reestablish primogeniture").[99] A jarring note came when a commission to the Count of Chambord was struck by his stubbornness: he refused to become the "legitimate king of the Revolution," but would stick to the white flag and would refuse to be bound by constitutional guarantees of a parliamentary regime. While monarchists fretted, it was only once the count published his position in a conservative newspaper that their hopes were dashed. All they could do was establish a conservative frame of government that would not preclude a later restoration.[100]

---

[98] Vivien Schmidt, *Democratizing France: The Political and Administrative History of Decentralization* (Cambridge: Cambridge University Press, 1990), 53.

[99] Kevin Passmore, *The Right in France from the Third Republic to Vichy* (Oxford, UK: Oxford University Press, 2013), 19; Reinach, *Discours et plaidoyers politiques de M. Gambetta*, vol. 2, pt. 2, 28–29.

[100] Robert Gildea, *Children of the Revolution: The French, 1799–1914* (Cambridge, MA: Harvard University Press, 2008), 248–50.

In November 1873, they voted that Mac-Mahon's term would be seven years, time enough to organize a conservative government and hold out the possibility of a restoration. But in the meantime, they would have to fortify and protect the government with conservative institutions. In December 1873, the National Assembly appointed a Commission of Thirty to draft the electoral laws. The commission was dominated by royalists, and its chair – Anselm Batbie – was explicit that the commission's goal was to coordinate an effective reaction "against the law of numbers" and universal suffrage.[101] Most conservatives agreed that a quarter-century of universal suffrage in France had been "an index of the most humiliating degradation."[102] Similar conclusions would be reached by most of those who testified before the commission or intervened in its debates. "If the France of the July Monarchy," argued one author "could embrace a perspective over the entire period that has gone by from '48 to our day, turned to look at universal suffrage," she would be appalled. "Universal suffrage," the author continued, "by direct and list ballot, is in itself irrational and absurd," it had never been respected in practice, because even its most "ardent promoters" recognized that it was a danger unless carefully manipulated. "The establishment of authoritarian socialism," he warned, "will depend on it."[103]

Another conceded that tax qualifications might "no longer have the flavor of the day," but insisted that the commission "conquer this repugnance and pronounce resolutely" in favor of a strict qualification. He suggested a draft franchise law, which he hoped might square the aversion to a tax qualification with the need to purge the electorate: the first article read, "Universal suffrage is maintained. But whoever does not pay taxes is not an elector."[104] Fernand Nicolaÿ had some advice for worried conservatives who were being told that "universal suffrage" was demanded by the people: "Stop listening." He called for plural votes in order to introduce a higher level of morality into the electorate by overrepresenting "intelligence," the family, and property.[105]

---

[101] Rosanvallon, *Le sacre du citoyen*, 316.

[102] Paul Lapeyre, *L'Esprit du suffrage universel* (Paris: V. Palmé, 1872), 3, 6.

[103] Félix Battanchon, *Le nombre et la raison, ou Revision du suffrage universel* (Bergerac: Faisandier, 1873), 3, 8.

[104] E. Dolbeau, *Le suffrage universel rationel et sans danger* (Le Mans: Imprimerie de La Chronique de l'Ouest, 1874), 4–5.

[105] Fernand Nicolaÿ, *Moralisation du suffrage universel par la représentation de l'intelligence, de la famille et de la propriété au moyen de la pluralité des votes* (Paris: Charles Noblet, 1875), 4.

Some Légitimists supported universal suffrage, believing that their constituents were devoted to the old Bourbon king: the popular memory of the revolution in many departments was of the church lands and the commons being confiscated by a small number of merchants, privatizing public resources and creating a source of wealth for the growth of the country's bourgeoisie but establishing a broad base of local resentment around which a popular Bourbonism could be organized. Even those Légitimists who supported universal suffrage, however, generally insisted that its practice and organization had to be reformed, as "the equality of intelligences is as impossible as the equality of wealth." The Count of Chambord's statement that "universal suffrage" should be maintained but "honestly practiced" was endlessly repeated in Légitimist writings and speeches. In order for universal suffrage to be a blessing, "it must be organized in such a manner that the most intelligent men enlighten those who are the least, and these, when it comes time to take a decision outside of their competence, listen to the councils of their fellow citizens."[106] A self-described "Picardy Peasant" suggested universal suffrage be reorganized so that it was based on the old feudal-era corporations, with "all the French artists electing artists, all the tailors electing tailors, all the men of letters electing men of letters," and so on.[107] Ferdinand Jacob referred back to the 1789 declaration of the rights of man and its preamble that "sovereignty resides in the nation," and noted that this was far preferable to subsequent declarations that "sovereignty resides in the universality of French citizens." The "nation" included women and children who spoke the same language, and had the patriarch-dominated family as its basis; citizenship, by contrast, encompassed adult men alone and considered them as individuals rather than part of an organic society. He proposed enfranchising the heads of all families, widows included.[108] Légitimists, with a very different conception of French nationality and its moral basis than that of republicans or liberal Orléanists, were the only group with substantial representation in the assembly whose members entertained the possibility of woman suffrage.

[106] R. De Roys, *Le suffrage universel* (Paris: E. de Beaufort, 1872), 1–2.
[107] Un paysan picard, *Le suffrage universel basé sur les corporations* (Paris: Coutant, 1875), 2.
[108] *Archives parlementaires* 68 (March 30, 1834): 193–94; Rosanvallon, *Le sacre du citoyen*, 318; Ferdinand Jacob, *Le Suffrage Universel établie Par Les Constituants de 1848 Est, 1. Un Mensonge; 2. Un Permanent Attentat Au Principe Fondamental Des Sociétés* (Antibes: J. Marchand, 1874), 3–4, 6–8, 13.

Some Bonapartists – who for decades had based their claim to govern on the voice of universal suffrage – now agreed that it posed a threat. Edouard Petit, a knight in the Legion of Honor, complained that under universal suffrage, "the man who has recourse to public assistance (often, alas, by his own fault), appears at the poll with those who contribute all their charges, even those which the miserable [welfare recipient] has imposed on them." This distasteful moment of social and political equality had been tolerable when it was controlled under the empire. "For twenty years, under the protection of a legendary name and the support of the countryside, France prospered. By our misfortunes, the charm is broken, and universal suffrage becomes every day more menacing."[109]

Most Bonapartists, however, seemed to hope that an appeal to the people would again place them in power. Louis-Napoleon had recently died, but his son had celebrated his eighteenth birthday celebration in England – Broglie had to ban French mayors and functionaries from attending – and called for an "appel au people," presumptuously declaring that "if the name of Napoleon emerges an eighth time from the popular vote, I am prepared to accept the responsibility imposed on me by the national will."[110] Royalists accused Bonapartists of striving to "excite once again the unintelligent masses to reconquer the lost ground and reconstitute the empire,"[111] while moderate republicans warned that "an appeal to the nation" would bring with it the possibility that "parliamentary government may disappear, and France along with it."[112] Bonapartist candidates now picked up additional seats in the ongoing special elections.

This was the context in which the Commission of Thirty was proceeding, a broadly shared worry that the "people" were too inclined toward radicalism or caesarism and a firm belief that some means of reducing and disciplining their influence was necessary. The commission debated restricting the suffrage to empower property holders, the rural countryside, and large Catholic families. Raising the minimum age to twenty-five had broad support, although some worried that it would not be enough: twenty-six-year-olds might be more mature, but they were just as often penurious extremists. An extension of the residence period was popular,

---

[109] Édouard Petit, *Quelques mots sur la pratique du suffrage universel* (Paris: Typographie Morris, 1873), 4–5, 8.
[110] Gildea, *Children of the Revolution*, 250.
[111] Jacob, *Le Suffrage Universel établie Par Les Constituants de 1848*, 3–4.
[112] *The Annual Register for 1875*, 153.

as was a distinction between those born in a commune and those born outside: for the former, six months' residence would suffice, while for the latter, three years would be required. This had the advantages of maintaining the franchise for small farmers, disenfranchising the urban proletariat, while securing the right to vote to those who knew their place within local patron-client relations. But the seasonal migration of many workers meant there was no sharp demarcation between the dangerous proletariat and the loyal peasantry, while a preference for those born in the commune would create the "absurdity" of enfranchising the returned vagabond at the expense of the newly installed merchant.[113] Other deputies hoped for a restoration of property-based tax qualifications, some form of education requirement, or multiple votes for those with diplomas, but were cautioned that restrictions based on property "did little to establish capacity" while education did little to establish judgment: if capacity "resides in good sense and reason, we see illiterate men who have more than baccalaureates. It would be dangerous to base it on diplomas; all the ambitious and the degenerate generally have these."[114]

Légitimists' faith in the Catholic peasantry and liberal Orléanists' faith in property and education meant that while both could agree on the necessity of exclusion, they could not agree on its terms: there was no unifying vision of who the "people" were and ought to be, what classes or groups represented its best nature – i.e., which would be most liable to support the policies desired by each faction or be most responsive to elite guidance – and how these could be defined institutionally.

Instead, the commission was becoming the site for competing visions with little common basis, and the Légitimists especially were constructing complicated designs by which their ideal of hierarchical but harmonious class relations could be achieved. The liberal *Revue de Deux Mondes*, which had strongly supported restricting the right to vote, had been totally unprepared for the spectacle of Légitimist deputies debating plural voting, family voting, corporate voting, or the creation of new staggered electoral colleges that reproduced the most baroque features of the ancien régime or the complexity of the late eighteenth-century revolutionary constitutions. The commission, it declared, was "obviously the victim of an illusion. It misunderstands: it was not created to deliver itself to the study of these fantasies," but to derive a practical and sensible plan for restricting the

---

[113] Huard, *Le suffrage universel en France*, 110.
[114] Meeting of the Commission, 4th sess., December 17, 1873, Archives Nationales, C*/II/611–613.

suffrage in such a way that would render it compatible with property and social order.[115] The Légitimist deputies were offering a coherent vision of the nation; but it had little appeal to other currents of conservative and liberal opinion, and they had done little of the outreach needed to build support for it. By indulging its members' utopian visions, the commission threatened to derail the broad support for disenfranchisement.

By 1874, a growing number of conservative republicans and liberals were coming out in favor of retaining the current system of manhood suffrage, a reflection of the extremism on display in the Batbie Commission and of the radicals' success in maintaining a tone of moderation and restraint.

The reinterpretation of the revolutionary tradition that radical republicans had developed, by contrast, now helped them dissuade their more extreme supporters against a *coup de force*, the massing of crowds in the street and the physical conquest of the central sites of national and local administration. The day after the Thiers government was deposed, radical newspapers emblazoned an appeal for calm on their front pages, with over fifteen hundred signatures, begging radical partisans to refrain from direct action. At the top of the list were the leaders of the union, with Gambetta and the aging socialist republican Louis Blanc foremost among them. A *coup de force*, they warned, would achieve nothing but the enmity of the liberals and conservative republicans who were more worried about the rise of the left than the strength of the right. As the government increased its harassment, surveillance, and imprisonment of republican and socialist activists, the *coup de force* became more appealing as possibly the only way to resist an intensifying reaction. But the radical leaders were generally able to quash suggestions of extralegal action, insisting that the proper response should be redoubled political efforts.[116]

Radicals continued to frame manhood suffrage as a conservative institution. In both the National Assembly and on the campaign trail, they argued that the exercise of manhood suffrage would not empower the "Red Sea" but the "new social strata," of small property-holding farmers, petit bourgeois, and skilled workers that were eager for social reforms or revisions of the tax code but were fundamentally committed to the rights of property.[117] "Universal suffrage," declared Gambetta, "has had as its

[115] Rosanvallon, *Le sacre du citoyen*, 322.
[116] Bury, *Gambetta and the Making of the Third Republic*, 154.
[117] *Annales de l'Assemblée Nationale* 1 (February 17, 1871): 64; Bury, *Gambetta and the Making of the Third Republic*, 136.

principal result the creation of a new social and political strata, since the goal of all electoral regimes is to create or defend classes, or to extend them, or to restrain them."

Every electoral system corresponds to a social system, and any time that an electoral regime operates for two, four, ten and fifteen years, it creates ... a new social and political class in its own image. ... This new social strata that we have seen everywhere for two years now, wise, moderate, patient, master of itself, capable of taking control of matters and directing them well, is repeating every day to those who represent the old political world: do you finally want to take your part of the indestructible and inevitable democratic state of France? Do you want to give us a share of the direction of the country? Do you want there to be no more hatred between classes? Then recognize the democracy! Recognize the democracy and a democracy with a form of government, a necessary form, essential, the Republic; recognize the Republic![118]

This "democracy" was a "new France" that had emerged due to new means of transportation, free exchange, and the "unfortunately too slow progress of public instruction." It had raised workers into property owners, and with each unit of "property that is created, it is a citizen that is formed. ... Property is, to our eyes, the superior sign and preparer of the moral and material emancipation of the individual." What the radical republicans were demanding was far from the abolition of property – which had its own base of support among the growing socialist movement[119] – but social and economic reforms that would facilitate its acquisition by republicanized citizens. The "democracy," the new republican people whom they claimed to recognize and represent, was to be found in this "world of small proprietors, small manufacturers, small shop-owners" who republicans said had been created, however gradually, by the revolution and manhood suffrage.[120]

The Dangerous Weapon

When Adolphe Thiers testified before the Commission of Thirty, his appearance caused a sensation. He announced that it would be wrong to proceed today as he had done in 1850, and conceded that he had made a catastrophic mistake by insisting on disenfranchisement back then. The Bonapartist coup "made clear to me that we had put a dangerous weapon in the hands of an adventurous man. This caused me considerable

---

[118] Reinach, *Discours et plaidoyers politiques de M. Gambetta*, vol. 4, pt. 3, 44–48.
[119] Robert Stuart, *Marxism at Work: Ideology, Class and French Socialism During the Third Republic* (Cambridge: Cambridge University Press, 1992).
[120] Ibid., 155.

reflection. There is always a danger of placing a weapon in the hands of those who can present themselves to the country announcing that they will re-establish universal suffrage." Thiers was still widely respected as a pragmatic statesman who would always protect the interests of property and social order, and his warning resonated with liberals and conservative republicans.[121] Hippolyte Taine, for instance, believed that fears of a popular reaction made "it very likely that universal suffrage will be maintained." "Liberal opinion, or at least, popular opinion, is for it; this is why many who do not like it very much will consent to keep it, so as to not remove the sympathies of the multitude from the new government." He hoped nonetheless that it would be "re-organized" to take account of the varying level of intelligence among "taxpayers."[122]

The claim that universal suffrage was too popular to be touched but nonetheless needed to be manipulated was repeated in an increasing number of tracts and forums. *Le Temps* noted the potential for revolution, arguing that "what has been conceded cannot be taken away or modified. Any restriction, any modification, would create a revolutionary risk." The general argument was that universal suffrage was an evil, but that its restriction would be dangerous. Conservatives took from this the implication that it should be "reorganized," by plural voting, voting in corporations, or various restrictions that could be defended as administrative in nature, such as requiring onerous voter identification procedures. "If we must respect universal suffrage in principle, it is at least permissible to organize it, to manage it."[123] "If universal suffrage could be suppressed," wrote Paul Ribot, "it would only be after plunging our country into an abyss of evil."[124] De Castellane reflected that "such is the power of this institution, that it requires a sort of courage to warn of its dangers. Like a colossus, the mere sight of which causes its adversaries to retreat, universal suffrage exercises an empire so considerable that many of those who present themselves before it as an enemy, prudently retire at

---

[121] M. Calmon, *Discours parlementaires de M. Thiers (1872–1877)*, vol. 15, pt. 4 (Paris: C. Lévy, 1879), 210–11; Louis Ulbach, *La France Parlementaire (1834–1851): Oeuvre Oratoires et écrits Politiques*, vol. 16 (Paris: Librairie Internationale, 1865), 204; Rosanvallon, *Le sacre du citoyen*, 330; Lasserre, *De la réforme et de l'organisation normale du suffrage universel*, 19, 60, 78.

[122] Hippolyte Taine, *Du suffrage universel et de la manière de voter* (Paris: Hachette et Cie, 1872), 8–9.

[123] Rosanvallon, *Le sacre du citoyen*, 330n3; Druon, *Le Suffrage Universel et La Loi électoral*, 6.

[124] Paul Ribot, *Du Suffrage universel et de la souveraineté du peuple* (Paris: Michel Lévy frères, 1874), 184.

the moment of the fight, and will even, out of fear of its resentment, let it be known to all that they are its allies and friends."[125] "What is the political party that would dare risk such unpopularity?" asked another. "We see that, despite the fears of some, universal suffrage imposes itself as a necessity and by that its future is assured."[126]

Conservatives on the commission worried that an open disenfranchisement would "raise a formidable resistance in the country. The institution of universal suffrage is a misfortune, no doubt, but it has existed for more than 20 years. It has set down deep roots in the country." The institution had "entered into our mores. The country holds to it. By mutilating it, we would raise passions and bring about cruel disappointments for us."[127] As one republican reflected years later, the conservatives "with their customary prudence," often refrained from openly stating their desires to abrogate universal suffrage, "but they cherished them at the bottom of their hearts."[128]

These anxieties were given concrete form in the mounting victories of the radicals in departments that had only recently elected royalists. The Société l'Union Républicaine inscribed "universal suffrage" at the top of their program, necessary to realize "the principles contained in the formula, Liberty, Equality, and Fraternity." The rapidly proliferating republican journals stated in their prospectuses that they were founded to "maintain the right of universal suffrage."[129] The new Bordeaux newspaper *Le Suffrage Universel*, for example, explained to its petit bourgeois and small farmer readership that its purpose was to defend "universal suffrage, the basis of our institutions and the only guarantee of our interests."[130]

Republican committees began requiring pledges from their candidates "of a more and more pressing character with reference to the suffrage."[131] An 1873 pamphlet, entitled "Le Suffrage Universel," was published and distributed by la Société d'instruction républicaine, with

[125] Castellane, *Essai sur l'organisation du suffrage universel en France*, 10–11.
[126] Lapeyre, *L'Esprit du suffrage universel*, 3–4.
[127] Meeting of the Commission of Thirty, 4th sess., December 17, 1873, Archives Nationale, C*/II/611-613; Rosanvallon, *Le sacre du citoyen*, 317.
[128] Gabriel Hanotaux, *Contemporary France*, vol. 1 (New York: Putnam's Sons, 1903), 37.
[129] La Société l'Union républicaine, *L'Union républicaine: programme* (Paris: Imprimerie de A. Chaix et Cie, n.d.); Auguste Vavasseur, *L'Union républicaine: société d'initiative* (Paris: Imprimerie de Dubuisson et Cie, 1871), 14.
[130] Georges Bouchon, *Histoire d'une imprimerie bordelaise, 1600–1900: les Imprimeries G. Gounouilhou, La Gironde, La Petite Gironde* (Bordeaux: G. Gounouilhou, 1901), 542.
[131] Hanotaux, *Contemporary France*, 620.

the goal of appealing to those constituencies that had returned a monarchial majority in 1871 and that the republicans were now seeking to organize. Universal suffrage was the "only legitimate authority" that could provide order in a time of turmoil. "The republic and universal suffrage are two words for the same proposition," they argued, for "hereditary monarchy excludes elections: republicanism demands them. Monarchy alienates the liberty of future generations and fatally condemns us to future revolutions; the Republic assures order through the constant exercise of national sovereignty."[132] And in all their campaigning, radicals insisted that any revision of universal suffrage would be an attack against popular sovereignty and the established institutions. "Let no one be fooled," wrote Gambetta's newspaper, La République française, "not since 31 May 1850 has a French assembly had to decide on a subject as grave or as dangerous."[133]

The Defense of Universal Suffrage

In March 1874, the Commission of Thirty released its report. The chair began by insisting that voting was not a right, but a public function. He regretted that France had "brusquely" jumped to universal suffrage during a revolution, and informed the deputies that the great majority of the commission believed that "it would be good to temper the power of numbers, until now without a counterweight, by adding the representation of interests." This was the clear desire of the commission. But Batbie was forced to concede that they had failed to agree on a comprehensive means by which they could accomplish this goal.[134]

He explained why the various proposals had been rejected. Multiple votes for fathers would probably not alter the proportions between different social classes, while multiple votes for those who paid a property tax would not be enough to "dominate universal suffrage." The same was true with the other proposals, including a personal taxpaying qualification, distinct representation of persons and property, or indirect elections. These reforms were also rejected because of "the fear of upsetting the most

[132] Edouard Millaud, Le Suffrage Universel (Paris: Société d'instruction républicaine, 1873), 30.
[133] La République française, June 3, 1874.
[134] Annexe no. 2320, Annales de l'Assemblée Nationale 30 (March 21, 1874): 202–17.

lively and suspicious feeling among us, equality."[135] "The right of suffrage is a function, it is not an absolute right," they would repeatedly claim, "but we cannot mutilate it, nor suppress it, but only regulate it."[136]

The defenders of the Batbie bill insisted in the report, the debates, and the provisions of the law that their project maintained universal suffrage.[137] The first article read, "Electors, for the nomination of deputies, are all French aged twenty-five years and enjoying their civil and political rights." With the exception of the increased age qualification, this was nearly identical to the constitution of 1848.[138]

It was only in the registration procedures that the task of disenfranchisement was to be accomplished. There would be different registration requirements for citizens born in or outside of the commune. All taxpayers were to be automatically registered, while those who did not pay a personal tax had to request registration. In small communes, a registration request needed to be supported by witnesses or written testimony confirming the voter's identity. In large cities, it needed to be supported by a registered lease, the declaration of a parent or senior relative living with the voter, the employers of live-in workers, or the testimony of three electors who were taxpayers themselves. New offenses were added to the list of crimes that would deprive a citizen of their political rights. Onerous residency requirements were imposed for officeholding, explicitly aimed at preventing the election of republican editors who were installing themselves in small towns or the countryside to disseminate republican ideology. The bill was well summarized by the moderate republican Achille Delorme: "Keep the label 'universal suffrage' while suppressing, by procedural means, two to three million voters."[139]

Opposing the bill in the assembly, radical republicans employed the rhetoric they had been using in campaigns across the country. The bill was

---

[135] Ibid.; Meeting of the Commission of Thirty, 7th sess., December 24, 1873, Archives Nationale, C*/II/611-613; Rosanvallon, *Le sacre du citoyen*, 324.

[136] *Annales de l'Assemblée Nationale* 31 (June 3, 1874): 271; *Annales de l'Assemblée Nationale* 31 (June 4, 1874): 289–90; *Annales de l'Assemblée Nationale* 32 (June 8, 1874): 43; *Annales de l'Assemblée Nationale* 32 (June 10, 1874): 97.

[137] *Annales de l'Assemblée Nationale* 31 (June 2, 1874): 258–59.

[138] One conservative believed manhood suffrage was "nothing else but the invasion of the barbarians into the political order," and that "many quietly desire [its suppression], without daring to admit as much in their speeches or to tempt it in their actions." Lasserre, *De la réforme et de l'organisation normale du suffrage universel*, 78, 19.

[139] *Annales de l'Assemblée Nationale* 31 (June 2, 1874): 258–59; Henri Rozy, *Le suffrage politique: observations sur le projet de loi électorale et le rapport de M. Batbie* (Paris: E. Thorin, 1874), 84; Rosanvallon, *Le sacre du citoyen*, 326.

a "mutilation" of universal suffrage, a "defiance against the entire country." Gambetta called it "an enterprise directed against universal suffrage," and highlighted how it would disenfranchise the "new social strata'.... There are four generations of Frenchmen that you will be removing from the circle of public life." They insisted on the conservative character of "universal suffrage," and recalled the dangers revealed in 1850. "We plead with you, as conservatives, to do nothing that could risk putting the people onto the revolutionary or plebiscitary path."[140] The aging Ledru-Rollin adhered to the radical script of a conservative suffrage, asking, "How in a country where there are as many property-owners as there are electors, can you worry that the Republic will not be conservative!"[141] "Must we remind you," asked socialist Louis Blanc, "of what came of the law of 31 May?"[142] Moderate republicans stressed that while the commission's ideas might be fascinating, they went against the grain of French political community as it had developed since the revolution. "Are they adapted to our mores?" asked Delorme, "are they adapted to our social system? Are they adapted to the country? It's that, it seems to me, which the authors of these projects have not sufficiently considered." Universal suffrage, republicans insisted with a united voice, was "the only peaceful and regular expression of the democracy and national sovereignty.... It is the great arbitrator and great pacifier."[143]

The disenfranchisement bill passed its second reading with 364 to 294 in favor. The extreme right and the center-right voted 315–3 in favor. But the different republican groups voted 240–4 against. Despite the hostility that many had expressed toward universal suffrage under the empire, and despite persistent misgivings about whether the electorate could be trusted, they were nearly unanimous. More important, the opposition included Thiers and Rémusat and a number of other liberals with varying commitments to either a conservative republic or a liberal monarchy: this bloc voted seventy-two to thirty-nine against the bill. Republicans had rallied around a male citizen suffrage and had managed to convince a majority of liberals to join them. But it was not enough, and they would need to flip at least thirty-five of those who had voted in favor.

[140] *Annales de l'Assemblée Nationale* 31 (June 4, 1874): 293, 303.
[141] *Annales de l'Assemblée Nationale* 31 (June 3, 1874): 285.
[142] *Annales de l'Assemblée Nationale* 31 (June 4, 1874): 293, 303.
[143] *Annales de l'Assemblée Nationale* 31 (June 2, 1874): 244–45, 250, 253; Annexe no. 2320, *Annales de l'Assemblée Nationale* 30 (Février 21–Mars 28, 1874): 202–17; Rosanvallon, *Le sacre du citoyen*, 324.

If the Commission of Thirty had shown some hesitation in disenfranchising the national electorate, the commission charged with drafting the laws regulating municipalities – the scope of their authority and the municipal franchise – was more audacious. Conservatives had earlier secured provisional restrictions on Paris's municipal authority and the right for the national government to appoint mayors and commune adjuncts, abandoning their historic commitment to local control in order to mute the growing influence of republicanism, resulting in the "revocation of many republican mayors solely because of their opinions."[144] They now proposed a municipal law that would entrench the right to appoint mayors while restricting and properly "organizing" the electorate. The proposed qualifications raised the voting age to twenty-five and made it much easier for taxpayers and persons born in the commune to register. The municipal franchise would also adopt some of the proposals rejected as too risky by the Commission of Thirty: additional representatives were to be elected by the most heavily taxed, and double votes were given to fathers with two or more children.[145]

The debate on the municipal election largely retrod the grounds covered during discussion on the Batbie proposal, until Joseph Bardoux – a centrist deputy who had supported disenfranchisement in 1850 – stood to propose an amendment. He proposed to reestablish a procedure from the July Monarchy, in which the most taxed citizens could be specially consulted in exceptional cases (such as large bond issues) but with the additional representation for taxpayers dropped. The republicans threw their support behind the amendment, which passed 361 to 316 with the support of liberal and centrist deputies.

The next day, the head of the commission tried to withdraw the bill, arguing that they would never have proposed as extensive a grant of powers to the municipalities had it not been for additional and permanent representation for taxpayers. "The guarantees offered to conservative interests" by the additional votes for wealthy taxpayers "had alone [persuaded] the majority of the commission to extend ... the municipal liberties." Republicans objected and were able to take control over the bill. With the help of the center-left, they now lowered the voting age to twenty-one, removed some of the

---

[144] This effectively overturned an earlier law that allowed the councils to elect the mayors in all communes other than Paris. Schmidt, *Democratizing France*, 54.

[145] Annexe no. 2268, *Annales de l'Assemblée Nationale* 30 (March 21, 1874): 71.

burdens to registration, and dropped the scheme for plural votes for fathers.[146]

Equal, direct, and near–manhood suffrage had been secured for the municipal councils. With this, support for the Batbie bill restricting the national franchise effectively collapsed: given the extent of authority being decentralized to the municipalities, it was clear that there was now a majority in support of having the qualifications for national elections broadly match the more liberal terms of the municipal bill. The rallying of the center and center-left – liberals who had been ambivalent about the regime type and suspicious of universal suffrage – had secured the principle of manhood suffrage. Gambetta's newspaper announced the next day that "universal suffrage is saved. It remains the fundamental law of French society. *It is a definitive conquest.*"[147]

The Batbie Commission resigned and a new one was appointed, a majority of its members having earlier voted against the disenfranchisement bill. From now on, the electoral laws would be in the hands of liberals and moderate republicans who had voted for manhood suffrage.

A year later, the commission issued its report, drafted by two center-left members who had now come out in favor of a republican regime. It was a modest restriction compared to the existing law. The electoral register for municipal elections would automatically include various classes of male taxpayers and men born in the commune, provided they were over the age of twenty-one, citizens, and not stripped of their political rights; male citizens who had been resident two consecutive years in the commune were not automatically included on the municipal electoral register but could request inclusion. The municipal list would form the basis for elections to the Chamber of Deputies, with an additional registry enfranchising male citizens resident six months in the commune. The disenfranchisement of soldiers was retained.

Figure 6.3 shows the estimated decline in the proportion of the population that was enfranchised in each department. In most regions of the country, the electoral law amounted to a modest disenfranchisement, although in Paris the combination of the restrictive municipal franchise, a growing noncitizen population, the political exclusion of persons who had been active in the commune, and a widespread working-class antipathy to the regime that had murdered their comrades led to a considerable drop in the proportion of persons registered.

[146] *Annales de l'Assemblée Nationale* 32 (June 19, 1874): 277–78.
[147] Rosanvallon, *Le sacre du citoyen*, 329.

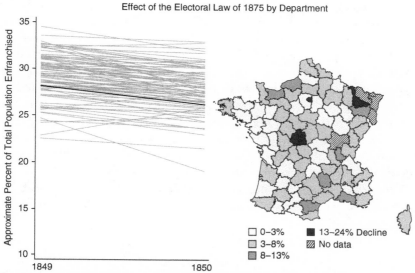

Effect of the Electoral Law of 1875 by Department

Grey lines represent Departments, and the black line represents the national total.

FIGURE 6.3 Modest Disenfranchisement of 1875

Gambetta was concerned above all with establishing the republic, but he and other radicals were furious at two additional features of the country's new electoral law: elections were for single member arrondisse- ments – small local districts – rather than voting by list at the larger department level.[148] "In small constituencies the influence of local mag- nates and clergy might be more effectively exercised than in large ones and the Republicans might have difficulty campaigning where they had no adequate nucleus of support."[149] More important, however, was that conservatives and liberals had united around the creation of a senate whose members would be chosen by an electoral college consisting of the departmental deputies, general councilors, arrondissement councilors, and delegates elected by each municipal council in the department. Senators were elected for nine-year terms, and a third of the senate stood for election every three years; sitting with deputies, they would help elect

---

[148] Gambetta was especially active in championing a list system of voting, which he had established in the early days of the Republic. Amel Ahmed, *Democracy and the Politics of Electoral Choice: Engineering Electoral Dominance* (Cambridge: Cambridge University Press, 2012), 147.

[149] Cole and Campbell, *French Electoral Systems and Elections since 1789*, 49.

the president, who could dissolve the Chamber of Deputies with the concurrence of the senate. A number of radicals broke with the republican coalition, denouncing their erstwhile allies and leaders as opportunists.

But the principle of manhood suffrage – in the Legislative Assembly at least – was secure. The first line of the commission report read, "Universal suffrage is the very foundation of our public law; it is through it that national sovereignty lives and reigns." It had been born of the ideas that "triumphed in 1789," and, when "ingenious minds had recently invented schemes whose object was more to suppress the right to vote than to organize it, we were able to judge just how much, in our day, such efforts must be in vain." "The principle of sovereignty of the people," announced the bill's manager in the assembly, "has risen to the state of political dogma in this country."[150]

CONCLUSION

The republic was not secure just yet. In May 1877, a rift opened up between the new Italian state and the papacy, leading French bishops and clergy to organize popular demands that France break off relations with Italy.[151] The conflict this caused between President Mac-Mahon and a newly installed republican cabinet headed by Jules Simon gave the president an opening to dismiss the government and install a new one headed by Broglie. When the assembly voted no-confidence in the new government, Mac-Mahon dissolved it, with the support of the royalist senate, and called for new elections. Once again, writes Jean-Marie Mayeur, "it was necessary to defend the Church and the old ruling classes against anti-clerical radicalism and the 'new strata of society.' The dominant groups of the France of days gone by were opposing, one last time, the rise of democracy."[152] The crisis of *"Seize Mai"* unified republicans and consolidated the support of liberals for the Republic.

---

[150] Annexes, *Annales de l'Assemblée Nationale* 41 (July 22, 1875): 17; *Annales de l'Assemblée Nationale* 42 (November 8, 1875): 38.

[151] Guy Thuillier, "Cohabitation et crise politique: les origines de la crise du 16 mai 1877," *La Revue administrative* 39, no. 233 (1986): 440–52; André Thuillier, "Aux origines du 16 mai 1877: Mgr de Ladoue et Lucien Gueneau," *Révue d'histoire de l'Eglise de France* 61, no. 166 (1975): 37–59.

[152] Jean-Marie Mayeur and Madeleine Reberioux, *The Third Republic from Its Origins to the Great War, 1871–1914*, trans. J. R. Foster (Cambridge: Cambridge University Press, 1984), 29.

"Even in some of the most Roman Catholic parts of the country," reported the *London Spectator*, "the Republican minority appears to be increasing into a steady majority." Republicans won the ensuing elections, and Mac-Mahon was forced to concede.[153]

Democratization in France in the 1870s was largely unaccompanied by mass disenfranchisement, although as Pierre Rosanvallon suggests, this was in large part "the result of resignation, the collapse of resistance."[154] But the triumph of male citizen suffrage also reflected the political and ideological work undertaken by republicans during the 1860s and 1870s, which enabled them to cohere around a narrative of political community that had appeal well beyond their traditional constituencies. By framing "universal suffrage" as an essentially conservative institution, they persuaded liberals and conservative republicans that its retention was not dangerous and certainly preferable to the risk of another Bonaparte. Gambetta could delight in the spectacle of "Republicans by birth sitting in opposition to Monarchists who have been converted and compelled by the cohesion of the Republican party and the legality of the Republic to accomplish the reforms which it demands."[155] As long as "universal suffrage" functioned, "there is no possibility of revolution, because there is no more revolution to tempt, no more coup d'état to dread when France has spoken."[156] As one radical republican put it, "Universal suffrage is among us a settled fact, one of the institutions accepted by all, which we will never reconsider, except but to consider perfecting its improvement. It is even the only institution that has become absolutely national, which is now one with the nation."[157]

Still, republicans could not rest easy. So long as the influence of anti-republican clericalism persisted, the republic would be in danger. Republican citizens would have to be made, through the institutions of the school, local government, and representative institutions that turned citizens' attention to the national level and away from the influence of local notables and a hostile clergy.[158] Republican anticlericalism was not

---

[153] *Chicago Tribune*, May 27, 1877, p. 4.   [154] Rosanvallon, *Le sacre du citoyen*, 324.

[155] Robert Nye, *Masculinity and Male Codes of Honor in Modern France* (New York: Oxford University Press, 1993), 154; Hanotaux, *Contemporary France*, 253.

[156] Rosanvallon, *Le sacre du citoyen*, 338.

[157] Paul Strauss, *Le suffrage universel* (Bruxelles: Librairie socialiste d'Henri Kistemaeckers, 1878), 10, 155.

[158] Eugen Weber, *Peasants into Frenchmen: The Modernization of Rural France, 1870–1914* (Palo Alto, CA: Stanford University Press, 1976); on representation, see Ahmed, *Democracy and the Politics of Electoral Choice: Engineering Electoral*

new, but it would become a central theme of citizenship as it was propounded in political discourse and disseminated by state institutions during the Third Republic.[159] Mandatory and strictly secular education was established in 1882 – with the clergy and members of ecclesiastical orders prohibited from teaching – soldiers were ordered not to frequent Catholic clubs (and the government secretly worked with freemason lodges to prevent the promotion of devout Catholics), diplomatic relations with the Vatican were severed, the Jesuits were expelled from the country, and in 1905 a strict separation of church and state was mandated, with state pensions for clergy abolished, church property liquidated, and resident members of clerical orders evicted.

The republican "people" being fashioned would be a secular one, the petit bourgeoisie and skilled workforce extolled by Gambetta. And in defense of this vision of political community, the regime would reinscribe certain exclusions. Soldiers were again disenfranchised, a compromise between antirepublican officers hoping the army could be insulated from politics and republicans anxious about the monarchical and Catholic officers' influence over the enlisted men.[160] The disenfranchisement of indigenous Muslim Algerians from the new municipal and departmental institutions was confirmed and, despite being a perennial source of complaint, would be only gradually and very modestly liberalized during the regime's existence.[161] The suppression of an uprising in Algeria in 1871 led to the intensification of colonialism there, with mass expropriations and transfers of land to settlers serving to punish the indigenous

---

Dominance, chap. 6; Didier Mineur, *Archéologie de la représentation politique: structure et fondement d'une crise* (Paris: SciencesPo. Les Presses, 2010), 204.

[159] Stone, *Sons of the Revolution*, 120; Maurice Larkin, *Church and State After the Dreyfus Affair: The Separation Issue in France* (London: Palgrave Macmillan, 1974).

[160] Douglas Porch, *The March to the Marne: The French Army, 1871–1914* (Cambridge: Cambridge University Press, 1981), chap. six; Stone, *Sons of the Revolution*, 133; Jean Charnay, *Société militaire et suffrage politique en France depuis 1789* (Paris: S.E.V.P.E.N., 1964); George Q. Flynn, *Conscription and Democracy: The Draft in France, Great Britain, and the United States* (Westport, CT: Greenwood Press, 2002), 19–20.

[161] Even the enfranchisements in the overseas departments that were maintained, such as that of indigenous Senegalese or Indians, were intended in part to sustain a vulnerable republicanism at home: "only one generalization seems possible concerning the twenty colonial deputies, namely, that they and their predecessors are and have been republicans, with the lone exception of the representative of French India in the National Assembly of 1871." Rudolph A. Winnacker, "Elections in Algeria and the French Colonies under the Third Republic," *American Political Science Review* 32, no. 2 (1938): 261–77, 262, 264.

populations, advance French control, and redistribute land to the republican settlers (including refugees from Alsace-Lorraine, ceded to Germany after 1871).[162] The new republican regime would soon pass the brutal *Code de l'indigénat*, authorizing the summary punishment of natives, forced labor, and the imposition of arbitrary taxes.

The disenfranchisement of women was also reinforced and given a resonant ideological justification: women supposedly remained under the guiding influence of an antirepublican clergy. Republicans were insistent that the exclusion of women was vital to maintaining the republican character of the regime.[163] In the 1870s, Léon Richer – who worked closely with a burgeoning feminist movement – argued that "at the present time it would be dangerous – in France – to give women the political ballot. They are in great majority reactionaries and clericals. If they voted today the Republic would not last six months."[164] A republican supporter of woman suffrage acknowledged in 1910 the force of the argument that "to give the suffrage to women in the commune or the state [would be] to throw onto the electoral balance an enormous weight that will go toward the side of reaction." He conceded that twenty or thirty years earlier, women were "under the influence, not to say the domination, of the clergy," although he insisted that this had changed.[165] Most were unconvinced, warning that woman suffrage would "capsize the boat. And the boat is the republican regime. ... After all, who can blame us republicans, who want to keep intact the Republic."[166]

The idea of "universal suffrage" would become a fundamental pillar of the republic, the means by which progressive reforms could be achieved without revolution. But to guard against the dangers of clericalism, monarchism, and caesarism, "universal suffrage" would have

---

[162] John Strachan, "Murder in the Desert: Soldiers, Settlers and the Flatters Expedition in the Politics and Historical Memory of European Colonial Algeria, 1830–1881," *French History and Civilization* 4, no. 1 (2011): 210–22.

[163] Stone, *Sons of the Revolution*, 53; Karen Offen, *Debating the Woman Question in the French Third Republic, 1870–1920* (Cambridge: Cambridge University Press, 2018), 17.

[164] Patrick K. Bidelman, "The Politics of French Feminism: Léon Richer and the Ligue Française pour le Droit des Femmes, 1882–1891," *Historical Reflections/Réflexions Historiques* 3, no. 1 (1976): 93–120, 106.

[165] Ferdinand Buisson insisted that this had changed, that "the secular school has spread many new habits: women are now accustomed to the formula, *the priest in Church, the instructor in the school, the mayor in city hall.*" They were now very far from the "peasants of Seize Mai when it comes to government by priests." Ferdinand Buisson, *Le Droit de Vote aux Femmes* (Paris: Martinet, 1910), 157–58.

[166] *Journal Officiel, Débats*, November 16, 1922, p. 1364.

to be contained, justifying exclusions that marked the boundary of the French people under the Third Republic.[167] The republic would expand the empire,[168] subjecting millions to a brutal exploitation while promising civilization and assimilation to the colonized; and to citizens, a republican education, piecemeal social reforms, and the redemption of national glory. To "make everyone educated and a soldier" was the self-appointed task of republicans, needed to break the hold of the priests. "Clericalism," Gambetta famously declared in 1877. "There's the enemy!"[169] This narrative of a regime imperiled would be the grounds upon which republicans would oppose women's suffrage for the next seventy years, the democracy of the Third Republic resting explicitly on their disenfranchisement.

[167] On the political process by which support for woman suffrage was organized, see Teele, *The Political Origins of the Female Franchise.*
[168] Efforts to republicanize the army undermined support for the first Radical governments, and they became increasingly supportive of imperialism: "The reason for the budding affection between the republic and the army was a simple one: soldiers were increasingly convinced that republicans sought to resurrect French military power." Porch, *The March to the Marne*, 9.
[169] Reinach, *Discours et plaidoyers politiques de M. Gambetta*, vol. 2, pt. 2, 23, 262.

Conclusion

What business, then, have we to fight for the old Union? We are not fighting for it. We are fighting for something incomparably better than the old Union. We are fighting for unity; unity of idea, unity of sentiment, unity of object, unity of institutions, in which there shall be no North, no South, no East, no West, no black, no white, but a solidarity of the nation, making every slave free, and every free man a voter.

—Frederick Douglass, 1863[1]

The question that opened this book was why the first wave of democratization in the United States became associated with black disenfranchisement, and I suggested that in answering this question, we might gain new insights into democratization as a more general political process. In summarizing these insights, it might be useful to ask the initial question in a slightly different way: Why did this association between democratization and disenfranchisement in the antebellum United States take the particular form that it did?

It could, for instance, have appeared in the form of what Stuart Chinn has called an "institutional recalibration," in which the ultimate terms of democratizing reforms are determined by a postreform implementation process that gives operational meaning to broad principles. Insofar as this process is controlled by the preexisting policy elite, or the reforms in question have the potential to disrupt a dense web of institutions, policies, and rights with vested and influential constituencies, then the likelihood of the reforms being moderated – possibly out of existence – is heightened.[2]

---

[1] *Proceedings of the American Anti-Slavery Society at Its Third Decade, Held in the City of Philadelphia* (New York: American Anti-Slavery Society, 1863), 118

[2] Stuart Chinn, "Institutional Recalibration and Judicial Delimitation," *Law & Social Inquiry* 37, no. 3 (2012): 535–64; Stuart Chinn, *Recalibrating Reform: The Limits of Political Change* (Cambridge: Cambridge University Press, 2014).

Chinn's argument dovetails with those advanced by Isabel Mares and Amel Ahmed and others in the comparative politics literature, that the design of electoral institutions allows elites to retain – through measures such as a nonsecret ballot or favorable representational schemes – some of the influence that democratization had threatened.[3]

It could also have taken the form of what Vesla M. Weaver has called a "frontlash," in which "formerly defeated groups" – such as regime-defending elites – "may become dominant issue entrepreneurs in light of the development of a new issue campaign."[4] By raising new issues, elites whose influence had been weakened or even dislodged by the democratizing reforms might be able to recapture some of their authority and in the process undermine the practical effects of democratization. This too is nòt exclusively an American phenomenon, and it finds parallels in Daniel Ziblatt's argument that democratic durability is in part a function of whether conservative parties can raise and manage new issue cleavages – such as religion or culture – that cut across the class divide.[5]

Finally, disenfranchisement in America could have been a more straightforward democratic reversal, as would eventually be the case in the South at the beginning of the twentieth century.[6] This was less an institutional recalibration or activation of new issue cleavage than the ending of democracy in the region altogether, as a coalition dominated by planter elites installed a form of authoritarian rule that allowed largely uncompetitive elections for political office and provided mechanisms for advancement and the regulation of differences within the dominant party.[7]

While these dynamics were present in the antebellum United States, the pattern by which white democratization was connected with black disenfranchisement at this juncture was different. It was not formerly defeated elites who limited democracy but the democratizers themselves, or rather a coalition that joined together actors who saw in democratization both an opportunity to advance politically and a resonant principle upon which to found a new political regime with others who were deeply concerned with the destabilizing possibilities of recognizing free black citizenship

---

[3] Isabela Mares, *From Open Secrets to Open Voting: Democratic Electoral Reforms and Voter Autonomy* (Cambridge: Cambridge University Press, 2015); Ahmed, *Democracy and the Politics of Electoral Choice.*

[4] Vesla M. Weaver, "Frontlash: Race and the Development of Punitive Crime Policy," *Studies in American Political Development* 21 (Fall 2007): 230–65, 230.

[5] Ziblatt, *Conservative Parties and the Birth of Democracy*, 43–44.

[6] Valelly, *The Two Reconstructions.*   [7] Mickey, *Paths Out of Dixie.*

when so much of the country's wealth was premised upon the labor of African-American slaves. Crucial to the success of this endeavor was the ability of members of this coalition to gradually work out a political and ideological logic by which black disenfranchisement and white democratization could be rendered compatible, a narrative of political community and purpose that could be offered to a broader (white) public sphere as a compelling rationale. By the end of the third decade of the nineteenth century, racial exclusion had become a constitutive feature of America's white democracy and racially defined nationality. America's purpose was to preserve a republican and democratic government for white people that should not be risked by injudicious inclusion of others.

Similar but distinct dynamics occurred in the United Kingdom and France, both of which debated political inclusions and exclusions in terms of the particular vision of the people that were to be defined and represented in government. Here as well we saw the organization of aspiring governing coalitions that had to decide how they would calibrate the composition of the electorate to the ambitions and priorities of their members. The conjoining of Irish disenfranchisement and Catholic emancipation in the United Kingdom resembles in some ways the pattern of institutional recalibration discussed above, while the post-1832 Conservative emphasis on Protestantism and anti-Irish sentiment might be understood as a case of "frontlash." The French disenfranchisement of 1850, by contrast, was more like a straightforward democratic reversal, and the ways in which the French political class interpreted the repercussions of this act would fundamentally shape the choices they made a quarter of a century later. But in both the United Kingdom in 1832 and France in the 1870s, the most important decisions over the parameters of the newly recomposed electorate were made by the democratizing coalitions, who were responsible for ratifying and often initiating the exclusions of the new regimes they established. And in each case, democratization was understood not simply as establishing a set of procedures and institutions for deciding upon political leadership, or an enfranchisement along a sliding scale of inclusion, but as an active effort to constitute and represent a *particular* "people."

I suggest that this is one of the more general insights of this study: *democratization is perhaps inseparable from processes of "people-making,"* and thus the affective, exclusionary, and discursive-institutional dimensions so important to the latter should be integrated into the study of the former. This has important implications for how we conceptualize and study democratization. Dankwart Rustow, for instance, famously argued that there was only one prerequisite to democratization, "a single background condition–national unity."

This implies nothing mysterious about *Blut und Boden* or daily pledges of allegiance, about personal identity in the psychoanalyst's sense, or about a grand political purpose pursued by the citizenry as a whole. It simply means that the vast majority of citizens in a democracy-to-be must have no doubt or mental reservations as to which political community they belong to. . ... As Ivor Jennings phrased it tersely, "The people cannot decide until somebody decides who are the people."

Rustow suggested further that the process by which national unity was constructed should ideally occur earlier and separately from democratization, or else the "total job of democratization [would be] quite unmanageable."[8]

But if democratization cannot be separated from processes of people-making, as I suggest, then "national" unity – as one form of political community – is not only *not* a prerequisite to democratization, but might never be a stable parameter of political life. In none of the cases examined here, for instance, was the question of political or national community resolved before democratization had begun; nor was the question raised primarily by an elite seeking to activate a new line of political conflict in order to diffuse a potent class dimension to politics. In fact, across the three cases it is difficult to neatly distinguish cleavages of race, ethnicity, or religion from ones of property and wealth, in large part because the actual distribution of the latter depended in part upon civic statuses that were defined in terms of the former. If civic statuses of class and ethnicity, race, or religion cannot be wholly disentangled, then the question for researchers is less whether elites were able to activate one cleavage over the other than it is of how the mutual imbrication of these statuses shaped the distribution of material interests, the content of ideologies, and the opportunities for coalition making. And if democratization always involves the reconstruction of the "people," then the possibility of its occurrence – or of a de-democratization – implies the potential for fragmenting any existing unity and replacing it with a new and recomposed one, a new "people" for a new regime, with newly defined civic statuses and the material opportunities and prerogatives these imply.

Nothing about the arc of the moral universe suggests that the new "peoples" that might be founded in the wake of regime change will be

---

[8] Dankwart Rustow, "Transitions to Democracy: Toward a Dynamic Model," *Comparative Politics* 2, no. 2 (1970): 337–63, 350–51, 361.

more inclusive, more emancipatory, more *democratic*, than those that preceded them. What the argument of this book suggests instead is that their boundaries, character, and purpose will reflect the particular goals of democratizing or disenfranchising coalitions, the institutional and ideological context in which they operate, and their capacity to create, out of the existing symbols and antagonisms of our collective lives, a vision of community that might be inscribed on the identities of "the people."

This observation raises a more fundamental question that this study could only partially evaluate: To what extent did the visions of political community described and documented in this work penetrate beyond a narrow stratum of politically attentive and engaged elites? It seems unlikely that the constitutional rationale for black disenfranchisement – that black Americans could not have been considered citizens, for this would never have been agreed to by Southern delegates – reached the attention of most Americans. But then it likely reached those for whom it was addressed: legislators, lawyers, and judges deciding on the civil and political rights of black Americans. And the more general arguments – that the United States is a country founded by and for white men, that the Protestant Constitution was the bulwark of English liberties and property, or that the Republic is the guarantor of the social equality made manifest in "universal suffrage," and yet threatened by a subversive clericalism – likely had wider circulation, perhaps especially when they were clearly tied to the sort of group and hierarchal differentiations into which we are socialized at an early age and that are reinforced over the course of our lives.

A related question then becomes whether these discourses and their institutional accompaniments can shape the attachments that are held toward the regime itself. After all, the cleavage in France between Catholics and republicans produced not only distinct partisan loyalties[9] but distinct postures toward the republican *regime*, even as parties representing different sides of this cleavage each claimed to represent the true and noblest French tradition. English dissenters and Irish Catholics were opposed not just to the Tory Party, but to the *regime* of the Protestant Constitution (although dissenters seem to have held a positive attachment to the English *state* that most Irish do not seem to have shared). And the political antislavery movement in America took issue not just with the Democratic Party, but with a slaveholding power that they argued had usurped the true purpose of the country and effectively constituted

---

[9] Lipset and Rokkan, "Cleavage Structures, Party Systems, and Voter Alignments."

a political regime – one dedicated to slavery and disenfranchisement rather than democracy and freedom.[10]

If attitudes toward a regime – whether democratic or authoritarian or some mix thereof – are rooted in perceptions of which particular configuration of "the people" it embodies, then it is easy to see how appeals to a particular democratic identity – an identification with the groups, persons, or communities valorized by a particular narrative of political community as constituting "the people" – can be turned against the processes and institutions of democracy itself.

In this, however, political parties or other forms of organized political coalitions are deliberate and consequential actors: they do not simply represent the perceived interests of their constituents. In each case studied here the forms in which democratization was connected to disenfranchisement were the result not of abstract a priori ideological commitments, but of deliberate efforts to reconcile the priorities of broad coalitions and work out shared principles that could sustain their joint projects over the long term. Political elites often seek to articulate and enshrine a public philosophy – a "legal and moral basis, or principle, on which the power of the political class rests."[11] "Democratic" elites in particular seek to anchor a claim to rule in the meaningful identities and real opportunities that a given regime affirms and enables. They define a "people," but with the expectation that it will uphold their authority and countenance their actions. It is the choices they make that in large part determine whether, and to what extent, the "democratic" peoples created will rest on disenfranchisement.

* * *

While this has been a study of nineteenth-century democratizations, I suggest the dynamic of disfranchising democracy has continuing relevance today. Throughout this book, democratization and disenfranchisement have been defined rather narrowly, as expansions or constrictions of the right to select the political leadership of the country. This has been in keeping with common usage in political science, in which democracy is often defined as the "institutional arrangement for arriving at political decisions in which individuals acquire the power to decide by means of a competitive struggle for the people's vote" or where democratization

---

[10] Langston was quoting Philemon Bliss, an early Republican judge and member of Congress. *State Proceedings of the Colored Men of the State of Ohio, Held in the City of Columbus, January 21st, 22d & 23d. 1857* (Columbus, OH: John Geary and Son, 1857), 24.

[11] Gaetano Mosca, *The Ruling Class* (New York: McGraw Hill, 1939), 70.

consists of reforms to either expand the scope of those who can participate politically or increase the opportunities for a meaningful competition.[12] But democratization and disenfranchisement have broader meaning than their particular operationalization in social scientific discourse, and it is important to not lose sight of the ways in which these can occur beyond the forms discussed here.

In recent years, the United States has seen a new wave of disenfranchisements, through ballot restrictions that make it more difficult for certain classes to vote; the denial of voting rights for ex-felons, persons under probation or on parole, or currently incarcerated inmates; the denial of citizenship rights and the inhumane threat of deporting people from the country in which they have made their home; by political assaults on the organizational life of the working class, carried out by political parties, private enterprises, as well as institutions heavily subsidized by taxpayers; and most glaringly, the aggressive police surveillance and harassment of communities of color and the policies that have made America a larger prison state than anywhere else in the world. There are other, more subtle forms of disenfranchisement as well, such as the systematic insistence that only a portion of the people are included within the boundaries of "the people" and the regular discursive constructions that wall off certain communities from "real Americans." These and other forms of language and state practice deny the reality of different groups' membership in the category of "the people" and their equal standing before the state, and systematically affirm that the country belongs to someone else. These too are disfranchisements, carried out by an ostensibly democratic government.

The nature of the relationship between these broader understandings of democracy and disfranchisement is once again a vital question of contemporary politics, with a surge of nationalist, ethnically exclusive, and often explicitly racist and religiously chauvinistic forms of so-called "populism" appearing in the United States and elsewhere. The political coalitions that have been brought to power have committed themselves to an intensification of these disenfranchisements, to build border walls, to exclude certain classes of immigrants on the basis of religion, to expand and aggressively pursue deportations, to give new vitality to "law and order" policies that disproportionately target particular communities – in the United States, communities of color above all. And they have often

---

[12] Joseph Schumpeter, *Capitalism, Socialism, Democracy* (New York: Harper and Row, 1942), 269; Dahl, *Polyarchy*, chap. 1.

done so while deploying the language of democracy, of empowering a particular and exclusive casting of "the people."

The term democracy, its content and affective associations, should not be ceded to these projects. In fact, even as these movements have grown, there have been ongoing counterprojects, efforts to imagine what a more egalitarian and free democratic life might look like and how it might be achieved. One of the lessons of *Disenfranchising Democracy*, I suggest, is that these projects will ultimately need to develop their own vision of political community, joint stories that connect the particular policies desired by a broad and diverse coalition with a meaningful sense of community and collective purpose that can appeal to a broad electorate. In this event, the response to exclusionary populism will play out in part – but only in part – on the terrain of people-making.

The responsibility falls on democrats – those who are committed to the belief that the people can and should govern, that we have the right to collectively exercise a determining influence over the conditions of our social, political, and working lives – to engage fully in this project. I do not believe this should take the form of a resurgent nationalism, insistent upon its exclusions and relative superiority but somehow kinder and gentler than those that have rattled liberal democrats across the world. Nor should it take the form of nostalgia for some mythical history in which politicians did not frame policies and collective purpose around the identities of potential constituents, in which their promises of a better life were supposedly directed at abstracted voters or toward members of an uncontested and singular community. Such misplaced nostalgia, after all, often seems to operate on the assumption that the representation of white men was somehow politically neutral.

Nor will stories of political community be enough. Instead, the task will be to craft a genuinely democratizing political program and to embed the real opportunities it provides within a compelling narrative of common purpose, a diverse "people" upon which a new democratization can rest. Whatever form this narrative will take, we do not lack for source material, for we need no longer be chained to the stale narrative of American exceptionalism.[13] Instead, we can draw on all our diverse histories, whose origins span the globe and that have been voiced by abolitionists, populists, unionists, civil rights

---

[13] Aziz Rana, "Goodbye, Cold War," *n+1* 30 (2018), https://nplusonemag.com/issue-30/politics/goodbye-cold-war/.

organizers, feminists, anti-imperialists, and many more. From these we can and should craft new stories and a new sense of political community premised upon burying the white man's republic for good and establishing – in institutions and public discourse – an emancipatory, solidaristic, and egalitarian collective purpose.

Index